Extending SSIS with .NET Scripting

A Toolkit for SQL Server
Integration Services

■■■

Joost van Rossum

Régis Baccaro

Apress®

Extending SSIS with .NET Scripting

ISBN-13 (pbk): 978-1-4842-0639-3

ISBN-13 (electronic): 978-1-4842-0638-6

Managing Director: Welmoed Spahr
Lead Editor: Jonathan Gennick
Development Editor: Douglas Pundick
Technical Reviewer: John Welch
Editorial Board: Steve Anglin, Mark Beckner, Gary Cornell, Louise Corrigan, Jim DeWolf, Jonathan Gennick, Robert Hutchinson, Michelle Lowman, James Markham, Susan McDermott, Matthew Moodie, Jeffrey Pepper, Douglas Pundick, Ben Renow-Clarke, Gwenan Spearing, Matt Wade, Steve Weiss
Coordinating Editor: Jill Balzano
Copy Editor: Kim Burton-Weisman
Compositor: SPi Global
Indexer: SPi Global
Artist: SPi Global
Cover Designer: Anna Ishchenko

Distributed to the book trade worldwide by Springer Science+Business Media New York, 233 Spring Street, 6th Floor, New York, NY 10013. Phone 1-800-SPRINGER, fax (201) 348-4505, e-mail orders-ny@springer-sbm.com, or visit www.springeronline.com. Apress Media, LLC is a California LLC and the sole member (owner) is Springer Science + Business Media Finance Inc (SSBM Finance Inc). SSBM Finance Inc is a Delaware corporation.

For information on translations, please e-mail rights@apress.com, or visit www.apress.com.

Apress and friends of ED books may be purchased in bulk for academic, corporate, or promotional use. eBook versions and licenses are also available for most titles. For more information, reference our Special Bulk Sales–eBook Licensing web page at www.apress.com/bulk-sales.

Any source code or other supplementary material referenced by the author in this text is available to readers at www.apress.com. For detailed information about how to locate your book's source code, go to www.apress.com/source-code/.

Contents at a Glance

Contents

About the Authors

Joost van Rossum has been a data warehouse/business intelligence consultant for more than 10 years; his focus is on the Microsoft SQL Server stack, especially SQL Server Integration Services. He speaks, writes, and blogs (http://microsoft-ssis.blogspot.com) about SSIS and related matters. He is a moderator for the Microsoft Developer Network on the SQL Server Integration Services forum and is an active volunteer for the PASS chapter in the Netherlands. In 2014, Joost received an MVP award for SQL Server. You can find him on twitter at @SSISJoost.

Régis Baccaro was born from the illegitimate alliance of C# and business intelligence in a SharePoint farm. He currently works as a principal consultant in Denmark, mainly doing architecture, mentoring, and performance tuning of large SQL Server data warehouse installations. He blogs at http://theblobfarm.wordpress.com. Régis is the founder of SQL Saturday Denmark, an active member of the European SQL Server community, and a top-rated speaker at SQL Server conferences. When not working on a SQL Server, you can find him cooking, running, or farming on his Danish island. He tweets at @regbac.

About the Technical Reviewer

John Welch works at Pragmatic Works, where he manages the development of a suite of BI products that make developing, managing, and documenting BI solutions easier. John has been working with business intelligence and data warehousing technologies since 2001, with a focus on Microsoft products in heterogeneous environments. He is a Microsoft Most Valued Professional (MVP), an award given due to his commitment to sharing his knowledge with the IT community, and an SSAS Maestro. John is an experienced speaker, having given presentations at Professional Association for SQL Server (PASS) conferences, the Microsoft Business Intelligence conference, Software Development West (SD West), Software Management Conference (ASM/SM), and others. He has also contributed to multiple books on SQL Server and business intelligence, including *Microsoft Big Data Solutions* (Wiley, 2014), *Smart Business Intelligence Solutions with Microsoft SQL Server 2008* (Microsoft Press, 2009), and the *SQL Server MVP Deep Dives* (Manning, 2009) series.

John writes a blog on business intelligence and SSIS topics at `http://agilebi.com/jwelch`. He is active in open source projects that help ease the development process for Microsoft BI developers, including ssisUnit (`http://ssisunit.codeplex.com`), a unit-testing framework for SSIS.

Acknowledgments

The writing of this book has been a great experience. I would like to thank Reza Rad for helping me initiate the writing process, and especially Régis Baccaro for joining me while the train was already moving. And just as important, I would like to thank my wife Merlijn and my sons Ruben, Jonathan, and Jasper for their support and for letting me write so often.

—Joost van Rossum

It has been a lot of rewarding work, mostly at night. This wouldn't have been possible without the continuous support of my wife, Annette—you make every day a better day.

—Régis Baccaro

Introduction

Microsoft SQL Server Integration Service (SSIS) is one of the leading tools for data integration, data consolidation, and data transformation. It is used by ETL developers, DBAs, and data analysts to extract, transform, and load data in ETL (Extract, Load and Transform) processes, or to do maintenance tasks. There are a lot of out-of-the-box tasks, sources, transformations, and destinations to solve the majority of everyone's needs, but they never cover 100 percent of everybody's needs.

Sometimes you need something very specific for your case, which isn't useful for the majority of the people; or the ever-continuing developments in ICT are just too fast for the SSIS version you are using; and of course, you sometimes just wonder why Microsoft didn't include a ZIP task, an SFTP task, or an XML destination. That is what this book is for.

Who This Book Is For

You have some experience with creating SSIS packages, but encountered some of the limitations of the out-of-the-box tasks and transformations. You are not an experienced programmer, but maybe you have adjusted an Excel macro or added some simple JavaScript to your web site. At least you're not afraid to use some scripting if you get some good guidance.

Or you might have a .NET developer background and you want to understand how SSIS scripting integrates with the rest of the SSIS components for data transfer and consolidation purposes; or maybe you are a DBA interested in using SSIS to perform some administrative tasks.

Regardless of your background and motivations for using SSIS scripting components, you need a proper fundamental and basic introduction to SSIS and scripting. Besides describing the fundamentals, this book also has a whole array of ready-made scripting examples for all common problems.

PART I

Getting Started

■ ■ ■

CHAPTER 1

Getting Started with SSIS and Scripting

This chapter walks you through a simple scenario where you will use .NET scripting to achieve the required functionality. The hope is that you learn how simple and how powerful it is to implement scenarios with .NET scripts. For each .NET version, new capabilities are added. You will also learn how these versions are correlated to the versions of SSIS.

In this chapter you will look at how to perform basic tasks using SSIS and how to use scripting to make these basic tasks easier.

Performing a Basic Action with SSIS Built-in Components

Learning by doing is often the easiest way to understand functionalities. So let's have a look at how it is possible to build a basic action with .NET scripting. But before you get started, let's set the scene and provide a formal introduction to SSIS.

What Is SSIS?

SQL Server Integration Services (SSIS) is an SQL Server service. The story started in SQL Server 2000 with DTS (Data Transformation Services). SSIS was first released with SQL Server 2005, and it has been enhanced for every version of SQL Server ever since—2008, 2008 R2, 2012, and 2014 at the time this book is being written. SSIS is a BI (business intelligence) developer's preferred tool for ETL (Extract, Transform, and Load). SQL developers use it for data transformation and DBAs use it for automation of some administrative tasks. Programmers use it to avoid having to do a huge amount of coding.

An SSIS project contains one or more packages. An SSIS project is developed in Business Intelligence Development Studio (BIDS) and on the later versions on SQL Server Data Tools (SSDT) with the BI templates installed. It is a bit confusing as to what tools are needed to develop SSIS packages. So to make it completely clear, here are the facts about SSDT, so that you can get started and create your first SSIS package:

- SSDT is available as a free component of the SQL Server platform and is available for all SQL Server users. It targets SQL Server 2005, 2008, 2008 R2, 2012, 2014, and Azure.

- SSDT full versions and updates are available online at https://msdn.microsoft.com/en-us/library/mt204009.aspx.

- SSDT can be installed stand-alone or together with Visual Studio.

To work with SSIS packages you need to download the BI templates that match your version of SSDT.

- SSDT 2012: `https://www.microsoft.com/en-us/download/details.aspx?id=36843`

- SSDT 2014: `https://www.microsoft.com/en-us/download/details.aspx?id=42313`

The following is a list of useful links for downloading the different versions of BIDS and SSDT. This book focuses on SSDT 2013.

- BIDS 2005: `http://www.microsoft.com/en-us/download/details.aspx?id=19413`. The Express Edition of SQL Server 2005 does not include BIDS.

- BIDS 2008 and 2008 R2 require Visual Studio 2010.

This web page at `https://msdn.microsoft.com/en-us/data/hh297027` sums up the several download possibilities, but the versions listed are a bit confusing.

Development Tool

Figure 1-1 shows the different elements of SSDT (BIDS has the same default layout but uses different colors).

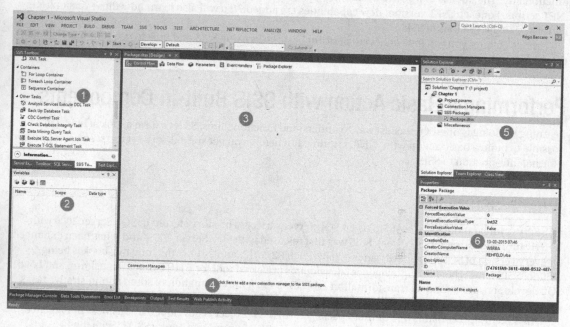

Figure 1-1. *SSDT development studio*

The callouts in Figure 1-1 highlight the following areas and aspects of the interface:

1. **SSIS Toolbox**: Has all available components and tasks.

2. **Variable pane**: Where you can create new variables and edit existing ones.

3. **Main design pane**: Where you add components and tasks, but also work with package parameters (SSIS 2012 and after) and define event handlers.

4. **Connection Managers pane**: For managing all connections to external resources for the current SSIS package.

5. **Solution Explorer**: For managing the solution, project, files, connection managers, and project parameters inside the project.

6. **Properties pane**: Lists and manages all properties for the selected object.

Control Flow Tasks

An SSIS package consists of one control flow and optionally one or several data flows. SSIS provides three types of control flow elements:

- Containers that provide structures in packages

- Tasks that provide functionality

- Precedence constraints that connect the executables

Figure 1-2 shows an example of the control flow in the designer pane.

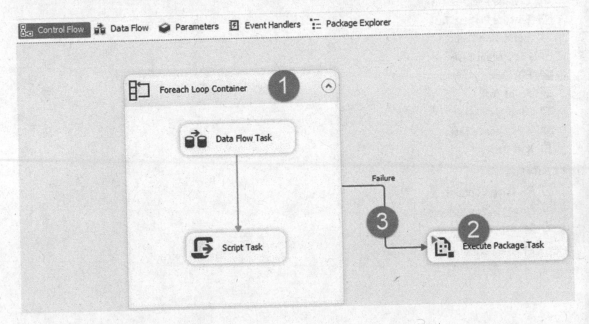

Figure 1-2. Control Flow design area

The following are the callouts in Figure 1-2:

1. A container that provides the structure of the package and some functionality that manages control flow.

2. A task that implements the functionality.

3. A precedence constraint that defines the flow of execution.

■ **Note**   As new versions of SSIS are released, new Control Flow Tasks appear and their graphical layouts are slightly different.

Figure 1-3 shows an example of the available Control Flow Tasks in the SSIS Toolbox.

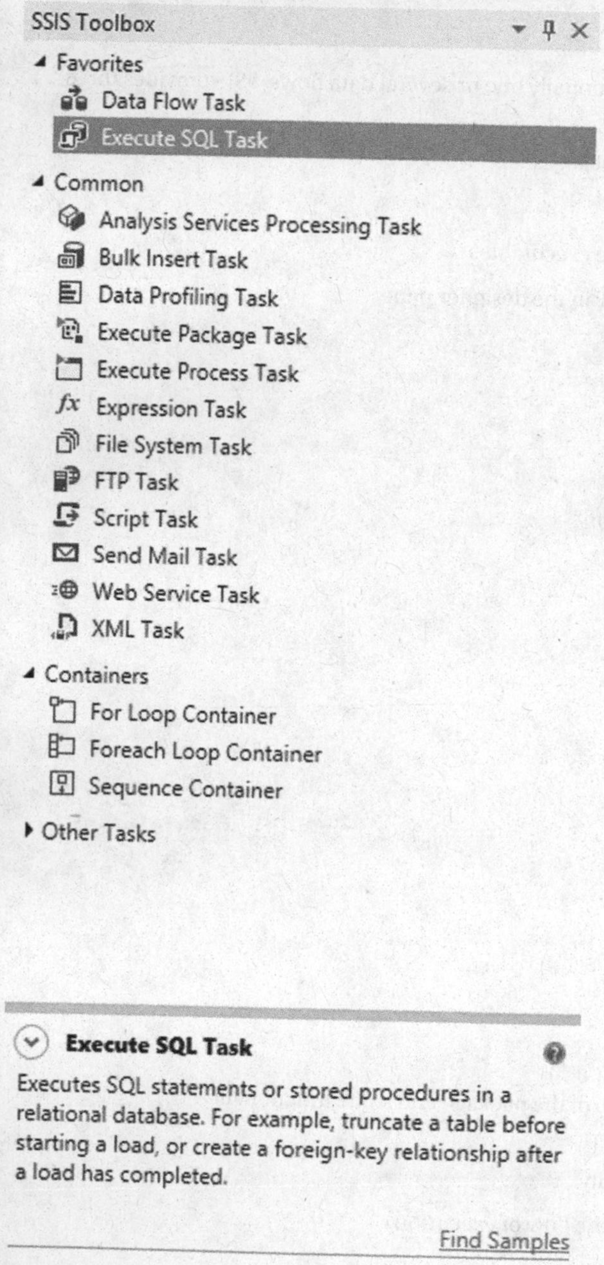

SSIS Toolbox   ▾ ⊥ ✕

▲ Favorites
  🖧 Data Flow Task
  🗗 Execute SQL Task

▲ Common
  📦 Analysis Services Processing Task
  📇 Bulk Insert Task
  📋 Data Profiling Task
  📑 Execute Package Task
  📂 Execute Process Task
  fx Expression Task
  📄 File System Task
  📭 FTP Task
  📂 Script Task
  ✉ Send Mail Task
  🌐 Web Service Task
  📜 XML Task

▲ Containers
  📁 For Loop Container
  📁 Foreach Loop Container
  📱 Sequence Container

▶ Other Tasks

  ⌄ **Execute SQL Task**   ❓

Executes SQL statements or stored procedures in a relational database. For example, truncate a table before starting a load, or create a foreign-key relationship after a load has completed.

Find Samples

Figure 1-3. *Control Flow Tasks*

As mentioned, Control Flow Tasks contain three types of elements: containers for structure, precedence constraints for connecting the executables, and tasks that provide functionality. From the tasks that provide functionality, there are elements for working with databases, such as the Execute SQL Task, the Bulk Insert Task, and the Analysis Services Processing Task; elements that operate with external systems include the File System Task and the Web Service Task; and database administration tasks include the Backup Database Task and the Shrink Database Task. The Execute Package Task is a task to call other packages. The Data Flow Task manages data transfer between the source and destination with various transformations. The Script Task is available for writing .NET scripts (and is one of the main subjects of this book).

A list of all the available Control Flow Tasks is at `http://msdn.microsoft.com/en-us/library/ms139892.aspx`.

Also notable, there are some structural elements in the control flow that can be used for grouping and looping. More information about containers in SSIS can be found at `https://msdn.microsoft.com/en-us/library/ms137728.aspx`.

Data Flow Components

Data flow is probably the most important task in SSIS. Data flow is the task that defines the data transformation from one or more sources into one or more destinations, through various transformations. Data flow is the cornerstone of building ETL and data integration solutions. There is a fundamental difference between data flow and control flow. Whereas control flows use precedence constraints for structuring the flow, data flow components use a data path for flowing data from one element to another. This is illustrated in Figure 1-4.

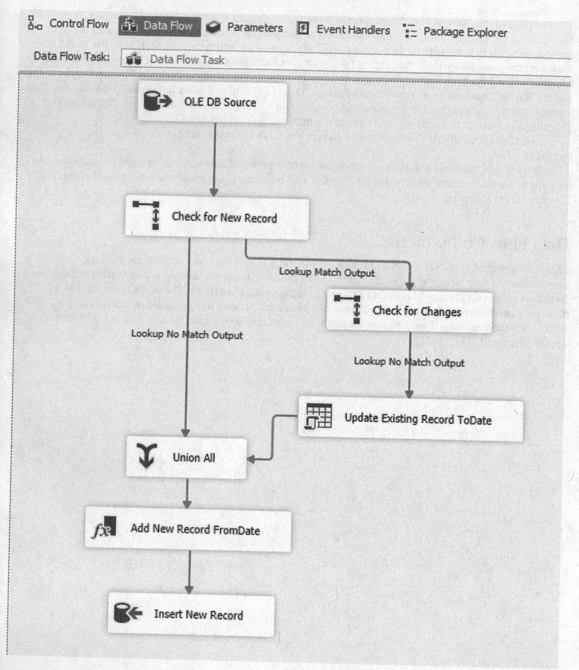

Figure 1-4. *Data Flow design pane*

As mentioned, there are three main stages in ETL: Extract, Transform, and Load. These three stages can be matched to the component types of the data flow.

Extract

The first stage is designed to fetch data from different data sources based on various data providers. Source data can come from databases like SQL Server, DB2, Oracle, MySQL, and so forth, or it might come from text files, XML datasets, Excel files, and so on. Figure 1-5 shows a list of available source components in the SSIS Data Flow Task (this list is for SQL Server 2012/2014, which is slightly different in prior versions).

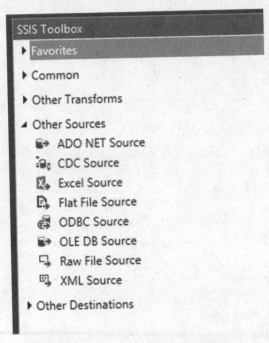

Figure 1-5. *Source components in data flow*

Transform

The second stage in ETL and probably the most challenging is the transformation required of data after it is extracted from source(s). There are many transformations available in SSIS data flow; it not within the scope of this book to describe them all. Some of the most commonly used transformations include creating new columns or replacing existing ones (Derived Column), converting data (Data Conversion), different types of joins (Lookup), pivoting and unpivoting data, and merging and sorting datasets. Figure 1-6 shows some data transformation components available in SSIS for SQL Server 2012/2014. You can find the complete list at http://msdn.microsoft.com/en-us/library/ms141713.aspx.

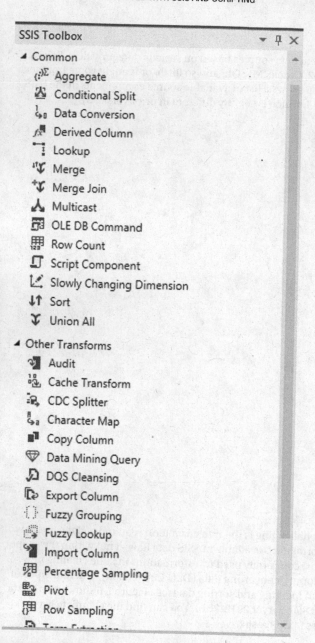

Figure 1-6. Transformation components in data flow

Load (Destination)

The final stage of ETL is to load data into destination(s). In the same manner that there is a wide range of available sources, there are many destinations. Figure 1-7 is an SQL Server 2012/2014 screenshot showing some of the available destinations.

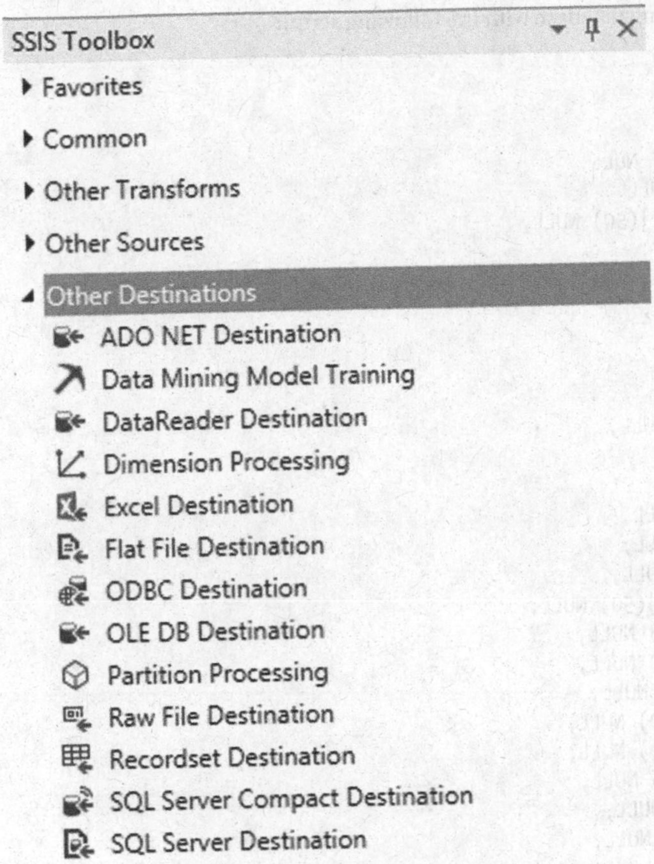

Figure 1-7. Destination components in SSIS

Example 1: Load .csv File into Database

The following example is an introduction to working with SSIS tasks and components. The purpose of this example is to build a simple SSIS package and illustrate how some of the features are better achieved by using scripting. It also points out which features can *only* be achieved using scripting in SSIS.

■ **Note** The package corresponding to this example is called Package1.dtsx, which can be found in the code for Chapter 1.

In this exercise, you will load a .csv file into a database. In SQL Server Management Studio (SSMS), create a database called Apress_SSIS_Scripting using your SQL Server default with the following script:

```
CREATE DATABASE [Apress_SSIS_Scripting]
CONTAINMENT = NONE
```

Create a table in the Apress_SSIS_Scripting database with the following script:

```
USE [Apress_SSIS_Scripting]
GO
CREATE TABLE [dbo].[Customer](
        [CustomerKey] [varchar](50) NOT NULL,
        [GeographyKey] [varchar](50) NULL,
        [CustomerAlternateKey] [varchar](50) NULL,
        [Title] [varchar](50) NULL,
        [FirstName] [varchar](50) NULL,
        [MiddleName] [varchar](50) NULL,
        [LastName] [varchar](50) NULL,
        [NameStyle] [varchar](50) NULL,
        [BirthDate] [varchar](50) NULL,
        [MaritalStatus] [varchar](50) NULL,
        [Suffix] [varchar](50) NULL,
        [Gender] [varchar](50) NULL,
        [EmailAddress] [varchar](50) NULL,
        [YearlyIncome] [varchar](50) NULL,
        [TotalChildren] [varchar](50) NULL,
        [NumberChildrenAtHome] [varchar](50) NULL,
        [EnglishEducation] [varchar](50) NULL,
        [SpanishEducation] [varchar](50) NULL,
        [FrenchEducation] [varchar](50) NULL,
        [EnglishOccupation] [varchar](50) NULL,
        [SpanishOccupation] [varchar](50) NULL,
        [FrenchOccupation] [varchar](50) NULL,
        [HouseOwnerFlag] [varchar](50) NULL,
        [NumberCarsOwned] [varchar](50) NULL,
        [AddressLine1] [varchar](50) NULL,
        [AddressLine2] [varchar](50) NULL,
        [Phone] [varchar](50) NULL,
        [DateFirstPurchase] [varchar](50) NULL,
        [CommuteDistance] [varchar](50) NULL,
        [SourceFile] [varchar](50) NULL
) ON [PRIMARY]
```

Open SSDT or BIDS and create a new SSIS project, as shown in Figure 1-8a. In the new SSIS package (created by default), drag and drop a Data Flow Task from the SSIS Toolbox into the main pane, and then double-click it to go to Data Flow tab. Figure 1-8b shows how to create a new SSIS project in SSDT-BI with Visual Studio 2013.

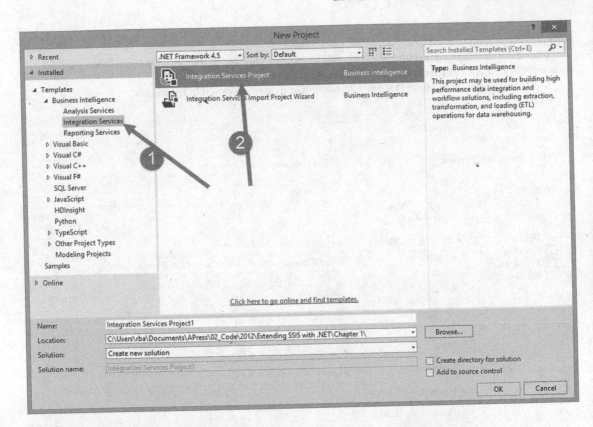

Figure 1-8a. *Flat File Connection Manager*

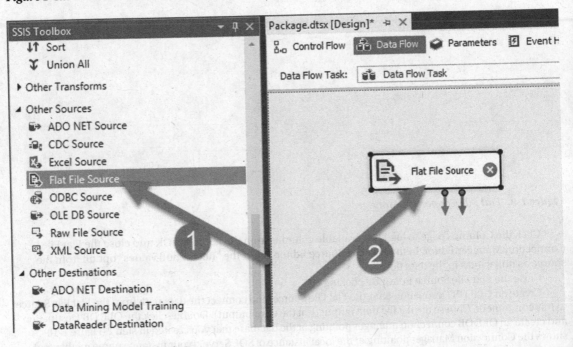

Figure 1-8b. *Creating a Flat File Source*

Drag a Data Flow Task on the design surface and double-click it. Within the Data Flow Task, drag a Flat File Source and double-click it to open its property dialog.

Click New to create a new Flat File Connection Manager pointing at the .csv file in the book's source code bundle at Chapter 01\Source Files\Customers.csv.

Configure the General tab of Flat File Connection Manager, as shown in Figure 1-9.

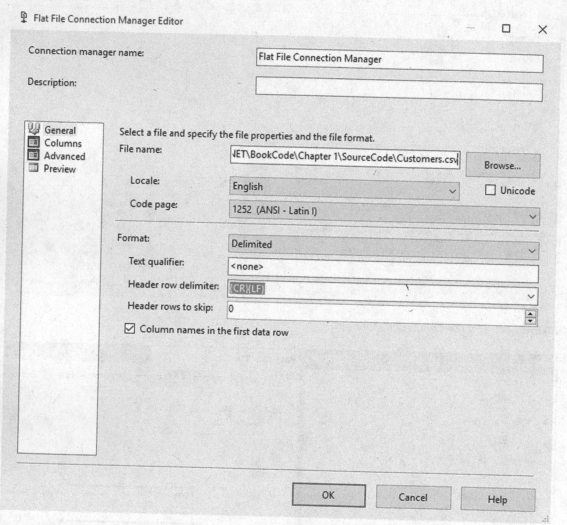

Figure 1-9. Flat File Connection Manager

Click the Columns page to load the available columns from the file. Click OK and close the Flat File Connection Manager Editor. In the Flat File Source Editor, select the "Retain null values" option from the source as null values in the data flow.

Close the Flat File Source Editor by clicking OK.

Create an OLE DB Destination after the Flat File Source, and connect the data path from the Flat File Source to this component. Choose the flat file data output (not the error output). Double-click the OLE DB Destination and create an OLE DB connection manager pointing at the database that you created in step 1. Figure 1-10 shows the Connection Manager pointing at the local instance of SQL Server (your instance name might vary).

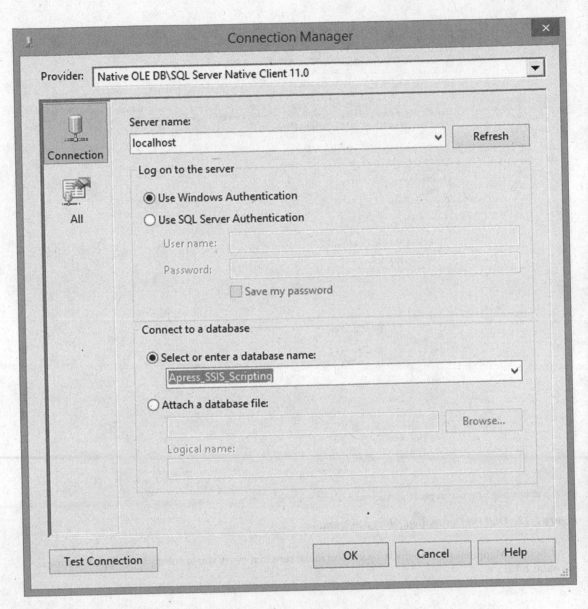

Figure 1-10. *Creating an OLE DB connection*

Select [dbo].[Customer] in the table and view drop-down menu, as shown in Figure 1-11.

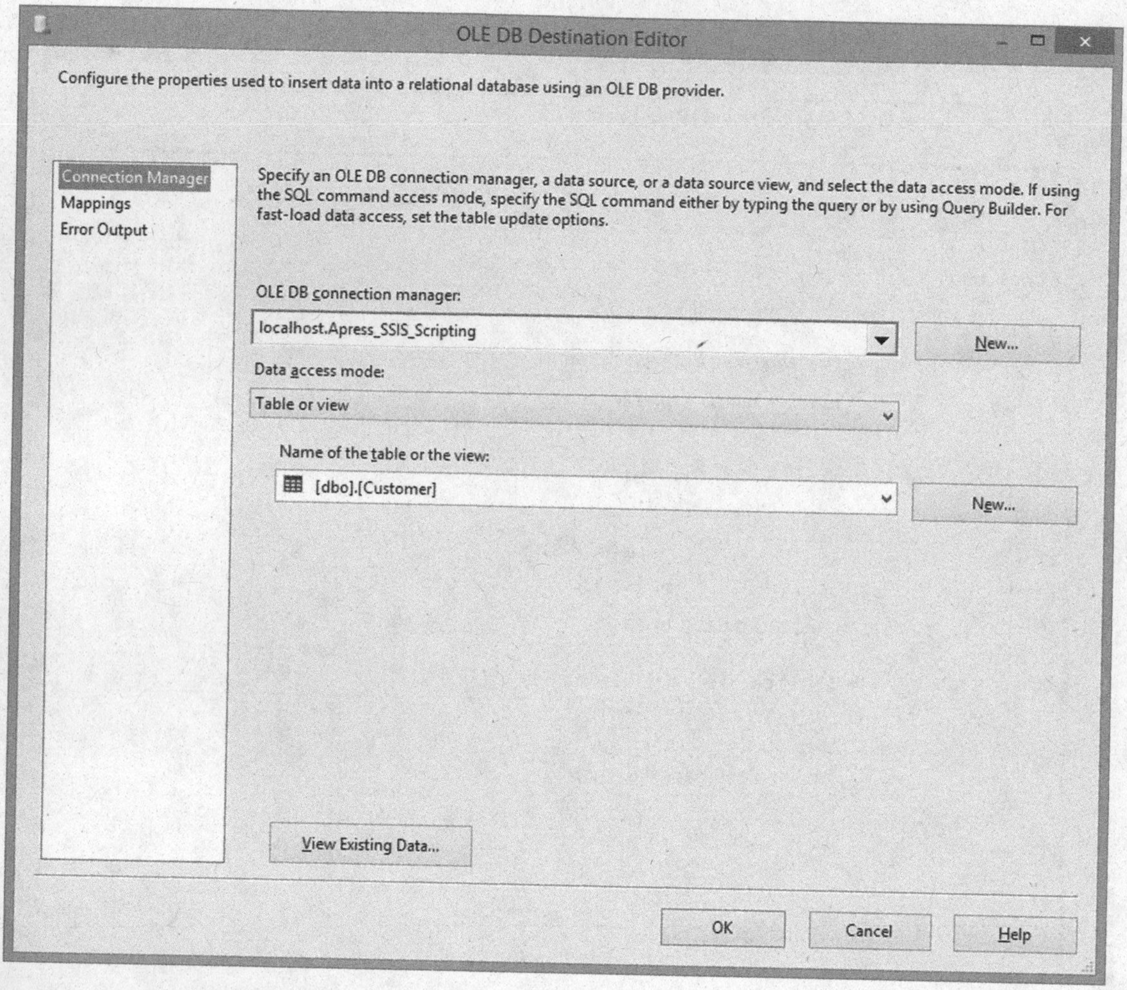

Figure 1-11. *OLE DB Destination Editor configuration*

Click the Mappings item on the left pane and make sure that every single column is mapped as shown in Figure 1-12.

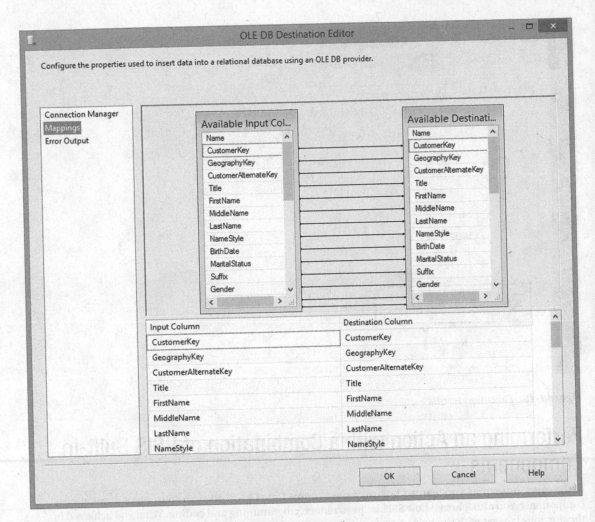

Figure 1-12. Column mappings in the destination component

Right-click the package in Solution Explorer and execute the package by clicking the Execute Package menu item. You see that 1,000 rows have transferred successfully from the .csv file into the database table (see Figure 1-13).

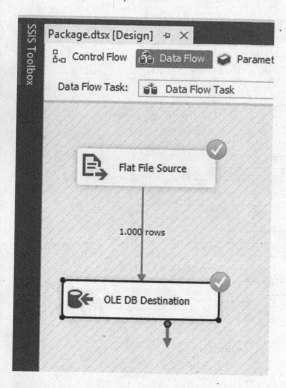

Figure 1-13. Execution results

Performing an Action with a Combination of SSIS Built-in Components

In the previous section, you learned how to create a simple Data Flow Task with source and destination components. You also learned how SSIS helps to reduce programming and coding. What you achieved in the previous lab was with the help of drag-and-drop and simple configuration on the user interface. One of the purposes of this lab (besides it being introductory) was to illustrate how easily SSIS can help reduce development time for data transfer and consolidation.

In the following section, you walk through an example where SSIS helps build a solution through built-in components. You will use the same Data Flow Task as before, and add a Foreach Loop Container and an Expression Task. You will also add a variable to the package to enable these components to communicate with each other in a more dynamic way.

The Foreach Loop Container defines a repeating control flow in a package. The loop implementation is very similar to the For looping in programming languages. The container enumerates each item in a collection. In this example, you use the File Enumerator to loop through all files in a specified directory.

The Expression Task (only available in SSIS 2012 and higher versions) creates and evaluates values of an expression at runtime. The Expression Task works with the SSIS Expression Language. This language includes operators and functions for working with dates, strings, numbers, and converting data types, and so forth. A full description of the language is available at http://msdn.microsoft.com/en-us/library/ms137547.aspx. In this lab, you will write an expression to compare the values of two variables for finding the most recent file.

Example 2: Find Files in a Folder and Load Them into the Database with Built-in Components

Please run the following code to truncate the destination table in SSMS:

```
Truncate table dbo.Customer
```

Copy and paste the package from the previous example. Go to the Control Flow designer, and then drag and drop a Foreach Loop Container in the main design area.

Create one new variable with datatypes and name it as specified in Figure 1-14. If you don't see the variables window, right-click an empty area in the control flow and choose Variables from the context menu.

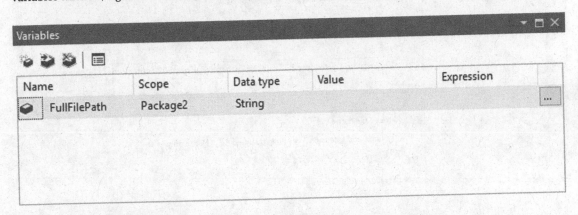

Figure 1-14. *Variables definition*

Go to the Foreach Loop Editor (double-click the Foreach Loop Container), and go to the Collection page. Set enumerator as Foreach File Enumerator, which displays the options for that enumerator. Then set the Folder to Chapter 01\Source Files (from the source code bundle of the book), and verify that you fetched the Fully Qualified file names, as shown in Figure 1-15.

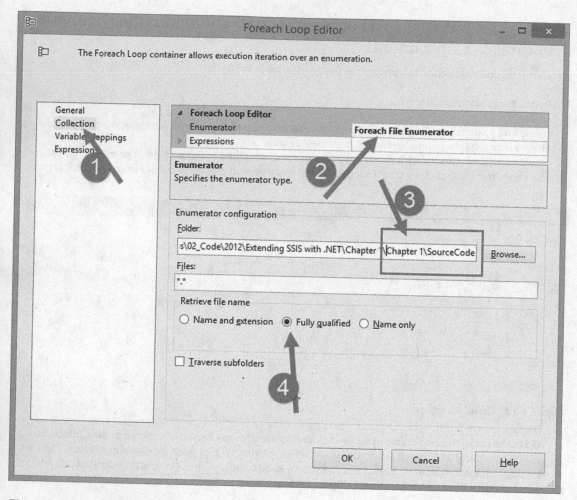

Figure 1-15. *Foreach File Enumerator*

For more granular filtering, you can add wildcards in the Files fields (for example, *.csv).

Go to the Variable Mappings page, and choose User::FullFilePath from the Variable column. Verify that the index is 0 (automatically set this time), as shown in Figure 1-16.

Foreach Loop Editor

The Foreach Loop container allows execution iteration over an enumeration.

General
Collection
Variable Mappings
Expressions

Select variables to map to the collection value.

Variable	Index
User::FullFilePath	0

Figure 1-16. Variable Mappings

Close the Foreach Loop Editor by clicking OK.

Drag and drop the Data Flow Task and the file destination from the previous chapter into the Foreach Loop Container so that everything looks like what's shown in Figure 1-17.

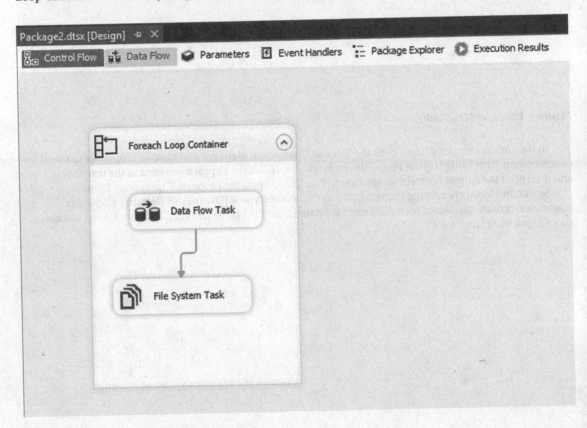

Package2.dtsx [Design]

Control Flow   Data Flow   Parameters   Event Handlers   Package Explorer   Execution Results

Foreach Loop Container

Data Flow Task

File System Task

Figure 1-17. Control Flow layout

Open the Data Flow Task by double-clicking it. It should look like what's shown in Figure 1-18.

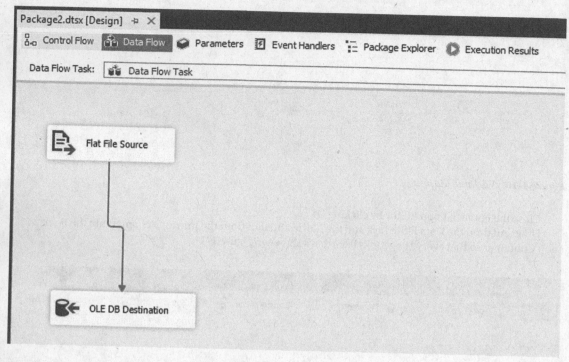

Figure 1-18. *Data Flow Task*

In the connection pane, right-click the Flat File Connection Manager and choose Properties in the context menu. This brings up the Properties tools window. Click the Expressions item in the property list, and then click the ellipsis button that appears to the right to open the Property Expressions Editor.

Select the ConnectionString property, and in Expression type **@[User::FullFilePath]**. (Now this connection is dynamic, based on the selected file name from the Foreach Loop Container.) What you see should look like Figure 1-19.

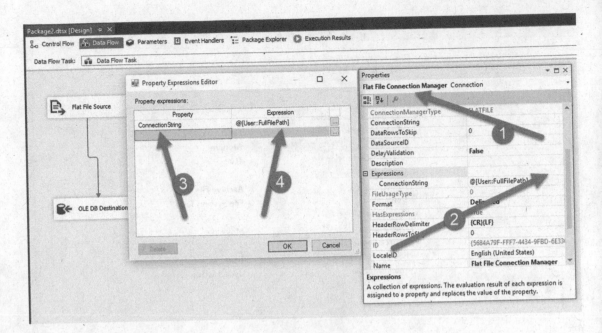

Figure 1-19. *Data Flow layout*

Open the File System Task Editor located inside the Foreach Loop Container by double-clicking the File System Task. Set the configuration to move the file from the User::FullFilePath source variable to an Archive folder. (For the Destination Connection, create a new connection to an existing folder and choose the Archive folder from the source code bundle of book.) The detailed configuration is shown in Figure 1-20.

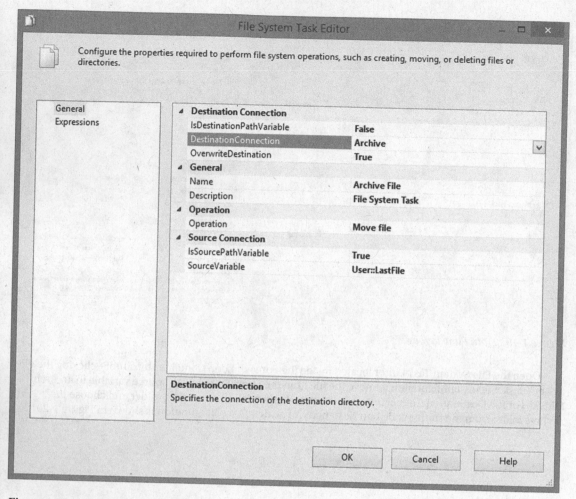

Figure 1-20. File System Task Editor

Close the File System Task Editor. There is still a red stop icon beside this task. Go to the Properties window and set the DelayValidation property to True. This happens because the variable used is only populated at runtime. When SSIS validates the value at design time, it fails, but it will succeed at runtime.

■ **Note**   You may want to truncate the destination table before executing the task because there might be some duplicate values in the CustomerKey column. Use this command:

```
TRUNCATE TABLE [Apress_SSIS_Scripting].[dbo].[Customer]
```

Execute the package and check the records in the customer table. You will see that data from all the customer files is loaded and that the archive folder contains the loaded files (see Figure 1-21).

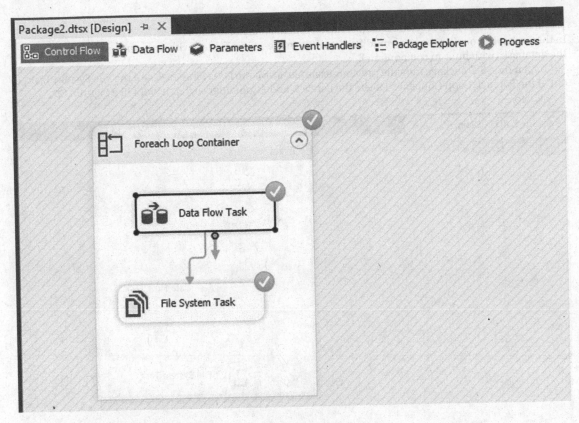

Figure 1-21. *Successful package execution*

.NET Scripting Makes Life Easier

In the previous section you saw how to solve problems using SSIS components and tasks. You found files, and then loaded and archived them. Now consider that you only want to find the latest file based on some of its properties, such as the modified date. Unfortunately, there is no built-in component in SSIS that allows you to do that. This is where SSIS scripting comes in handy.

In the next section, you will create a Script Task and a .NET script to find the latest modified file. The rest of the package will be unchanged. After finding the latest modified file, you will load it into the customer table and archive it.

The Script Task is a Control Flow Task that allows you to write a .NET script. Then you can set the execution order of that .NET script by placing the Script Task somewhere in the control flow with precedence constraints.

This section is meant to be introductory; therefore, there are some sections of this lab that will be covered in greater detail later in the book. The purpose of this section is to give you a basic understanding of the Script Task.

Example 3: Find the Latest Modified .csv File

In this example, you find the latest modified .csv file in the source folder (with scripting), and load it into the database (with built-in components).

Open the SSIS package from the previous example. Move the Data Flow Task and the File System Task out of the Foreach Loop Container. Delete the Foreach Loop Container so that it looks like Figure 1-22.

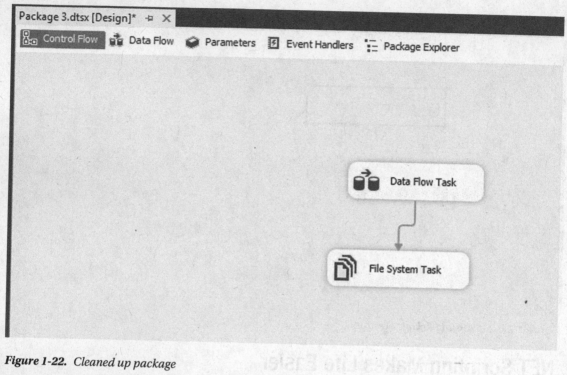

Figure 1-22. *Cleaned up package*

Remove the FileFullPath variable.

If necessary, move the Customer files from the Archive folder back to the source folder. Truncate the customer table with the code:

```
TRUNCATE TABLE [Apress_SSIS_Scripting].[dbo].[Customer]
```

Add a Script Task. Go to the Script Task Editor by double-clicking the Script Task. Leave the script language as C#. Choose User::FullFilePath in the ReadWriteVariables as shown in Figure 1-23.

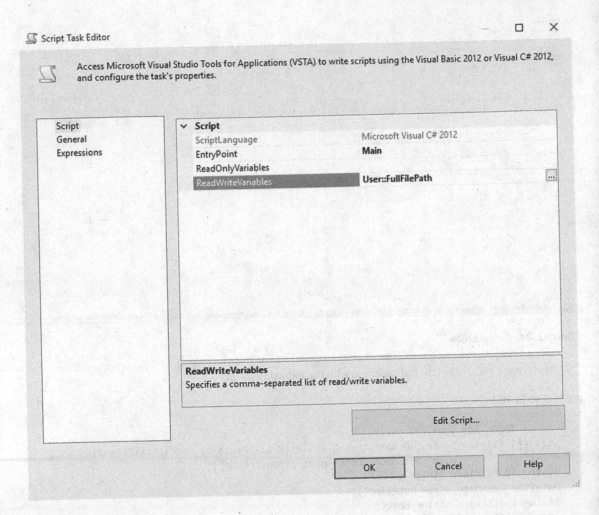

Figure 1-23. *Script Task Editor*

Click the Edit Script... button. A new Visual Studio window opens with a C# project and an autogenerated name. A ScriptMain.cs file opens in the main section (see Figure 1-24).

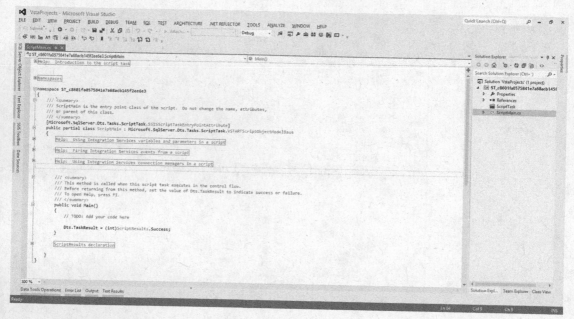

Figure 1-24. *Script Editor*

Replace the contents of the Main method with the following script:

```
public void Main()
{

      // TODO: Add your code here
    string[] files = System.IO.Directory.GetFiles(@"C:\APress\02_Code\2014\Extending SSIS
                with .NET\BookCode\Chapter 1\SourceCode");
    System.IO.FileInfo finf;
    DateTime lastDate = new DateTime();
    string lastFile = string.Empty;
    foreach (string f in files)
    {

        finf = new System.IO.FileInfo(f);
        //let's find the last file and only csv files
        if (finf.LastWriteTime > lastDate && finf.Name.Contains("csv"))
        {
            lastDate = finf.CreationTime;
            lastFile = f;
        }
    }


    Dts.Variables["User::FullFilePath"].Value = lastFile;
    Dts.TaskResult = (int)ScriptResults.Success;

        Dts.TaskResult = (int)ScriptResults.Success;
}
```

Save the script by exiting the VSTA editor (click the X in the top-right corner). Close the Script Task Editor. Connect the Script Task to the Data Flow Task with a success precedence constraint.

Execute the package. You see that `Customer_2.csv` is loaded into the customer table and moved to the archive, as this file is the latest modified file (see Figure 1-25).

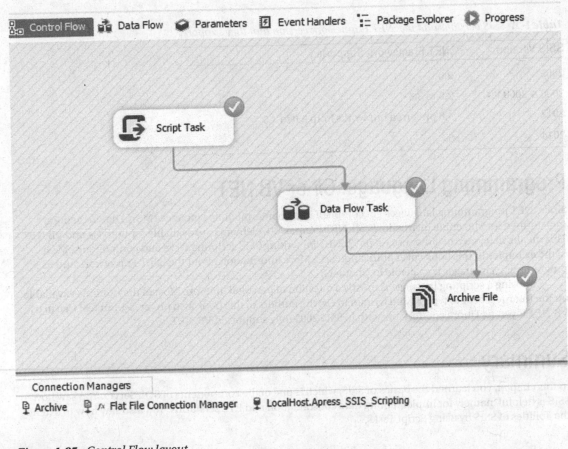

Figure 1-25. Control Flow layout

■ **Note**   You might want to open `Customer_2.csv` in Notepad and save it again to modify its timestamp because the downloaded files all have the same timestamp.

You've seen how helpful Script Task and scripting are in SSIS. In this lab you used C# code to loop through files in the source folder and find the latest modified file—a task that cannot be achieved with built-in SSIS tasks. You then used data flow to transfer the data from that file to an SQL Server database table, which is much easier to do in SSIS rather than with scripting. The combination of SSIS and scripting is important; it greatly extends the capabilities of the SSIS packages that you build.

In this book, you will go through scripting samples in SSIS and you will learn how to create a custom task based on a script, so that you can reuse it in other packages and projects.

SSIS Versions and .NET Library Limitations

Each version of SSIS is compatible with specific versions of the .NET libraries. SSIS 2005 was the first version of SSIS to support a version of the .NET Framework. The Table 1-1 lists the SSIS versions and the .NET Framework version that they support.

Table 1-1. *SSIS versions and the .NET Framework version that they support*

SSIS Version	.NET Framework Supported
2005	2.0
2008 & 2008 R2	2.0 to 3.5
2012	4.0 preferred but works from 2.0 to 4.0
2014	5

Programming Language: C# or VB.NET

Since .NET programming languages get compiled into an intermediate language (MSIL) before being transformed into machine instructions, all .NET Framework elements are available for both C# and VB.NET. This means that you can either use C# or VB.NET for writing SSIS scripting tasks and components. Most of the examples in this book cover both languages. More information about the .NET Framework and its programming languages is available in Chapter 3.

Choosing a scripting language is mostly a question of personal opinion. Most of the examples available on the Internet seem to typically be written in C#; the authors of this book also prefer C#. But feel free to use VB.NET if you feel more comfortable with it. SSIS 2005 only supported VB.NET.

Summary

In this chapter, you learned the basics of SSIS, which is one of the components of SQL Server. You saw how SSIS is helpful, namely for implementing data consolidation and ETL scenarios. You also saw how to extend the abilities of SSIS by using Script Tasks.

CHAPTER 2

Script Task vs. Script Component

Within SSIS, .NET scripts can be written in a Script Task or in a Script Component. The purpose of the Script Task and Script Component is to extend the functionality of SSIS with your own custom code when the out-of-the-box tasks and components don't meet your requirements. And there are more similarities between Script Task and Script Component. They both have a general editor such as in Figure 2-1 to specify properties such as scripting language and the usages of variables. And they both have a VSTA editor to write Visual C# or Visual Basic code.

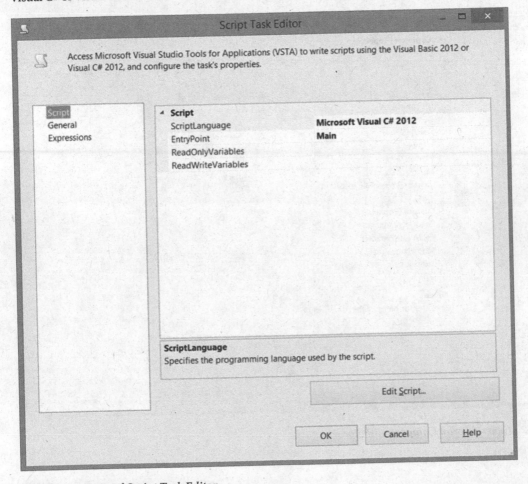

Figure 2-1. General Script Task Editor

■ **Note**   Since SSIS 2008, the code for both Script Task and Script Component are precompiled into binary code and stored in your package to permit faster execution.

In the various SSIS forums on Internet, Script Task and Script Component are often confused because they look alike and share all these features, but they are, in fact, fundamentally different. A Script Task is part of the SSIS Control Flow and executes a certain task, such as checking the size of a file, unzipping a source file, or sending a formatted email to let the analysts know that the cube was successfully processed. The Script Task can pretty much do anything, but it is not used for row-based transformations or actions. That is what the Script Component is used for. Figure 2-2 shows the Script Component editor.

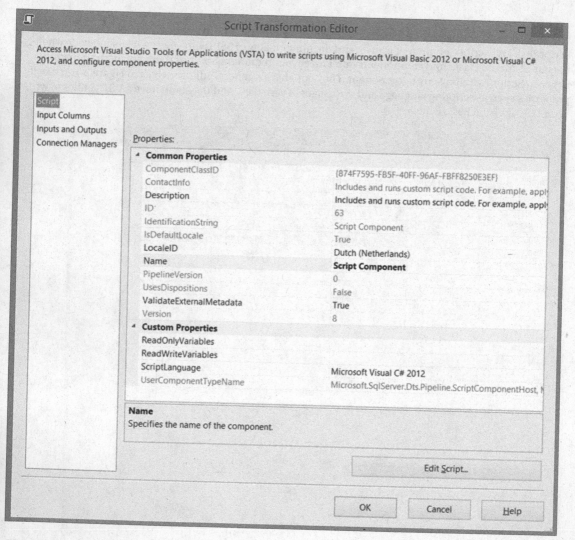

Figure 2-2. *General Script Component Editor*

A Script Component is part of the SSIS Data Flow Task. It can be used as a source, a transformation, or a destination. The transformation type is probably the most popular type for row-based transformations or actions such as validating an email address or encrypting a sensitive column value.

Introduction to Script Task

To demonstrate the possibilities of the Script Task, let's look at a very simplified example; but when you have finished this book, you will be able to create a more sophisticated and more stable version of it. For this first case, let's check the file size of a flat file before processing it in the Data Flow Task. When the size is zero bytes, let's send an email to the person responsible.

Package Design

Create a Data Flow Task that uses a flat file as source. What the data flow does isn't important for this example, but make sure that the name of the Flat File Connection Manager is myFlatFile. Also add a Send Mail Task for sending the error email. Now add the Script Task and connect it to both the Data Flow Task and the Send Mail Task. Change the precedence constraint to Failure for the Send Mail Task. It should look something like Figure 2-3. You can also use the Script Task starter package from the solution folder.

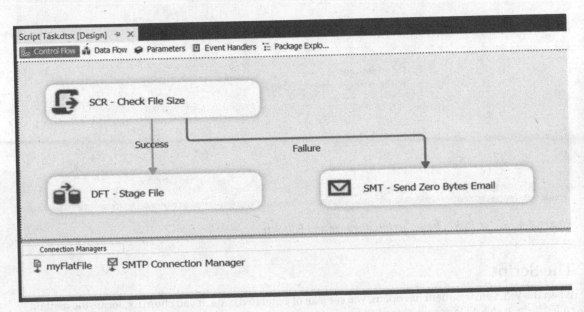

Figure 2-3. Script Task to check file size

Edit Script Task

Now edit the Script Task by double-clicking it or by right-clicking it, and then choose Edit. On the first tab, called Script, choose your scripting language (C# or VB.NET) as shown in Figure 2-4. You don't have to change any other options of the Script Task. On the same tab, locate the Edit Script... button in the lower-right corner and click it to open the VSTA environment, where you are adding your .NET code. A new Visual Studio window will open.

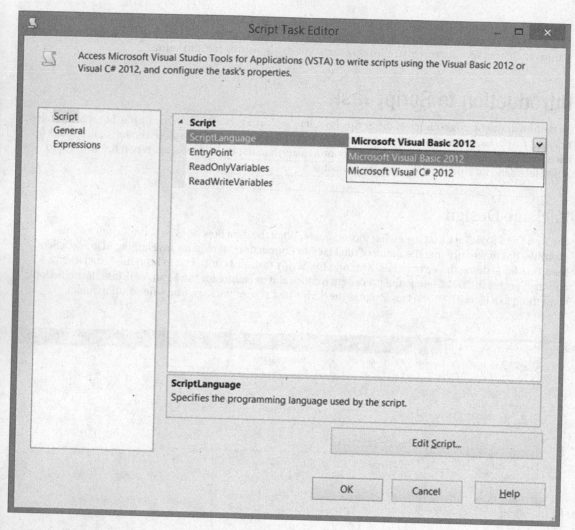

Figure 2-4. *Script Task: Choose ScriptLanguage and Edit Script...*

The Script

When the VSTA environment has opens, you see a lot of generated code. If you chose C#, locate the method called Main. It should look something like this:

```
public void Main()
{
        // TODO: Add your code here

        Dts.TaskResult = (int)ScriptResults.Success;
}
```

Now replace that code with the following code. Afterward, close the newly opened Visual Studio window so that you return to the Script Task Editor. Click OK to close it.

```csharp
public void Main()
{
    // Fill variable with the filepath from a Flat File Connection Manager
    string filePath;
    filePath = Dts.Connections["myFlatFile"].ConnectionString;

    // Use the FileInfo class to check the length of the file
    System.IO.FileInfo fi = new System.IO.FileInfo(filePath);

    // Fail the Script Task if the length is not greater than zero
    if (fi.Length > 0)
    {
        Dts.TaskResult = (int)ScriptResults.Success;
    }
    else
    {
        Dts.TaskResult = (int)ScriptResults.Failure;
    }
}
```

If you chose VB.NET, locate the method called Main. It should look something like this:

```vbnet
Public Sub Main()
    '
    ' Add your code here
    '
    Dts.TaskResult = ScriptResults.Success
End Sub
```

Replace this code with the following code. Afterward, you close the newly opened Visual Studio window so that you return to the Script Task Editor. Click OK to close it.

```vbnet
Public Sub Main()
    ' Fill variable with the filepath from a Flat File Connection Manager
    Dim filePath As String
    filePath = Dts.Connections("myFlatFile").ConnectionString

    ' Use the FileInfo class to check the length of the file
    Dim fi As System.IO.FileInfo = New System.IO.FileInfo(filePath)

    ' Fail the Script Task if the length is not greater than zero
    If (fi.Length > 0) Then
        Dts.TaskResult = ScriptResults.Success
    Else
        Dts.TaskResult = ScriptResults.Failure
    End If
End Sub
```

35

Testing

Now you're ready for the coding part. In Chapter 4 and beyond, you learn how to extend this example code with other file properties, logging, and error handling.

Make sure that the Data Flow Task and the Send Mail Task are working properly. Also make sure that the text file mentioned in the Flat File Connection Manager contains data. If you don't have an SMTP server, then replace the Send Mail Task with another task, such as the Execute SQL Task. Now run the package. If the file contains data, then the Script Task should be successful and continue with the data flow. See Figure 2-5 for an example.

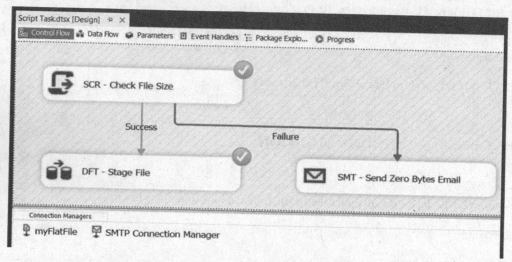

Figure 2-5. *The result of your first Script Task with a filled text file*

Open the text file in Notepad and remove all text. Save the file and run the package again. The Script Task should fail and continue with the Send Mail Task. Figure 2-6 shows this behavior.

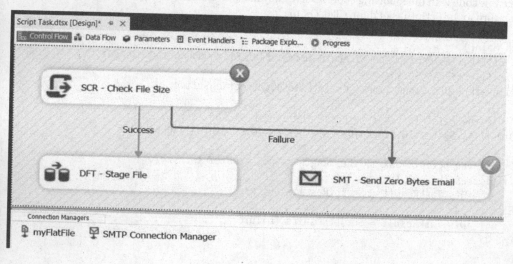

Figure 2-6. *The result of your first Script Task with an empty text file*

Introduction to Script Component

To introduce the Script Component, let's add a surrogate key column in the Data Flow Task. A surrogate key is an automatically incremented row number, similar to the identity column in an SQL Server table. Again, this is a very simplified example that you will be able to extend after reading this book.

Flat File

For this example, you will use a text file with some bicycle types in it as a source in the data flow. Add a Flat File Source component to your data flow as shown in Figure 2-7. Specify a connection manager that refers to a text file with the following content:

```
BikeTypes
Mountainbike
City bike
BMX
Unicycle
Racing bike
```

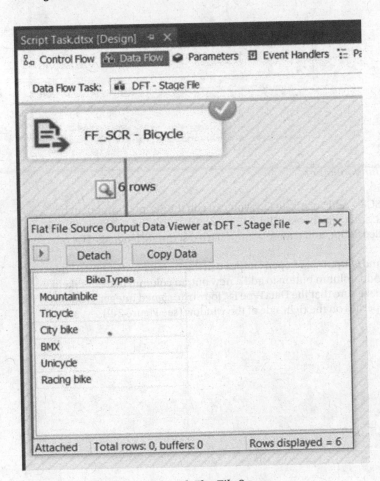

Figure 2-7. *Data Flow Task with Flat File Source*

Script Component

Add a Script Component to the Data Flow Task and choose Transformation as the Script Component Type as in Figure 2-8. Next, connect the Flat File Source to your new Script Component.

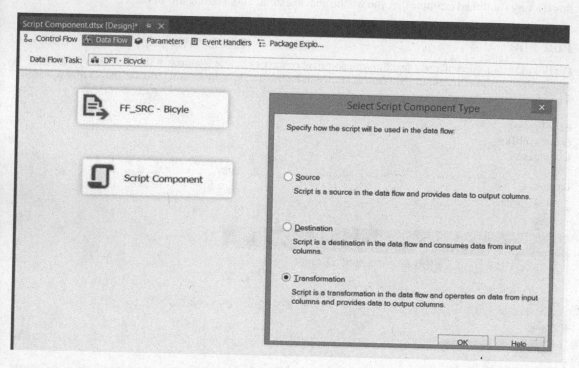

Figure 2-8. *Script Component Type: Transformation*

After giving it a useful name, like SCR – Add Surrogate Key, you can edit the Script Component by double-clicking it or by right-clicking it, and then choosing Edit. Chapter 9 discusses all the options and pages. For now, go to the first page, called Script, and choose your preferred scripting language (C# or VB.NET) under Custom Properties.

Next, go to the third page, Inputs and Outputs, and open Output 0 in the "Inputs and outputs:" treeview. Then click Output Columns. Click the Add Column button to add a new output column; name it BikeId. The new column stores a number, so make sure that the DataType is "four-byte signed integer" You can change the DataType in Data Type Properties on the right side of the window (see Figure 2-9).

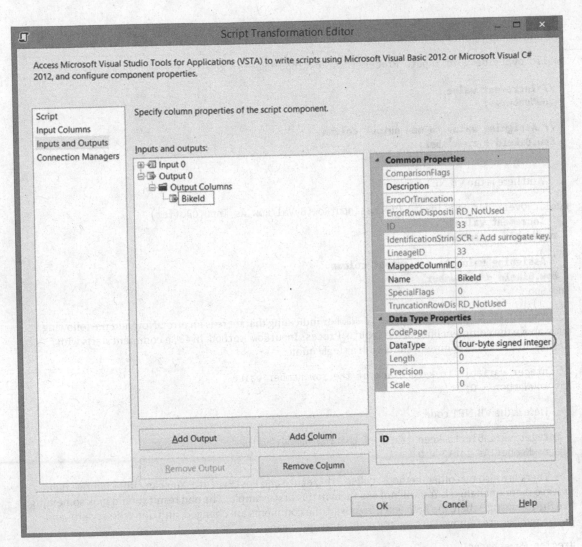

Figure 2-9. *Script Component: Add new output column and set the datatype*

After adding the new output column, go back to the Script page and click the Edit Script... button. A new Visual Studio window opens with the so-called VSTA environment.

You will see a lot of generated code. First, locate the method called `Input0_ProcessInputRow`. Depending on the chosen language, the code should look something like the following:

```
public override void Input0_ProcessInputRow(InputOBuffer Row)
```

And the VB.NET code would look like this:

```
Public Overrides Sub Input0_ProcessInputRow(ByVal Row As InputOBuffer)
```

Add the following five lines of code (including one empty row and two comment rows) to this method. The end result should look like this:

```
public override void Input0_ProcessInputRow(InputOBuffer Row)
{
  // Increment value
  rowNumber++;

  // Assigning value to new output column
  Row.BikeId = rowNumber;
}
```

And here is the VB.NET code:

```
Public Overrides Sub Input0_ProcessInputRow(ByVal Row As InputOBuffer)
  ' Increment value
  rowNumber = rowNumber + 1

  ' Assigning value to new output column
  Row.BikeId = rowNumber
End Sub
```

You will see some red lines under rowNumber indicating that there is an error. Now add the following code above the comment lines of the Input0_ProcessInputRow method. In C#, a comment starts with slashes. In VB.NET, a comment starts with a single quote.

```
// Integer variable to keep track of the row number value
int rowNumber = 0;
```

Here is the VB.NET code:

```
' Integer variable to keep track of the row number value
Dim rowNumber As Int32 = 0
```

There are also two other methods, called PreExecute and PostExecute. You can either remove them or leave them unchanged. You will not use them in this first example. The end result should look something like the following, where the help text is removed, the comments are changed, and unnecessary pre- and post- methods are removed to keep the code short and clean:

```
#region Namespaces
using System;
using System.Data;
using Microsoft.SqlServer.Dts.Pipeline.Wrapper;
using Microsoft.SqlServer.Dts.Runtime.Wrapper;
#endregion

/// <summary>
/// This is the class to which to add your code.
/// Do not change the name, attributes, or parent
/// of this class.
/// </summary>
[Microsoft.SqlServer.Dts.Pipeline.SSISScriptComponentEntryPointAttribute]
public class ScriptMain : UserComponent
{
  // Integer variable to keep track of the row number value
  int rowNumber = 0;
```

```csharp
/// <summary>
/// This method is called once for every row that
/// passes through the component from Input0.
///
/// Increment and assign variable to new output column
/// </summary>
/// <param name="Row">The row that is currently passing
/// through the component</param>
public override void Input0_ProcessInputRow(Input0Buffer Row)
{
    // Increment value
    rowNumber++;

    // Assigning value to new output column
    Row.BikeId = rowNumber;
}

}
```

This is the VB.NET code:

```vbnet
#Region "Imports"
Imports System
Imports System.Data
Imports System.Math
Imports Microsoft.SqlServer.Dts.Pipeline.Wrapper
Imports Microsoft.SqlServer.Dts.Runtime.Wrapper
#End Region

' This is the class to which to add your code.
' Do not change the name, attributes, or parent
' of this class.
<Microsoft.SqlServer.Dts.Pipeline.SSISScriptComponentEntryPointAttribute> _
<CLSCompliant(False)> _
Public Class ScriptMain
  Inherits UserComponent

  ' Integer variable to keep track of the row number value
  Dim rowNumber As Int32 = 0

  'This method is called once for every row that
  'passes through the component from Input0.
  '
  'Increment and assign variable to new output column
  Public Overrides Sub Input0_ProcessInputRow(ByVal Row As Input0Buffer)
    ' Increment value
    rowNumber = rowNumber + 1

    ' Assigning value to new output column
    Row.BikeId = rowNumber
  End Sub

End Class
```

■ **Note**   The generated code varies per SSIS version, so there could be some changes in text or in position.

With only three lines of code, you have created a perfect surrogate key. You could extend this code with, for example, a variable starting number and increment. Chapter 11 will continue with this example.

Now you can close the VSTA environment and the Script Component editor. You are now ready to test it. Add a dummy derived column after the new script component so that you can add a data viewer to see the result of the script. Then execute the Data Flow Task and check the result in the data viewer. It should look like Figure 2-10.

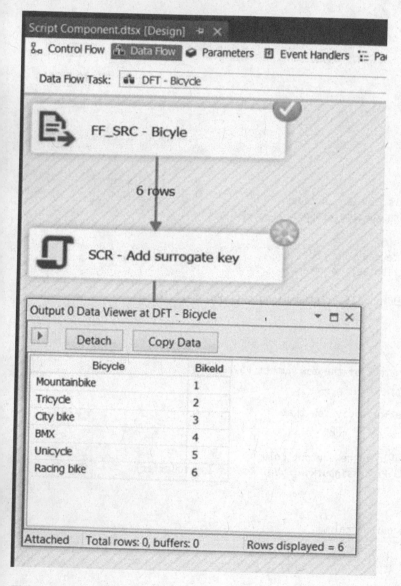

Figure 2-10. *New surrogate key added*

When to Use a Script Task/Component

The two introduction examples, although very simple, showed how useful scripting can be as an addition to SSIS, but there are a few disadvantages to using them. The most important drawback is maintainability. You might have excellent coding skills, but a colleague who works on the same project or the person that will maintain your packages when you finish them, might not. In fact, many SSIS developers and administrators do not have any C# or VB.NET coding skills at all.

Another drawback is clarity. When you see a Send Mail Task or an Execute Package Task, you can tell at a glance what the task does and what to expect when you edit the task. With the Script Task, you only have the name that the developer gave it, and then you probably still have to edit the Script Task and study the code to see what it is doing exactly. SCR – Unzip File looks very straightforward, but where is the zip file located? Is it extracting all files? Where does it put the unzipped files? Is it deleting, moving, or ignoring the original zipped file afterward? The same applies to the Data Flow Task transformations. A Merge Join or a Conditional Split is very clear, but with SCR – Validate Email, you might want to know how it is validating an email address and what it does with email addresses that are not valid.

The conditions for using Script Tasks and Script Components are very easy: only use them if they offer an advantage over the built-in tasks and components. Don't use them if you don't have to. Deleting a single file with a Script Task is not a good idea because you can easily do that with a File System Task. But what if you want to delete all *.txt and *.csv files in a folder? You could use two For each Loop Containers with a File System Task in them to delete the files, but you could also do that more easily and faster in a single Script Task. And what if you want to delete all files older than seven days? Then you are stuck with a Script Task because that is very hard to accomplish with the built-in tasks.

You should also not use the Script Task or Script Component when you have to use that same script in multiple packages. Solving a bug or adding a feature in a Script Component that is used in several packages could be very annoying and tiresome. In this case, you should consider creating a custom task or transformation. Chapters 16 through 19 xplain how this works.

Building Code

When your code is syntactically not correct, Visual Studio warns you in a couple of ways. First, you see some red wavy lines under your code. You can see those in Figure 2-11, under the ConnectionStrings identifier. When you move your mouse pointer to the error, the interface shows the error message.

```
// Fill variable with the filepath from a Flat File Connection Manager
string filePath;
filePath = Dts.Connections["myFlatFile"].ConnectionStrings;
```

Figure 2-11. *Wavy red lines under ConnectionStrings indicates an error*

Some errors—like a missing semicolon in C#—are less visible, especially in a large script. When you close the Script Task or Script Component editor, Visual Studio warns you again as in Figure 2-12. And if you choose to ignore this error, then the famous red circle with a cross in it indicates the error.

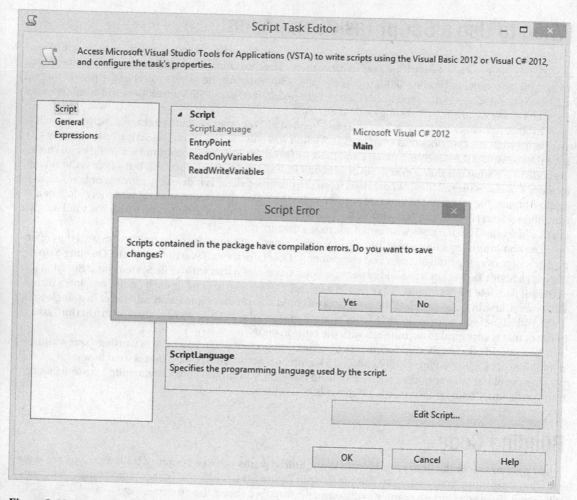

Figure 2-12. *A compilation error occurs because the script contains an error*

To make sure that your code is syntactically correct before you close the VSTA environment, you can build the code (see Figure 2-13) in the Build menu of Visual Studio. Any errors will show up in the Error pane. You can click these error messages to jump to the actual error in the code.

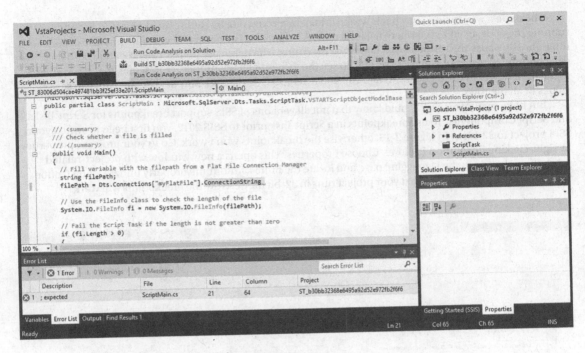

Figure 2-13. *Building the code to check for syntax errors*

Debugging in Visual Studio

When your .NET code is syntactically correct, but still not working properly, or when you get a vague runtime error such as *Exception has been thrown by the target of an invocation* or *Object reference not set to an instance of an object*, you want to know what is wrong with your code. Figure 2-14 shows an example of such an error.

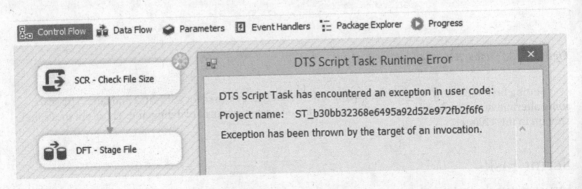

Figure 2-14. *This is a vague error for most people*

The easiest way to find out what is wrong is to debug your code by setting breakpoints in it, and then running the code again to see where it goes wrong. A *breakpoint* is a point that you add on a line of code to intentionally pause the script on that line while executing. The debugger pauses the execution, and then you can continue to run your code, line by line, to see the values of all the properties in scope. It works similar to the data viewer in the data flow. When you add a data viewer, the data flow pauses, and you can see the values of all the rows.

But before going on, you should know that not all versions of SSIS support breakpoints for Script Tasks and Script Components. To use breakpoints in a Script Task prior to SSIS 2012, you first need to switch your SSIS project to 32-bit as in Figure 2-15, otherwise the breakpoints won't work. Go to your project's properties by right-clicking in Solution Explorer. Choose Properties. This opens a new window with project-related properties. Now go to the Debugging page and locate the Run64BitRuntime property under Debug Options. Set it to False and click OK so that your project runs in 32-bit mode. Now the breakpoints will work.

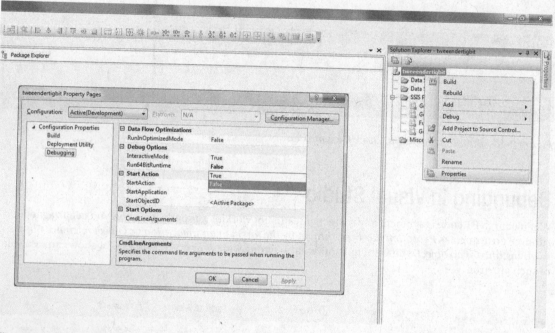

Figure 2-15. *Switch SSIS 2008 project to 32-bit*

Setting breakpoints in Script Components unfortunately only works for SSIS 2012 and later. There are some alternatives—like firing events and trace logging—to get some form of debugging. These are described later on in this chapter.

Script Task

First, start with the Script Task example that checks whether the size of a file is at least 1 byte in size. We created a package called debug.dtsx with this script, but we intentionally added an error. Try to find it and correct it. The scripts builds successfully, but when running it, you get an error: *Exception has been thrown by the target of an invocation*. See Figure 2-16.

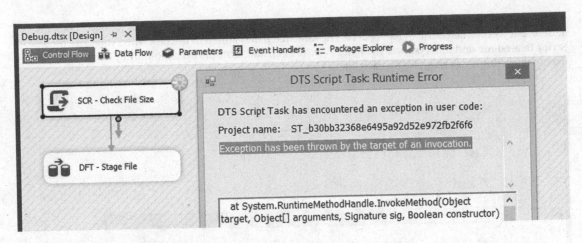

Figure 2-16. *Our intentionally added error*

You should edit the Script Task and click the Edit Script... button to see the code in the VSTA environment. Go to the line where you want the debugger to break. This could be the first line of code in the Main method or a line just before the place where you suspect your script will fail. In the Debug menu you find the Toggle Breakpoint option shown in Figure 2-17, but you can also hit F9 or click the light-gray column on the left side to add a breakpoint. You cannot add breakpoints on empty lines or comment lines.

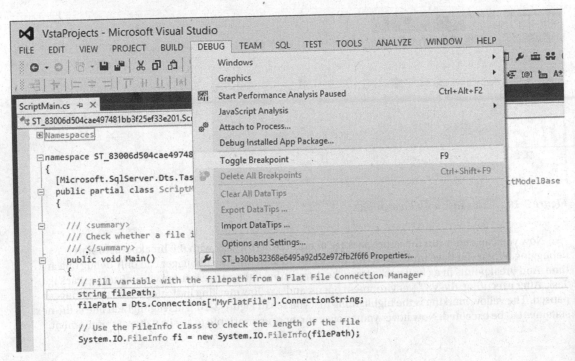

Figure 2-17. *Add a breakpoint in a Script Task*

When you add a breakpoint, it is clearly visible in the code. A red ball and a red background color are added, and you can see those in Figure 2-18. The same red ball is added in the task when you close the Script Task editor, and that is shown in Figure 2-19. You can add multiple breakpoints in your code, but don't overdo it by adding a breakpoint on each line.

```csharp
/// <summary>
/// Check whether a file is filled
/// </summary>
public void Main()
{
    // Fill variable with the filepath from a Flat File Connection Manager
    string filePath;
    filePath = Dts.Connections["MyFlatFile"].ConnectionString;

    // Use the FileInfo class to check the length of the file
    System.IO.FileInfo fi = new System.IO.FileInfo(filePath);

    // Fail the Script Task if the length is not greater than zero
    if (fi.Length > 0)
```

Figure 2-18. Breakpoint added

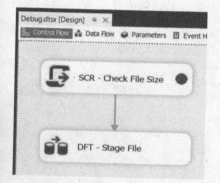

Figure 2-19. Script Task with breakpoint

Now you can either run the entire package or only the Script Task with the breakpoint to start debugging. When you have multiple Script Tasks with breakpoints, the debugger can only debug one at a time. And breakpoints in a child package will be disregarded if they are executed via an Execute Package Task. After executing, the VSTA environment opens, and a yellow marking indicates where the debugger paused. The yellow marking is the highlighting that you see in Figure 2-20. This highlighted line is the next statement to be executed. Now hover your mouse cursor over a variable to see its value at this moment.

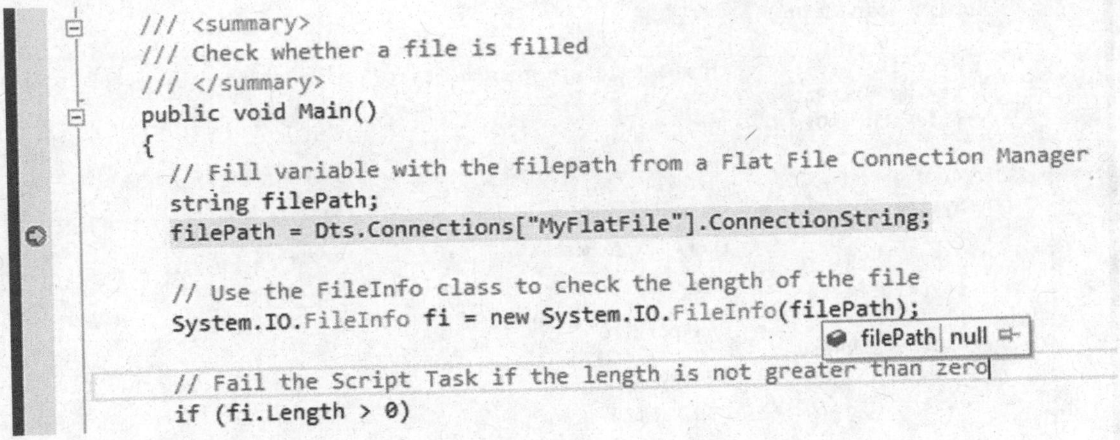

```
/// <summary>
/// Check whether a file is filled
/// </summary>
public void Main()
{
    // Fill variable with the filepath from a Flat File Connection Manager
    string filePath;
    filePath = Dts.Connections["MyFlatFile"].ConnectionString;

    // Use the FileInfo class to check the length of the file
    System.IO.FileInfo fi = new System.IO.FileInfo(filePath);
                                                         filePath   null

    // Fail the Script Task if the length is not greater than zero
    if (fi.Length > 0)
```

Figure 2-20. *Hitting a breakpoint and pause execution*

By pressing Debug…Step Over (F10), the currently selected line of code is executed. The yellow marking moves to the next code line and then you can check the values again. You can repeat this until there are no code lines left. You can also press F5 (continue), and then execution of the code proceeds until the next breakpoint, or if there are no more breakpoints, until the end of the script.

By now you probably found the error in the script. Our error is shown in Figure 2-21. It tells us that MyFlatFile is not found. Some further research will tell you that the name of the flat file doesn't start with a capital letter and that the code is case sensitive.

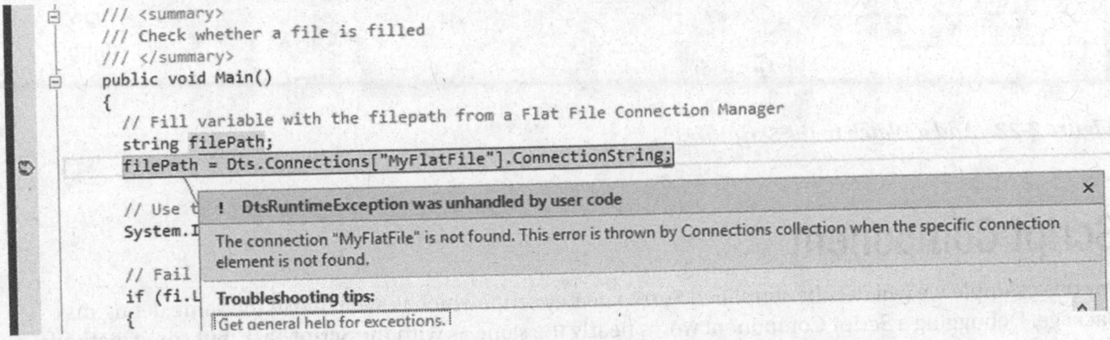

```
/// <summary>
/// Check whether a file is filled
/// </summary>
public void Main()
{
    // Fill variable with the filepath from a Flat File Connection Manager
    string filePath;
    filePath = Dts.Connections["MyFlatFile"].ConnectionString;
```
┌──┐
│ ! DtsRuntimeException was unhandled by user code   × │
│   │
│ The connection "MyFlatFile" is not found. This error is thrown by Connections collection when the specific connection │
│ element is not found.   │
│   │
│ Troubleshooting tips: │
│ Get general help for exceptions.   │
└──┘

Figure 2-21. *An error message that makes more sense*

You can also add a watch on a variable or a piece of code. Select the filePath variable from the example. Right-click it and select Add Watch as shown in Figure 2-22. The variable is added to the Watch window. Now you can step through your code by pressing F10 to see the value change in the Watch window without hovering your mouse pointer above the variable. If the Watch window isn't visible, then go to the Debug menu, and choose Windows ➤ Watch ➤ Watch 1, or press Ctrl + Alt + W, 1.

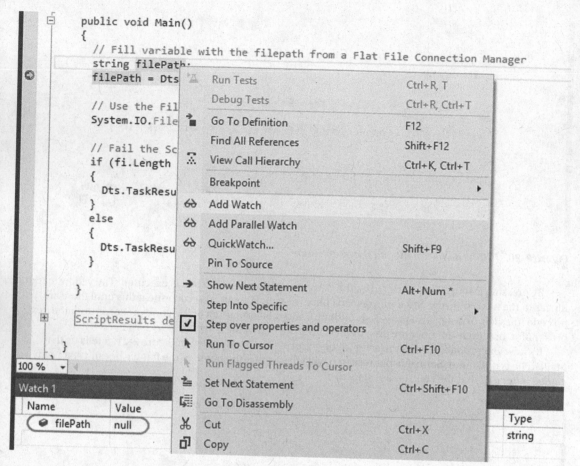

Figure 2-22. *Add a Watch to the Script Task*

Script Component

For this example we will use the simplified Surrogate Key script which is available in the same debug.dtsx package. Debugging a Script Component works nearly the same as with the Script Task, but some methods are executed multiple times. Edit the Script Component and click on the Edit Script... button to open the VSTA environment with our Surrogate Key script. Select a code line within the Input0_ProcessInputRow method and add a breakpoint as illustrated in Figure 2-23. The breakpoint will be clearly visible within the VSTA environment but not on the transformation itself like with the Script Task.

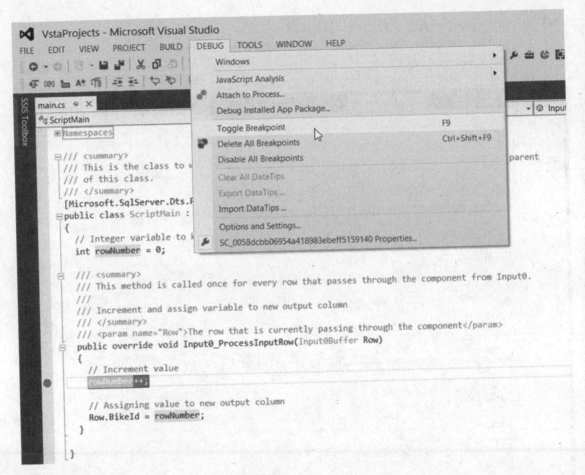

Figure 2-23. *Adding a breakpoint in a Script Component*

Now close the VSTA environment and execute the Data Flow Task or the entire package. Because you added a breakpoint within the ProcessInputRow method, which executes for each row, the debugger will continue with the second row after finishing the first row, and continue until all rows have been processed. Try this by pressing F5 (continue), and then checking the value of the rowNumber variable. Repeat this until all rows are processed. The watch functionality also works within the Script Component. For example, select the rowNumber variable, right-click it, and add a Watch. Figure 2-24 shows the result.

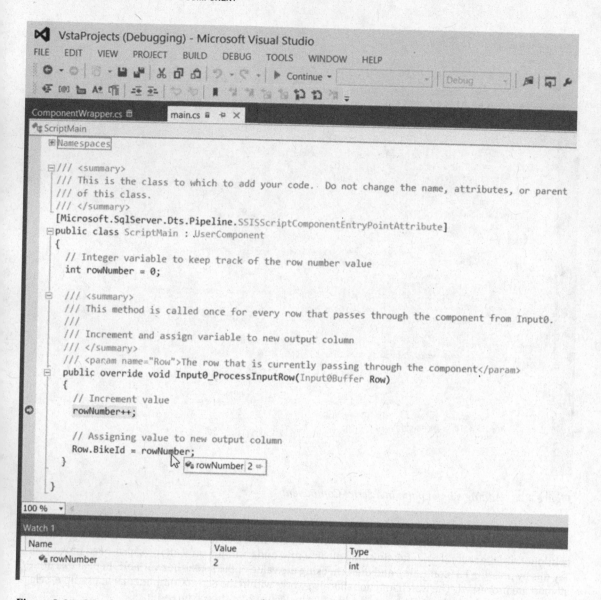

Figure 2-24. Watch in Script Component

When using an SSIS version prior to SSIS 2012, you cannot use breakpoints in the Script Component. There are a few workarounds to get some form of debugging. The good-old message box is a simple and quick way of displaying a value.

The message box is useful and traditional, but can get a little annoying when processing a large of records. No one wants to click OK 10,000 times. There is also the chance that you might accidentally leave a message box in the code when going to production.

The following code example implements a message box for debugging. Figure 2-25 shows that message box being used to display the current row number.

```
public override void Input0_ProcessInputRow(InputOBuffer Row)
{
  // Increment value
  rowNumber++;

  // MessageBox for a quick and dirty debug workaround
  System.Windows.Forms.MessageBox.Show(rowNumber.ToString());

  // Assigning value to new output column
  Row.BikeId = rowNumber;
}
```

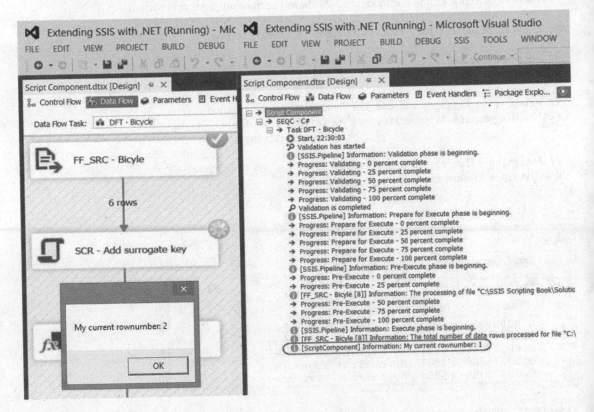

Figure 2-25. *Result debug alternatives*

A better alternative is to fire events to show the value in the Execution Result tab. Firing events are described in more depth in Chapter 4.

```
public override void Input0_ProcessInputRow(InputOBuffer Row)
{
  // Increment value
  rowNumber++;
```

```
// Firing events for a more fancy debug workaround
bool fireAgain = true;
this.ComponentMetaData.FireInformation(0, "ScriptComponent",
                               "My current rowNumber: " +
                               rowNumber.ToString(),
                               string.Empty, 0, ref fireAgain);

// Assigning value to new output column
Row.BikeId = rowNumber;
}
```

Another good alternative for breakpoints is to write trace messages to a listener. You can capture these messages with a free tool like DebugView (http://technet.microsoft.com/en-us/sysinternals/bb896647.aspx).

Following is a code example, and Figure 2-26 shows the trace output that is written.

```
public override void Input0_ProcessInputRow(Input0Buffer Row)
{
  // Increment value
  rowNumber++;

  // Write trace messages and use the DebugView to watch them
  System.Diagnostics.Trace.WriteLine("My current rownumber: " +
                                rowNumber.ToString());

  // Assigning value to new output column
  Row.BikeId = rowNumber;
}
```

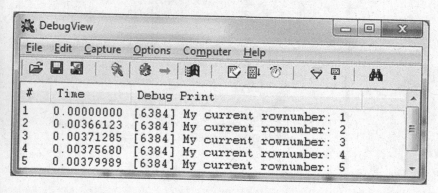

Figure 2-26. Watching trace messages with DebugView

Summary

This chapter explained the differences between the Script Task and the script component. It also showed some very basic examples to get an idea of what you can accomplish with coding. And it explained how you can solve errors in your script. The next chapter explains some C# and VB.NET basics.

CHAPTER 3

∎∎∎

.NET Fundamentals

If you are not familiar with the .NET Framework, or if you haven't written VB.NET or C# code before, this chapter is for you. In this chapter, you learn the basics and fundamentals of .NET development. You learn about data types, variables, and the structure of writing code in .NET; you learn this in both C# and VB.NET. The main purpose of this chapter, as one of the very first chapters in the book, is to help you understand .NET scripting. You'll enhance your knowledge in future chapters, because as you continue reading this book, you'll see more complex lines of code that need a good understanding of .NET fundamentals. If you are familiar with .NET, or if you are coming from a C#/VB.NET developer background, then you can simply skip this chapter.

Introduction

The .NET Framework is a proprietary and partial open source framework (the .NET Core is open source, including the runtime and the framework libraries) developed by Microsoft; it runs primarily on the Microsoft Windows platform. Its two main components are a large Framework Class Library (FCL) and the Common Language Runtime (CLR), which provides language interoperability, meaning that each language can use code written in other languages. The CLR is a managed software environment that allows programs and applications written with the .NET Framework to execute. The CLR is a kind of application virtual machine that deals with security, memory management, and exception handling. The FCL and CLR form the .NET Framework.

Microsoft provides an integrated development environment for the .NET Framework called Visual Studio.

More information about the basic concepts of the .NET Framework can be found on MSDN at `https://msdn.microsoft.com/en-us/library/ff361664(v=vs.110).aspx`.

.NET Data Types .vs Data Flow Data Types

Although there are similarities between them, there are also several fundamental differences between the data types used in .NET and the data types used in SSIS. The data types used in SSIS are data flow, which are supported by the pipeline buffer and are exposed using a dedicated type system.

This type system is different from the one used by SSIS variables or by data providers such as OLE DB and ADO.NET. Table 3-1 shows comparisons between the data types found in .NET and SSIS pipeline buffer types.

Table 3-1. *Data Types in .NET and in SSIS Pipeline*

.NET Type	SSIS Pipeline Buffer Type
Int64	DT_I8
Array of Byte	DT_BYTES
Boolean	DT_BOOL
String	DT_STR
DateTime	DT_DBDATE
DateTime	DT_DBTIMESTAMP
DateTime	DT_DBTIMESTAMP2
DateTimeOffset	DT_DBTIMESTAMPOFFSET
Prior to SQL Server 2012 : Object* from SQL Server 2012 : Decimal	DT_NUMERIC
Double	DT_R8
Object*	DT_IMAGE
Int32	DT_I4
String	DT_WSTR
String	DT_NTEXT
Single	DT_R4
Int16	DT_I2
TimeSpan	DT_DBTIME2
Byte	DT_UI1
GUID**	DT_GUID

All the data types in the .NET Framework derive from the Object type. Therefore, all data types can be converted to Object. This means that if you have a data type in SSIS that lacks an appropriate counterpart, you can always convert it to the Object type.

Even though GUID is a native .NET, it is not a part of the available SSIS variable type system. To create GUID you must resort to Script Tasks or Script Components. If you want to assign a GUID to a variable, you have to convert it to a string first; for example:Dts.Variable["MyGUID"].Value = "{" + Guid.NewGuid(). Tostring() + "}";

Data Types

The data type of an element indicates what kind of data the element can hold and how the data is stored. All the values that can be part of the evaluation of an expression or that can be stored into the computer memory have a data type. These elements can be variables, constants, enumerations, parameters, arguments, and properties. Procedure return values also have a data type. In the .NET Framework, you must declare the data types beforehand. The syntax varies whether you are using C# or VB.NET as a programming language. Table 3-2 shows how elements are declared in both languages.

Table 3-2. *Net Declaring Data Types*

Programming Element	C# Declaration	VB.NET Declaration
Variable	Double Amount; String Name;	Dim Amount as Double Dim Name as String
Literal	Double Amount = 10.5; String Name = "Regis";	Dim Amount as Double = 10.5 Dim Name as String = "Regis"
Constant	const Double VAT = 18.6;	Const VAT as Double = 18.6
Enumeration	Enum Colors{ blue, green}	Enum Colors Green Blue End Enum
Property	public int MyProperty { get; set; }	Public Property MyProperty() As Integer Get Return m_MyProperty End Get Set m_MyProperty = Value End Set End Property Private m_MyProperty As Integer
Parameter	public void myMethod (string parameter1)	Sub myMethod(ByVal parameter1 As String)
Argument	newString = inputArgument. Substring(0,2);	newString = Left(inputArgument, 2)
Return value	public string myNewMethod (String parameter)	Function myNewMethod(ByVal parameter as String) As String

Variables

A variable is a storage location that contains a known or unknown quantity of information called a *value*. In VB.NET, a variable is dimensioned, hence the name *Dim*. Variables can have access modifiers indicating their scope. At a class level, a variable with a public scope is exposed to all instances of the class, as well as other objects—including other classes. If the variable is private, it is only available inside the class. The same rules apply to properties: a public property is exposed to all other objects. A variable declared inside a method or a function is scoped to this method or function and cannot be used outside the scope of the function. Furthermore, if the variable is declared inside an if or a loop construct in a function, it is only scoped to the if or the loop construct.

Operators

There are different categories of operators in the .NET Framework, as shown in Table 3-3.

Table 3-3. *Operators Categories*

Category	Example
Primary	x.y, typeof, x++, x--
Unary	!x, ++x, --x
Multiplicative	x*y, x/y, x%y
Additive	x+y, x-y
Shift	x>>y, x<<y
Relational	x>y, x>y, x<=y, x>=y
Type testing	is, as
Equality	x==y, x!=y
Logical AND	x&y
Logical XOR	x^y
Logical OR	x|y
Conditional AND	x&&y
Conditional OR	x||y
Null-coalescing	x??y
Conditional	?:
Assignment and lambda expressions	x = y, x += y, x -= y, x *= y, x/=y, x %= y, x &= y, x |= y, x ^= y, 1. x <<= y, x >>= y, =>

For more information about operators and their usage, please visit MSDN at https://msdn.microsoft.com/en-us/library/6a71f45d.aspx; and for more information regarding VB.NET, go to https://msdn.microsoft.com/en-us/library/a1w3te48.aspx.

Using/Import, Classes, and Namespaces

To enable type names to be referenced without having to qualifying them with their namespace, you need to use the using (C#) or Imports (VB.NET) keywords. This is done at the file level and can also be done inside namespaces, classes, and so forth. Each source file can contain any number of Imports or usings.

■ **Note** Neither Import nor using make elements from other projects or assemblies available to your project. You still need to set a reference to the projects or assemblies. The using or Imports keywords only remove the need for qualifying names that are already available to your project.

The following is an example of a using statement in C#:

```
using System;
using System.Collections.Generic;
using System.Data;
using System.Linq;
using System.Text;
using System.Threading.Tasks;
```

In VB.NET, the equivalent is an Import statement; for example:

```
Import System;
Import System.Collections.Generic;
Import System.Data;
Import System.Linq;
Import System.Text;
Import System.Threading.Tasks;
```

Arrays

Arrays in C# and VB.NET are zero-indexed, meaning that the index starts at zero. When declaring an array in C#, the square brackets come after the type. In the following, note the identifier as illustrated in C#:

```
int[] myArray;
```

Or write it as follows in VB.NET:

```
Dim myArray as int[];
```

Another thing that makes arrays in C# or VB.NET different from arrays in other languages is that the size of the array is not part of its type. This way, it is possible to declare an array and assign objects to it, regardless of the array's length.

```
int[] myArray; // declares an array of int of any size
myNumberedArray = new int[10]; // number is a 10-elements array
myNumberedArray = new int[15]; // number is now a 15-elements array
```

The Different Types of Arrays

In C# and VB.NET, you can declare different type of arrays: single-dimensional, multi-dimensional, and array of arrays. Table 3-4 lists these types.

Table 3-4. Types of Array

Array Type	Example Declaration
Single dimensional array	`int[ ] myArray;`
Multidimensional array	`String[,] myArray;`
Array of arrays	`Byte[ ][ ] matrix;`

As illustrated in Table 3-1, declaring arrays does not actually create them. In C# and VB.NET, arrays are objects and must be instantiated like any other objects. Table 3-5 provides some examples.

Table 3-5. Instantiating Arrays

Array Type	Example Instantiation
Single dimensional array	`int[] myArray = new int[5];`
Multidimensional array	`String[,] myArray = new string[2,3];`

Array of arrays	`Byte[][] matrix = new byte[5][];`
	`2. For(int I = 0; I < matrix.length; i++)`
	`3. {`
	`4. matrix[x] = new byte[4];`
	`5. }`

It is also possible to have larger arrays; for example, a three-dimensional array can be written in C# as follows:

```
int[,,] 3DArray = new int[3,4,5];
```

And in VB.NET it is as follows:

```
Dim anArray As Integer(,,) = New Integer(2, 3, 4) {}
```

Initializing Arrays

Initializing arrays is simple and straightforward; it is done at declaration time by enclosing the values in curly brackets.

```
Int[] numbers = new int[]{1,2,3,4,5};
```

This is the VB.NET version:

```
Dim numbers As Int() = New Integer() {1, 2, 3, 4, 5}
```

Accessing Array Members

Accessing array members is also straightforward; it is very much like what is found in other programming languages. The following C# code declares an array and assigns a value of 12 to the fifth element.

```
Int[] numbers = new int[]{1,2,3,4,5,6,7,8,9};
numbers[4] = 12;
```

And here is the same example written in VB.NET:

```
Dim numbers As Int() = New Integer() {1, 2, 3, 4, 5, 6, 7, 8, 9}
numbers(4) = 12
```

As mentioned, arrays are objects that all descend from the base type System.Array. As such, they have properties and methods; for example, the length property lets you retrieve the number of elements in an array.

■ **Note** Arrays are 0-indexed but the length is 1-based.

Collections

Collections contain interfaces and classes that you can use to define collections of objects. These collections can be generic or non-generic and can hold various objects, such as lists, queues, arrays, dictionaries, and hash tables.

Lists

Lists are dynamic, strongly typed collections of objects that can be accessed by index. Lists have methods that help you search, sort, and work with data. It is ideal for elements accessed by indices. The following example in C# creates a list of four elements of type int.

```
List<int> myList = new List<int>();
myList.Add(1);
myList.Add(2);
myList.Add(3);
myList.Add(4);
```

■ **Note** The angle brackets are part of the declaration type in C#; they are not the operators (lesser than and greater than).

The same example is written in VB.NET as follows:

```
Dim myList As New List(Of Integer)()
myList.Add(1)
myList.Add(2)
myList.Add(3)
myList.Add(4)
```

Generics

The preceding examples added a primitive type to a list, but you can add object types and reference types as elements.

Lists are objects that are derived from the System.Collection.Generic class, and as such they have properties and methods that make them great types to work with. While the number of elements of an array is obtained with its length property, the number of elements in a list is obtained via its count property.

Generic lists are strongly typed, which usually gives them better safety and performance compared to non-generic lists; for example, List<T> is the generic version of the non-generic ArrayList.

For more information about lists, visit MSDN at https://msdn.microsoft.com/en-us/library/6sh2ey19 (v=vs.110).aspx.

Loops

Loops are obviously a very helpful programming artifact. With loops you can apply logic to every single element of a collection, a list, or an array.

Let's begin by discussing the while loop.

The while Loop

The while loop executes until the while condition evaluates to false. And because the test for the while condition executes before the content, a while loop executes zero or more times.

The following is an example of a while loop in C#:

```
int i = 0;
while(i++ < 10)
{
// do something
}
```

In VB.NET you can write the same loop as follows:

```
Dim index As Integer = 0
While index <= 10
    Debug.Write(index.ToString & " ")
    index += 1
End While
```

■ **Note**   If you want a loop that executes one or more times, then there is a construct called the do loop, which is explained in detail at https://msdn.microsoft.com/en-us/library/370s1zax.aspx.

The .NET Framework has two types of loop found in SSIS: the foreach loop and the for loop.

The for Loop

A for loop is typically used for looping over an array or a list. Arrays have a length property and lists have a count property; both can be used in the initialization of the loop. The following example has a single-dimensional array with three elements, as well as a list with five elements. You want to iterate through all of their elements:

```
//instantiate the array
int[] numberArray = new int[]{1,2,3};

//instantiate the List
List<string> numberList = new List<string>();

//Add elements to the list
numberList.Add("a");
numberList.Add("b");
numberList.Add("c");
numberList.Add("d");
numberList.Add("e");

//iterate through the elements of the array
for(int i = 0; i < numberArray.Length;i++)
{
//print out the value
Console.WriteLine(numberArray[i]);
}

//iterate through the elements of the list in the same manner
for(int i = 0; i < numberList.Count;i++)
{
//print out the value
Console.WriteLine(numberList[i]);
}
```

The prior example is in C#. You can achieve the same effect in VB.NET by writing this:

```
'instantiate the array
Dim numberArray As Integer() = New Integer() {1, 2, 3}

'instantiate the List
Dim numberList As New List(Of String)()

'Add elements to the list
numberList.Add("a")
numberList.Add("b")
numberList.Add("c")
numberList.Add("d")
numberList.Add("e")
```

```
'iterate through the elements of the array
For i As Integer = 0 To numberArray.Length - 1
    'print out the value
    Console.WriteLine(numberArray(i))
Next


'iterate through the elements of the list in the same manner
For i As Integer = 0 To numberList.Count - 1
    'print out the value
    Console.WriteLine(numberList(i))
Next
```

At any point during the iteration you can break out of the loop by using the break keyword, or you can step to the next iteration with the continue keyword. It is also possible to exit a for loop by using the following keywords : goto, return, throw.

■ **Note** If you want to iterate through a list or an array backward, you just need to count down in the following way: for(int i = myArray.Length -1; i = 0; i--).

The foreach Loop

Just like the for loop, the foreach loop repeats a statement or a group of statements for each element of an array or a collection. The foreach loop is used to execute those statements in the order provided by the list or the array, but the statements cannot alter the list or the array because they are iterated to avoid side effects.

At any point during the iteration, you can break out of the loop by using the break keyword, or you can step to the next iteration with the continue keyword. It is also possible to exit a foreach loop by using the following keywords : goto, return, throw.

The only condition your list or collection you want to iterate over need to fulfill is that it must implement the IEnumerable interface. Generic lists and collections do exactly that. They are available in System.Collections.Generic.

The following illustrates using the foreach loop to iterate over elements of an array.

```
int[] numbers = { 1, 2, 4, 6, 7, 9, -3, -1, 0 };

foreach (int i in numbers)
{
    Console.Write("{0} ", i);
}
// Output: 1 2 4 6 7 9 -3 -1 0
```

Here is the same loop type in VB.NET:

```
Dim numbers As Integer() = {1, 2, 4, 6, 7, 9, -3, -1, 0}

For Each i As Integer In numbers
    Console.Write("{0} ", i)
Next
' Output: 1 2 4 6 7 9 -3 -1 0
```

It is also possible to use foreach loops to iterate over items in multidimensional arrays, but using a nested for loop gives you more control over the elements.

Error Handling

A well-designed script must handle errors and exceptions to prevent crashes. The following are guidelines on how to handle errors and raise exceptions.

The throw Statement

The throw statement is used to signal a situation where there is an anomaly during program execution. It is used to raise exceptions. Exceptions are always objects that are derived from the System.Exception class; for example, in C# it is as follows:

```
class exampleException : System.Exception{}
// ... do something
throw new exampleException();
```

And in VB.NET, you throw an exception as follows:

```
Private Class exampleException      Inherits System.Exception
End Class
' ... do something
Throw New exampleException()
```

Ultimately, the fact that exceptions are derived from the System.Exception class means that you can create your own exception classes and throw them in your code, depending on the situation. The result could look like the following C# code snippet:

```
try
{
    // Do something and throw different type of exceptions.
}
catch (CustomException ce)
{
    ...
}
catch (AnotherCustomException ace)
{
    ...
}
catch (Exception ex)
{
    //the generic exception
}
```

In VB.NET, it would look like this:

```
Try
' Do something and throw different type of exceptions.
Catch ce As CustomException
'do something
Catch ace As AnotherCustomException
' do somerhing
Catch ex As Exception
'the generic exception

End Try
```

The try-catch Statement

By using `try-catch` you can programmatically check for and handle an exception that is likely to occur. The `try-catch` statement always consists of a `try` block followed by one or several `catch` clauses that specify how to handle different types of exceptions. When an exception is caught, the CLR looks for the `catch` statement that will handle that exception. If the executed method doesn't contain a catch statement, then the errors bubble up to the method calling this method, and so on until the CLR meets a `catch` block that it can use. If there are no `catch` blocks, then the program or application will return an unhandled error exception. There are several types of exceptions that can be raised; for more granular exception handling, you can check for several types in one try-catch block. Of course, by deriving from the base class `System.Exception`, you can always build your own exception classes to handle errors that suit your application or program.

The try-catch-finally Statement

A common usage of `try-catch-finally` is to obtain a resource in `try`, deal with exceptions in `catch`, and release the resource in `finally`. By using finally, you ensure that whether the code executed successfully or raised an exception, the finally clause will be executed. This is a great way to deal with connections, blocking IO resources and objects that you want to use and release afterward.

Another way of doing this—and generally a better approach—is to use the `using(){}` block in C# since it ensures that resources are cleaned up, as long these resources implement the `iDisposable` interface.

■ **Note** In VB.NET it is possible to filter exceptions and build conditional catch clauses. It is not possible in C# until .NET Framework 4.6 (which ships with SQL Server 2016).

Summary

The goal of this chapter was to provide an introduction to the data types and the most used constructs used in SSIS when scripting with C# and VB.NET. As you can imagine, there is a lot more to the framework than what can be written in a single chapter. We've merely scratched the surface. You are encouraged to read more about the .NET Framework, its capacities, and its strength on MSDN, starting at www.microsoft.com/net.

PART II

Script Tasks

CHAPTER 4

■ ■ ■

Script Task

If you want to work through SFTP (SSH File Transfer Protocol), or if you want to automate sending a highly customized email, or applying passwords on files, or checking file properties such as creation date and modified date, then the Script Task is one of your best choices. This chapter dives into the Script Task and some of its most common usages, including how to use it with variables and connection managers, how to use it with logging and error handling, and how to reference custom assemblies.

Editor

When you add a Script Task to the Control Flow and edit it, you first have to choose the Script Language: C# or VB.NET (see Figure 4-1). If you still work with SSIS 2005, then you can only select VB.NET. This option is write-once. After hitting the Edit Script... button, this option is grayed out and you cannot change the Script Language anymore. The only way to change it is to delete the entire Script Task, add a new Script Task to the Control Flow, and then start over again.

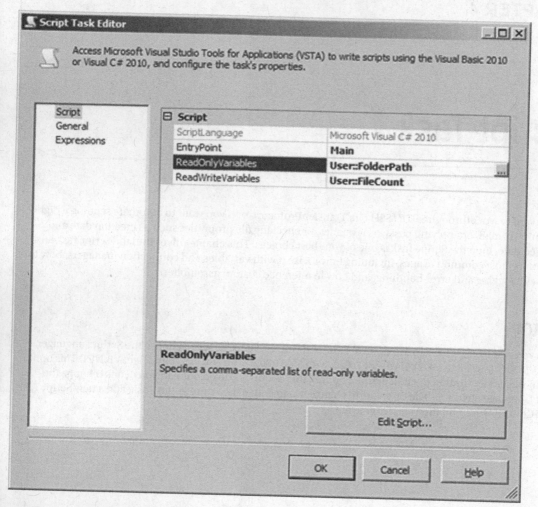

Figure 4-1. *The Script Task Editor*

You can change the default programming language to your own preference. In Visual Studio, go to the Tools menu and select Options.... Expand the Business Intelligence Designer section and then the Integration Services Designer. The default Language option appears on the right side (see Figure 4-2).

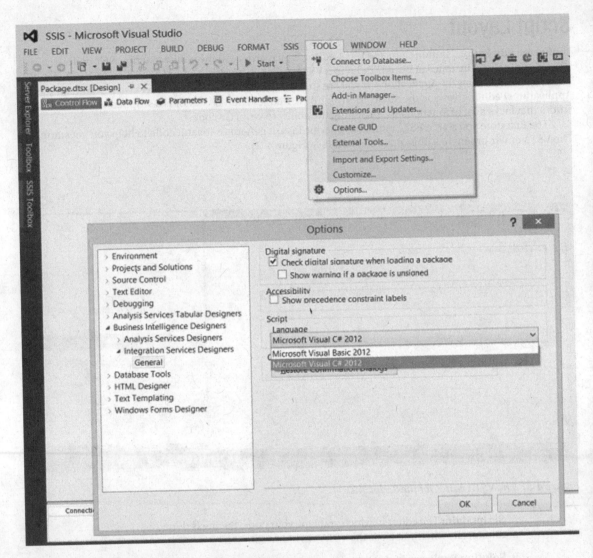

Figure 4-2. Changing the default Script Language

The second property in the editor is the Entry Point. With this property, you can change the name of the method that will be the starting point for your script. The default is the Main method. Unless you have a good reason, changing it could perhaps be a little confusing for others. *ReadOnlyVariables* and *ReadWriteVariables* give you the ability to read and change variables within the Script Task code, but you can also use them to read package and project parameters if you are using the project deployment model (available since SSIS 2012). You can either enter the variable names manually or use the pop-up window. These fields are optional, but more information and examples are provided later in this chapter.

Script Layout

Hitting the Edit Script... button starts the VSTA editor, which gives you the ability to write .NET code. This editor is a new instance of Visual Studio in a VSTA project with either C# or VB.NET code. VSTA stands for Visual Studio Tools for Applications. If you are still using SSIS 2005, then the VSA (Visual Studio for Applications) editor gives you the ability to write VB.NET code. The VSA editor is a stripped version of Visual Studio that lacks a lot of functionality, including the ability to write C# code.

The first time you start a VSTA editor for a Script Task, it generates default code to help you get started. The VSTA environment has three main sections (see Figure 4-3).

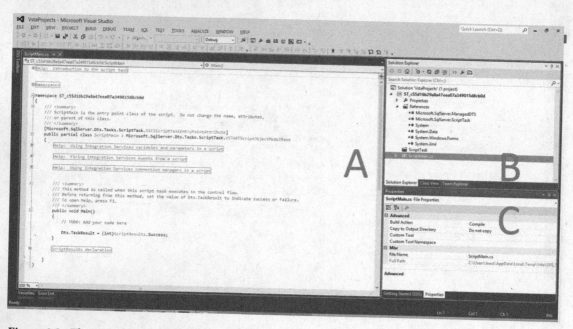

Figure 4-3. The VSTA editor for the Script Task

A. **ScriptMain:** The editor in which you type your code. Saving is done automatically when you close the VSTA environment.

B. **Solution Explorer:** In this section, you can add extra references to other .NET libraries, such as LINQ or to custom libraries. You could also change project properties, such as the target framework, and optionally add extra C# or VB.NET files. Changes should be saved with the Save All button; otherwise, they will be lost when you close the VSTA editor.

C. **Properties:** Here you can see the properties of the item you selected in the Solution Explorer. You can see where the (temporary) VSTA project is stored on disk, for example.

The script in section A is generated and the code varies per SSIS version and, of course, per scripting language (see Figures 4-4 and 4-5).

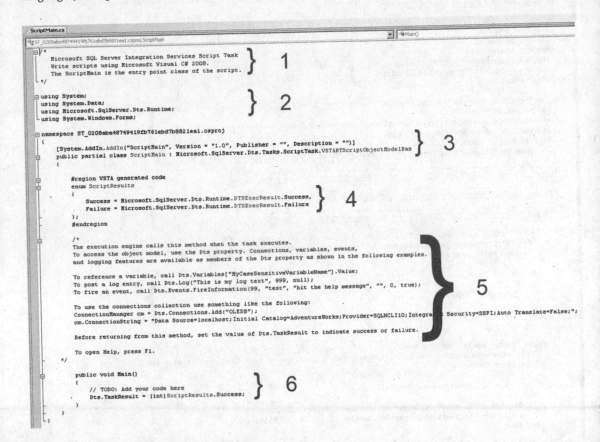

Figure 4-4. *SSIS 2008 C# Script Task code*

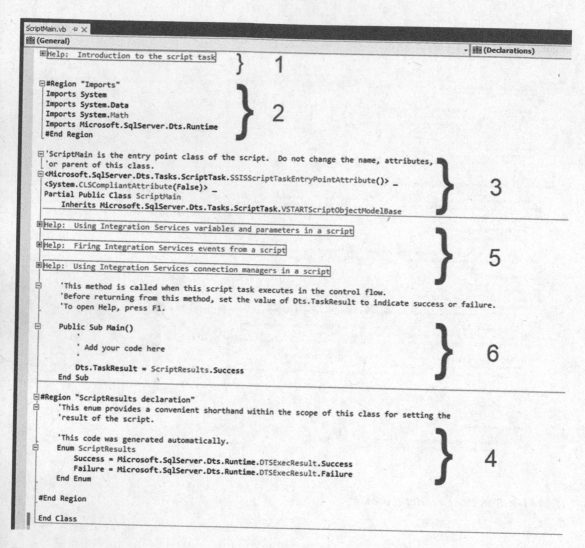

Figure 4-5. *2012 VB.NET Script Task code*

The Script Task always starts with a general comment. The text changes between SSIS versions. Remove these, or even better, replace them with a useful comment about the file/script. Why did you use a Script Task and what is your code doing? In 2012, regions were added to make the code more orderly. You could also add them manually to SSIS 2008 script.

```
#region Help: Introduction to the script task
/* The Script Task allows you to perform virtually any operation that can be
 * accomplished in a .Net application within the context of an Integration
 * Services control flow.
 *
 * Expand the other regions which have "Help" prefixes for examples of specific
 * ways to use Integration Services features within this script task.
 */
#endregion
```

This is the VB.NET code:

```
#Region "Help:  Introduction to the script task"
'The Script Task allows you to perform virtually any operation that can be
'accomplished in a .Net application within the context of an Integration
'Services control flow.

'Expand the other regions which have "Help" prefixes for examples of specific
'ways to use Integration Services features within this script task.
#End Region
```

Next part are the using directives or import statements. In C# they are called *using directives* and in VB.NET they are called *Imports statements*. For example:

```
#region Namespaces
using System;
using System.Data;
using Microsoft.SqlServer.Dts.Runtime;
using System.Windows.Forms;
#endregion
```

And here is the VB.NET code:

```
#Region "Imports"
Imports System
Imports System.Data
Imports System.Math
Imports Microsoft.SqlServer.Dts.Runtime
#End Region
```

Which namespaces are included varies per SSIS version and even per scripting language. You can add extra usings/imports to make your code more compact. They enable/allow the use of types in a given namespace. See Chapter 3 for more information about .NET fundamentals.

The third part is the namespace and class declaration. These are generated. Don't change these unless you are an experienced .NET developer with a good reason to do it.

```
namespace ST_abfa556bdb974f78a26e3c3af4606e6e
{
  /// <summary>
  /// ScriptMain is the entry point class of the script. Do not change the
  /// name, attributes, or parent of this class.
  /// </summary>
  [Microsoft.SqlServer.Dts.Tasks.ScriptTask.SSISScriptTaskEntryPointAttribute]
  public partial class ScriptMain : Microsoft.SqlServer.Dts.Tasks.ScriptTask.
  VSTARTScriptObjectModelBase
  {
```

And here is the VB.NET code:

```
'ScriptMain is the entry point class of the script. Do not change the name, 'attributes, or
parent of this class.
<Microsoft.SqlServer.Dts.Tasks.ScriptTask.SSISScriptTaskEntryPointAttribute()> _
<System.CLSCompliantAttribute(False)> _
Partial Public Class ScriptMain
   Inherits Microsoft.SqlServer.Dts.Tasks.ScriptTask.VSTARTScriptObjectModelBase
```

Next is the Script Result declaration (in SSIS 2012 these were moved to the bottom of the script; they don't exist in SSIS 2005). This generated code is for assigning a result to the Script Task: Success or Failure. Don't change this. To save space, the book examples do no show this code, but you can't delete it from the actual code!

```
#region ScriptResults declaration
/// <summary>
/// This enum provides a convenient shorthand within the scope of this class
/// for setting the result of the script.
///
/// This code was generated automatically.
/// </summary>
enum ScriptResults
{
    Success = Microsoft.SqlServer.Dts.Runtime.DTSExecResult.Success,
    Failure = Microsoft.SqlServer.Dts.Runtime.DTSExecResult.Failure
};
#endregion
```

And this is the VB.NET code:

```
#Region "ScriptResults declaration"
  'This enum provides a convenient shorthand within the scope of this class
  'for setting the result of the script.

  'This code was generated automatically.
  Enum ScriptResults
    Success = Microsoft.SqlServer.Dts.Runtime.DTSExecResult.Success
    Failure = Microsoft.SqlServer.Dts.Runtime.DTSExecResult.Failure
  End Enum
#End Region
```

The fifth part consists of help text and example code. You can leave it, remove it, or change it to general comments about your class and its methods.

The final part is the Main method. This is the method that starts when you run the Script Task and where you add your custom code. The Main method should always result in either ScriptResults.Success or ScriptResults.Failure. In SSIS 2005, you see a different syntax. To succeed the Script Task, it is Dts.TaskResult = Dts.TaskResult.Success and to fail the Script Task, it is Dts.TaskResult = Dts.TaskResult.Failure.

Variables and Parameters

The package variables in SSIS 2012 introduced parameters that can be used in a Script Task. You can use them to avoid hard-coded values in the script itself, or you can adjust the variable values in the script so that they can be used in other tasks or expressions. There are two different methods. In this example, you are counting the number of files in a folder. The folder path will be provided by a string variable or parameter, and the number of files will be stored in an integer variable.

■ **Note** Parameters are read-only. You can't change them, and you will get this error if you try to: Exception has been thrown by the target of an invocation.

First, create a new package called `variables.dtsx` and add a Script Task to the Control Flow. Give the Script Task a useful name like SCR – Count Files. Next, create a string variable (or a string package parameter or a string project parameter), name it FolderPath, and fill it with the path of an existing directory. Also create an integer (Int32) variable called FileCount for storing the number of files. Figure 4-6 shows the two variables.

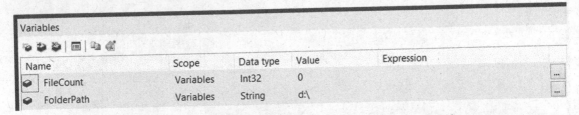

Figure 4-6. *Use variables for the FileCount and FolderPath*

Method 1: ReadOnlyVariables and ReadWriteVariables

For the first method, you need to fill the ReadOnlyVariables and ReadWriteVariables properties in the Script Task Editor so that these variables are locked by the Script Task during runtime. This can be done by typing the name or using the selection window (click the button with the three dots that appears when you select the field). Add the string variable name FolderPath (or one of the string parameters) as the read-only variable and add the integer variable FileCount as the read-write variable.

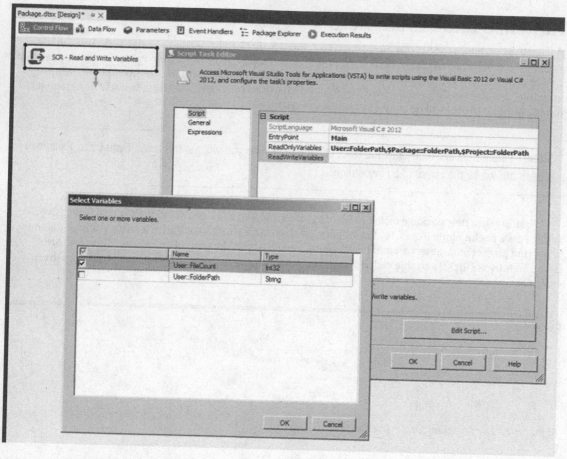

Figure 4-7. *Select the variables (or parameters) that you want to use*

After filling the ReadOnlyVariables and ReadWriteVariables properties, you can click the Edit Script... button to open the VSTA environment. First, add an extra using/import for System.IO on top so that you can do IO operations such as counting all the files in a folder.

```
using System.IO;
```

And here is the VB.NET code:

```
Imports System.IO
```

Next, add the actual code to the Main method. First you need to get the folder path from the variable and store it in a local .NET variable.

```
string myFolder = Dts.Variables["User::FolderPath"].Value.ToString();
```

And this is the VB.NET code:

```
Dim myFolder As String = Dts.Variables("User::FolderPath").Value.ToString()
```

Then you need to use that local variable in the actual file counting code and store the file count directly in the SSIS integer variable FileCount.

```
Dts.Variables["User::FileCount"].Value = Directory.GetFiles(myFolder, "*.*",
                                         SearchOption.TopDirectoryOnly).Length;
```

And this is the VB.NET code:

```
Dts.Variables("User::FileCount").Value = Directory.GetFiles(myFolder, "*.*", _
                                         SearchOption.TopDirectoryOnly).Length
```

Your total script now should look something like the following, but the namespace has a different name because it is generated. And the ScriptResults declaration is not shown in this code.

```
#region Namespaces
using System;
using System.Data;
using Microsoft.SqlServer.Dts.Runtime;
using System.Windows.Forms;
#endregion

#region customNamespaces
using System.IO;
#endregion

namespace ST_a0107ad99e244d5ca57c869184dd6a52
{
    /// <summary>
    /// This is an example on how to use variables and parameters in a Script
    /// Task. It gets a folder from a variable or parameter. Counts the number of
    /// files in it and fill the read write integer variable with the filecount.
    /// </summary>
    [Microsoft.SqlServer.Dts.Tasks.ScriptTask.SSISScriptTaskEntryPointAttribute]
    public partial class ScriptMain : Microsoft.SqlServer.Dts.Tasks.ScriptTask.
    VSTARTScriptObjectModelBase
    {
        /// <summary>
        /// Get folder and count the number of files in it.
        /// Pass te file count to the SSIS variable
        /// </summary>
        public void Main()
        {
            // First create a .NET string variable to store the path in. A little
            // redundant in this example but you could add extra steps to for
            // example validate the existance of the folder. Then choose which
            // variable or parameter you want to use to get the path from. In this
            // case I used the variable
            string myFolder = Dts.Variables["User::FolderPath"].Value.ToString();
```

```
        // If you rather want to use a parameter then use one of these codelines instead
        // of the variable line above. One of the three lines should be uncommented.
        //string myFolder = Dts.Variables["$Package::FolderPath"].Value.ToString();
        //string myFolder = Dts.Variables["$Project::FolderPath"].Value.ToString();

        // Get the file count from the my folder and store that number
        // in the SSIS integer variable.
        Dts.Variables["User::FileCount"].Value = Directory.GetFiles(myFolder, "*.*",
                                            SearchOption.TopDirectoryOnly).Length;

        // Close the script with result success.
        Dts.TaskResult = (int)ScriptResults.Success;
    }
  }
}
```

And here is the VB.NET code:

```
#Region "Imports"
Imports System
Imports System.Data
Imports System.Math
Imports Microsoft.SqlServer.Dts.Runtime
#End Region

#region customNamespaces
Imports System.IO
#endregion

<Microsoft.SqlServer.Dts.Tasks.ScriptTask.SSISScriptTaskEntryPointAttribute()> _
<System.CLSCompliantAttribute(False)> _
Partial Public Class ScriptMain
  Inherits Microsoft.SqlServer.Dts.Tasks.ScriptTask.VSTARTScriptObjectModelBase

  ' This is an example on how to use variables and parameters in a Script Task.
  ' It gets a folder from a variable or parameter. counts the number of files
  ' in it and fill the read write integer variable with the file count.
  Public Sub Main()
    ' First create a .NET string variable to store the path in. A little
    ' redundant in this example but you could add extra steps to for
    ' example validate the existance of the folder. Then choose which
    ' variable or parameter you want to use to get the path from. In this
    ' case I used the variable
    Dim myFolder As String = Dts.Variables("User::FolderPath").Value.ToString()

    ' If you rather want to use a parameter then use one of these codelines instead
    ' of the variable line above. One of the three lines should be uncommented. ' string
    myFolder = Dts.Variables("$Package::FolderPath").Value.ToString()
    ' string myFolder = Dts.Variables("$Project::FolderPath").Value.ToString()
```

```
    ' Get the file count from the my folder and store that number in the SSIS
    ' integer variable.
    Dts.Variables("User::FileCount").Value = Directory.GetFiles(myFolder, "*.*", _
                                             SearchOption.TopDirectoryOnly).Length

    ' Close the script with result success.
    Dts.TaskResult = ScriptResults.Success
  End Sub
End Class
```

When you copy and paste a lot of code to other Script Tasks, it is also possible to check if a variable exists in the collection of ReadOnlyVariables and ReadWriteVariables, and then log a meaningful error if it isn't available:

```
if (Dts.Variables.Contains("FileCount"))
{
  // Get the file count from the my folder and store that number in the SSIS integer
  variable. Dts.Variables["User::FileCount"].Value = Directory.GetFiles(myFolder, "*.*",
                                           SearchOption.TopDirectoryOnly).Length;

}
else
{
  // Handle error
}
```

And here is the VB.NET code:

```
If (Dts.Variables.Contains("FileCount")) Then
  ' Get the file count from the my folder and store that number in the SSIS ' integer variable.
  Dts.Variables("User::FileCount").Value = Directory.GetFiles(myFolder, "*.*", _
                                           SearchOption.TopDirectoryOnly).Length

Else
  ' Handle error
End If
```

And it is also possible to loop through the collection of variables that are added to the ReadOnlyVariables and ReadWriteVariables properties. In this example, you use a message box, but in one of the next paragraphs, you see a more elegant way to show the variables:

```
foreach (Variable myVar in Dts.Variables)
{
  MessageBox.Show(myVar.Namespace + "::" + myVar.Name);
}
```

And this is the VB.NET code:

```
For Each myVar As Variable In Dts.Variables
  MessageBox.Show(myVar.Namespace & "::" & myVar.Name)
Next
```

81

However, it is not possible to loop through all package variables and parameters because the Script Task doesn't support enumerating the list of all variables and parameters. You always have to hard-code the names unless you hard-code a reference to your package, and then you can iterate through all package variables and parameters. You should be aware that in this case it will create a second instance in the memory of the package. If you want to try this code, change the file path of the package.

```
Microsoft.SqlServer.Dts.Runtime.Application app = new Microsoft.SqlServer.Dts.Runtime
.Application();
Package myPackage = app.LoadPackage(@"Y:\SSIS\Variables.dtsx", null);

// Loop through package variables and parameters
foreach (Variable myVar in myPackage.Variables)
{
  // Filter System variables
  if (!myVar.Namespace.Equals("System"))
  {
    MessageBox.Show(myVar.Name);
  }
}
```

And this is the VB.NET code:

```
Dim app As Microsoft.SqlServer.Dts.Runtime.Application = _
                            New Microsoft.SqlServer.Dts.Runtime.Application()
Dim myPackage As Package = app.LoadPackage("Y:\SSIS\Variables.dtsx", Nothing)

' Loop through package variables and parameters
For Each myVar As Variable In myPackage.Variables
  ' Filter System variables
  If Not myVar.Namespace.Equals("System") Then
    MessageBox.Show(myVar.Name)
  End If
Next
```

If you want to get the value of a sensitive parameter, then you have to slightly change the code. Instead of using .Value.toString(), you need to use .GetSensitiveValue().ToString(). But be aware that you're now responsible for not accidently leaking sensitive values like passwords.

```
// Create string variable to store the parameter value
string mySecretPassword = Dts.Variables["$Package::MySecretPassword"].GetSensitiveValue()
.ToString();

// Show the parameter value with a messagebox
MessageBox.Show("Your secret password is " + mySecretPassword);
```

And here is the VB.NET code:

```
' Create string variable to store the parameter value
Dim mySecretPassword as string = _
              Dts.Variables("$Package::MySecretPassword").GetSensitiveValue().ToString()

' Show the parameter value with a messagebox
MessageBox.Show("Your secret password is " + mySecretPassword)
```

Method 2: Variable Dispenser

For the second method, you don't use the ReadOnlyVariables and ReadWriteVariables properties in the Script Task Editor. Instead you lock the variables in the script using the variable dispenser with the LockForRead and LockForWrite methods. A different method than earlier, but it has the same end result.

Add a new Script Task to your variables.dtsx package and connect it to the existing Script Task to make sure that the two Script Tasks don't execute at the same time; otherwise, they will both try to lock the same variables.

Edit the Script Task and open the VSTA environment. Add an extra using/import for System.IO on top so that you can do IO operations such as counting all the files in a folder.

```
using System.IO;
```

And this is the VB.NET code:

```
Imports System.IO
```

Now go to the Main method and add the following lines to lock the variables by code. The FolderPath variable is locked for read and the FileCount variable is locked for write.

```
Dts.VariableDispenser.LockForRead("User::FolderPath");
Dts.VariableDispenser.LockForWrite("User::FileCount");
```

And here is the VB.NET code:

```
Dts.VariableDispenser.LockForRead("User::FolderPath")
Dts.VariableDispenser.LockForWrite["User::FileCount"]
```

Then read the FolderPath variable and store its content in a local string variable.

```
Variables vars = null;
Dts.VariableDispenser.GetVariables(ref vars);
string myFolder = vars["User::FolderPath"].Value.ToString();
```

And here is the VB.NET code:

```
Dim vars As Variables = Nothing
Dts.VariableDispenser.GetVariables(vars)
Dim myFolder As String = vars("User::FolderPath").Value.ToString()
```

The next step is to count the number of files in the folder and store it in the SSIS integer variable FileCount.

```
vars["User::FileCount"].Value = Directory.GetFiles(myFolder, "*.*",
SearchOption.TopDirectoryOnly).Length;
```

And this is the VB.NET code:

```
vars("User::FileCount").Value = Directory.GetFiles(myFolder, "*.*",
SearchOption.TopDirectoryOnly).Length
```

Now the last part: releasing the lock on the variables.

```
vars.Unlock();
```

And here is the VB.NET code:

```
vars.Unlock()
```

The finale code should look something like this:

```csharp
#region Namespaces
using System;
using System.Data;
using Microsoft.SqlServer.Dts.Runtime;
using System.Windows.Forms;
#endregion

#region customNamespaces
using System.IO;
#endregion

namespace ST_fb03c633e7fc4e20a58e8e1ffc40b68e
{
    /// <summary>
    /// This is an example on how to use variables and parameters in a Script
    /// Task. It gets a folder from a variable or parameter. Counts the number
    /// of files in it and fill the read write integer variable with the file
    /// count.
    /// </summary>
    [Microsoft.SqlServer.Dts.Tasks.ScriptTask.SSISScriptTaskEntryPointAttribute]
    public partial class ScriptMain : Microsoft.SqlServer.Dts.Tasks.ScriptTask
    .VSTARTScriptObjectModelBase
    {
        /// <summary>
        /// Get folder and count the number of files in it. Pass te file count to
        /// the SSIS variable
        /// </summary>
        public void Main()
        {
            // Lock variables for read or for write
            Dts.VariableDispenser.LockForRead("User::FolderPath");
            Dts.VariableDispenser.LockForWrite("User::FileCount");

            // If you want to use a parameter instead of a variable then change the code to one of
            these lines.
            //Dts.VariableDispenser.LockForRead("$Package::FolderPath");
            //Dts.VariableDispenser.LockForRead("$Project::FolderPath");

            // Create a variable 'container' to store variables
            Variables vars = null;
```

```
// Add variables from the VariableDispenser to the variables container
Dts.VariableDispenser.GetVariables(ref vars);

// First create a .NET string variable to store the path in. A little
// redundant in this example but you could add extra steps to for
// example validate the existance of the folder. Then choose which
// variable or parameter you want to use to get the path from. In
// this case I used the variable
string myFolder = vars["User::FolderPath"].Value.ToString();

// Same alternative for using a parameter instead of a variable. Only use one of these
three lines.
//string myFolder = vars["$Package::FolderPath"].Value.ToString();
//string myFolder = vars["$Project::FolderPath"].Value.ToString();
// Get the file count from the my folder and store that number in the
// SSIS integer variable.
vars["User::FileCount"].Value = Directory.GetFiles(myFolder, "*.*",
                                        SearchOption.TopDirectoryOnly).Length;

// Release the locks
vars.Unlock();

// Close the script with result success.
Dts.TaskResult = (int)ScriptResults.Success;
    }

  }
}
```

And this is the VB.NET code:

```
#Region "Imports"
Imports System
Imports System.Data
Imports System.Math
Imports Microsoft.SqlServer.Dts.Runtime
#End Region

#region customNamespaces
Imports System.IO
#endregion

' This is an example on how to use variables and parameters in a Script
' Task. It gets a folder from a variable or parameter. Counts the number
' of files in it and fill the read write integer variable with the file
' count.
<Microsoft.SqlServer.Dts.Tasks.ScriptTask.SSISScriptTaskEntryPointAttribute()> _
<System.CLSCompliantAttribute(False)> _
Partial Public Class ScriptMain
   Inherits Microsoft.SqlServer.Dts.Tasks.ScriptTask.VSTARTScriptObjectModelBase
```

```vb
' Get folder and count the number of files in it. Pass te file count to
' the SSIS variable
Public Sub Main()
    ' Lock variables for read or for write
    Dts.VariableDispenser.LockForRead("User::FolderPath")
    Dts.VariableDispenser.LockForRead("$Package::FolderPath")
    Dts.VariableDispenser.LockForRead("$Project::FolderPath")
    Dts.VariableDispenser.LockForWrite("User::FileCount")

    ' Create a variable 'container' to store variables
    Dim vars As Variables = Nothing

    ' Add variables from the VariableDispenser to the variables container
    Dts.VariableDispenser.GetVariables(vars)

    ' First create a .NET string variable to store the path in. A little
    ' redundant in this example but you could add extra steps to for example
    ' validate the existance of the folder. Then choose which variable or
    ' parameter you want to use to get the path from. In this case I used the
    ' variable
    Dim myFolder As String = vars("User::FolderPath").Value.ToString()

    ' Get the file count from the my folder and store that number in
    ' the SSIS integer variable.
    vars("User::FileCount").Value = Directory.GetFiles(myFolder, "*.*", _
                                        SearchOption.TopDirectoryOnly).Length

    ' Release the locks
    vars.Unlock()

    ' Close the script with result success.
    Dts.TaskResult = ScriptResults.Success
End Sub

End Class
```

If you only need to lock one variable for read or for write, then you can use the LockOneForRead and LockOneForWrite methods. You need a little less code, but the result is similar. Here you only show the alternative code from the Main method. The extra using/import is the same as before.

```csharp
public void Main()
{
    // Create a variable 'container' to store variables
    Variables vars = null;

    // Lock variable for read and add it to the variables 'container'
    Dts.VariableDispenser.LockOneForRead("User::FolderPath", ref vars);

    // First create a .NET string variable to store the path in. A little
    // redundant in this example but you could add extra steps to for example
    // validate the existance of the folder. Then choose which variable or
```

```csharp
// parameter you want to use to get the path from. In this case I used
// the variable
string myFolder = vars["User::FolderPath"].Value.ToString();

// Release the lock
vars.Unlock();

// Lock variable for write and add it to the variables container
Dts.VariableDispenser.LockOneForWrite("User::FileCount", ref vars);

// Get the file count from the my folder and store that number in the
// SSIS integer variable.
vars["User::FileCount"].Value = Directory.GetFiles(myFolder, "*.*",
                                    SearchOption.TopDirectoryOnly).Length;

// Release the lock
vars.Unlock();

// Close the script with result success.
Dts.TaskResult = (int)ScriptResults.Success;
}
```

And here is the VB.NET code:

```vbnet
Public Sub Main()

' Create a variable 'container' to store variables
Dim vars As Variables = Nothing

' Lock variable for read and add it to the variables 'container'
Dts.VariableDispenser.LockOneForRead("User::FolderPath", vars)
' Dts.VariableDispenser.LockOneForRead("$Package::FolderPath", vars)
' Dts.VariableDispenser.LockOneForRead("$Project::FolderPath", vars)

' First create a .NET string variable to store the path in. A little
' redundant in this example but you could add extra steps to for example
' validate the existence of the folder. Then choose which variable or
' parameter you want to use to get the path from. In this case I used the
' variable
Dim myFolder As String = vars("User::FolderPath").Value.ToString()

' Release the locks
vars.Unlock()

' Lock variable for write and add it to the variables 'container'
Dts.VariableDispenser.LockOneForWrite("User::FileCount", vars)

' Get the file count from the my folder and store that number in the
' SSIS integer variable.
vars("User::FileCount").Value = Directory.GetFiles(myFolder, "*.*",
SearchOption.TopDirectoryOnly).Length
```

```
' Release the locks
vars.Unlock()

' Close the script with result success.
Dts.TaskResult = ScriptResults.Success
End Sub
```

Advantages and Disadvantages of Both Methods

With the variable dispenser method, you have a little more control when you lock and unlock your variables. The big downside is that you cannot quickly see which variables you are using. You have to check the entire code. Another disadvantage is that you need more code to accomplish the same thing. Therefore, the first method should be your preferred method. And you can also unlock the variables manually when you use the first method:

```
if (Dts.Variables.Count > 0)
{
  Dts.Variables.Unlock();
}
```

And here is the VB.NET code:

```
If (Dts.Variables.Count > 0) Then
  Dts.Variables.Unlock()
End If
```

Parent Package Variables

A *parent package* is a package that executes another package (a child) via the Execute Package Task. In the child package, you can read and write variables from a parent package with a Script Task, but the variables are only available in run-time mode and not in design-time mode. This means you cannot use the selection window, but you can type it manually. You can use both methods to read/write parent package variables in a Script Task.

There is one downside: without proper error handling, you won't be able to run the child package without the parent package, because it expects a variable that is not available. An alternative for reading parent package variables is to use parent package configurations, but that is only for reading and not for writing.

Referencing Assemblies

Sometimes you reuse a piece of code in multiple Script Tasks. If for some reason you have to change that piece of code, then you have to edit all the Scripts Tasks that use that code. To avoid this, you could create an assembly and reference it in your Script Tasks. An *assembly* is a piece of precompiled code that can be used by .NET applications. You can create an assembly to store your often-used methods. If you have to change one of those methods, then you only have to change the assembly (and not all of those Script Tasks).

Third-party companies (including Microsoft) can create assemblies for you as well; for example, an assembly to unzip files or to download files via SFTP. So, you don't have to reinvent the wheel. In some of the following chapters, you will learn how to use these third-party assemblies. In this chapter, you will learn how to create a simple assembly and use it in a Script Task.

Creating an Assembly

If you want to create your own assembly, then you need the "full" version of Visual Studio, or at least a version that supports a C# or VB.NET project. (So not just BIDS or SSDT BI.) In this example, you will create an assembly with a method to validate the format of an email address. Start Visual Studio and create a new Class Library project called myMethodsForSSIS. This template can be found under Visual Basic and Visual C# (see Figure 4-8). Make sure that you choose the right .NET Framework version (see Table 4-1); otherwise, you cannot reference it. Referencing a lower .NET version is possible with some extra steps, but you can't reference an assembly with a higher .NET version.

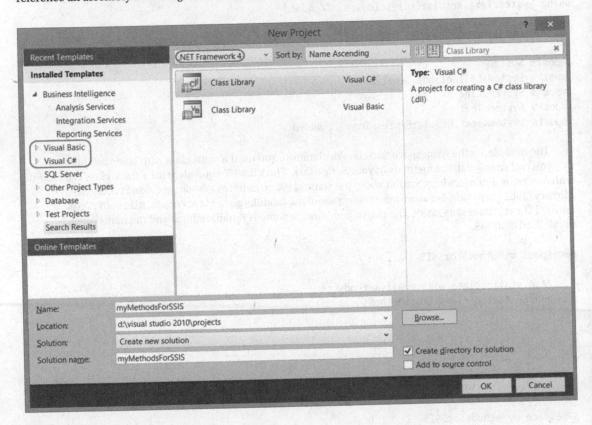

Figure 4-8. *New Class Library project*

Table 4-1. *Choose the Correct .NET Framework Version*

SSIS Version	Supported Framework
2005	2.0
2008 (R2)	2.0 => 3.5
2012	2.0 => 4.0
2014	2.0 => 4.5.1

When you create the new project, the Class1.cs or Class1.vb file is pretty empty. Start with adding the usings or imports at the top of the Class1 file. The C# file already has some usings, but the VB.NET file has none. They are in the project properties, but to keep the examples the same, you are adding them to the file as well.

```
using System;
using System.Collections.Generic;
using System.Linq;
using System.Text;
using System.Text.RegularExpressions;    // Added
```

And this is the VB.NET code:

```
Imports System
Imports System.Collections.Generic
Imports System.Linq
Imports System.Text
Imports System.Text.RegularExpressions   ' Added
```

The next step is the namespace and class declaration. You used a static class with static methods so that you can simply call the methods in your Script Task. The VB.NET equivalent for a static class is a module with functions. For more information about the static class, go to http://msdn.microsoft.com/en-us/library/79b3xss3.aspx. For more information about the module, go to http://msdn.microsoft.com/en-us/library/aaxss7da.aspx. The classname/modulename is EmailMethods and the namespace is myMethodsForSSIS.

```
namespace myMethodsForSSIS
{
    // A static class with email methods
    public static class EmailMethods
    {

    }
}
```

And here is the VB.NET code:

```
Namespace myMethodsForSSIS
    ' A module with email methods
    Public Module EmailMethods

    End Module
End Namespace
```

And the last step for the code is to add a public static method that validates the email address format to the C# class, or a public function to the VB.NET module. It is called IsCorrectEmail and it takes an email address as input and returns either true or false, indicating whether the format is correct. You can copy the method from the sources added to this book. When you are finished, the complete code should look like this.

```csharp
using System;
using System.Collections.Generic;
using System.Linq;
using System.Text;
using System.Text.RegularExpressions;    // Added

namespace myMethodsForSSIS
{
  // A static class with email methods
  public static class EmailMethods
  {
    // A boolean method that validates an email address
    // with a regex pattern.
    public static bool IsCorrectEmail(String emailAddress)
    {
      // The pattern for email
      string emailAddressPattern = @"^(([^<>()[\]\\.,;:\s@\""]+"
          + @"(\.[^<>()[\]\\.,;:\s@\""]+)*)|(\"".+\""))@"
          + @"((\[[0-9]{1,3}\.[0-9]{1,3}\.[0-9]{1,3}"
          + @"\.[0-9]{1,3}\])|(([a-zA-Z\-0-9]+\.)+"
          + @"[a-zA-Z]{2,}))$";
      // Create a regex object with the pattern
      Regex emailAddressRegex = new Regex(emailAddressPattern);
      // Check if it is match and return that value (boolean)
      return emailAddressRegex.IsMatch(emailAddress);
    }
  }
}
```

And this is the VB.NET code:

```vbnet
Imports System.Collections.Generic
Imports System.Linq
Imports System.Text
Imports System.Text.RegularExpressions  ' Added
Namespace myMethodsForSSIS
  ' A module with email methods
  Public Module EmailMethods
    ' A boolean method that validates an email address
    ' with a regex pattern.
    Public Function IsCorrectEmail(emailAddress As [String]) As Boolean
      ' The pattern for email
      Dim emailAddressPattern As String = "^(([^<>()[\]\\.,;:\s@\""]+" &
          "(\.[^<>()[\]\\.,;:\s@\""]+)*)|(\"".+\""))@" &
          "((\[[0-9]{1,3}\.[0-9]{1,3}\.[0-9]{1,3}" &
          "\.[0-9]{1,3}\])|(([a-zA-Z\-0-9]+\.)+" &
          "[a-zA-Z]{2,}))$"
```

91

```
        ' Create a regex object with the pattern
        Dim emailAddressRegex As New Regex(emailAddressPattern)
        ' Check if it is match and return that value (boolean)
        Return emailAddressRegex.IsMatch(emailAddress)
    End Function
  End Module
End Namespace
```

Strong Name

Before you can use the new assembly in an SSIS Script Task, you first have to strong name it. Go to the properties of the project and then to the Signing page. Check the "Sign the assembly" check box and then add a new key file in the drop-down list. The name for this example is PublicPrivateKeyFile.snk with sha256RSA as signature algorithm, and no password (see Figure 4-9). After clicking the OK button, the new key file will be visible in the Solution Explorer.

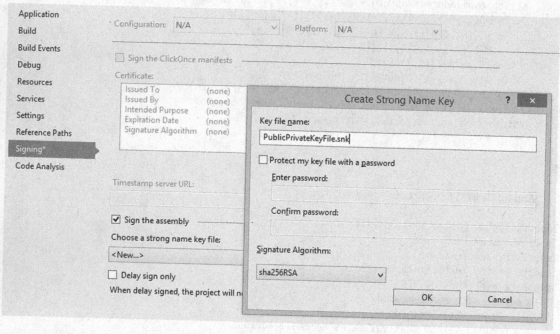

Figure 4-9. *Add key file (C# project, but VB.NET looks similar)*

Now close the project properties and build the project as a Release instead of the default Debug mode. You can change this in the Visual Studio toolbar. When you build the project, the assembly is signed with this new keyfile.

■ **Note** Adding a strong name is not a security measure. It only provides a unique identity.

Global Assembly Cache

The last step for preparing the assembly is to add it to the Global Assembly Cache (GAC) on the SSIS machine. SSIS can only use assemblies that are available via the GAC. Open the Visual Studio (2008/2010/ etc.) command prompt, but run it as administrator; otherwise, you can't add assemblies to the GAC. Go to the Bin\Release folder of your project, where you will find the .dll file of your newly created assembly. Execute the following command to add it to the GAC (see Figure 4-10):

```
gacutil /i myMethodsForSSIS.dll
```

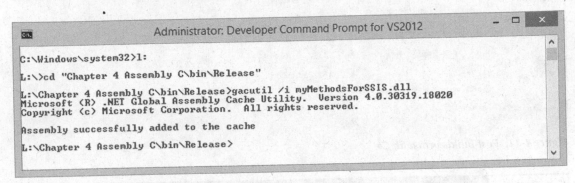

Figure 4-10. *.NET Global Assembly Cache Utility*

If you don't have gacutil on your server, which is often the case if don't have Visual Studio installed on a server, then you can use PowerShell to deploy your assembly (an example script is available with the source code for this book), or you can create a Setup and Deployment project in Visual Studio to create an installer for your assembly. Depending on the Visual Studio version installer, projects are located in Other Project Types ➤ Setup ➤ Deployment Projects. For Visual Studio 2013 and above, you need to download this project template: https://visualstudiogallery.msdn.microsoft.com/9abe329c-9bba-44a1-be59-0fbf6151054d.

Build Events

If you don't want to use the command prompt to add the assembly to the GAC each time you change it, then you could also add a post-build event to your Visual Studio project. Go to the properties of your assembly project by right-clicking it in the Solution Explorer. For C#, you can go to the Build Events tab and locate the post-build event command line (see Figure 4-11). For VB.NET, you need to go to the Compile tab and hit the Build events button in the lower-right corner, and then locate the same post-build event command line (see Figure 4-12).

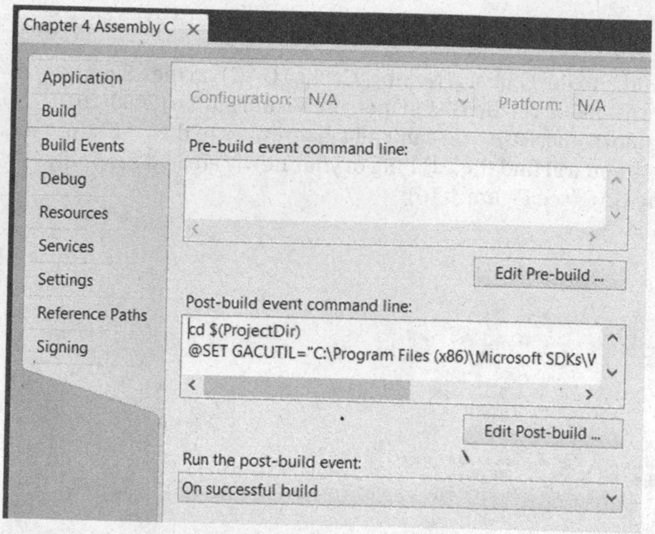

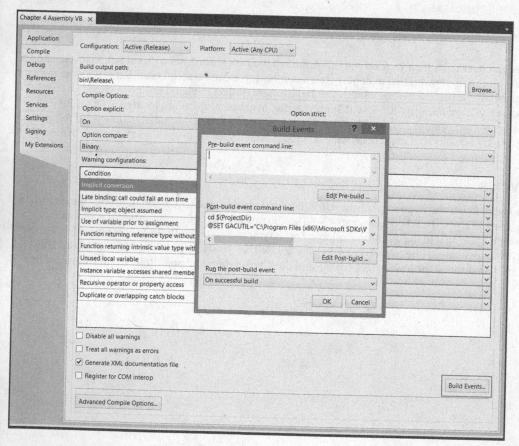

Figure 4-11. *Post-build event with C#*

Figure 4-12. *Post-build event with VB.NET*

Now copy the following command, but change the path of the gacutil. The path depends on the .NET Framework version and even the Windows version. This example is for .NET 3.5 on Windows 7.

```
cd $(ProjectDir)
@SET GACUTIL="C:\Program Files (x86)\Microsoft SDKs\Windows\v7.0A\bin\gacutil.exe"
Echo Installing dll in GAC
Echo $(OutDir)
Echo $(TargetFileName)
%GACUTIL% -if "$(OutDir)$(TargetFileName)"
```

Here are some alternative paths:

```
C:\Program Files (x86)\Microsoft SDKs\Windows\v7.0A\Bin\NETFX 4.0 Tools\gacutil.exe
(4.0 on Win7)
C:\Program Files (x86)\Microsoft SDKs\Windows\v8.1A\bin\NETFX 4.5.1 Tools\gacutil.exe
(4.5.1 on Win8.1)
```

Now you can add the assembly to the GAC by building the assembly project, but you need to run Visual Studio as an administrator, otherwise it won't work. To use the assembly in a Script Task you also need to think of a location for the actual dll file. For SSIS 2005, it is mandatory to put the .dll file in the Assemblies folder of SQL Server: C:\Program Files\Microsoft SQL Server\90\SDK\Assemblies\. For newer versions, you can put it anywhere. You can do that manually, but you could also add some extra lines to the post-build event:

```
@SET DLLDIR="C:\Program Files (x86)\Microsoft SQL Server\100\DTS\Assemblies\"
Echo Copying files to Assemblies
copy "$(OutDir)$(TargetFileName)" %DLLDIR%
```

Add a Reference in the Script Task

Now you can add a reference in the Script Task to the newly created assembly. For C#, right-click References in the Solution Explorer and choose Add Reference (see Figure 4-13). For VB.NET, right-click the project in the Solution Explorer and choose Add Reference (see Figure 4-14). Now browse to your .dll file and click OK to add it. The location of the browse button varies per version of Visual Studio. After adding the new reference, you need to click Save All to save the internal project and its new references. In newer versions of Visual Studio (2014), this mandatory Save All step isn't necessary anymore.

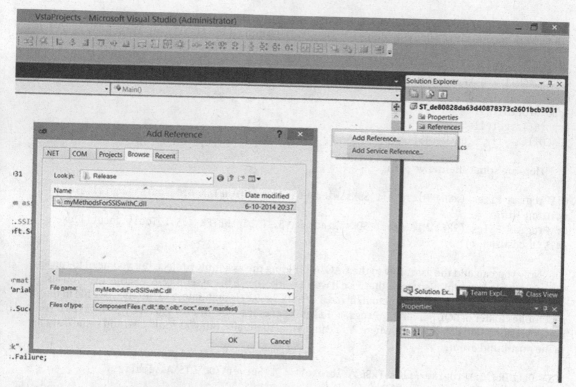

Figure 4-13. *Add reference in C# Script Task*

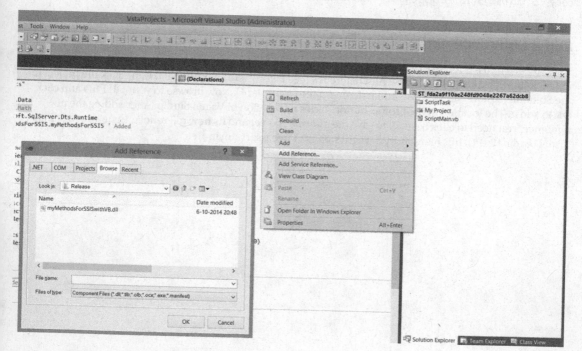

Figure 4-14. *Add reference in VB.NET Script Task*

■ **Note** Adding a reference to a third-party assembly works the same as adding a reference to your own assembly.

The following is some example code for using the assembly in a Script Task. To test this code, you first need to create an SSIS string variable named emailaddress and fill it with a valid email address. Then add a new Script Task and select the string variable as a ReadOnlyVariable in the Script Task Editor.

Now go to the VSTA environment and add the assembly myMethodsForSSIS as a reference. To create more compact code, you can add an extra using/import. Note that the import of the VB assembly in the VB.NET code is slightly different.

```
#region customNamespaces
using myMethodsForSSIS;
#endregion
```

And here is the VB.NET code:

```
#region customNamespaces
Imports myMethodsForSSIS.myMethodsForSSIS
#End Region
```

Now comes the actual code in the Main method. The script uses a variable as the parameter for the email method that checks the format with a regular expression. If the format is correct, then it succeeds the Script Task. If it's not correct, it fails the Script Task, but it also fires an error event explaining why the Script Task failed. Firing events for logging purposes is explained in detail in the last part of this chapter.

```
public void Main()
{
  // Get email address from variable
  string email = Dts.Variables["User::emailaddress"].Value.ToString();

  // Let the script task fail if the format of the email is incorrect
  if (EmailMethods.IsCorrectEmail(email))
  {
    Dts.TaskResult = (int)ScriptResults.Success;
  }
  else
  {
    // Show why the Script Task is failing by firing an error event
    Dts.Events.FireError(0, "Email check", "Incorrect format:" + email, string.Empty, 0);
    Dts.TaskResult = (int)ScriptResults.Failure;
  }
}
```

And this is the VB.NET code:

```vb
Public Sub Main()
    ' Get email address from variable
    Dim email As String = Dts.Variables("User::emailaddress").Value.ToString()

    ' Let the script task fail if the format of the email address is incorrect
    If (IsCorrectEmail(email)) Then
        Dts.TaskResult = ScriptResults.Success
    Else
        Dts.Events.FireError(0, "Email check", "Incorrect format:" + email, String.Empty, 0)
        Dts.TaskResult = ScriptResults.Failure
    End If
End Sub
```

Connection Managers

Integration Services uses connection managers to provide access to various data sources, such as flat files and databases, but also to web servers or FTP servers, or a message queue. You can use these connection managers in a Script Task to avoid hard-coded paths and connection strings. When used in the correct way, you can even let them participate in MSDTC transactions, but only for connection managers that support it.

File Connection Managers

Let's first cover the connection managers for files and folders such as File, Flat File, and Excel. There are two different methods for using connection managers in a Script Task. The first one is just getting properties from the connection manager, such as the ConnectionString property from a flat file connection manager or the ExcelFilePath property of an Excel connection manager.

In the first code example, you need a File or Flat File Connection Manager to an existing text file. The content doesn't matter as long as the connection manager is called myFlatFile and the file contains some data. The script gets the file path and checks whether it contains data by checking the file size. It uses FileInfo from the System.IO namespace, which you will add as using/import.

```
#region customNamespaces
using System.IO;
#endregion
```

And this is the VB.NET code:

```vb
#region customNamespaces
Imports System.IO
#End Region
```

Now the actual code from the Main method:

```csharp
public void Main()
{
  // Declare string variable and fill it with the connection string of the Flat File.
  string filePath = Dts.Connections["myFlatFile"].ConnectionString;

  // Declare file info object and fill it with the filepath from the string variable.
  // Then fill a bigint variable with the actual filesize for the next if-statement
  FileInfo fi = new FileInfo(filePath);
  Int64 length = fi.Length;

  // Let the script fail when the filesize is 0 bytes
  if (length.Equals(0))
  {
    Dts.TaskResult = (int)ScriptResults.Failure;
  }
  else
  {
    Dts.TaskResult = (int)ScriptResults.Success;
  }
}
```

And here is the VB.NET code:

```vbnet
Public Sub Main()
    ' Declare string variable and fill it with the connection string of the Flat File.
    Dim filePath As String = Dts.Connections("myFlatFile").ConnectionString

    ' Declare file info object and fill it with the filepath from the string variable.
    ' Then fill a bigint variable with the actual filesize for the next if-statement
    Dim fi As FileInfo = New FileInfo(filePath)
    Dim length As Int64 = fi.Length

    ' Let the script fail when the filesize is 0 bytes
    If (length.Equals(0)) Then
        Dts.TaskResult = ScriptResults.Failure
    Else
        Dts.TaskResult = ScriptResults.Success
    End If
End Sub
```

When you are using an Excel file, you cannot use the whole ConnectionString property because it contains more than just the file path. The next example extracts the file path from a connection string of an Excel connection manager named myExcel by using a substring method. It is stored in a string variable that you can use in your actual code.

```
// Declare string variable and fill it with the connection string of the Excel File.
string filePath = Dts.Connections["myExcel"].ConnectionString;

// For Excel connection you only need a part of the connectionstring:
// =======================================================================
// Provider=Microsoft.Jet.OLEDB.4.0;Data Source=D:\MyExcelFile.xls;
// Extended Properties="Excel 8.0;HDR=YES";
// Provider=Microsoft.ACE.OLEDB.12.0;Data Source=D:\MyExcelFile.xlsx;
// Extended Properties="Excel 12.0 XML;HDR=YES";
// =======================================================================
// You only want the part after 'Source=' until the next semicolon (;)
filePath = filePath.Substring(filePath.IndexOf("Source=") + 6);
filePath = filePath.Substring(1, filePath.IndexOf(";") - 1);
```

And here is the VB.NET code:

```
' Declare string variable and fill it with the connection string of the Excel File.
Dim filePath As String = Dts.Connections("myExcel").ConnectionString

' For Excel connection you only need a part of the connectionstring:
' =======================================================================
' Provider=Microsoft.Jet.OLEDB.4.0;Data Source=D:\MyExcelFile.xls;
' Extended Properties="Excel 8.0;HDR=YES";
' Provider=Microsoft.ACE.OLEDB.12.0;Data Source=D:\MyExcelFile.xlsx;
' Extended Properties="Excel 12.0 XML;HDR=YES";
' =======================================================================
' You only want the part after 'Source=' until the next semicolon (;)
filePath = filePath.Substring(filePath.IndexOf("Source=") + 6)
filePath = filePath.Substring(1, filePath.IndexOf(";") - 1)
```

Another trick is to first create a connection manager variable and fill it a reference to the Excel connection manager. Then you can read the ExcelFilePath property to get the file path instead of the complete connection string. It then stores the file path in a string variable that you can use in your actual code.

```
// Get the Excel connection manager to read its properties
ConnectionManager myExcelConn = Dts.Connections["myExcel"];

// Declare string variable and fill it with the ExcelFilePath property of the Excel
connection manager.
string filePath = myExcelConn.Properties["ExcelFilePath"].GetValue(myExcelConn).ToString();
```

And this is the VB.NET code:

```
' Get the Excel connection manager to read its properties
Dim myExcelConn As ConnectionManager = Dts.Connections("myExcel")

' Declare string variable and fill it with the ExcelFilePath property of the Excel
connection manager.
Dim filePath As String = myExcelConn.Properties("ExcelFilePath").GetValue(myExcelConn)
.ToString()
```

The big downside with this first method is that it doesn't validate expressions on the connection manager. If you are using it within a Foreach Loop Container, it could cause some unexpected results. By using the AcquireConnection method, you can overcome this because it forces SSIS to re-evaluate any expressions on the connection manager. Here are two examples that fill the same string variable with the file path of the flat file:

```
// Declare string variable and fill it with the connection string of the Flat File.
string filePath = Dts.Connections["myFlatFile"].AcquireConnection(Dts.Transaction)
.ToString();

// Or a little more complicated version that applies to more to all connection manager types

// Declare object variable to reference a connection manager
object rawConnection = Dts.Connections["myFlatFile"].AcquireConnection(Dts.Transaction);

// Declare string variable and fill it with the connection string of the Flat File.
string filePath = rawConnection.ToString();
```

And here is the VB.NET code:

```
// And optional release the connection manager manually to let SSIS know you're done
Dts.Connections["myFlatFile"].ReleaseConnection(rawConnection);

' Declare string variable and fill it with the connection string of the Flat File.
Dim filePath As String = Dts.Connections("myFlatFile").AcquireConnection(Dts.Transaction)
.ToString()

' Or a little more complicated version that applies to more to all connection manager types

' Declare object variable to store a Connection Manager
Dim rawConnection As Object = Dts.Connections("myFlatFile").AcquireConnection(Dts.Transaction)

' Declare string variable and fill it with the connection string of the Flat File.
Dim filePath As String = rawConnection.ToString()

' And optional release the connection manager manually to let SSIS know you're done
Dts.Connections("myFlatFile").ReleaseConnection(rawConnection)
```

> ■ **Note** If you don't want to use MSDTC transactions, then you can replace the AcquireConnection parameter Dts.Transaction with null.

The same can be done for OLE DB and ADO.NET Connection Managers, but beware of using database connection managers in a Script Task. Don't use them unnecessarily if you can also use an Execute SQL Task, such as for executing a query or stored procedure. The preferred connection manager for connecting databases in a Script Task is the ADO.NET Connection Manager. OLE DB is also possible, but it is a lot more difficult and it has some limitations, like not being able to pass current transactions, and it doesn't honor the Retain Same Connection property. This is because the Script Task has managed code that interacts better with other managed code, and the OLE DB provider is made with unmanaged code. The following code is a very simplified example of using a database connection manager in a Script Task. It could have been accomplished more easily with an Execute SQL Task, but more sophisticated examples will follow later in this book. For this example, you have added an SSIS string variable named sqlServerVersion in the ReadWriteVariables property. It will be filled with the SQL Server version information by the Script Task. Also make sure that you have an ADO.NET Connection Manager in your package named myADONETConnection.

This example uses the SqlClient assembly, which you will add as using/import to shorten the code.

```
#region customNamespaces
using System.Data.SqlClient;
#endregion
```

And here is the VB.NET code:

```
#region customNamespaces
Imports System.Data.SqlClient
#End Region
```

And now the actual code in the Main method.

```
public void Main()
{
  // Declare a SqlClient connection and assign your ADO.NET Connection Manager to this
  connection.
  SqlConnection myADONETConnection = (SqlConnection)
              Dts.Connections["myADONETConnection"].AcquireConnection(Dts.Transaction);

  // Create string variable with query
  string myQueryText = "SELECT @@version as SqlVersion";

  // Create a SqlClient command to store a query in it. In this case a simple query to get
  the SQL version
  SqlCommand myQuery = new SqlCommand(myQueryText, myADONETConnection);

  // Execute the query and store the result in a SqlClient datareader object
  SqlDataReader myQueryResult = myQuery.ExecuteReader();

  // Go to the first record of the datareader
  myQueryResult.Read();

  // Store the value of the 'SqlVersion' column in an SSIS string variable
  Dts.Variables["User::sqlServerVersion"].Value = myQueryResult["SqlVersion"].ToString();

  // Close Script Task with success
  Dts.TaskResult = (int)ScriptResults.Success;
}
```

And this is the VB.NET code:

```vb
Public Sub Main()
    ' Declare a SqlClient connection and assign your ADO.NET Connection Manager to this connection
    Dim myADONETConnection As SqlConnection = DirectCast(Dts.Connections("myADONETConnection") _
                                    .AcquireConnection(Dts.Transaction), SqlConnection)


    ' Create string variable with query
    Dim myQueryText As String = "SELECT @@version as SqlVersion"

    ' Create a SqlClient command to store a query in it. In this case a simple query to get
    the SQL version
    Dim myQuery As SqlCommand = New SqlCommand(myQueryText, myADONETConnection)

    ' Execute the query and store the result in a SqlClient datareader object
    Dim myQueryResult As SqlDataReader = myQuery.ExecuteReader()

    ' Go to the first record of the datareader
    myQueryResult.Read()

    ' Store value of the SqlVerion column in an SSIS string variable
    Dts.Variables("User::sqlServerVersion").Value = myQueryResult("SqlVersion").ToString()

    ' Close Script Task with success
    Dts.TaskResult = ScriptResults.Success
End Sub
```

As I said earlier, getting the OLE DB version to work is a lot more difficult. The `AcquireConnection` method cannot be used for OLE DB connection managers because it returns a native COM object. In this example, you need an OLE DB Connection Manager named myOLEDBConnection, and the same sqlServerVersion string variable as in the previous example in the ReadWriteVariable property. The work-around is casting the OLE DB connection manager's InnerObject to the IDTSConnectionManagerDatabaseParameters100 interface (SSIS 2005 uses 90 instead of 100). To do that, you first have to add a reference to `Microsoft.SqlServer` `.DTSRuntimeWrap.dll` in the VSTA project. That assembly can be found in the GAC 64-bit folder. The folder path should look something like this: `C:\Windows\Microsoft.NET\assembly\GAC_64\Microsoft.SqlServer` `.DTSRuntimeWrap\v4.0_11.0.0.0__89845dcd8080cc91\`.

For C#, go to the Solution Explorer of the VSTA project and right-click References. Choose Add Reference to open the Add Reference window (see Figure 4-15). You can search for it in newer versions of Visual Studio or browse to it. In the Browse tab, you can browse to the correct folder. Select the assembly and click OK to add the new reference. After adding the reference, it is necessary to click the Save All button if you are using Visual Studio 2010 or lower!

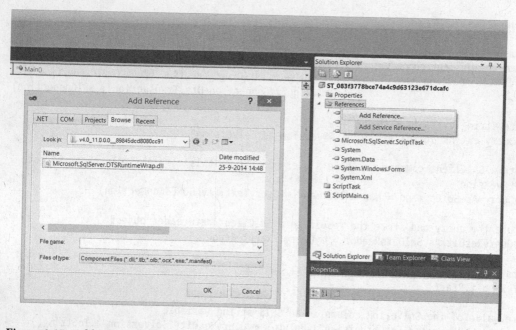

Figure 4-15. *Add reference to DTSRuntimeWrap.dll in C# project*

For VB.NET, go to the Solution Explorer of the VSTA project and right-click the project. Choose Add Reference to open the Add Reference window (see Figure 4-16). In the Browse tab, you can browse to the correct folder. Select the assembly and click OK to add the new reference. After adding the reference, it is necessary to click the Save All button!

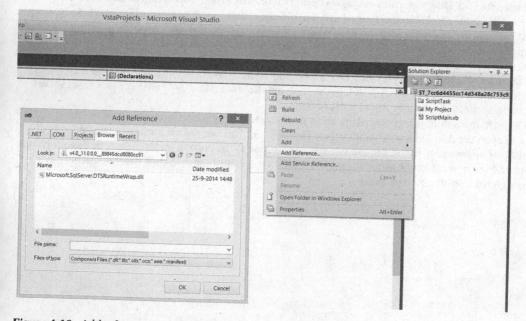

Figure 4-16. *Add reference to DTSRuntimeWrap.dll in VB project*

Add two extra usings/imports for shorter code: one for the OLE DB and one for the newly added reference.

```
#region customNamespaces
using System.Data.SqlClientOleDb;
using Microsoft.SqlServer.Dts.Runtime.Wrapper;
#endregion
```

And here is the VB.NET code:

```
#region customNamespaces
Imports System.Data.SqlClient
using Microsoft.SqlServer.Dts.Runtime.Wrapper
#End Region
```

Next is the actual code for the Main method. The major code difference is mainly in the beginning of the code. The rest looks very similar to the ADO.net example.

```
public void Main()
{
    // Store the connection in a Connection Manager object
    ConnectionManager myConnectionManager = Dts.Connections["myOLEDBConnection"];

    // Cast the Connection Managers's InnerObject to the
    // IDTSConnectionManagerDatabaseParameters100
    // interface (SSIS 2005 uses 90 instead of 100).
    IDTSConnectionManagerDatabaseParameters100 cmParams;
    cmParams = myConnectionManager.InnerObject as IDTSConnectionManagerDatabaseParameters100;

    // Get the connection from the IDTSConnectionManagerDatabaseParameters100 object
    OleDbConnection myConnection = cmParams.GetConnectionForSchema() as OleDbConnection;

    // Create string variable with query
    string myQueryText = "SELECT @@version as SqlVersion";

    // Create a new OleDbCommand object to store a query in it.
    OleDbCommand myQuery = new OleDbCommand(myQueryText, myConnection);

    // Execute the query and store the result in an OleDb DataReader object
    OleDbDataReader myQueryResult = myQuery.ExecuteReader();

    // Go to the first record of the datareader
    myQueryResult.Read();

    // Store the value of the SqlVersion column in an SSIS
    // string variable
    Dts.Variables["User::sqlServerVersion"].Value = myQueryResult["SqlVersion"].ToString();

    // Close Script Task with success
    Dts.TaskResult = (int)ScriptResults.Success;
}
```

And here is the VB.NET code:

```vbnet
Public Sub Main()
    ' Store the connection in a Connection Manager object
    Dim myConnectionManager As ConnectionManager = Dts.Connections("myOLEDBConnection")

    ' Cast the Connection Managers's InnerObject to the IDTSConnectionManagerDatabaseParameters100
    ' interface (SSIS 2005 uses 90 instead of 100).
    Dim cmParams As IDTSConnectionManagerDatabaseParameters100
    cmParams = TryCast(myConnectionManager.InnerObject, IDTSConnectionManagerDatabaseParameters100)

    ' Get the connection from the IDTSConnectionManagerDatabaseParameters100 object
    Dim myConnection As OleDbConnection = DirectCast(cmParams.GetConnectionForSchema(), _
    OleDbConnection)

    ' Create a new OleDbCommand object to store a query in it.
    Dim myQuery As OleDbCommand = New OleDbCommand("SELECT @@version as SqlVersion", _
    myConnection)

    ' Execute the query and store the result in an OleDb DataReader object
    Dim myQueryResult As OleDbDataReader = myQuery.ExecuteReader()

    ' Go to the first record of the datareader
    myQueryResult.Read()

    ' Store the value of the SqlVersion column in an SSIS string variable
    Dts.Variables("User::sqlServerVersion").Value = myQueryResult("SqlVersion").ToString()

    ' Close Script Task with success
    Dts.TaskResult = ScriptResults.Success
End Sub
```

■ **Note** If you don't want to use this complicated method, you could always just use the ConnectionString property of the OLE DB connection manager and create a new connection.

Logging Events

When you want to log messages from a Script Task into the SSIS log, you have to raise events with code. Whether they will show up in the log depends on the chosen log level (project deployment) or on the chosen logging configuration (package deployment). The Script Task can raise events by calling event firing methods on the Events property of the Dts object. In this example, you will check whether a file from a File Connection Manager exists and contains data.

Create a File or Flat File Connection Manager named myFile that points to a random text file. The content doesn't matter. Because you will try to get some file properties, you need the System.IO assembly. You will add this to the usings/imports.

```
#region customNamespaces
using System.IO;
#endregion
```

And this is the VB.NET code:

```
#region customNamespaces
Imports System.IO
#End Region
```

Next is the actual code for the Main method. First get the file path from the connection manager and then check if the file exists and contains data.

```
public void Main()
{
  // Get filepath from File Connection Manager and store it in a string variable
  string filePath = Dts.Connections["myFile"].AcquireConnection(Dts.Transaction).ToString();

  // Create File Info object with filepath variable
  FileInfo fi = new FileInfo(filePath);

  // Check if file exists
  if (fi.Exists)
  {
    // File exists, but check size
    if (fi.Length > 0)
    {
      // Boolean variable indicating if the same event can fire
      // multiple times
      bool fireAgain = true;

      // File exists and contains data. Fire Information event
      Dts.Events.FireInformation(0, "Script Task File Check", "File exists and contains data.",
      string.Empty, 0, ref fireAgain);
    }
    else
    {
      // File exists, but contains no data. Fire Warning event
      Dts.Events.FireWarning(0, "Script Task File Check", "File exists, but contains no
      data.", string.Empty, 0);
    }
    // Succeed Script Task
    Dts.TaskResult = (int)ScriptResults.Success;
  }
  else
  {
    // File doesn't exists. Fire Error event and fail Script Task
    Dts.Events.FireError(0, "Script Task File Check", "File doesn't exists.", string.Empty, 0);

    // Fail Script Task
    Dts.TaskResult = (int)ScriptResults.Failure;
  }
}
```

And here is the VB.NET code:

```vb
Public Sub Main()
    ' Get filepath from File Connection Manager and store it in a string variable
    Dim filePath As String = Dts.Connections("myFile").AcquireConnection(Dts.Transaction)
    .ToString()

    ' Create File Info object with filepath variable
    Dim fi As FileInfo = New FileInfo(filePath)

    ' Check if file exists
    If (fi.Exists) Then
        ' File exists, but check size
        If (fi.Length > 0) Then
            ' Boolean variable indicating if the same event can fire multiple times
            Dim fireAgain As Boolean = True

            ' File exists and contains data. Fire Information event
            Dts.Events.FireInformation(0, "Script Task File Check", "File exists and
            contains data.", _
            String.Empty, 0, fireAgain)
        Else
            ' File exists, but contains no data. Fire Waring event
            Dts.Events.FireWarning(0, "Script Task File Check", "File exists, but contains no
            data.", _
            String.Empty, 0)
        End If

        ' Succeed Script Task
        Dts.TaskResult = ScriptResults.Success
    Else
        ' File doesn't exists. Fire Error event and fail Script Task
        Dts.Events.FireError(0, "Script Task File Check", "File doesn't exists.", String.Empty, 0)

        ' Fail Script Task
        Dts.TaskResult = ScriptResults.Failure
    End If
End Sub
```

Now you can test the script by emptying or deleting the file that is referenced in the connection manager, and then run the package and watch the Execution Results tab. Besides the common FireInformation, FireWarning, and FireError, there are more firing event methods available, but they are less used:

- FireBreakpointHit: Raises an event indicating a breakpoint has been hit in the Script Task

- FireCustomEvents: Raises a custom event

- FireProgress: Raises an event that shows the progress of the Script Task

- FileQueryCancel: Raises an event that indicates whether the Script Task should shut down prematurely

■ **Note** Because firing events is expensive, you shouldn't use it excessively. Some firing event methods have a Boolean parameter, fireAgain, to suppress firing the same event multiple times.

FireCustomEvents

Once in a while you end up in a situation where SSIS lacks some of the enterprise skills that a complete ETL solution offers, such as when you want to implement a custom metadata driven logging solution.

Let's say that you want to centrally configure the logging setup for all the running packages. What happens with the logging logic has to be transparent for all the child packages.

The only thing a package has to do is notify the master package by firing a custom event. A good way to handle that on the master package is to use the event handling functionality. There are several types of events at your disposal (see Figure 4-17).

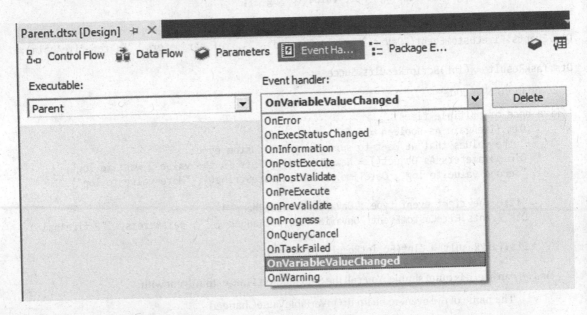

Figure 4-17. Events at our disposal

A good candidate for this example is the OnVariableValueChanged because

- It has some built-in variables you can use.

- It is not fired automatically, even when a variable changes.

Basically, you want to be able to catch a custom event fired in the child packages by using an event handler of the parent package.

Let's start by building the child package.

Child Package

Create a new SSIS package called Child and add a Script Task called SCR_FireCustomEvent to it.

The code for the event is simple and does nothing else than take some of the available variables to the package and fire them in an event.

The Script

In the Main method of the class, add the following:

```
// fire once or multiple times
bool fireAgain = false;
// the values that we want to surface in the custom event
object[] parameters = new object[] { "This is the value I want to log", "Second value to log",
DateTime.Now.ToLongDateString(), "More value to log" };

//fire the right event type : OnVariableValueChanged
Dts.Events.FireCustomEvent("OnVariableValueChanged", "", ref parameters, "", ref fireAgain);

Dts.TaskResult = (int)ScriptResults.Success;
```

And in VB.NET code:

```
' fire once or multiple times
    Dim fireAgain As Boolean = False
    ' the values that we want to surface in the custom event
    Dim parameters As Object() = New Object() {"This is the value I want to log", -
    "Second value to log", DateTime.Now.ToLongDateString(), "More value to log"}

    'fire the right event type : OnVariableValueChanged
    Dts.Events.FireCustomEvent("OnVariableValueChanged", "", parameters, "", fireAgain)

    Dts.TaskResult = CInt(ScriptResults.Success)
```

As you can see, it is quite simple. You call the SSIS method FireCustomEvent with:

- The name of the event to be fired: OnVariableValueChanged
- The event text, which you don't need, so it is ""
- An object array with some string parameters (can also be other types)
- The name of a subcomponent (not needed)
- Instruction about firing the event again, false in this case

This is all that you need for the Script Task.
Now let's create a second package called Parent.

The Parent Package

This package invokes the child package; so for that you need an Execute Package Task that points at the child package as shown in Figure 4-18.

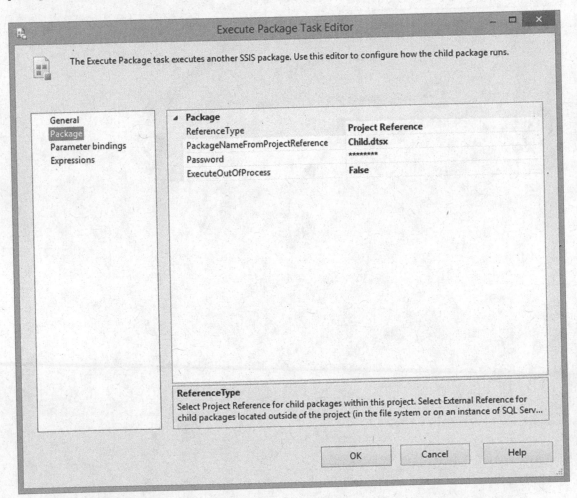

Figure 4-18. *Execute Package Task Editor*

On the Event handler tab of the package surface, choose the OnVariableValueChanged event in the drop-down list. It opens the designer surface for this specific event and you can place a Script Component on the surface of the event handler (see Figure 4-19).

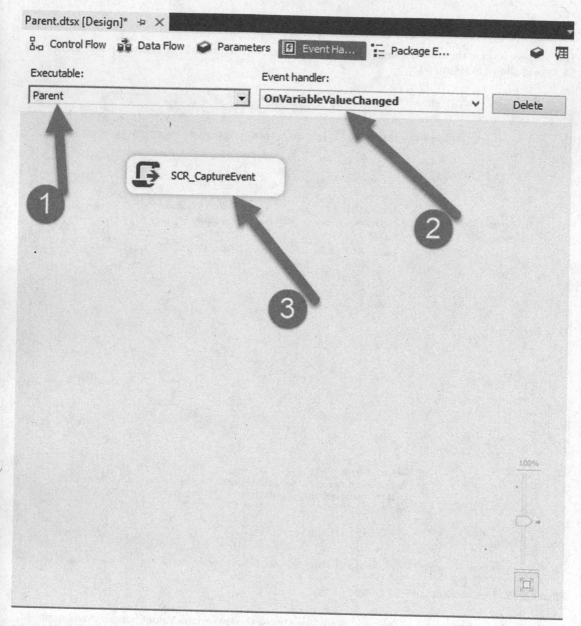

Figure 4-19. *Configuring the event handler*

Here is the callout for Figure 4-19:

1. The Executable is set to the top level element (the package).

2. The event handler is OnVariableValueChanged.

3. The Script Task that you use for capturing the event.

The Script Task

You added a Script Task on the surface of the event handler, which you called SCR_CaptureEvent.
Inside the script, you need to set some of the available system variables as read-only:

- System::TaskName

- System::SourceName

- System::VariableDescription

- System::VariableID

- System::VariableName

- System::VariableValue

The last four variables are the ones that you populated with the object array from the child package.

The Code

You open the script by clicking the Edit Script... button on the Script page of the Script Component Editor.
Next, you add the following lines of code to the Main method:

```
//Building a string that gets the values of the variables
// from the event fired in the child package
string result = "VariableName: " + Dts.Variables["System::VariableName"].Value.ToString() +
Environment.NewLine;
result += "VariableID: " + Dts.Variables["System::VariableID"].Value.ToString() +
Environment.NewLine;

result += "VariableDescription: " + Dts.Variables["System::VariableDescription"].Value
.ToString() + Environment.NewLine;

result += "VariableValue: " + Dts.Variables["System::VariableValue"].Value.ToString() +
Environment.NewLine;

result += "TaskName: " + Dts.Variables["System::TaskName"].Value.ToString() +
Environment.NewLine;

result += "SourceName: " + Dts.Variables["System::SourceName"].Value.ToString();

//Showing the string value as a message box
MessageBox.Show(result);
```

And in VB.NET:

```
'Building a string that gets the values of the variables
' from the event fired in the child package
Dim result As String = "VariableName: " + Dts.Variables("System::VariableName").Value
.ToString() + Environment.NewLine
```

113

```
result += "VariableID: " + Dts.Variables("System::VariableID").Value.ToString() +
Environment.NewLine
result += "VariableDescription: " + Dts.Variables("System::VariableDescription").Value
.ToString() + Environment.NewLine
result += "VariableValue: " + Dts.Variables("System::VariableValue").Value.ToString() + _
Environment.NewLine
result += "TaskName: " + Dts.Variables("System::TaskName").Value.ToString() +
Environment.NewLine
result += "SourceName: " + Dts.Variables("System::SourceName").Value.ToString()

'Showing the string value as a message box
MessageBox.Show(result)
```

Running the parent package invokes the child package, which in turn fires a custom event that is captured by the event handler of the parent package, and shows the results in Figure 4-20.

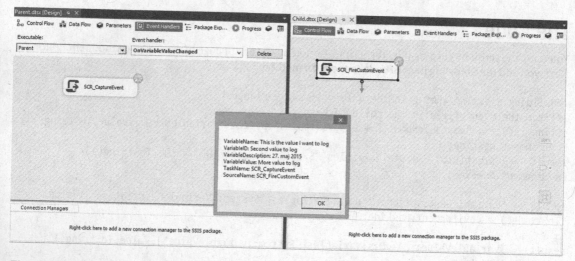

Figure 4-20. *The results of running the package*

In this example, you kept it really simple, but it wouldn't be a problem to create a metadata framework to control the logging or to implement some custom auditing using FireCsutomEvents.

Summary

In this chapter you learned the basic functionality of the Script Task, such as the use of variables and connection managers to avoid hard-code values in your scripts, and logging useful information by firing events. And you saw how you can reference custom or third-party assemblies.

In the next few chapters you will see solutions for all the common problems. With the knowledge of this Script Task chapter, you can now customize those examples by logging or by using a different connection manager.

CHAPTER 5

■ ■ ■

File Properties

The built-in File System Task in SSIS does basic operations on files, such as copy, move, and delete. Sometimes, however (especially in data transfer scenarios), you want to find the most recent file, or you want to check whether a file is locked or if it is read-only. In these situations, Script Task is useful in getting help from .NET libraries such as System.IO.File. This chapter presents some very common usage examples of working with files within Script Task.

Getting All Properties

As shown in Figure 5-1, the built-in File System Task is good for copying/moving files and directories, and also for setting attributes, but it cannot be used to work with file properties such as sorting by modified date.

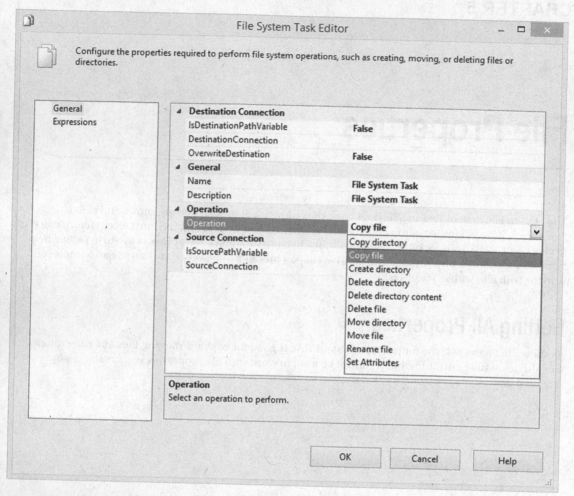

Figure 5-1. *Built-in File System Task operations*

One of the limitations is that you cannot read all the file attributes (i.e., file system information such as read-only flags or permissions) and properties (i.e., metadata about the file itself). This built-in task uses System.IO.File and System.IO.Directory as the core of operations, but these two namespaces include more features that can be used when you work with them directly in .NET scripts.

In this section, you learn how to read file and directory properties, and attributes from .NET scripts. The scripts used in this chapter use System.IO.File and System.IO.Directory, which exist in all versions of .NET framework (with some minor differences).

Usually a file contains detailed properties such as attributes, date created, modified date, owner, file size, and so forth. Figure 5-2 shows how you can view file properties.

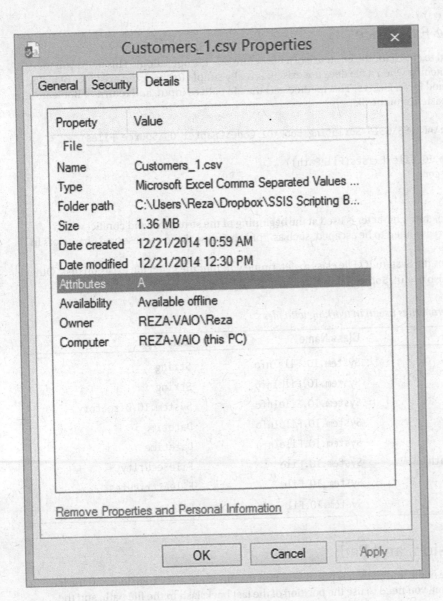

Figure 5-2. File properties

The built-in File System Task won't provide any of this information. In real-world ETL or data transformation scenarios, you need to find last modified file, or all files from a specific owner, or only files smaller than a specific size. So the ability to read the details of file properties are important, and fortunately, it is possible with a few lines of .NET scripts.

Checking for File Existence

It is always recommended to check for the existence of a file before any file operations. This helps you to reduce the risk of error catching when a file does not exist. It is really simple to check the existence of a file; System.IO.File has a method for it: Exists. This method gets the file path as input, and returns a Boolean value that indicates the existence of the file.

```
string FilePath = @"C:\APRESS\SSIS Scripting Book\02_Code\Chapter 05\Source Files\
Customers_1.csv";
            if (System.IO.File.Exists(FilePath))
            { \\ some code
            }
```

In the preceding code, the @ character is used at the beginning of the string to avoid conflict with a character that would otherwise need to be escaped, such as " or \, because these are reserved characters in the code.

The example here uses the System.IO.File class to determine whether the given file exists on disk. Other classes and methods are also useful. Some of these are listed in Table 5-1.

Table 5-1. *Methods and properties useful in working with files*

Method or Property Name	Class Name	Data Type
Name	System.IO.FileInfo	String
Extension	System.IO.FileInfo	String
Directory.FullName	System.IO.FileInfo	System.IO.Directory
CreationTime	System.IO.FileInfo	Datetime
LastWriteTime	System.IO.FileInfo	Datetime
GetAccessControl(filePath)	System.IO.File	FileSecurity
FileAttributes	System.IO.File	FileAttributes
FileSize	System.IO.FileInfo	FileInfo

File Name, Extension, and Path

In SSIS, with a complete file name and path, it is possible to find the file name, the extension, and the file path. To find this information, you need to use the position of the last backslash in the file path, and the position of the last dot in the string.

For example, if you have a variable with a qualified file name called strFilePath, you use the following expression to get the file name:

```
REVERSE(SUBSTRING(REVERSE( @[User::strFilePath] ), 1, FINDSTRING(REVERSE( @
[User::strFilePath] ),"\\", 1)-1))
```

Not an easy to read solution! .NET provides a much more readable and elegant solution using System.IO.FileInfo.

File Created and Modified Time

System.IO.FileInfo also has four properties to read a file's creation time, and also its last modified time. There are two properties for creation time: `CreationTime` and `CreationTimeUtc`. The same type of UTC and local timing is available for modified time: `LastWriteTime` and `LastWriteTimeUtc`.

File Owner

Information about the owner of a file is accessed with the `GetAccessControl` method of the `System.IO.File` class. This method takes the file's path as the input parameter and returns an object of type `FileSecurity`. This object has a method for fetching the file's owner: `GetOwner`. `GetOwner` returns the Security Identifier (SID) of the user, and then it can be translated into a network account.

File Attributes and ReadOnly

`GetAttributes` is the method in the `System.IO.File` class that returns enumeration of a file's attributes. There is also an `IsReadOnly` property in System.IO.FileInfo that returns a Boolean value indicating the `ReadOnly` property of the file.

File Size

You can read a file's size with the Length property of the System.IO.FileInfo object. The length value is returned as bytes, so if you want to convert it to kilobytes, megabytes, or other scales, you have to do it after fetching the value.

Examples of the File Properties Mentioned

For the following script to work, you first need to add a reference to the System.Security.Principal namespace.

The following code shows the `Main` method of the Script Task used in this example. Figure 5-3 shows the output window for the FireInformation event:

```
public void Main()
                {
                        string FilePath = @"C:\APRESS\SSIS Scripting Book\02_Code\Chapter 05\
Source Files\Customers_1.csv";

//Check for file existence
if (File.Exists(strFilePath))
{
//Get file informations
FileInfo objFileInfo = new FileInfo(strFilePath);

//Get the creation time
DateTime createdTime = objFileInfo.CreationTime;
```

```
// What is the length (in bytes) of the file
long FileLength = objFileInfo.Length;

//Gets the name of the file (with the extension)
string fileName = objFileInfo.Name;

//Get the directory
string Directory = objFileInfo.Directory.Name;

//Get the path and the name of the file
string PathAndName = objFileInfo.FullName;

//Get the extension for the file
string Extension = objFileInfo.Extension;

//is the file Read Only?
bool isReadOnly = objFileInfo.IsReadOnly;

//When was the file opened for the last time (and date)
DateTime lastAccessTime = objFileInfo.LastAccessTime;

//When was the file written for the last time (and date)
DateTime lastWriteTime = objFileInfo.LastWriteTime;

//gets the owner
string owner = System.IO.File.GetAccessControl(strFilePath).GetOwner(typeof(System.Security.
Principal.NTAccount)).ToString();

string status ="Creation time: " + createdTime.ToString() + Environment.NewLine +
"Directory: " +Directory + Environment.NewLine +
"Owner: " + owner + Environment.NewLine +
"Extension: " + Extension + Environment.NewLine +
"PathName: " + PathAndName + Environment.NewLine +
"is file ReadOnly: " + isReadOnly.ToString() + Environment.NewLine +
"last accessed: " + lastAccessTime.ToString() + Environment.NewLine +
"last written: " + lastWriteTime.ToString() + Environment.NewLine +
"Length (in Bytes): " + FileLength.ToString() + Environment.NewLine +
"File name: " + fileName;

bool fireagain = false;
Dts.Events.FireInformation(0, "File properties example", status, string.Empty,
0,ref fireagain);
```

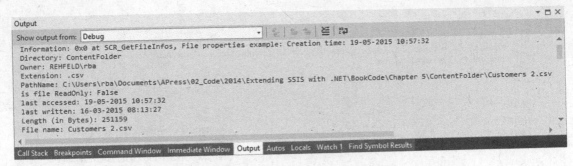

Figure 5-3. *Output window with FireInformation text and file properties*

Deleting Files Older Than X Days

If you're familiar with the Foreach Loop Container in SSIS, you know that there is an enumerator for looping through files in a directory, called the Foreach File Enumerator. This option works in most scenarios, but there are also scenarios that you want to do a conditional search (through a folder, for example) for searching for files modified within a specific date range. Or you might want to read some folder properties that cannot be done using the File System Task. System.IO.Directory and System.IO.DirectoryInfo give you the most usability when you work with folders.

An example of a conditional loop is looping through files that are older than X days ago. With a Script Task and few lines of .NET code, you can loop through files in a directory and check their LastWriteTime, and then remove every file last modified more than X days ago.

The following example uses a couple of variables in the package: one for FolderPath and one for DaysToKeep. Figure 5-4 shows the variable definitions.

Name	Scope	Data type	Value	Expression
DaysOfRetention	DeleteOldFiles	Int32	1	
SourceFolder	DeleteOldFiles	String	C:\APress\02_Code\2014\Extending SSIS with .NET\Chapter 5\ContentFolder	

Figure 5-4. *Variable definitions*

A Script Task is used to accept these two variables as input parameters. Figure 5-5 shows the input parameters for a Script Task.

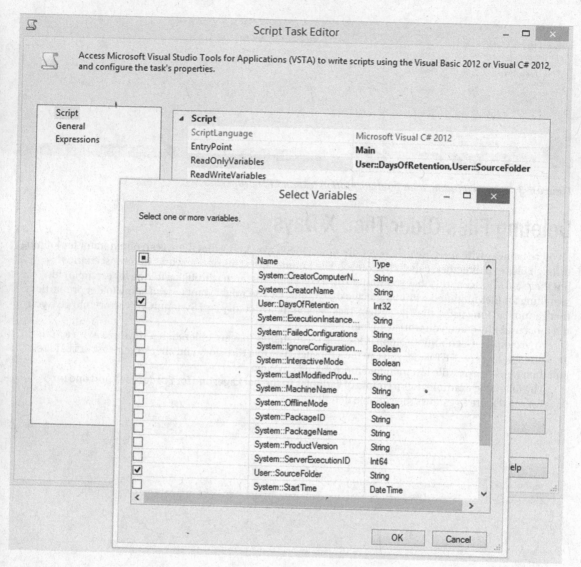

Figure 5-5. *Input parameters for Script Task*

■ **Note** The entire code is in the downloadable code for this book. In the following, only the relevant parts were highlighted.

First, two lines of code read input variable values from the package (there are other methods for reading a package variable's values, which are described in Chapter):

```
string DirectoryPath = Dts.Variables["User::FolderPath"].Value.ToString();
int DaysToKeep=(int) Dts.Variables["User::DaysToKeep"].Value;
```

After checking for the existence of a directory, a list of existing files is fetched into an array of strings. This line of defensive programming allows you to take another course of action should the directory not exist.

```
//check directory existance
if (System.IO.Directory.Exists(DirectoryPath))
{
                //fetch files
                string[] files=System.IO.Directory.GetFiles(DirectoryPath);
```

Then in a loop structure, all the files are checked, one by one, creating a FileInfo object for the specified file path.

```
//loop through files
 foreach (var file in files)
 {
      //read file information
      System.IO.FileInfo finf = new System.IO.FileInfo(file);
```

Then FileInfo object is able to return a file's LastWriteTime. The TimeSpan object has been used to identify the difference between the file's LastWriteTime and today's date, which indicates how long it has been since the file was last modified. If the days since the last modification date are greater than the DaysToKeep value, the file will be removed. TimeSpan is a structure representing a time interval.

```
//calculate difference between file creation date and today
TimeSpan span = DateTime.Now.Subtract(finf.LastWriteTime);

//compare difference with DaysToKeep variable
if ((int)span.TotalDays>DaysToKeep)
{
    //remove old file
    System.IO.File.Delete(file);
}
```

Here is the full VB.NET code:

```
'read parameters
Dim DirectoryPath As String = Dts.Variables("User::FolderPath").Value.ToString

Dim DaysToKeep As Integer = Convert.ToInt32(Dts.Variables("User::DaysToKeep").Value)

'check existance of directory
If System.IO.Directory.Exists(DirectoryPath) Then
        'fetch files in the directory
        Dim files() As String = System.IO.Directory.GetFiles(DirectoryPath)

        'loop through files
        For Each file As String In files
        'read file information
            Dim finf As System.IO.FileInfo = New System.IO.FileInfo(file)
```

```
            'calculate difference between file modified date and today
            Dim span As TimeSpan = DateTime.Now.Subtract(finf.LastWriteTime)

            'compare difference with DaysToKeep variable
            If Convert.ToInt32(span.TotalDays) > DaysToKeep Then
                'remove old file
              System.IO.File.Delete(file)
            End If
          Next

     End If

     Dts.TaskResult = ScriptResults.Success
```

■ **Note** The screenshots show an example run on December 22, 2014, so you expect the two older files to be removed. If you want to run this package yourself, you might want to use a more recent date; otherwise, all the files will be moved/deleted.

Figure 5-6 shows the list of the files in the example before running the package.

Name	Date modified	Type	Size
Customers_1.csv	12/21/2014 12:30 ...	Microsoft Excel C...	1,396 KB
Customers_2.csv	10/9/2014 6:45 PM	Microsoft Excel C...	1,748 KB
Customers_3.csv	6/25/2013 9:38 PM	Microsoft Excel C...	1,895 KB

Figure 5-6. *List of all the files in the directory*

And Figure 5-7 shows the same folder *after* running the packages.

Name	Date modified	Type	Size
Customers_1.csv	12/21/2014 12:30 ...	Microsoft Excel C...	1,396 KB

Figure 5-7. *The remaining files after running the package*

Checking for a Locked File

An ETL process or a data transfer process can fail because a file (or files) that is the source of the data is open or in use, resulting in the file being locked. It is essential to have the process of checking for locked files as part of your ETL scenario. Fortunately, with a few lines of C# or VB.NET code, you can identify whether a file is locked or not.

In this example, you use a variable called `FilePath` to store the path of the file, and then you check this file in the script to identify whether or not the file exists; the result of this is stored in another package variable called `Exists`. Then you check the file against locking, so if file is locked, a variable called `IsLocked` is written as true. The result of checking this against the file is used in precedence constraint for the following actions;

- If the file exists and it is not locked, then move it to an archive folder.

- If the file does not exists or is locked, then log this situation in a log table with the date and time of checking and the status of existence and locking.

- Add two variables, as shown in Figure 5-8. Set the value of the `FilePath` variable to the `Customers_1.csv` file.

Figure 5-8 shows the variables used in the package.

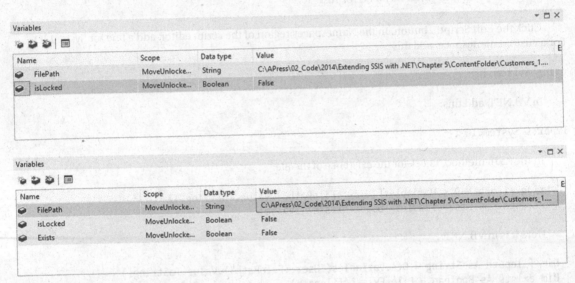

Figure 5-8. *Variables*

Add a new Script Task to the control flow. Set the language as C# or VB.NET. The FilePath variable is ReadOnlyVariables (because you want to only read it). Exists and isLocked are ReadWriteVariables (because you want to write into these variables), as shown in Figure 5-9.

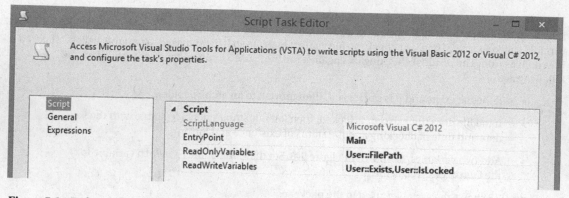

Figure 5-9. Define input variables for Script Task

Click the Edit Script... button. In the Namespaces region of the script editor, add a line for System.IO. For a custom namespace, add this:

```
using System.IO;
```

In VB.NET, add this:

```
Imports System.IO
```

In the Main method, check for the existence of the file:

```
string filepath=Dts.Variables["User::FilePath"].Value.ToString();
bool exists = Dts.Variables["User::Exists"].Value;
```

Here it is in VB.NET:

```
Dim filepath As String = Dts.Variables("User::FilePath").Value.ToString()
Dim exists As Boolean = File.Exists(filepath)
```

Set the Exists package variable accordingly:

```
if (File.Exists(filepath))
{
    Dts.Variables["User::Exists"].Value = true;
    // rest of the code will be here
}
else
{
    Dts.Variables["User::Exists"].Value = false;
}
```

And here it is in VB.NET:

```
If exists Then
            Dts.Variables("User::Exists").Value = True
' rest of the code will be here
Else
            Dts.Variables("User::Exists").Value = False
End If
```

If the file exists, you want to check for locking, so define a FileStream variable and try to fill it. If you faced an error of type IOexception, it means that the file is locked for read or write, or a process is using it.

```
FileStream fs = null;
try
{
        fs = File.Open(filepath, FileMode.Open, FileAccess.ReadWrite, FileShare.None);
}
catch (IOException ex)
{
        Dts.Variables["User::IsLocked"].Value = true;
}
```

Here it is in VB.NET:

```
Dim fs As FileStream = Nothing

Try
    fs = File.Open(filepath, FileMode.Open, FileAccess.ReadWrite, FileShare.None)

Catch ex As IOException
    Dts.Variables("User::IsLocked").Value = True
End Try
```

If the file opened successfully, then it will return an object of FileStream type, which means file is not locked. Using a finally block ensures that the file is released before the Script Task exits.

```
Finally
{
        if (fs != null)
        {
                fs.Close();
                Dts.Variables["User::IsLocked"].Value = false;
        }
}
```

And here it is in VB.NET:

```
If Not (fs Is Nothing) Then
        fs.Close()
        Dts.Variables("User::IsLocked").Value = False
End If
```

127

Moving the File

Now that the previous script has identified whether the file exists or if it is locked, the Exists and IsLocked package variables show the values accordingly. By checking these values, you can take the necessary action move the file or not.

You need to define a connection manager called Archive for stating where to move the file(s). Once this is done, add a File System Task after the Script Task, and connect a precedence constraint from the Script Task to this task. Next, go to the task editor and assign the right connection to archive the file by moving it to an archive folder, as shown in Figure 5-10.

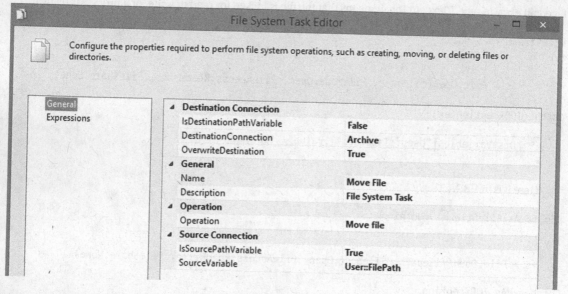

Figure 5-10. *Configure the File System Task Editor to Move File*

Right-click the precedence constraint between the Script Task and the File System Task. From the context menu, choose Edit. In the Precedence Constraint Editor, change Evaluation Operation to Expression and Constraint. Confirm the value to be a success, and write the following expression to check that the file exists and is not locked.

```
@[User::Exists] && !(@[User::IsLocked])
```

Figure 5-11 shows the Precedence Constraint Editor with the Expression filled in.

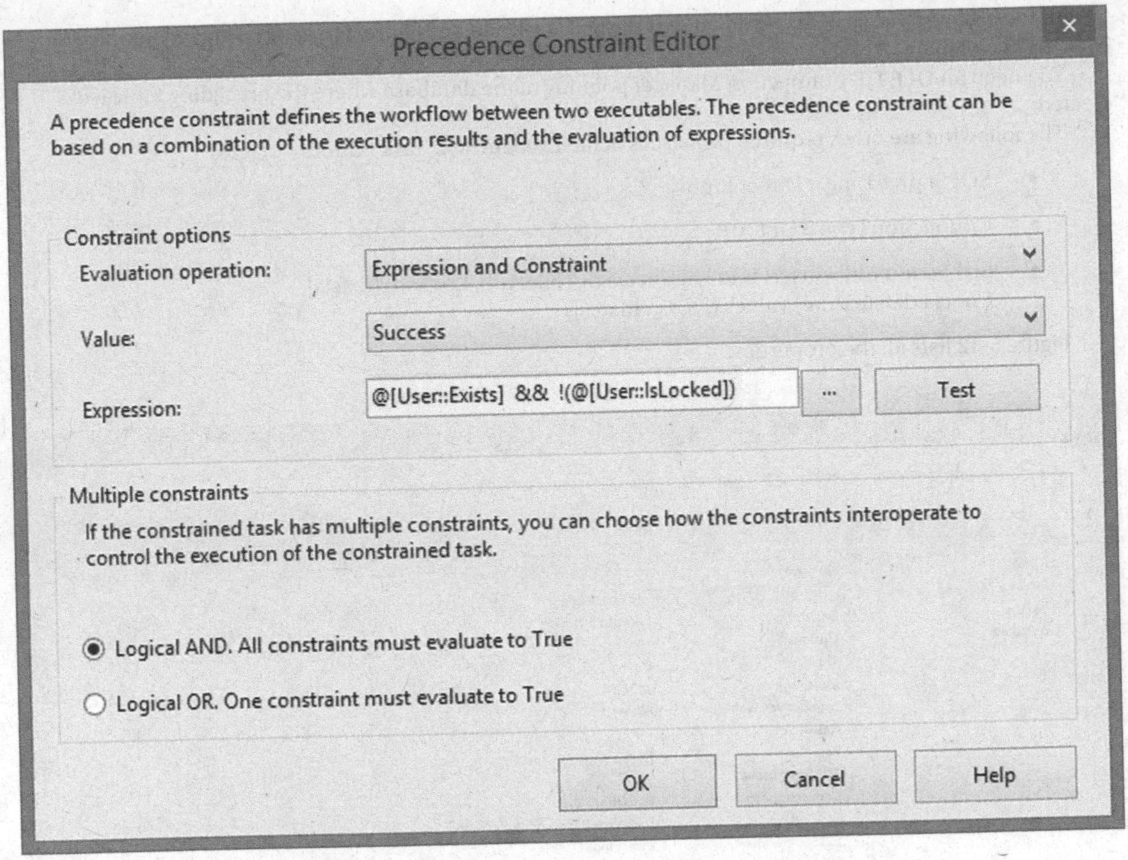

Figure 5-11. *The file exists and it is not locked*

If file does not exist or it is locked, you want to log this status (with the date and time) into a log table in database; in this example, the Apress_SSIS_Scripting database. Run the following script to create the FileCheckLog table (run the script in Management Studio).

■ **Note** The table creation script is also included in the Chapter 5 source code.

```
CREATE TABLE [dbo].[FileCheckLog](
    [ID] [int] IDENTITY(1,1) NOT NULL,
    [FilePath] [varchar](4000) NULL,
    [Locked] [bit] NULL,
    [Exists] [bit] NULL,
    [CheckedDateTime] [datetime] NULL,
 CONSTRAINT [PK_FileCheckLog] PRIMARY KEY CLUSTERED
(
    [ID] ASC
)WITH (PAD_INDEX = OFF, STATISTICS_NORECOMPUTE = OFF, IGNORE_DUP_KEY = OFF, ALLOW_ROW_
LOCKS = ON, ALLOW_PAGE_LOCKS = ON) ON [PRIMARY]
) ON [PRIMARY]
```

In the package's control flow, add an Execute SQL Task and configure it to insert a log record into the FileCheckLog table.

You need an OLE DB Connection Manager pointing at the database where the preceding table was created.

The following are other required properties of the Execute SQL Task Editor:

- SQLSourceType = Direct Input

- ConnectionType = OLE DB

- SQLStatement = insert into FileCheckLog (FilePath, Locked, [Exists], CheckedDateTime) values (?,?,?,getdate())

Figure 5-12 lists all the properties.

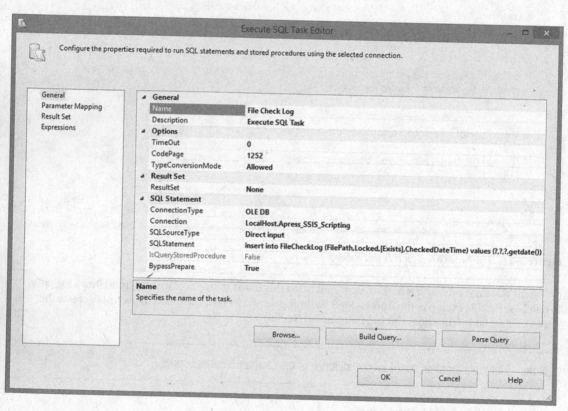

Figure 5-12. *Configure Execute SQL Task to write log entry*

Because FilePath, the Locked status, and the Exists status come from package variables, go to the Parameter Mapping tab and add mappings, as shown in Figure 5-13.

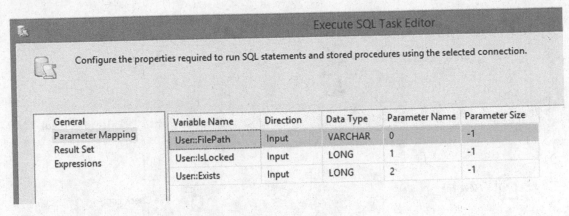

Figure 5-13. *Parameter mapping for file check log*

Because an OLE DB connection is used in this example, parameter names should be indexed 0-based (0, 1, 2...). To learn more about the parameter names of other connection types, read the article at http://msdn.microsoft.com/en-us/library/ms140355.aspx.

Connect a success precedence constraint from Script Task to the execute SQL task. Go to the Precedence Constraint Editor window to configure it (see Figure 5-14) and determine if a file does not exists or is locked. The Expression is: **!(@[User::Exists]) && @[User::IsLocked]**.

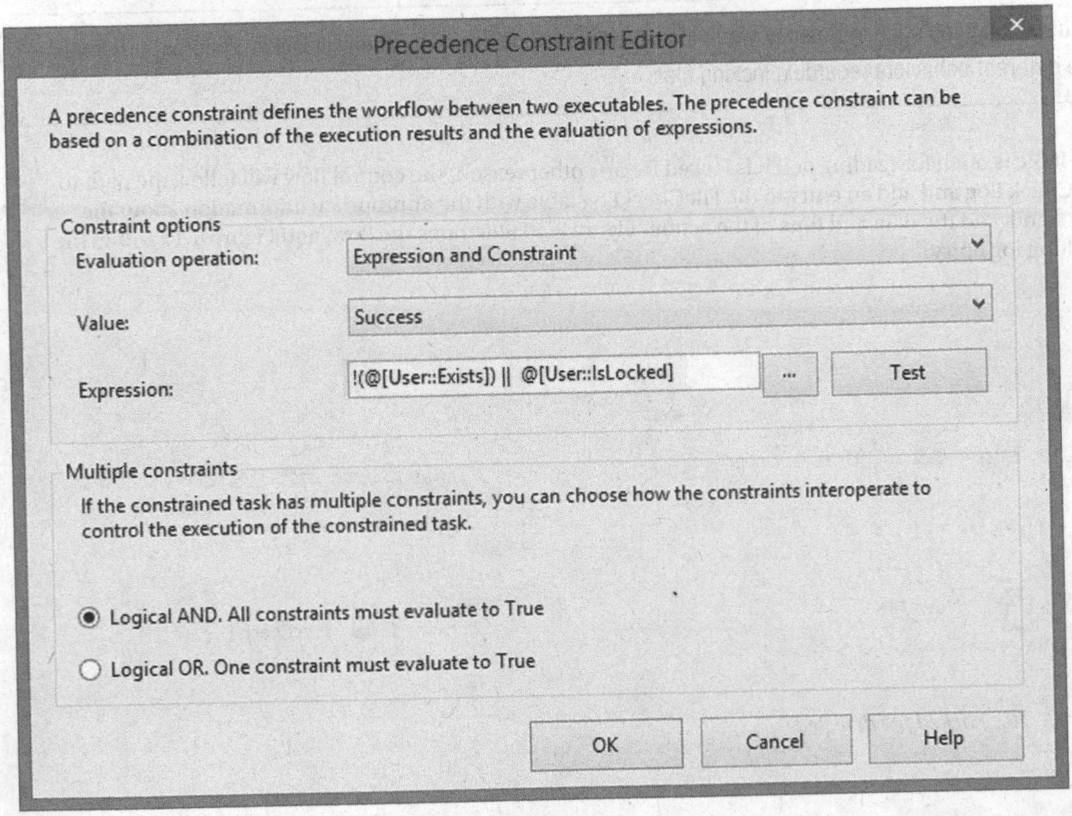

Figure 5-14. *Check if the file does not exists or is locked*

Figure 5-15 shows the schema for the package's control flow (i.e., an annotation was added to explain the behavior more clearly).

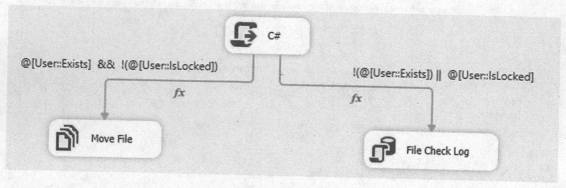

Figure 5-15. *Control flow schema or the check file is locked package*

Now it is time to run and test the example. If you run the code when the Customers_1.csv file is not opened, you will see that the control flow follows the path to the Move File task, and the file will be moved to an archive directory.

■ **Note** Opening a file in Notepad won't lock it; whereas opening it in Excel will lock it. Different programs have different behaviors regarding locking files.

If file is open for reading or if it is locked for any other reason, the control flow will follow the path to File Check Log and add an entry to the FileCheckLog table with the appropriate information about the file's status and the date and time of the action. Figure 5-16 illustrates the flow, and Figure 5-17 shows the resulting log entry.

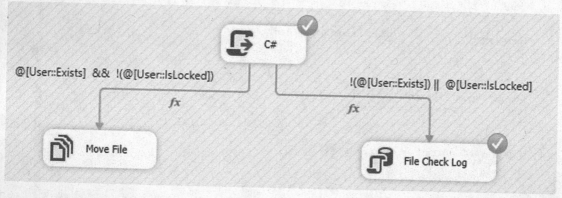

Figure 5-16. *Locked file detected*

ID	FilePath	Locked	Exists	CheckedDateTime
1	C:\Users\Reza\Dropbox\SSIS Scripting Book\02_Cod...	1	1	2015-01-02 13:40:08.400

Figure 5-17. *A log entry added to FileCheckLog table*

You can use the method that you learned in this exercise in data transfer scenarios to determine whether or not a file is locked.

Foreach Loop Ordered File Enumerator

There is a container in the SSIS control flow called the *Foreach Loop*. Foreach Loop allows you to develop a control flow that loops through the items of an enumerator. There are seven types of enumerators, including a File Enumerator to loop through files in a directory, and an ADO enumerator to loop through records of a data table in an object variable.

The File Enumerator provides basic search functionalities, such as a mask on a file name or extension, or the ability to traverse subfolders. But there are some requirements that cannot be handled with the built-in file enumerator; for example, when you want to load files in a folder in a specific order, such as by creation date (i.e., you want to load files into the database based on their datetime order).

In the next section, you learn how to empower the Foreach Loop Container with scripts (you are already familiar with most of them from examples earlier in this chapter) to create a data table with columns and rows, and then using that data table as the source object for enumeration in the Foreach Loop.

Foreach Ordered File Enumerator

In this example, you loop through .csv files in the specified directory, and load them based on their created date and time order. You will archive each file, and then write a log entry to a file load table at the end.

Create package variables and set the directory path to the folder that contains .csv files in this book's code bundle.

The following is a list of the values and names used. Change it so that it matches your setup. It is also shown in Figure 5-18.

- FilePath (String): C:\APress\02_Code\2014\Extending SSIS with .NET\ BookCode\Chapter 5\ContentFolder\Customer.csv

- OrderedeFiles (Object): defaults to System.Object

- SourceFolder (String): C:\APress\02_Code\2014\Extending SSIS with .NET\ Chapter 5\ContentFolder

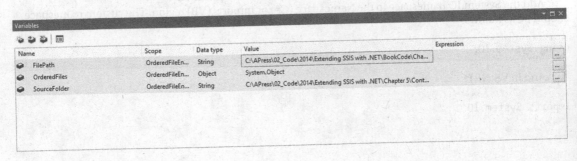

Figure 5-18. *Variables definition*

Create a Script Task, set User::SourceFolder as ReadOnlyVariables, and User::OrderedFiles as ReadWriteVariables, as shown in Figure 5-19.

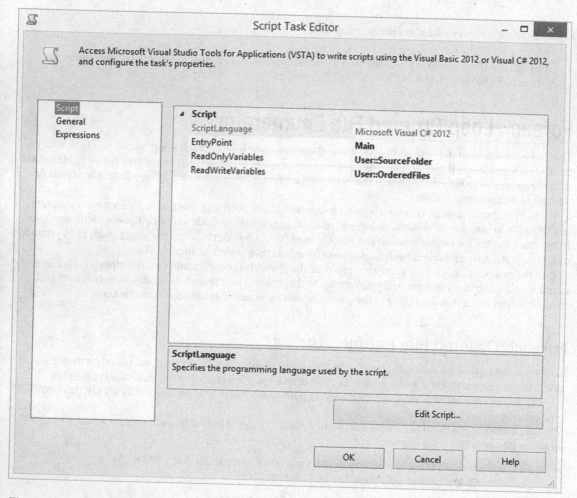

Figure 5-19. Setting variables

Choose the language, and then click Edit Script to open the script editor.

Add the System.IO namespace to the Namespace (C#) or Imports (VB) region. The custom namespace should be as follows:

```
using System.IO;
```

And in VB.NET:

```
Imports System.IO
```

Creating a Dataset

In the Main method, create a DataSet object. A dataset object can contain one or more data tables.

```
DataSet dsUnsorted = new DataSet();
```

And here it is in VB.NET:

```
Dim dsUnsorted As New DataSet()
```

Add a data table for keeping file information:

```
DataTable filelistTable = dsUnsorted.Tables.Add();
```

After adding the table, you can add the columns to the table, specifying a name for the column and a datatype:

```
filelistTable.Columns.Add("FilePath", typeof(string));
filelistTable.Columns.Add("FileName", typeof(string));
filelistTable.Columns.Add("FileDate", typeof(DateTime));
```

And here it is in VB.NET:

```
Dim filelistTable As DataTable = dsUnsorted.Tables.Add()
filelistTable.Columns.Add("FilePath", GetType(String))
filelistTable.Columns.Add("FileName", GetType(String))
filelistTable.Columns.Add("FileDate", GetType(DateTime))
```

Loading Files

Read all the files in the directory and load them into a string array:

```
string[] allFiles = Directory.GetFiles(Dts.Variables["User::DirectoryPath"].Value.
ToString());
```

Here it is in VB.NET:

```
Dim allFiles As String() = Directory.GetFiles(Dts.Variables("User::DirectoryPath").Value.
ToString())
```

Loop through each file in the array, and then create each file's FileInfo object. Next, insert a new record in the data table with information loaded from FileInfo object.

```
FileInfo fileInfo;
foreach (string currentFile in allFiles)
{
fileInfo = new FileInfo(currentFile);
    // Columns: FilePath,FileName,FileDate
filelistTable.Rows.Add(fileInfo.FullName, fileInfo.Name, fileInfo.CreationTime);
}
```

Here it is in VB.NET:

```
Dim fileInfo As FileInfo

For Each currentFile As String In allFiles
        fileInfo = New FileInfo(currentFile)
      ' Columns: FilePath,FileName,FileDate
   filelistTable.Rows.Add(fileInfo.FullName, fileInfo.Name, fileInfo.CreationTime)
Next
```

Define a new set of DataRows based on the desired filter condition and the order of the files (FileDate ASC in this example):

```
DataRow[] rows = dsUnsorted.Tables[0].Select("FileName like '*.csv'", "FileDate ASC");
```

Here it is in VB.NET:

```
Dim rows As DataRow() = dsUnsorted.Tables(0).[Select]("FileName like '*.csv'", "FileDate ASC")
```

Create a new dataset and a data table with only a FilePath column (this new dataset will be used to store ordered and filtered list):

```
DataSet dsSorted = new DataSet();
DataTable filelistTableSorted = dsSorted.Tables.Add();
filelistTableSorted.Columns.Add("FilePath", typeof(string));
```

And here it is in VB.NET:

```
Dim dsSorted As New DataSet()
Dim filelistTableSorted As DataTable = dsSorted.Tables.Add()
filelistTableSorted.Columns.Add("FilePath", GetType(String))
```

Adding Rows to the Dataset

Add rows, one by one, to the new data table in a foreach loop:

```
foreach (DataRow row in rows)
{
        filelistTableSorted.Rows.Add(row["FilePath"].ToString());
}
```

And here it is in VB.NET:

```
For Each row As DataRow In rows
        filelistTableSorted.Rows.Add(row("FilePath").ToString())
Next
```

Writing the Result

Write the result dataset into the FileList package variable:

```
Dts.Variables["User::OrderedFiles "].Value = dsSorted;
```

Here it is in VB.NET:

```
Dts.Variables("User::OrderedFiles ").Value = dsSorted
```

■ **Note**   The code for this example is available in the Source code/Downloads area for this book at www.apress.com. An alternative method is to use a generic list instead of a dataset, and then sort it.

Putting It All Together

Save and close the script. Add a Foreach Loop Container after the Script Task, and a precedence constraint connecting the script to the foreach loop.

Set the enumerator for the Foreach Loop to ADO enumerator. Select the User::OrderedFiles variable as the ADO object source variable, as shown in Figure 5-20.

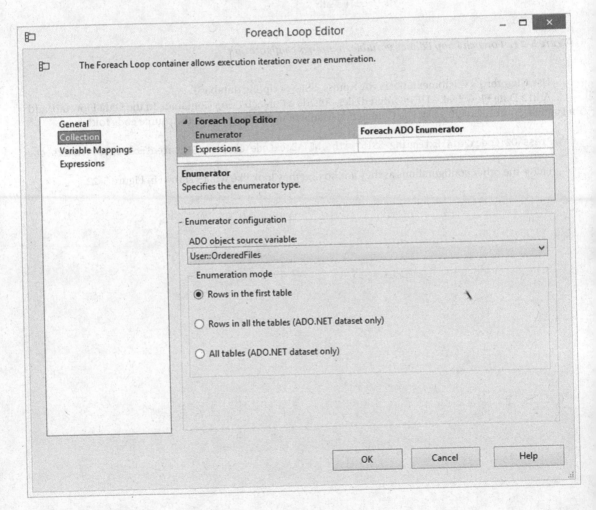

Figure 5-20. Foreach ADO enumerator

137

Go to the Variable Mappings page and map the User::FilePath variable with index 0. (Columns in the dataset's table are indexed based on their order from 0). Click OK to close the Foreach Loop Editor, as illustrated in Figure 5-21.

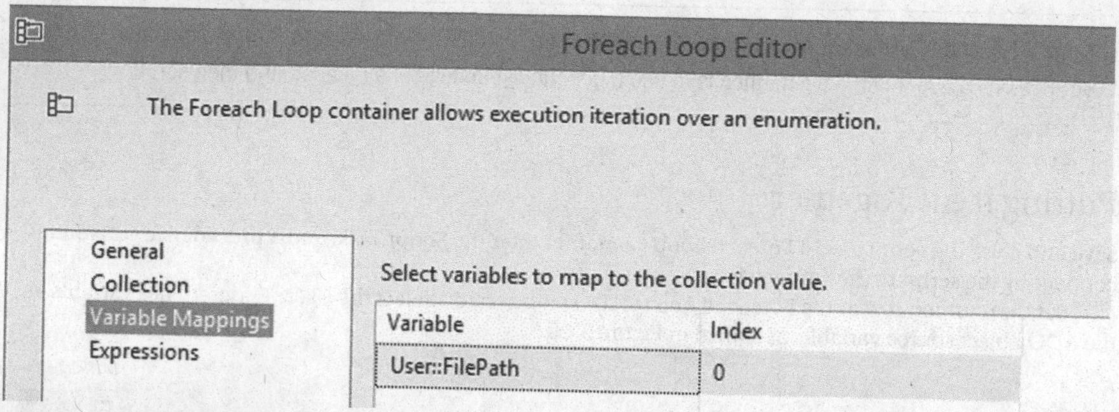

Figure 5-21. Foreach Loop Editor's variable mappings configuration

Use Chapter 1's Customer table in the Apress_SSIS_Scripting database.

Add a Data Flow Task – DFT_OrderedFiles - inside a Foreach Loop Container. In the Data Flow tab, add a Flat File Source. Create a Flat File Connection Manager to a .csv file from the source code folder:

`C:\APress\02_Code\2014\Extending SSIS with .NET\BookCode\Chapter 5\ContentFolder\Customers.csv`

Leave the other configurations as they are, so that they look like what's shown in Figure 5-22.

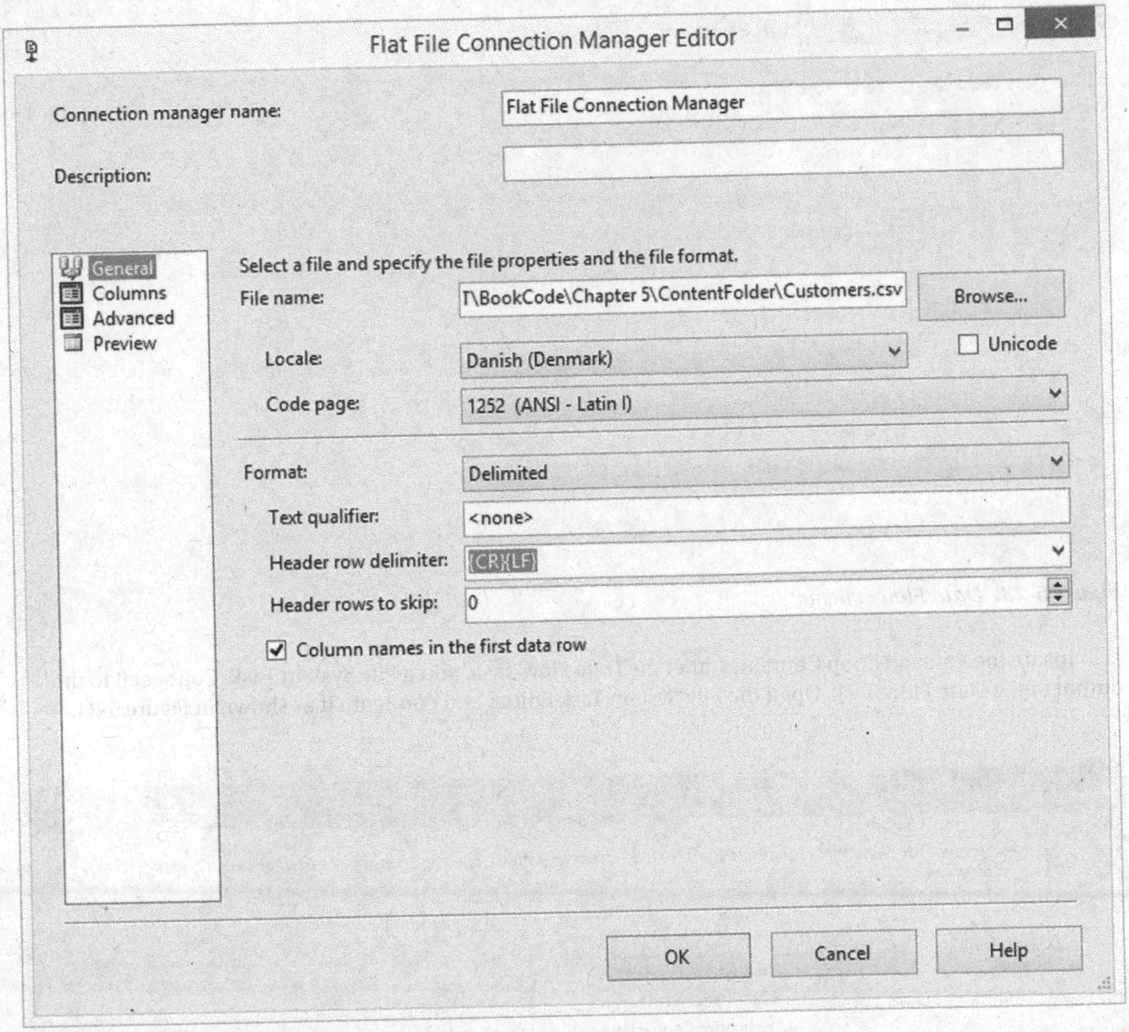

Figure 5-22. *File Connection Manager configuration*

Click the Columns item in the left pane to generate column mappings. Close the editor by clicking OK. In the Data Flow Task, add OLE DB Destination connected to Apress_SSIS_Scripting database, and Customer Table. Use the default mappings. Connect it to the source, as shown in Figure 5-23.

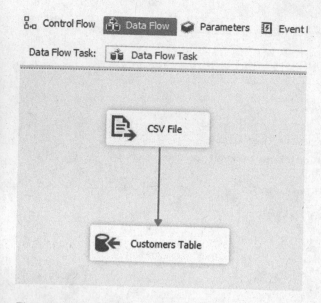

Figure 5-23. *Data Flow schema*

Inside the Foreach Loop Container, after the Data Flow Task, add a File System Task. Connect it to the output of the Data Flow Task. Open the File System Task Editor, and configure it as shown in Figure 5-24.

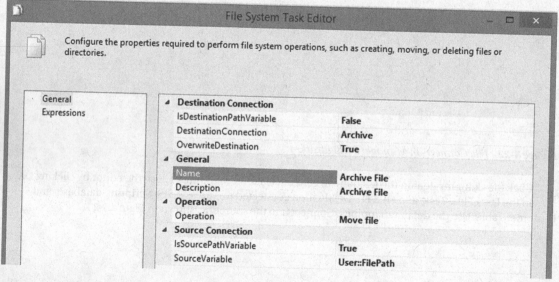

Figure 5-24. *File System Task Editor for archiving file*

Create a FileLoadLog table to store information about loading files into the database. Run the following script in SSMS in the Apress_SSIS_Scripting database:

```
CREATE TABLE [dbo].[FileLoadLog](
    [ID] [int] IDENTITY(1,1) NOT NULL,
    [FilePath] [varchar](4000) NULL,
    [LoadDateTime] [datetime] NULL,
) ON [PRIMARY]
```

Add an Execute SQL Task after the Archive File task. Add a precedence constraint to the Archive File task. Write an insert command to add the log entry into FileLoadLog table as follows:

```
INSERT INTO FileLoadLog (FilePath,LoadDateTime) values (?,getdate())
```

Figure 5-25 shows the final task configuration.

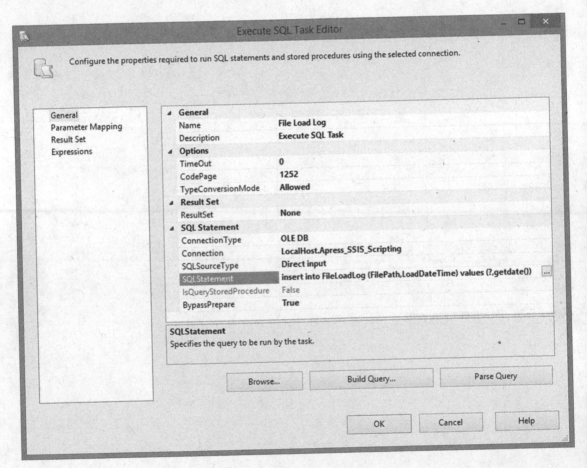

Figure 5-25. *File Load Log execute SQL Task configuration*

On the Parameter Mapping page, set the User::FilePath variable to parameter name 0 with data type VARCHAR, as shown in Figure 5-26.

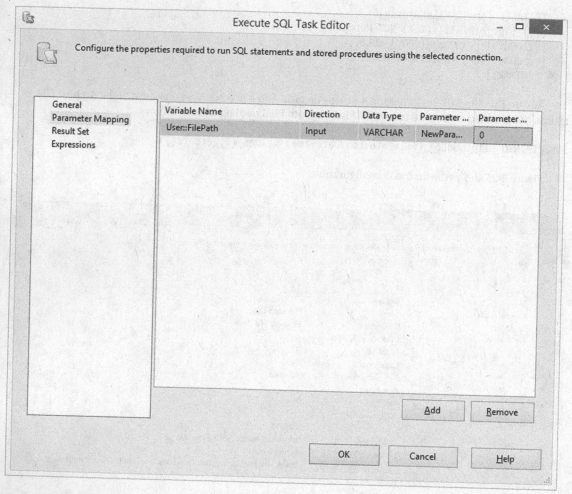

Figure 5-26. *Parameter mapping*

Figure 5-27 shows the full layout of the package.

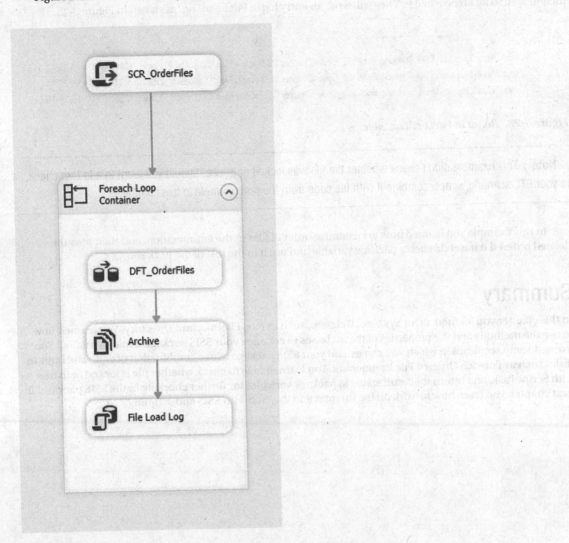

Figure 5-27. *Schema of Package 04 - Foreach Ordered File Enumerator*

Run the package. You will see that all the files from the source folder are loaded into the database, and then moved to an archive folder. They will write an entry log in FileLoadLog, as shown in Figure 5-28.

ID	FilePath	LoadDateTime
1	C:\Users\Reza\Dropbox\SSIS Scripting Book\02_Code\Chapter 05\Source Files\Customers_1.csv	2015-01-04 15:26:13.073
2	C:\Users\Reza\Dropbox\SSIS Scripting Book\02_Code\Chapter 05\Source Files\Customers_2.csv	2015-01-04 15:26:14.627
3	C:\Users\Reza\Dropbox\SSIS Scripting Book\02_Code\Chapter 05\Source Files\Customers_3.csv	2015-01-04 15:26:16.533

Figure 5-28. *Result in FileLoadLog table*

■ **Note** This example didn't check whether the file was locked or in use. Should you want to add that check to your ETL scenario, simply combine it with the code from the first example in this chapter.

In this example you learned how to customize order of files in the enumeration, and then pass the desired ordered dataset through a package variable and use it in the rest of the package.

Summary

In this chapter you learned about System.IO classes, such as File, FileInfo, and Directory. You learned how to use the methods and the properties of these classes to enhance your SSIS package implementation. You learned some scenarios in which you can extend your SSIS package with a combination of code and built-in tasks, such as Foreach Ordered File Enumerator. You learned how to check whether file is locked or in use with Script Task, and return the result status to package variables for further checking in the SSIS package. In next chapter, you learn how to work on the Internet and the Web with SSIS and scripting.

CHAPTER 6

■ ■ ■

Working Through the Internet and the Web

The Web is an important source for data. Data might come from files that are located on a web site or on an (S)FTP server. In this chapter, you learn how to work with files through the Web, how to download files, and how to work with FTP and SFTP. Scenarios in this chapter cannot be done easily with built-in tasks, such as the FTP Task.

Sending HTML-Formatted Email

One of the drawbacks of the out-of-the-box Send Mail Task is that it doesn't support HTML-formatted emails. The associated SMTP Connection Manager doesn't support more-advanced settings like changing port and setting basic credentials. The Script Task could help you here, however.

An alternative is to use an Execute SQL Task that calls sp_send_dbmail, but the Script Task gives you more possibilities and you don't have to ask your database administrator (DBA) to enable this in the database.

SMTP Connection Manager

For storing the SMTP server address, let's use the SMTP Connection Manager shown in Figure 6-1. You can add it by right-clicking the Connection Manager pane, choosing New Connection, and then choosing SMTP. Enter the server address and optionally change other settings. Make sure that the name of the connection manager is SMTP Mail Server. You can change it, but remember to change it in the script as well. The alternative is to use an extra SSIS string variable in the next step for storing the SMTP Server name or IP address.

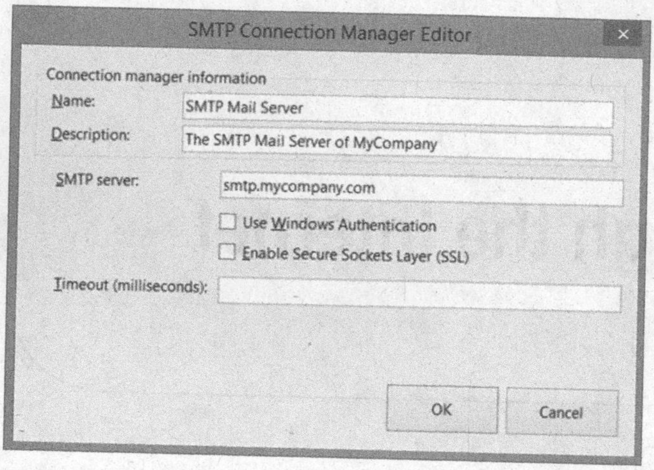

Figure 6-1. *SMTP Connection Manager*

If your company or provider don't have an SMTP server, then you can search for public SMTP servers like gmail.com or outlook.com, but they often require authentication or have other limitations.

■ **Note**   If sending HTML-formatted emails is your only reason for using the Script Task, then it is a best practice to use the SMTP Connection Manager. If you also want to change the port or the credentials, then it is probably a little confusing to use both variables and an SMTP Connection Manager as an input for the Script Task.

Variables

For storing an email's From, To, Subject, and Body, you need four string variables as shown in Figure 6-2. If you also want to change the default port number, then you need an additional integer variable. The same applies for adding authentication, for which you need additional string variables to store the username and password.

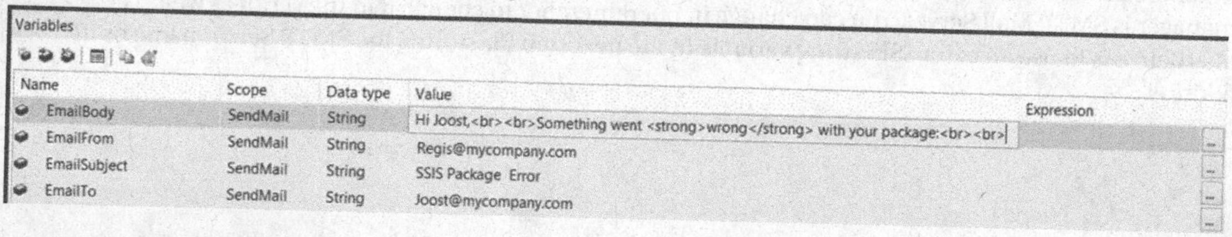

Figure 6-2. *String variables for storing email parts*

Script Task

Add a Script Task to the control flow (or one of the event handlers, if you prefer that) and give it a suitable name, like SCR - Send Error Mail. You don't need additional tasks to test this, but you could, for example, connect it to your Data Flow Task with an error precedence constraint. Edit the Script Task and add the variables from the previous step as shown in Figure 6-3. Make these ReadOnlyVariables so that you can use them in the script code.

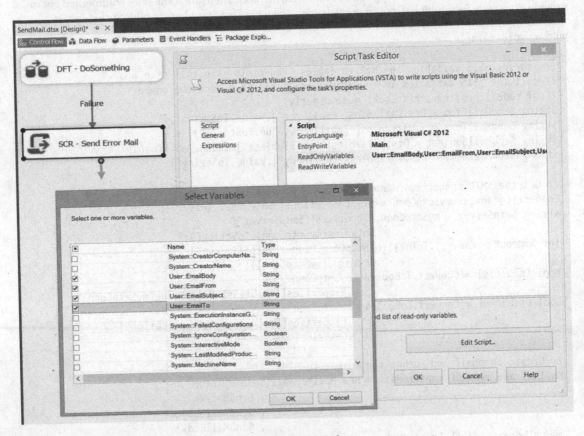

Figure 6-3. Adding variables (or parameters) to the Script Task

The Code

Click the Edit Script. . . button to open the VSTA environment. First, add the extra namespaces to shorten the code:

```
#region customNamespaces
using System.Net;
using System.Net.Mail;
#endregion
```

And here is the VB.NET code:

```
#Region "customNamespaces"
Imports System.Net
Imports System.Net.Mail
#End Region
```

Now it's time to add the following code to your Main method. There are some lines commented out to provide extra code for additional requirements, such as changing port numbers or adding credentials.

```
public void Main()
{
  // Storing SSIS variables in .Net variables. You could skip this step and
  // call the SSIS variables in the actual mail code to reduce the number
  // of code lines, but this looks more orderly.
  String SendMailFrom = Dts.Variables["EmailFrom"].Value.ToString();
  String SendMailTo = Dts.Variables["EmailTo"].Value.ToString();
  String SendMailSubject = Dts.Variables["EmailSubject"].Value.ToString();
  String SendMailBody = Dts.Variables["EmailBody"].Value.ToString();

  // Get the SMTP connection manager read its properties
  ConnectionManager mySmtpConn = Dts.Connections["SMTP Mail Server"];
  string SmtpServer = mySmtpConn.Properties["SmtpServer"]
                            .GetValue(mySmtpConn).ToString();
  int Timeout = Convert.ToInt32(mySmtpConn.Properties["Timeout"]
                            .GetValue(mySmtpConn));
  bool EnableSsl = Convert.ToBoolean(mySmtpConn
                                .Properties["EnableSsl"].GetValue(mySmtpConn));
  bool UseWinAut = Convert.ToBoolean(mySmtpConn
                                .Properties["UseWindowsAuthentication"]
                                .GetValue(mySmtpConn));

  // Create an email and change the format to HTML
  MailMessage myHtmlFormattedMail = new MailMessage(SendMailFrom
                                      , SendMailTo
                                      , SendMailSubject
                                      , SendMailBody);
myHtmlFormattedMail.IsBodyHtml = true;

  // Create a SMTP client to send the email
  SmtpClient mySmtpClient = new SmtpClient(SmtpServer);
  mySmtpClient.EnableSsl = EnableSsl;
  mySmtpClient.UseDefaultCredentials = UseWinAut;
  // Check other properties like portnumber
  // mySmtpClient.Port = 587; // Get value from variable
  // or credentials with an username/email and password
  // mySmtpClient.Credentials = new NetworkCredential("username", "password");
```

```csharp
// Try sending the email
try
{
  // Send email
  mySmtpClient.Send(myHtmlFormattedMail);

  // Close Script Task with success
  Dts.TaskResult = (int)ScriptResults.Success;
}
catch (Exception ex)
{
  // Fire an error for logging purposes
  string Error = "Error: " + ex.Message + " ";
  Error += ((ex.InnerException != null) ? ex.InnerException.Message : "");
  Dts.Events.FireError(0, "Send Mail Task", Error, string.Empty, 0);

  // Close Script Task with Failure
  Dts.TaskResult = (int)ScriptResults.Failure;
}
}
```

Here is the VB.Net code:

```vbnet
Public Sub Main()
  ' Storing SSIS variables in .Net variables. You could skip this step and
  ' call the SSIS variables in the actual mail code to reduce the number
  ' of code lines, but this looks more orderly.
  Dim SendMailFrom As String = Dts.Variables("EmailFrom").Value.ToString()
  Dim SendMailTo As String = Dts.Variables("EmailTo").Value.ToString()
  Dim SendMailSubject As String = Dts.Variables("EmailSubject").Value _
                                  .ToString()
  Dim SendMailBody As String = Dts.Variables("EmailBody").Value.ToString()


  ' Get the SMTP connection manager read its properties
  Dim mySmtpConn As ConnectionManager = Dts.Connections("SMTP Mail Server")
  Dim SmtpServer As String = mySmtpConn.Properties("SmtpServer") _
                                  .GetValue(mySmtpConn).ToString()
  Dim Timeout As Integer = Convert.ToInt32(mySmtpConn.Properties("Timeout") _
                                  .GetValue(mySmtpConn))
  Dim EnableSsl As Boolean = Convert.ToBoolean(mySmtpConn _
                      .Properties("EnableSsl") _
                      .GetValue(mySmtpConn))
  Dim UseWinAut As Boolean = Convert.ToBoolean(mySmtpConn _
                      .Properties("UseWindowsAuthentication") _
                      .GetValue(mySmtpConn))


  ' Create an email and change the format to HTML
  Dim myHtmlFormattedMail As New MailMessage(SendMailFrom _
                                  , SendMailTo _
                                  , SendMailSubject _
                                  , SendMailBody)
```

```
    myHtmlFormattedMail.IsBodyHtml = True

    ' Create a SMTP client to send the email
    Dim mySmtpClient As New SmtpClient(SmtpServer)
    mySmtpClient.EnableSsl = EnableSsl
    mySmtpClient.UseDefaultCredentials = UseWinAut

    ' Check other properties like portnumber
    ' mySmtpClient.Port = 587; // Get value from variable
    ' or credentials with an username/email and password
    ' mySmtpClient.Credentials = New NetworkCredential("username", "password")

    ' Try sending the email
    Try
      ' Send email
      mySmtpClient.Send(myHtmlFormattedMail)

      ' Close Script Task with success
      Dts.TaskResult = ScriptResults.Success
    Catch ex As Exception
      ' Fire an error for logging purposes
      Dim ErrorStr As String = "Error: " + ex.Message & " "
      ErrorStr = ErrorStr + ex.InnerException.Message.Replace(vbNullString, "")
      Dts.Events.FireError(0, "Send Mail Task", ErrorStr, String.Empty, 0)

      ' Close Script Task with Failure
      Dts.TaskResult = ScriptResults.Failure
    End Try
End Sub
```

The Results

Now close the Script Task and execute it to see the results. You should see an image and a message such as in Figure 6-4.

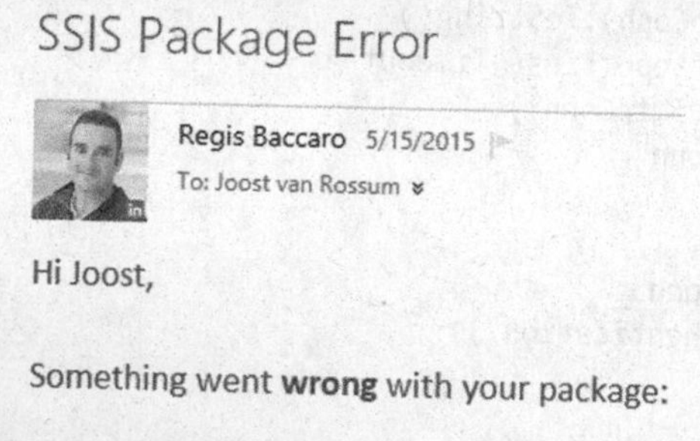

SSIS Package Error

 Regis Baccaro 5/15/2015
To: Joost van Rossum ⌄

Hi Joost,

Something went **wrong** with your package:

Figure 6-4. Email from Régis

Downloading a File from a Web Server

Downloading a file from an FTP Server is easy with the FTP Task, but sometimes you need a file from a web server. This example shows how to do that with a Script Task. Logging in or other manual actions are beyond the scope of this book. One starting point is a publicly downloadable file. For testing purposes, you can use the following URL: `https://sites.google.com/site/ssisblogspot/products.csv`.

Data Flow Task

The Starting situation is a simple Data Flow Task such as in Figure 6-5 that reads a flat file, but you want to refresh that flat file and download a new version from a web site. You will use the Flat File Connection Manager, named Products, to determine the download location. There is a starter package available that already has the data flow in it.

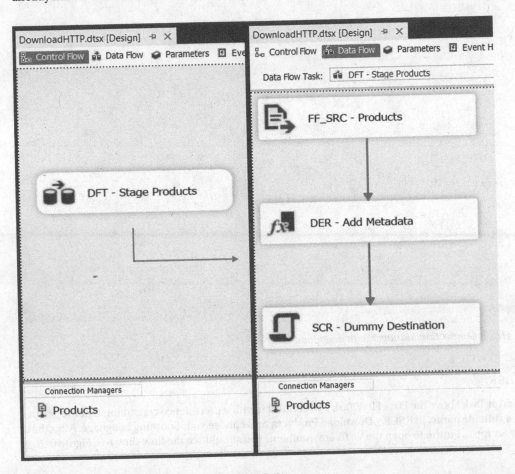

Figure 6-5. *Simple Data Flow Task with Flat File Source*

HTTP Connection Manager

To store the source file's URL, use an HTTP Connection Manager. For this example, only fill in the URL of the file that you want to download; leave all other values in their defaults. See Figure 6-6 for an example.

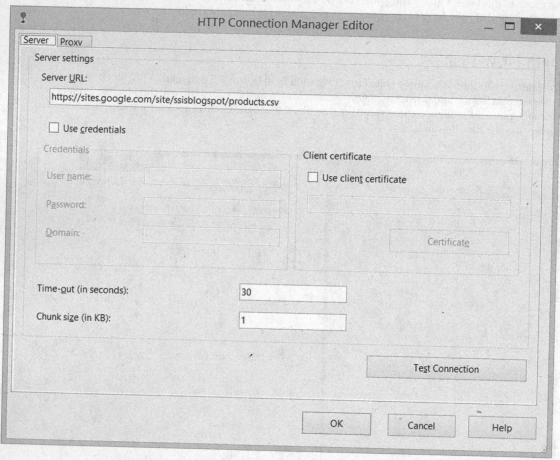

Figure 6-6. *HTTP Connection Manager with download URL*

Script Task

Now add a Script Task above the Data Flow Task and connect it with a precedence constraint. Edit the Script Task. Give it a suitable name, like SCR – Download Products, and choose your Scripting Language. After that, click the Edit Script. . . button to open the VSTA environment. You should see the flow shown in Figure 6-7.

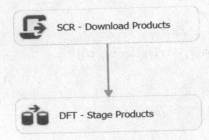

Figure 6-7. *Adding the Script Task*

The Code

Now go to the Main method and add the following code:

```
public void Main()
{
  // Get your newly added HTTP Connection Manager
  Object HTTPConnectionManager =
              Dts.Connections["WebProducts"].AcquireConnection(null);

  // Create a new connection
  HttpClientConnection WebProductConnection =
                      new HttpClientConnection(HTTPConnectionManager);

  // Get the location from the Flat File Connection Manager
  string DownloadLocation = Dts.Connections["Products"].
                      AcquireConnection(Dts.Transaction).ToString();


  try
  {
    // Logging start of download (optional)
    bool fireAgain = true;
    Dts.Events.FireInformation(0, "Download", "Downloading " +
          WebProductConnection.ServerURL, string.Empty, 0, ref fireAgain);

    // Download the file and replace the current CSV
    WebProductConnection.DownloadFile(DownloadLocation, true);

    // Logging end of download (optional)
    Dts.Events.FireInformation(0, "Download", "Saved " + DownloadLocation,
                              string.Empty, 0, ref fireAgain);

    // Quit Script Task succesful
    Dts.TaskResult = (int)ScriptResults.Success;
  }
```

```
  catch (Exception ex)
  {
    // Logging why download failed
    Dts.Events.FireError(0, "Download", "Failed: " + ex.Message, string.Empty, 0);

    // Quit Script Task unsuccesful
    Dts.TaskResult = (int)ScriptResults.Failure;
  }
}
```

Here is theVB.Net code:

```
Public Sub Main()
  ' Get your newly added HTTP Connection Manager
  Dim HTTPConnectionManager As [Object] = _
        Dts.Connections("WebProducts").AcquireConnection(Nothing)

  ' Create a new connection
  Dim WebProductConnection As New HttpClientConnection(HTTPConnectionManager)

  ' Get the location from the Flat File Connection Manager
  Dim DownloadLocation As String = _
        Dts.Connections("Products"). _
        AcquireConnection(Dts.Transaction).ToString()

Try
    ' Logging start of download (optional)
    Dim fireAgain As Boolean = True
    Dts.Events.FireInformation(0, "Download", "Downloading " + _
          WebProductConnection.ServerURL, String.Empty, 0, fireAgain)

    ' Download the file and replace the current CSV
    WebProductConnection.DownloadFile(DownloadLocation, True)

    ' Logging end of download (optional)
    Dts.Events.FireInformation(0, "Download", "Saved " & DownloadLocation, _
          String.Empty, 0, fireAgain)

    ' Quit Script Task succesful
    Dts.TaskResult = ScriptResults.Success
  Catch ex As Exception
    ' Logging why download failed
    Dts.Events.FireError(0, "Download", "Failed: " + ex.Message, _
        String.Empty, 0)

    ' Quit Script Task unsuccesful
    Dts.TaskResult = ScriptResults.Failure
  End Try
End Sub
```

154

The Results

Now close the Script Task and execute it to see the results.

Downloading the Latest File from an FTP Server

The FTP Task is an often-used task to download a specific file from an FTP server. But what if you want to download the latest file from an FTP folder and you don't know the exact name? This is not possible with the out-of-the-box FTP task. For this example, you use a wildcard filter to select all the appropriate files, and then loop through these files to determine the newest file. This example is for a Windows-based FTP server. And if there are multiple files with the same maximum file date, you only get one.

Variables

In most cases, it's preferable to use a connection manager to pass on login information to the script, but in this case, you need a password, which you can't extract from the FTP Connection Manager object because it is a sensitive property. In this case, you will use variables (or parameters) to store the connection data in. Make sure to remove the value from the password variable when you are ready. Replace its value with configurations, otherwise the password will be visible in your package.

First, create five SSIS string variables and fill them with correct connection data from your own FRP server. The names and example values are shown in Figure 6-8.

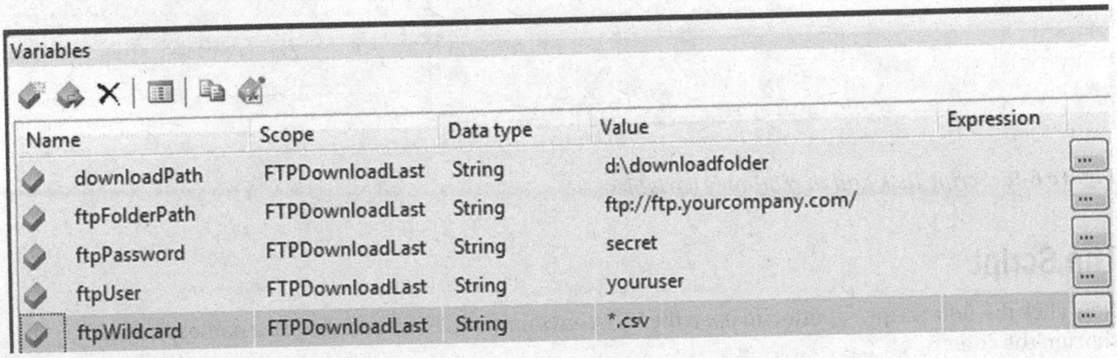

Figure 6-8. SSIS string variables

Script Task

Add a Script Task to the Control Flow to download the latest file. Give it a suitable name, like SCR – Get Latest FTP File. Next, edit it and add the five SSIS string variables as ReadOnlyVariables. See Figure 6-9.

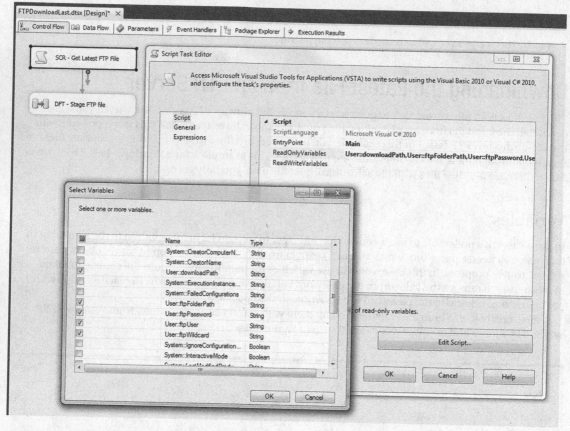

Figure 6-9. *Script Task and its read-only variables*

The Script

Now click the Edit Script. . . button to open the VSTA environment. First, add the extra namespaces to shorten the code.

```
#region customNamespaces
using System.Globalization;
using System.IO;
using System.Text.RegularExpressions;
#endregion
```

And here is the VB.NET code:

```
#Region "customNamespaces"
Imports System.Globalization
Imports System.IO
Imports System.Text.RegularExpressions
#End Region
```

Now add the following code to your `Main` method; also add the two extra methods to your class. The first custom method is for determining the latest file on your FTP server. Make sure that the `ListDirectoryDetails` output format in that method is equal to yours; otherwise, you need to change the datetime format. The second custom method is for downloading the file from your FTP server.

```
public void Main()
{
  // String variable to store the ftp connection data
  string ftpFolderPath = Dts.Variables["User::ftpFolderPath"].Value.ToString();
  string ftpUser = Dts.Variables["User::ftpUser"].Value.ToString();
  string ftpPassword = Dts.Variables["User::ftpPassword"].Value.ToString();
  string ftpWildcard = Dts.Variables["User::ftpWildcard"].Value.ToString();
  string downloadFolder = Dts.Variables["User::downloadPath"].Value.ToString();

  try
  {
    // Determine latest file
    string latestFile = GetLatestFile(ftpFolderPath, ftpUser, ftpPassword, ftpWildcard);

    // Now you can either fill an SSIS string variable (see chapter 4) and use
    // the FTP Task to download the file or you can use a piece of code to
    // download it.
    DownloadFile(latestFile, ftpUser, ftpPassword, downloadFolder);

    // Succeed Script Task
    Dts.TaskResult = (int)ScriptResults.Success;
  }
  catch (Exception ex)
  {
    // No file found
    Dts.Events.FireError(0, "Most recent file", ex.Message + Environment.NewLine +
                      ex.InnerException.Message, string.Empty, 0);

    // Fail Script Task
    Dts.TaskResult = (int)ScriptResults.Failure;
  }
}

// Method to determine the latest file
private string GetLatestFile(string ftpFolderPath,
                      string ftpUser,
                      string ftpPassword,
                      string ftpWildcard)
{
  // DateTime variable to check the highest date
  DateTime highestDateTime = Convert.ToDateTime("1-1-1900");

  // String variable to store the latest file
  string fileWithHighestDate = "";
```

```csharp
// Create an FTP Web Request
FtpWebRequest ftpRequest;
ftpRequest = (FtpWebRequest)FtpWebRequest.Create(ftpFolderPath);

// Provide credentials and set settings
ftpRequest.Credentials = new NetworkCredential(ftpUser, ftpPassword);
ftpRequest.UseBinary = true;
ftpRequest.UsePassive = true;
ftpRequest.KeepAlive = true;

// Specify the Type of FTP Request. This type
// returns a string containing file details.
// For Windows based FTP sites it looks like:
// 08-09-14  07:35PM                 435279 fileA.csv
// 08-10-15  07:34PM                 443808 fileB.csv
// 08-11-16  07:33PM                 424118 fileC.csv
// 07-06-13  03:53PM      <DIR>             foldername
ftpRequest.Method = WebRequestMethods.Ftp.ListDirectoryDetails;

// Try to connect to the server
try
{
  // Establish connection and return communication
  FtpWebResponse ftpResponse;
  ftpResponse = (FtpWebResponse)ftpRequest.GetResponse();

  // Create stream and get FTP Server's Response stream
  Stream ftpStream;
  ftpStream = ftpResponse.GetResponseStream();

  // Put stream in streamreader
  StreamReader ftpReader = new StreamReader(ftpStream);

  // Set the format of the datetime: 08-09-14 07:35PM
  // Verify that your ftp server uses the same format
  string dtFormat = "MM-dd-yy hh:mmtt";
  CultureInfo ci = CultureInfo.InvariantCulture;

  // Read each line of the response and check
  // which file is the most recent file
  while (ftpReader.Peek() != -1)
  {
    // Fill variable with 1 line of response
    string textLine = ftpReader.ReadLine();

    // If you want to check the row layout you could
    // add something like this and comment out the
    // rest of the code in and after the while loop:
    // MessageBox.Show(textLine);
```

```
    // Remove all duplicate spaces
    textLine = Regex.Replace(textLine, @"\s+", " ");

    // Split textLine on space and fill array
    string[] fileDetails = textLine.Split(" ".ToCharArray());

    // Change wildcard into regex pattern
    string wildcardPattern = "^" + Regex.Escape(ftpWildcard).Replace("\\*",
                             ".*").Replace("\\?", ".") + "$";

    // Create wildcard regular expression
    Regex wildcardRegex = new Regex(wildcardPattern,
                                    RegexOptions.IgnoreCase);

    // Check if file matches wildcard and skip subfolders
    if (wildcardRegex.IsMatch(fileDetails[3]) &&
        !fileDetails[2].Trim().ToLower().Equals("<dir>"))
    {
        // Compose filedatetime with date and time column
        string fileDateTxt = fileDetails[0] + " " + fileDetails[1];
        DateTime fileDate = DateTime.ParseExact(fileDateTxt, dtFormat, ci);

        // Check if the current file is the most recent one
        if (fileDate > highestDateTime)
        {
            // If it is, replace the most recent file variables
            highestDateTime = fileDate;
            fileWithHighestDate = fileDetails[3];
        }
    }
}

    // Resource cleanup
    ftpReader.Close();
    ftpStream.Close();
    ftpResponse.Close();
    ftpRequest = null;
}
catch (Exception ex)
{
    // Error in ftp response or in peak
    throw new Exception("Error in ftp response or peak", ex);
}

if (fileWithHighestDate.Equals(""))
{
    // No file found
    throw new Exception("No file found matching wildcard");
}

return ftpFolderPath + fileWithHighestDate;
}
```

```csharp
// Method to download a file
private void DownloadFile(string ftpFilePath,
                         string ftpUser,
                         string ftpPassword,
                         string downloadFolder)
{
  // Create an FTP Web Request
  FtpWebRequest ftpRequest;
  ftpRequest = (FtpWebRequest)FtpWebRequest.Create(ftpFilePath);

  // Provide credentials and set settings
  ftpRequest.Credentials = new NetworkCredential(ftpUser, ftpPassword);
  ftpRequest.UseBinary = true;
  ftpRequest.UsePassive = true;
  ftpRequest.KeepAlive = true;

  // Specify the Type of FTP Request.
  ftpRequest.Method = WebRequestMethods.Ftp.DownloadFile;

  // Try to connect to the server
  try
  {
    // Establish connection and return communication
    FtpWebResponse ftpResponse;
    ftpResponse = (FtpWebResponse)ftpRequest.GetResponse();

    // Create stream and get FTP Server's Response stream
    Stream ftpStream;
    ftpStream = ftpResponse.GetResponseStream();

    // Determine filename in FTP path
    string downloadFile = Path.Combine(downloadFolder,
                                    Path.GetFileName(ftpFilePath));

    // Specify the size of the buffer
    int bufferSize = 2048;

    // Create filestream to save the FTP file in
    FileStream localFileStream = new FileStream(downloadFile, FileMode.Create);

    // Create buffer to download data
    byte[] byteBuffer = new byte[bufferSize];

    // Integer variable to store the number of read bytes in
    int bytesRead = ftpStream.Read(byteBuffer, 0, bufferSize);

    // Start downloading until all bytes are downloaded
    while (bytesRead > 0)
    {
      // Write current buffer to local file
      localFileStream.Write(byteBuffer, 0, bytesRead);
```

```
    // Download next buffer
    bytesRead = ftpStream.Read(byteBuffer, 0, bufferSize);
  }

  // Resource cleanup
  localFileStream.Close();
  ftpStream.Close();
  ftpResponse.Close();
  ftpRequest = null;
}
catch (Exception ex)
{
  // Error in ftp response or in peak
  throw new Exception("Error in ftp response or peak", ex);
}
}
```

This is the VB.NET code:

```
Public Sub Main()
  ' String variable to store the ftp connection data
  Dim ftpFolderPath As String = _
                      Dts.Variables("User::ftpFolderPath").Value.ToString()
  Dim ftpUser As String = Dts.Variables("User::ftpUser").Value.ToString()
  Dim ftpPassword As String = _
                      Dts.Variables("User::ftpPassword").Value.ToString()
  Dim ftpWildcard As String = _
                      Dts.Variables("User::ftpWildcard").Value.ToString()
  Dim downloadFolder As String = _
                      Dts.Variables("User::downloadPath").Value.ToString()


  Try
    ' Determine latest file
    Dim latestFile As String = GetLatestFile(ftpFolderPath, _
                                             ftpUser, _
                                             ftpPassword, _
                                             ftpWildcard)


    ' Now you can either fill an SSIS string variable (see chapter 4) and use
    ' the FTP Task to download the file or you can use a piece of code to
    ' download it.
    DownloadFile(latestFile, ftpUser, ftpPassword, downloadFolder)

    ' Succeed Script Task
    Dts.TaskResult = ScriptResults.Success
```

```vbnet
    Catch ex As Exception
      ' No file found
      Dts.Events.FireError(0, "Most recent file", ex.Message & _
                          Environment.NewLine & ex.InnerException.Message, _
                          String.Empty, 0)
      ' Fail Script Task
      Dts.TaskResult = ScriptResults.Failure
    End Try
End Sub


' Method to determine the latest file
Private Function GetLatestFile(ftpFolderPath As String, ftpUser As String, ftpPassword As _
                              String, ftpWildcard As String) As String
    ' DateTime variable to check the highest date
    Dim highestDateTime As DateTime = Convert.ToDateTime("1-1-1900")

    ' String variable to store the latest file
    Dim fileWithHighestDate As String = ""

    ' Create an FTP Web Request
    Dim ftpRequest As FtpWebRequest
    ftpRequest = DirectCast(FtpWebRequest.Create(ftpFolderPath), FtpWebRequest)

    ' Provide credentials and set settings
    ftpRequest.Credentials = New NetworkCredential(ftpUser, ftpPassword)
    ftpRequest.UseBinary = True
    ftpRequest.UsePassive = True
    ftpRequest.KeepAlive = True

    ' Specify the Type of FTP Request. This type
    ' returns a string containing file details.
    ' For Windows based FTP sites it looks like:
    ' 08-09-14  07:35PM                 435279 fileA.csv
    ' 08-10-15  07:34PM                 443808 fileB.csv
    ' 08-11-16  07:33PM                 424118 fileC.csv
    ' 07-06-13  03:53PM         <DIR>           foldername
    ftpRequest.Method = WebRequestMethods.Ftp.ListDirectoryDetails

    ' Try to connect to the server
    Try
      ' Establish connection and return communication
      Dim ftpResponse As FtpWebResponse
      ftpResponse = DirectCast(ftpRequest.GetResponse(), FtpWebResponse)

      ' Create stream and get FTP Server's Response stream
      Dim ftpStream As Stream
      ftpStream = ftpResponse.GetResponseStream()

      ' Put stream in streamreader
      Dim ftpReader As New StreamReader(ftpStream)
```

```vb
' Set the format of the datetime: 08-09-14 07:35PM
Dim dtFormat As String = "MM-dd-yy hh:mmtt"
Dim ci As CultureInfo = CultureInfo.InvariantCulture

' Read each line of the response and check
' which file is the most recent file
While ftpReader.Peek() <> -1
  ' Fill variable with 1 line of response
  Dim textLine As String = ftpReader.ReadLine()

  ' If you want to check the row layout you could
  ' add something like this and comment out the
  ' rest of the code in and after the while loop:
  ' MessageBox.Show(textLine);

  ' Remove all duplicate spaces
  textLine = Regex.Replace(textLine, "\s+", " ")

  ' Split textLine on space and fill array
  Dim fileDetails As String() = textLine.Split(" ".ToCharArray())

  ' Change wildcard into regex pattern
  Dim wildcardPattern As String = "^" & _
                Regex.Escape(ftpWildcard).Replace("\*", ".*") _
                .Replace("\?", ".") & "$"

  ' Create wildcard regular expression
  Dim wildcardRegex As New Regex(wildcardPattern, RegexOptions.IgnoreCase)

  ' Check if file matches wildcard and skip subfolders
  If wildcardRegex.IsMatch(fileDetails(3)) AndAlso _
    Not fileDetails(2).Trim().ToLower().Equals("<dir>") Then
    ' Compose filedatetime with date and time column
    Dim fileDateTxt As String = fileDetails(0) & " " & fileDetails(1)
    Dim fileDate As DateTime = DateTime.ParseExact(fileDateTxt, _
                        dtFormat, ci)

    ' Check if the current file is the most recent one
    If fileDate > highestDateTime Then
      ' If it is, replace the most recent file variables
      highestDateTime = fileDate
      fileWithHighestDate = fileDetails(3)
    End If
  End If
End While

' Resource cleanup
ftpReader.Close()
ftpStream.Close()
ftpResponse.Close()
ftpRequest = Nothing
```

```vb
  Catch ex As Exception
    ' Error in ftp response or in peak
    Throw New Exception("Error in ftp response or peak", ex)
  End Try

  If fileWithHighestDate.Equals("") Then
    ' No file found
    Throw New Exception("No file found matching wildcard")
  End If


  Return ftpFolderPath & fileWithHighestDate
End Function


' Method to download a file
Private Sub DownloadFile(ftpFilePath As String, ftpUser As String, ftpPassword As String,
                         downloadFolder As String)
  ' Create an FTP Web Request
  Dim ftpRequest As FtpWebRequest
  ftpRequest = DirectCast(FtpWebRequest.Create(ftpFilePath), FtpWebRequest)

  ' Provide credentials and set settings
  ftpRequest.Credentials = New NetworkCredential(ftpUser, ftpPassword)
  ftpRequest.UseBinary = True
  ftpRequest.UsePassive = True
  ftpRequest.KeepAlive = True

  ' Specify the Type of FTP Request.
  ftpRequest.Method = WebRequestMethods.Ftp.DownloadFile

  ' Try to connect to the server
  Try
    ' Establish connection and return communication
    Dim ftpResponse As FtpWebResponse
    ftpResponse = DirectCast(ftpRequest.GetResponse(), FtpWebResponse)

    ' Create stream and get FTP Server's Response stream
    Dim ftpStream As Stream
    ftpStream = ftpResponse.GetResponseStream()

    ' Determine filename in FTP path
    Dim downloadFilePath As String = Path.Combine(downloadFolder, _
                             Path.GetFileName(ftpFilePath))

    ' Specify the size of the buffer
    Dim bufferSize As Integer = 2048

    ' Create filestream to save the FTP file in
    Dim localFileStream As New FileStream(downloadFilePath, FileMode.Create)

    ' Create buffer to download data
    Dim byteBuffer As Byte() = New Byte(bufferSize - 1) {}
```

```
  ' Integer variable to store the number of read bytes in
  Dim bytesRead As Integer = ftpStream.Read(byteBuffer, 0, bufferSize)

  ' Start downloading until all bytes are downloaded
  While bytesRead > 0
      ' Write current buffer to local file
      localFileStream.Write(byteBuffer, 0, bytesRead)

      ' Download next buffer
      bytesRead = ftpStream.Read(byteBuffer, 0, bufferSize)
  End While

  ' Resource cleanup
  localFileStream.Close()
  ftpStream.Close()
  ftpResponse.Close()
  ftpRequest = Nothing
Catch ex As Exception
  ' Error in ftp response or in peak
  Throw New Exception("Error in ftp response or peak", ex)
End Try
End Sub
```

The Results

Now close the Script Task and execute it to see the results. The newest file that meets the filter will be downloaded. If you want a Data Flow Task behind it to process that newest file, you need to know the file name and path in the connection manager. The easiest way to do this is to write that path to an SSIS string variable in the Main method; something like this:

```
Dts.Variables["NewestFile"].Value = Path.Combine(downloadFolder, latestFile);
```

And here is the VB.NET code:

```
Dts.Variables("NewestFile").Value = Path.Combine(downloadFolder, latestFile)
```

Downloading a File from an SFTP Server

Secure FTP is not supported by the SSIS FTP Task, and it isn't even supported by the .NET Framework. So for this example you need to use a third-party SFTP library in the Script Task. There are plenty commercial libraries available, but for this example, you will use the SSH.NET library from CodePlex (http://sshnet.codeplex.com).

CodePlex is Microsoft's open source project hosting site. Although all projects are open source, check the project licenses before you start using an assembly or a piece of code. Some projects have limitations on commercial use.

Download and Install

Go to http://sshnet.codeplex.com and download the appropriate SSHNet Binary (SSHNet .NET 3.5 Binary for SSIS 2008 and SSHNet .NET 4.0 Binary for SSIS 2012 and later). Via the Visual Studio Command prompt, you can use the gacutil to add this library to the Global Assembly Cache: `gacutil -i Renci.SshNet.dll` (see Chapter 4). Afterward, it is ready to be used in the Script Task.

Variables

In most cases, it's preferable to use a connection manager, but since there is no SFTP Connection Manager available, you need to use variables (or parameters). For this example, you will use variables to store the connection data. Make sure to remove sensitive data, such as passwords and keys, from the variable values when you are ready. Replace these values with configurations; otherwise, they will be visible in your package.

First, create five SSIS string variables and fill them with the correct connection data. Table 6-1 describes the variables and their usage. Figure 6-10 shows them populated with data.

Table 6-1. *Variables for holding connection data*

Name	Data Type	Description
sftpServer	String	Contains the name or IP address of the SFTP server
sftpUser	String	Contains the username that has access on the SFTP server
sftpPassword	String	The corresponding password
sftpFilePath	String	The file path of the file you need to download: /export/source.zip
downloadPath	String	The path of the local download folder: d:\downloadfolder

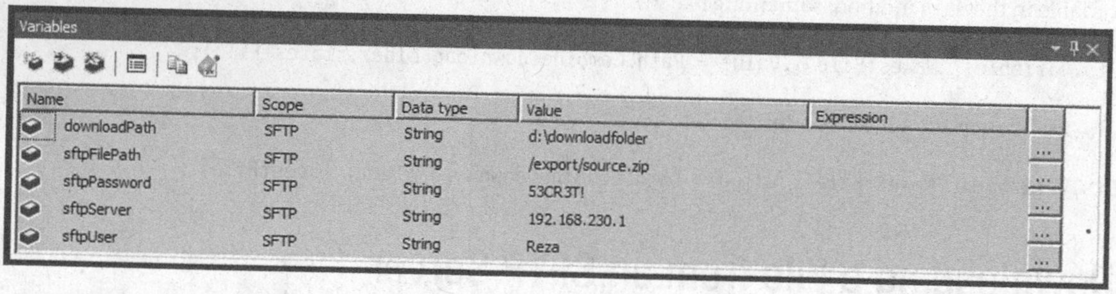

Figure 6-10. *Variable for SFTP connection: Download*

Script Task

Add a Script Task to the Control Flow to download the file from the SFTP server. Give it a suitable name, such as SCR – Download SFTP File. Afterward, edit it and add the five SSIS string variables as ReadOnlyVariables. Figure 6-11 shows the dialog from wich to add the variables.

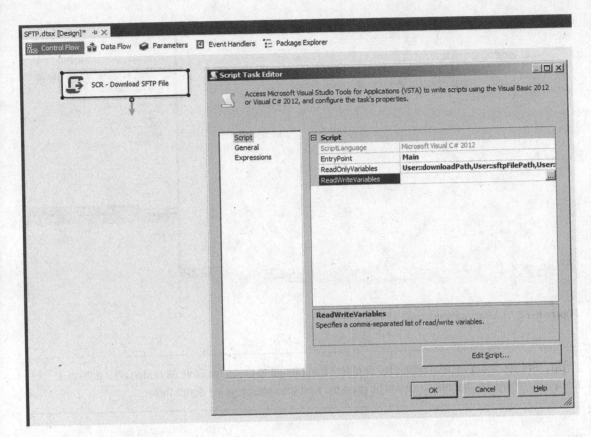

Figure 6-11. *Add variables for read-only lock*

Add Reference

Edit the Script Task and add a new reference to the Renci.SshNet.dll assembly located in the Global Assembly Cache (GAC) (see Chapter 4 for more information). The location could vary per assembly version, but is should look something like this:

C:\Windows\Microsoft.NET\assembly\GAC_MSIL\Renci.SshNet\v4.0_2014.4.6.0__1cee9f8bde3db106\

Figure 6-12 shows reference in place in the Reference Manager dialog.

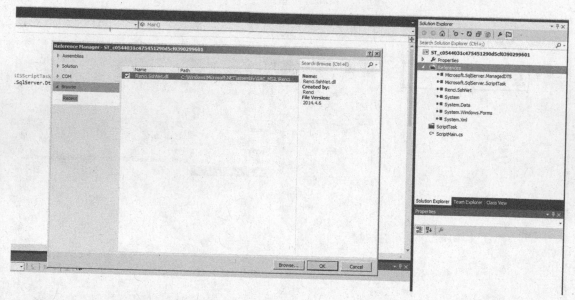

Figure 6-12. *Adding reference to SFTP assembly (C#)*

■ **Tip** Are you using Visual Studio 2010 or older? Don't forget to press the Save All button after adding a reference; otherwise, that reference will be gone the next time you open the Script Task.

The Code

Now click the Edit Script. . . button to open the VSTA environment. First, add the extra namespaces to shorten the code.

```
#region customNamespaces
using System.IO;
using Renci.SshNet;
#endregion
```

And here is the VB.NET code:

```
#Region "customNamespaces"
Imports System.IO
Imports Renci.SshNet
#End Region
```

Then add the following code to your Main method:

```
public void Main()
{
  // Store values of SSIS variables in local variable
  string sftpServer = Dts.Variables["User::sftpServer"].Value.ToString();
  string sftpUser = Dts.Variables["User::sftpUser"].Value.ToString();
  string sftpPassword = Dts.Variables["User::sftpPassword"].Value.ToString();
  string sftpFilePath = Dts.Variables["User::sftpFilePath"].Value.ToString();
  string downloadPath = Dts.Variables["User::downloadPath"].Value.ToString();

  try
  {
    // Specify SFTP Connection
    using (SftpClient mySftpClient = new SftpClient(sftpServer,
                                                    sftpUser,
                                                    sftpPassword))
    {
      // Connect to server
      mySftpClient.Connect();

      // Combine the remote filename and the download path
      string localFilePath = Path.GetFileName(sftpFilePath);
      localFilePath = Path.Combine(downloadPath, localFilePath);

      // Create a file stream for the local file
      using (Stream localFile = File.OpenWrite(localFilePath))
      {
        // Download the remote file and store it in the filestream
        mySftpClient.DownloadFile(sftpFilePath, localFile);

        // Cleanup
        localFile.Dispose();
      }
      // Disconnect and Cleanup
      mySftpClient.Disconnect();
      mySftpClient.Dispose();
    }
    // Succeed Script Task
    Dts.TaskResult = (int)ScriptResults.Success;
  }
  catch (Exception ex)
  {
    // Fire error message
    Dts.Events.FireError(-1, "SFTP Download", ex.Message, string.Empty, 0);

    // Fail Script Task
    Dts.TaskResult = (int)ScriptResults.Failure;
  }
}
```

Here is the VB.NET code:

```vbnet
Public Sub Main()
    ' Store values of SSIS variables in local variable
    Dim sftpServer As String = Dts.Variables("User::sftpServer").Value.ToString()
    Dim sftpUser As String = Dts.Variables("User::sftpUser").Value.ToString()
    Dim sftpPassword As String = _
                    Dts.Variables("User::sftpPassword").Value.ToString()
    Dim sftpFilePath As String = _
                    Dts.Variables("User::sftpFilePath").Value.ToString()
    Dim downloadPath As String = _
                    Dts.Variables("User::downloadPath").Value.ToString()

    Try
        ' Specify SFTP Connection and connect to server
        Using mySftpClient As New SftpClient(sftpServer, sftpUser, sftpPassword)
            mySftpClient.Connect()

            ' Combine the remote filename and the download path
            Dim localFilePath As String = Path.GetFileName(sftpFilePath)
            localFilePath = Path.Combine(downloadPath, localFilePath)

            ' Create a file stream for the local file
            Using localFile As Stream = File.OpenWrite(localFilePath)

                ' Download the remove file and store it in the filestream
                mySftpClient.DownloadFile(sftpFilePath, localFile)

                ' Cleanup
                localFile.Dispose()
            End Using
            ' Disconnect and Cleanup
            mySftpClient.Disconnect()
            mySftpClient.Dispose()
        End Using

        ' Succeed Script Task
        Dts.TaskResult = ScriptResults.Success
    Catch ex As Exception
        ' Fire error message
        Dts.Events.FireError(-1, "SFTP Download", ex.Message, String.Empty, 0)

        ' Fail Script Task
        Dts.TaskResult = ScriptResults.Failure
    End Try
End Sub
```

Upload

If you want to upload files via SFTP (instead of downloading), then you need to change a couple of variables and, of course, the code. The rest of the steps are similar. Table 6-2 describse the variables needed, and Figure 6-13 shows them populated.

Table 6-2. *Descriptions of the variables for SFTP connections*

Name	Data Type	Description
sftpServer	String	Contains the name or IP address of the SFTP server
sftpUser	String	Contains the username that has access on the SFTP server
sftpPassword	String	The corresponding password
sftpFolderPath	String	The folder path of the SFTP server for storing the files: /export/
localFilePath	String	The path of the local file which you want to upload: d:\somefile.txt

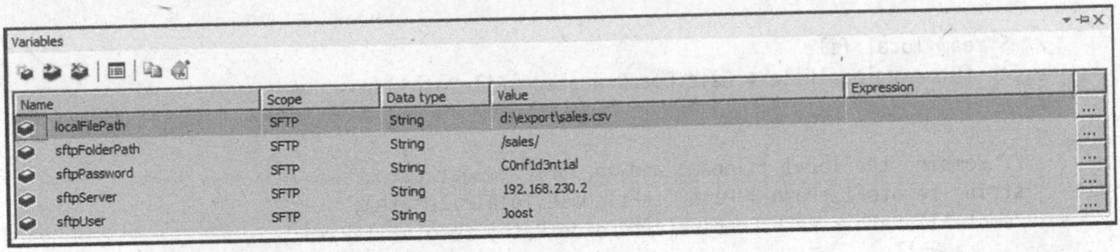

Figure 6-13. *Variable for SFTP connection: Upload*

The Code: Upload

First, add the extra namespaces to shorten the code.

```
#region customNamespaces
using System.IO;
using Renci.SshNet;
#endregion
```

This is the VB.NET code:

```
#Region "customNamespaces"
Imports System.IO
Imports Renci.SshNet
#End Region
```

Now you can add the following code to the Main method:

```
public void Main()
{
  // Store values of SSIS variables in local variable
  string sftpServer = Dts.Variables["User::sftpServer"].Value.ToString();
  string sftpUser = Dts.Variables["User::sftpUser"].Value.ToString();
  string sftpPassword = Dts.Variables["User::sftpPassword"].Value.ToString();
  string sftpFolderPath = Dts.Variables["User::sftpFolderPath"].Value.ToString();
  string localFilePath = Dts.Variables["User::localFilePath"].Value.ToString();

  try
  {
    // Specify SFTP Connection
    using (SftpClient mySftpClient = new SftpClient(sftpServer, sftpUser, sftpPassword))
    {
      // Connect to server
      mySftpClient.Connect();

      // Stream local file
      using (Stream localFile = File.OpenRead(localFilePath))
      {

        // Combine the local filename and the SFTP folder path
        string remoteFilePath = Path.GetFileName(localFilePath);
        remoteFilePath = Path.Combine(sftpFolderPath, remoteFilePath);

        // Upload local file to SFTP Server (and overwrite)
        mySftpClient.UploadFile(localFile, remoteFilePath, true);

        // Cleanup
        localFile.Dispose();
      }
      // Disconnect and Cleanup
      mySftpClient.Disconnect();
      mySftpClient.Dispose();
    }

    // Succeed Script Task
    Dts.TaskResult = (int)ScriptResults.Success;
  }
  catch (Exception ex)
  {
    // Fire error message
    Dts.Events.FireError(-1, "SFTP Upload", ex.Message, string.Empty, 0);

    // Fail Script Task
    Dts.TaskResult = (int)ScriptResults.Failure;
  }
}
```

This is the VB.NET code:

```vbnet
Public Sub Main()
    ' Store values of SSIS variables in local variable
    Dim sftpServer As String = Dts.Variables("User::sftpServer").Value.ToString()
    Dim sftpUser As String = Dts.Variables("User::sftpUser").Value.ToString()
    Dim sftpPassword As String = Dts.Variables("User::sftpPassword").Value.ToString()
    Dim sftpFolderPath As String = Dts.Variables("User::sftpFolderPath").Value.ToString()
    Dim localFilePath As String = Dts.Variables("User::localFilePath").Value.ToString()

    Try
        ' Specify SFTP Connection
        Using mySftpClient As New SftpClient(sftpServer, sftpUser, sftpPassword)
            ' Connect to server
            mySftpClient.Connect()

            ' Stream local file
            Using localFile As Stream = File.OpenRead(localFilePath)

                ' Combine the local filename and the SFTP folder path
                Dim remoteFilePath As String = Path.GetFileName(localFilePath)
                remoteFilePath = Path.Combine(sftpFolderPath, remoteFilePath)

                ' Upload local file to SFTP Server (and overwrite)
                mySftpClient.UploadFile(localFile, remoteFilePath, True)

                ' Cleanup
                localFile.Dispose()
            End Using
            ' Disconnect and Cleanup
            mySftpClient.Disconnect()
            mySftpClient.Dispose()
        End Using

        ' Succeed Script Task
        Dts.TaskResult = ScriptResults.Success
    Catch ex As Exception
        ' Fire error message
        Dts.Events.FireError(-1, "SFTP Upload", ex.Message, String.Empty, 0)

        ' Fail Script Task
        Dts.TaskResult = ScriptResults.Failure
    End Try
End Sub
```

The Results

Now close the Script Task and execute it to see the results. In the upload example, you could also replace the localFilePath variable with a connection manager if you are already using it; for example, a data flow. See Chapter 4 for connection manager code examples.

Summary

In this chapter you learned how to use the Script Task for web-based tasks, where the built-in tasks simply come up short. You also experienced your first example of a third-party assembly.

CHAPTER 7

■ ■ ■

Working with Web Services and XML

According to World Wide Web Consortium (W3C), a web service is a software system designed to support interoperable machine-to-machine interaction over a network. Furthermore, W3C specifies that a web service must have a described interface and that other systems interact with this web service using Simple Object Access Protocol (SOAP) typically over HTTP using XML serialization. This very short introduction clearly describes that you don't have a web service without XML. In SSIS you can consume web services using scripting tasks and the .NET Framework, namely by using .NET and Windows Communication Foundation.

Windows Communication Foundation

Windows Communication Foundation (WCF) is a framework for building service-oriented applications. WCF makes the development and usage of web services easier because it offers a manageable approach to the creation of web services and web services clients.

WCF offers the following features:

- Service orientation
- Security
- Interoperability
- Multiple message patterns
- Service metadata
- Data contracts
- Multiple transports and encodings
- Durable, reliable, and queued messages
- Transactions
- Support for REST and AJAX
- Extensibility

A lot has already been written about WCF; it is a very vast subject. For more information, you can read about it on MSDN at `https://msdn.microsoft.com/en-us/library/ms730846(v=vs.110).aspx` or read *Pro WCF 4* by Nishith Pathak (Apress, 2011).

Web Services

In SSIS there is a built-in Web Service Task that you can use for calling web services. The component is pretty straightforward. You can save the result to a file or a variable, as shown in Figure 7-1.

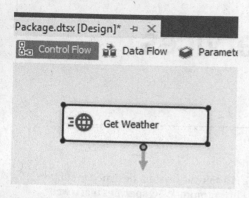

Figure 7-1. *The built-in Web Service Task*

As you've seen many times in the previous chapters, sometimes the capabilities of the built-in tasks in SSIS are not enough; this is when you need the flexibility and power of scripting.

Let's assume that you want to call a WCF web service that is communicating over NetTCP rather than HTTP. NetTCP offers the advantage of binary-encoded communication and interprocess and across-computer communication over the TCP protocol. This option is not available from within the standard Web Service Task.

Figure 7-2 is a schema that shows which protocol to use and when. All the cases where HTTP is not an option, you need to use a Script Task Component to call your web service.

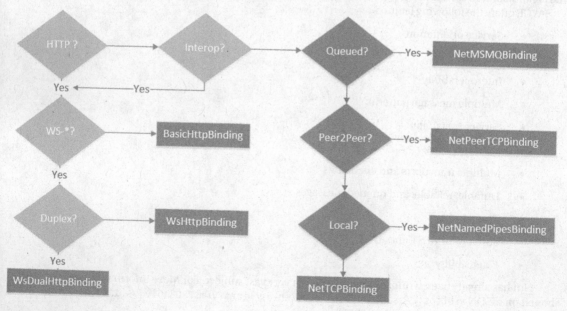

Figure 7-2. *WCF protocol chart*

Creating Variables

You need the following variables to get started:

- City of type string to store the city name

- Country of type string to store the country name

- ResultString of type string to store the XML result from the web service call

- WeatherServiceURL is also a string in the web service URL. The main advantage of saving the web service URL address in a variable is that you are able to change it without having to open the package. For example, when the web service (or the package) goes from development to production, you might want to control which address to use; one way to do this is to use parameters or to configure it dynamically.

The Script

Create a new Script Task Component and call it SCR_Get Weather. Add the four variables created previously. City, Country, and ResultString should be ReadWrite and the WeatherServiceURL should be ReadOnly.

Service Reference

When working with web services, you need to generate a contract. This is done by adding a service reference in the VSTA project. The service reference generates the interface needed to call the web service with the methods and types available for the call.

■ **Note** This is only available from SSIS on SQL Server 2008 and later. Prior to that, VSTA didn't support adding service references.

There are several things that you need to be aware of when you add a service reference. In the following example, you use a reference to the weather web service available at http://www.webservicex.net/globalweather.asmx?WSDL.

Initially, there is no Service Reference folder—just the Reference folder. You have to add a service reference for the folder to show up. To add a reference to a web service, right-click the Reference folder in the VSTA Solution Explorer and choose Add Service Reference. This opens the dialog window shown in Figure 7-3.

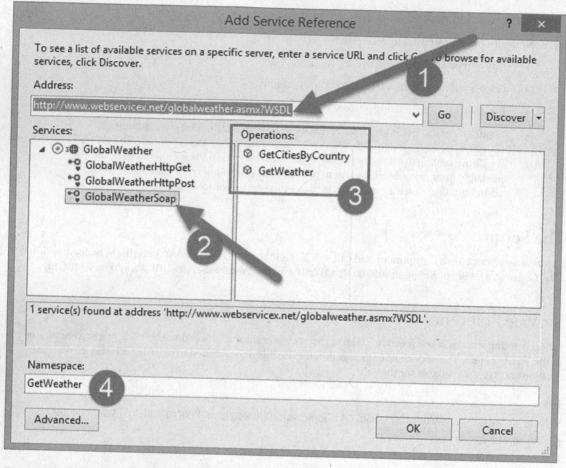

Figure 7-3. *Add Service Reference dialog*

Here are the steps to complete in the Add Service Reference dialog shown in Figure 7-3.

1. Enter the address of the web service you want to connect to.

2. In Services, since you are using WCF, select the SOAP implementation.

3. In Operations, you have two methods to choose from.

4. Enter a namespace, which is the name that you will use when calling the service from your script.

Once the dialog is filled out, press the OK button. A few things are happening behind the scenes: VSTA generates the metadata necessary to use the web service. The methods, properties, signature, interfaces, and all the artifacts necessary to call the web service are autogenerated.

■ **Note** Since it is autogenerated code, you shouldn't alter it, because the changes will be lost if you refresh the service reference.

If you want to find out how the metadata is generated and learn the intrinsic nature of the web service, you have a look at the autogenerated files. In most cases, this is not necessary because VSTA provides the necessary IntelliSense to call the service. Together with the code files, an `app.config` file is added to the project with the information needed for the contract and the binding to the web service.

The following is the `app.config` for the reference to the weather web service:

```xml
<?xml version="1.0" encoding="utf-8" ?>
<configuration>
  <system.serviceModel>
    <bindings>
      <basicHttpBinding>
        <binding name="GetCitiesByCountry" />
      </basicHttpBinding>
    </bindings>
    <client>
      <endpoint address="http://www.webservicex.net/globalweather.asmx"
          binding="basicHttpBinding" bindingConfiguration="GlobalWeatherSoap"
          contract="GetCitiesByCountry.GlobalWeatherSoap" name="GlobalWeatherSoap" />
    </client>
  </system.serviceModel>
</configuration>
```

Custom Namespace

System.ServiceModel is the namespace where all the WCF implementation lives. You need to add that to the namespace region; or even better, add a custom namespace region, as follows:

```
#region CustomNamespace

using System.ServiceModel;
using System.Xml;
using ST_1211e492c97246a9947e241a0234dce6.GetWeather;
using System.IO;

#endregion
```

The System.ServiceModel was first introduced in .NET Framework 3.0.

■ **Note**   If you are working with an earlier version of the .NET Framework, you need to manually generate the WSDL, the .disco file, the XSD schemas, and more artifacts. For more information on how to do this, go to https://msdn.microsoft.com/en-us/library/7h3ystb6%28v=vs.80%29.aspx.

Config or Not Config

After having generated the code, things get a bit more complicated because there are two ways of calling WCF web services. Now you have two options for configuring and debugging: modify a bunch of .config files, or do the configuration in C#/VB.NET. The first one is the most portable, whereas the second one is best suited for debugging. Both solutions are described next.

Solution 1: Modifying .config Files

This solution involves two steps.

Changes Required for Debugging

When debugging, you need to modify the DtsDebugHost.exe.Config file. DtsDebugHost.exe is the file used by SSDT when executing a package in debug mode. Therefore, its .config file needs to be modified to reflect the changes made to the app.config in the VSTA project. The file can be found in the 64-bits folder and the 32-bits folder. SSDT is only 32-bits, but the debugger supports both modes, making things even more confusing. The Run64BitRuntime can be changed in the Debugging pane of the project properties. On an SQL Server 2014 installation, the file is located at C:\Program Files\Microsoft SQL Server\120\DTS\Binn.

Changes Required After Debugging Is Done

This section should probably be called "Where is my app.config?" because you might need to change several more files, depending on how you are calling your packages.

- DTExec.exe.config: The .config file to the stand-alone DTExec.exe application used for calling packages. It has both a 32-bits and a 64-bits version; in SQL Server 2014 it is found in C:\ProgramFiles\MicrosoftSQLServer\120\DTS\Binn.

- DtsHost.exe.config: The file used by the SQL Server Agent when it is calling a package. There is a 32-bits version and a 64-bits version of the file. On SQL Server 2014, it is typically located at C:\ProgramFiles\MicrosoftSQLServer\120\DTS\Binn.

- DTExecUI.exe.config: The file used by the DTExec.exe UI. It is also typically located in C:\ProgramFiles\MicrosoftSQLServer\120\DTS\Binn on an SQL Server 2014 installation.

- ISServer.exe.config: The file used by SSISDB and ISServer.exe when using the package deployment model and executing the package from SSMS. The file is found in C:\Program Files\Microsoft SQL Server\120\DTS\Binn.

As you can imagine, it can be pretty tough to keep all of those files up-to-date. Table 7-1 lists all the files and where to find them.

Table 7-1. *.config Files and Their Locations*

File Name	32-bit	64-bit
DtsDebugHost.exe.config	C:\Program Files (x86)\Microsoft SQL Server\120\DTS\Binn	C:\Program Files\Microsoft SQL Server\120\DTS\Binn
DTExec.exe.config	C:\Program Files (x86))\Microsoft SQL Server\120\DTS\Binn	C:\Program Files\Microsoft SQL Server\120\DTS\Binn
DtsHost.exe.config	C:\Program Files (x86))\Microsoft SQL Server\120\DTS\Binn	C:\Program Files\Microsoft SQL Server\120\DTS\Binn
ISServer.exe.config	C:\Program Files (x86))\Microsoft SQL Server\120\DTS\Binn	C:\Program Files\Microsoft SQL Server\120\DTS\Binn

> ■ **Note**   The folder named 120 is for SQL Server 2014, 110 is for SQL Server 2012, and 100 is for SQL Server 2008.

This brings you to solution 2 for implementing web service calls in Script Tasks.

Solution 2: The In-Code Method

With this method, you don't need to change a single .config file. It is also an easy way to figure out how web services are configured and called without needing to keep several .config files in sync and up-to-date. The only downside is that you need to recompile the script should the service change its endpoint address or authentication method.

The code is basically the C# or VB.NET representation of what is described in the .config file. The code for the GetWeather application is shown later.

The Code

> ■ **Note**   The following code snippets show different parts of the script. The whole script is shown further down; it is also available in the Chapter 7 source code.

The Channel Factory type to use is of the interface generated when adding a reference to the web service. In this case, it is the GlobalWeatherSoap public interface.

```
//Create a Channel Factory with the type of the
//Web Service.
ChannelFactory<GlobalWeatherSoap> channelFactory = null;
```

And here it is in VB.NET:

```
'Create a ChannelFactory of the right type
Dim channelFactory As ChannelFactory(Of GlobalWeatherSoap) = Nothing
```

You also need a variable to store the endpoint for later usage.

```
EndpointAddress ep = null;
```

And here it is in VB.NET:

```
Dim ep As EndpointAddress = Nothing
```

To call a web service, you need an endpoint address, which is basically the address that you used when adding the service reference. You are using a variable for more flexibility.

```
//Specify what the address is
string epAdr = "http://www.webservicex.net/globalweather.asmx";
```

181

Here it is in VB.NET:

```
'Specify what the address is
Dim epAdr As String = "http://www.webservicex.net/globalweather.asmx"
```

After this, you can start specifying the binding to use and create the endpoint to be used with the ChannelFactory:

```
//Get the right binding
BasicHttpBinding httpb = new BasicHttpBinding();
channelFactory = new ChannelFactory<GlobalWeatherSoap>(httpb);

//The necessary endpoint with our address
ep = new EndpointAddress(epAdr);
```

Here it is in VB.NET:

```
'Get the right binding
Dim httpb As New BasicHttpBinding()
channelFactory = New ChannelFactory(Of GlobalWeatherSoap)(httpb)

'The necessary endpoint with our address
ep = New EndpointAddress(epAdr)
```

Once you have the elements ready, you are ready for the important part of the web service: calling the service itself and getting the result.

```
//Ready to create the representation of the web svc
GlobalWeatherSoap weatherSvcObj = channelFactory.CreateChannel(ep);
//Getting some geographic info about a country
string result = weatherSvcObj.GetCitiesByCountry("France");
//Save the result in a variable for later use.
Dts.Variables["ResultString"].Value = result;
```

And here it is in VB.NET:

```
'The necessary endpoint with our address
'Ready to create the representation of the web svc
Dim weatherSvcObj As GlobalWeatherSoap = channelFactory.CreateChannel(ep)
'Getting some geographic info about a country
Dim result As String = weatherSvcObj.GetCitiesByCountry("France")
'Save the result in a variable for later use.
Dts.Variables("ResultString").Value = result
```

Since a web service usually isn't something that is under your control, it is a really good idea to be ready to handle errors, which can happen many places along the lines to the endpoint. So a try-catch is very necessary here.

The following is the entire Main method in C#:

```
//Create a ChannelFactory of the right type – a using is necessary to use the service
reference in the code
// in our case it is :
```

182

```csharp
// using ST_751e10ef586a4cd9ac45c6d1c84c526c.GetWeather;
ChannelFactory<GlobalWeatherSoap> channelFactory = null;
EndpointAddress ep = null;

string City = Dts.Variables["City"].Value.ToString();
string Country = Dts.Variables["Country"].Value.ToString();

//Specify what the address is
string epAdr = Dts.Variables["WeatherServiceURL"].Value.ToString();
try
{
    //Get the right binding
    BasicHttpBinding httpb = new BasicHttpBinding();
    channelFactory = new ChannelFactory<GlobalWeatherSoap>(httpb);

    //The necessary endpoint with our address
    ep = new EndpointAddress(epAdr);

    //Ready to create the representation of the web svc
    GlobalWeatherSoap weatherSvcObj = channelFactory.CreateChannel(ep);
    //Getting some geographic info about a country
    string result = weatherSvcObj.GetWeather(City, Country);

    ////make sure that you are dealing with an XML document
    //XmlDocument doc = new XmlDocument();
    //doc.LoadXml(result);

    ValidateXML(result);
    //Save the result in a variable for later use.
    Dts.Variables["ResultString"].Value = result;

    MessageBox.Show(result);

}
catch (Exception ex)
{
    Dts.TaskResult = (int)ScriptResults.Failure;
    throw ex;
}
```

And this is it in VB.NET:

```vbnet
'Create a ChannelFactory of the right type - a using is necessary to use the service
reference in the code
' in our case it is :
' using ST_751e10ef586a4cd9ac45c6d1c84c526c.GetWeather;
Dim channelFactory As ChannelFactory(Of GlobalWeatherSoap) = Nothing
Dim ep As EndpointAddress = Nothing

Dim City As String = Dts.Variables("City").Value.ToString()
Dim Country As String = Dts.Variables("Country").Value.ToString()
```

```
'Specify what the address is
Dim epAdr As String = Dts.Variables("WeatherServiceURL").Value.ToString()
Try
        'Get the right binding
        Dim httpb As New BasicHttpBinding()
        channelFactory = New ChannelFactory(Of GlobalWeatherSoap)(httpb)

        'The necessary endpoint with our address
        ep = New EndpointAddress(epAdr)

        'Ready to create the representation of the web svc
        Dim weatherSvcObj As GlobalWeatherSoap = channelFactory.CreateChannel(ep)
        'Getting some geographic info about a country
        Dim result As String = weatherSvcObj.GetWeather(City, Country)

        '''/make sure that you are dealing with an XML document
        'XmlDocument doc = new XmlDocument();
        'doc.LoadXml(result);

        ValidateXML(result)
        'Save the result in a variable for later use.
        Dts.Variables("ResultString").Value = result

        MessageBox.Show(result)
Catch ex As Exception
        Dts.TaskResult = CInt(ScriptResults.Failure)
        Throw ex
End Try
```

Once you have called the web service as described here, you should get a result that looks like this (shortened for simplicity):

```
<NewDataSet>
  <Table>
    <Country>France</Country>
    <City>Le Touquet</City>
  </Table>
  <Table>
    <Country>France</Country>
    <City>Agen</City>
  </Table>
...
</NewDataSet>
```

So now that you have an XML structure representing the cities in France where weather data is available for this web service, you want to loop on each City element and get the weather for every single one.

The Foreach Loop to Handle XML

When creating the Foreach Loop Container, you need to specify the type of enumeration you are dealing with. The container needs a precedence constraint on the script. Figure 7-4 shows the collection settings for the container.

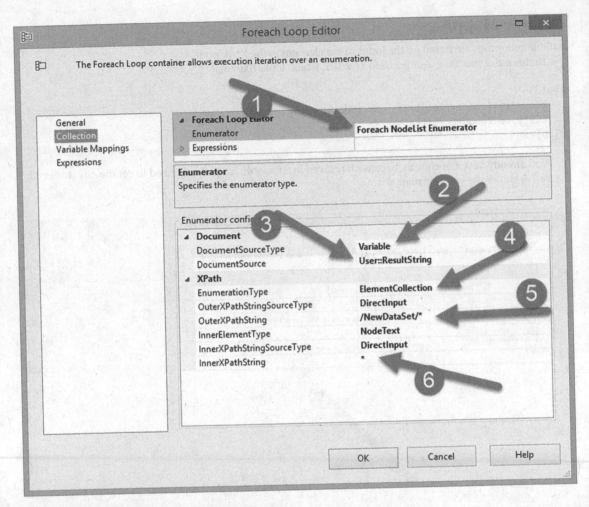

Figure 7-4. *Foreach Loop Container Collection settings*

The following explains the callouts for Figure 7-4:

1. You want to enumerate over a NodeList to get every city in the XML node list.

2. The node list is specified in a variable.

3. The variable name that holds the XML (of type string or even Object since every type inherits from the Object type).

4. The enumeration type is an element collection.

5. Where to find the elements. From the root (indicated by the first /) and every node below (indicated by the second /), node-by-node.

6. Each element in the node is index based and specified in the next pane of the Foreach Loop Editor.

Now that you have a loop over the `<Table>` element of the XML document, you need to get the element that you need. In this case, the `<City>` element. It is specified in Variable Mappings in the Foreach Loop Editor.

Variable Mappings

Variable mappings are based on the index of the element in the XML node.

In this case, you have a node called <Table>, which looks like this:

```
<Table>
    <Country>France</Country>    ← index 0
    <City>Le Touquet</City>      ← index 1
</Table>
```

You already have the country because it is saved in a variable, so you only need to get the city (index 1). Figure 7-5 shows the variable mapping.

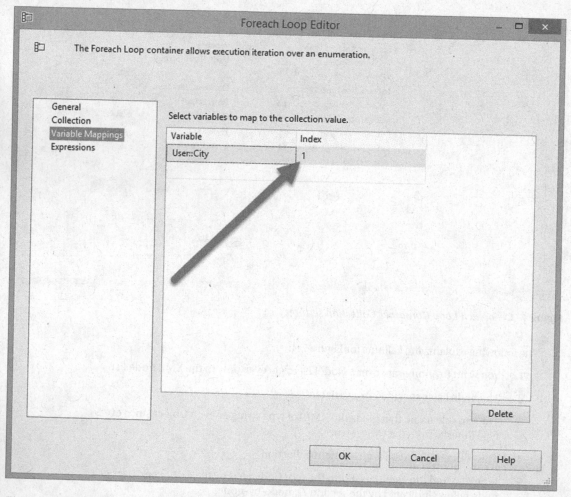

Figure 7-5. *Variable Mappings pane in the Foreach Loop Editor*

So now that everything is set in the Foreach Loop, you can iterate over the XML node list and get every city name. This demonstrates how to validate XML against a schema.

Validating XML Against Schemas

Before working with XML documents, it is often very useful to validate the content and make sure that the provided XML can adhere to the schema that it is supposed to represent. XML schema syntax and usage is outside the topic of this book, but it is very interesting and useful information; if you want to learn more about the topic, you are encouraged to take a look at the following:

- W3C schema recommendation: www.w3.org/TR/xmlschema-1/

- More information about XML Schema is on MSDN (in the System.XML.Schema namespace): https://msdn.microsoft.com/en-us/library/System.Xml.Schema(v=vs.110).aspx

XML Schemas can contain subparts that are declaratively included in the schema; these are called schema include elements, which look like this:

```
<xs:include schemaLocation="CityWeather_include.xsd"/>
```

The schemaLocation attribute points at the file to include. Other attributes are the id and "any attributes".

■ **Note** The include element is used to add multiple schemas with the same target namespace to a document.

An XML source honors schema include elements. But if you work with an XML task, it fails, and you get a statement that the include element is not a valid element. This is where a scripting task is handy. In the following examples, you use two schemas and the XML input from the GetWeather web service for all the cities that where returned for the country that you chose.

The first schema is for validating the <CurrentWeather> element in WeatherSchema.xsd.

```
<?xml version="1.0"?>
<xs:schema xmlns:xs="http://www.w3.org/2001/XMLSchema">
<xs:include schemaLocation="CityWeather_include.xsd"/>
  <xs:element name="CurrentWeather">
    <xs:complexType>
      <xs:sequence>
        <xs:element name="Location" type="LimitedString" />
        <xs:element name="Time" type="xs:string" />
        <xs:element name="Wind" type="xs:string" />
        <xs:element name="Visibility" type="xs:string" />
        <xs:element name="Temperature" type="xs:string" />
        <xs:element name="DewPoint" type="xs:string" />
        <xs:element name="RelativeHumidity" type="xs:string" />
        <xs:element name="Pressure" type="xs:string" />
        <xs:element name="Status" type="xs:string" />
      </xs:sequence>
    </xs:complexType>
  </xs:element>
</xs:schema>
```

The second schema is the one that is included in the first schema: CityWeather_include.xsd.

```xml
<?xml version="1.0"?>
<xs:schema xmlns:xs="http://www.w3.org/2001/XMLSchema">
  <xs:simpleType name="LimitedString">
    <xs:restriction base="xs:string">
      <xs:maxLength value="200" />
    </xs:restriction>
  </xs:simpleType>
</xs:schema>
```

It defines the length of a string type called LimitedString. The length shouldn't exceed 200 characters. The XML that is used for validation looks like the following:

```xml
<?xml version="1.0" encoding="utf-8"?>
<CurrentWeather>
  <Location>Le Touquet, France (LFAT) 50-31N 001-37E 14M</Location>
  <Time>Apr 27, 2015 - 04:00 PM EDT / 2015.04.27 2000 UTC</Time>
  <Wind> from the NNW (330 degrees) at 3 MPH (3 KT):0</Wind>
  <Visibility> greater than 7 mile(s):0</Visibility>
  <Temperature> 46 F (8 C)</Temperature>
  <DewPoint> 33 F (1 C)</DewPoint>
  <RelativeHumidity> 61%</RelativeHumidity>
  <Pressure> 29.91 in. Hg (1013 hPa)</Pressure>
  <Status>Success</Status>
</CurrentWeather>
```

As you can see, it contains all the elements specified in the schema.

Validating XML with Schemas

There are different approaches for validating XML. Let's have a look at a rather simple one where you get the schema file from a connection.

Connections

First, you need a connection to the schema file, so let's create a connection manager called WeatherSchema for that purpose, as shown in Figure 7-6.

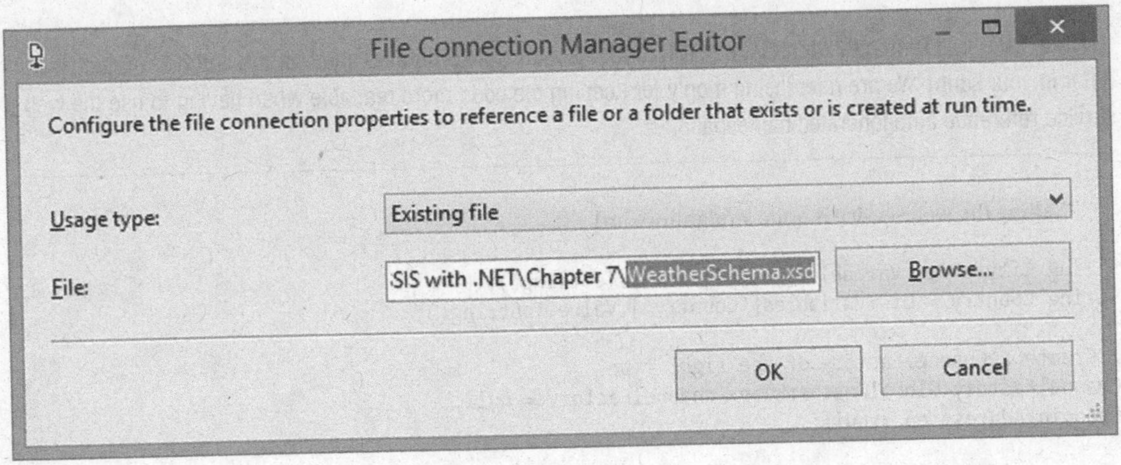

Figure 7-6. *Connection manager pointing at the XSD file*

You don't need a connection manager for the second schema since it is declaratively included in the first one.

The Code

Add a Script Task inside the Foreach Loop and configure its variable as follows:

- read-only variables: User::City and User::Country

- read-write variables: User::ResultString

Once you've chosen the language to use, C# or VB.NET, click Edit Script... and create a service reference to the GetWeather service, as described in the "Service Reference" section. Call the reference GetWeather.

Custom Namespaces

You need to reference to the following namespaces. This is C#:

```
#region CustomNamespace

using System.ServiceModel;
using System.Xml;
using ST_1211e492c97246a9947e241a0234dce6.GetWeather;
using System.IO;

#endregion
```

And this is VB.NET:

```
#Region "CustomNameSpace"

Imports ST_64feb36f55b24388a6c2553c036e36a6.GetWeather
Imports System.ServiceModel
Imports System.Xml

#End Region
```

■ **Note**   ST_1211e492c97246a9947e241a0234dce6 is the autogenerated name of the authors' project. It will differ in your script. We are referencing it only for keeping the code more readable when having to use the web service reference autogenerated namespace.

Calling the web service is quite straightforward.

```
string City = Dts.Variables["City"].Value.ToString();
string Country = Dts.Variables["Country"].Value.ToString();

//Create a ChannelFactory of the right type
ChannelFactory<GlobalWeatherSoap> channelFactory = null;
EndpointAddress ep = null;

//Specify what the address is
string epAdr = Dts.Variables["WeatherServiceURL"].Value.ToString();
try
  {
    //Get the right binding
    BasicHttpBinding httpb = new BasicHttpBinding();
    channelFactory = new ChannelFactory<GlobalWeatherSoap>(httpb);

    //The necessary endpoint with our address
    ep = new EndpointAddress(epAdr);

    //Ready to create the representation of the web svc
    GlobalWeatherSoap weatherSvcObj = channelFactory.CreateChannel(ep);
    //Getting some geographic info about a country
    string result = weatherSvcObj.GetWeather(City, Country);

    //Calling the validation method
    ValidateXML(result);
    //Save the result in a variable for later use.
    Dts.Variables["ResultString"].Value = result;

    Boolean fireagain = false;
    Dts.Events.FireInformation(0,"Calling web service",result,String.Empty,0,
    ref fireagain);

  }
  catch (Exception ex)
  {
    Dts.TaskResult = (int)ScriptResults.Failure;
    throw ex;
  }
```

And here it is in VB.NET:

```vbnet
'Create a ChannelFactory of the right type
Dim channelFactory As ChannelFactory(Of GlobalWeatherSoap) = Nothing
Dim ep As EndpointAddress = Nothing

'Specify what the address is
Dim epAdr As String = Dts.Variables("WeatherServiceURL").Value.ToString
Dim city As String = Dts.Variables("City").Value.ToString
Dim country As String = Dts.Variables("Country").Value.ToString

Try
    'Get the right binding
    Dim httpb As New BasicHttpBinding()
    channelFactory = New ChannelFactory(Of GlobalWeatherSoap)(httpb)

    'The necessary endpoint with our address
    ep = New EndpointAddress(epAdr)

    'Ready to create the representation of the web svc
    Dim weatherSvcObj As GlobalWeatherSoap = channelFactory.CreateChannel(ep)

    'Getting some weather info about the city
    Dim result As String = weatherSvcObj.GetWeather(city, country)

    Validate(result)
    'Save the result in a variable for later use.
    Dts.Variables("ResultString").Value = result

    Dim fireagain As [Boolean] = False
    Dts.Events.FireInformation(0, "Calling web service", result, [String].Empty, 0,
    fireagain)

Catch ex As Exception
    Dts.TaskResult = CInt(ScriptResults.Failure)
    Throw ex
End Try
```

Validating the XML

In the code, you added a method called ValidateXML, which takes a string as input and validates the XML against the schema provided. The following is the entire code for the method:

```csharp
private void ValidateXML(string xmlToValidate)
{
// Try reading the XML file using the XSD. Use the
// Connection Manager to get the path from the XML file
try
{
    // create object for the XSD file that will be used
    // for validating the XML file. Use the Connection
```

```
        // Manager to get the path from the XSD file.
        XmlReaderSettings xmlrs = new XmlReaderSettings();
        xmlrs.ValidationType = ValidationType.Schema;
        xmlrs.Schemas.Add(null, Dts.Connections["WeatherSchema"].ConnectionString);
        xmlrs.Schemas.Compile();

        XmlReader xmlr = XmlReader.Create(new StringReader(xmlToValidate),xmlrs);
        while (xmlr.Read())
        {
        }
        // The XML file was succesfully read.

        // Close XML file
        xmlr.Close();
}
catch (Exception ex)
{
        // Validation failed, throw error
        Dts.Events.FireError(-1, "Validate XML", "Validation error: " + ex.Message,
        string.Empty, 0);
}
}
```

And here it is in VB.NET:

```
Private Sub ValidateXML(xmlToValidate As String)
        ' Try reading the XML file using the XSD. Use the
        ' Connection Manager to get the path from the XML file
        Try
                ' create object for the XSD file that will be used
                ' for validating the XML file. Use the Connection
                ' Manager to get the path from the XSD file.
                Dim xmlrs As New XmlReaderSettings()
                xmlrs.ValidationType = ValidationType.Schema
                xmlrs.Schemas.Add(Nothing, Dts.Connections("WeatherSchema").
                ConnectionString)
                xmlrs.Schemas.Compile()

                Dim xmlr As XmlReader = XmlReader.Create(New StringReader(xmlToValidate),
                xmlrs)
                While xmlr.Read()
                End While
                ' The XML file was succesfully read.

                ' Close XML file
                xmlr.Close()
        Catch ex As Exception
                ' Validation failed, throw error
        Dts.Events.FireError(-1, "Validate XML", "Validation error: " + ex.Message,
        String.Empty, 0)
        End Try

End Sub
```

The important elements in the XML validation include the schema to add to the XmlReaderSettings object.

```
xmlrs.Schemas.Add(null, Dts.Connections["WeatherSchema"].ConnectionString);
```

(This is it in VB.NET):

```
xmlrs.Schemas.Add(Nothing, Dts.Connections("WeatherSchema").ConnectionString)
```

As well as the fact that you add the XmlReaderSettings to the XmlReader, forcing it to validate against the schema.

```
XmlReader xmlr = XmlReader.Create(new StringReader(xmlToValidate),xmlrs);
```

And here it is in VB.NET:

```
Dim xmlr As XmlReader = XmlReader.Create(New System.IO.StreamReader(xmltoValidate), xmlrs)
```

If you were to read a file instead of passing an XML string to the XmlReader.Create method, the code would be more straightforward (without the need to use the System.IO namespace), and the XmlReader would look like this:

```
XmlReader xmlr = XmlReader.Create(pathToXmlFile,xmlrs);
```

And this is it in VB.NET:

```
Dim xmlr As XmlReader = XmlReader.Create(PathtoXmlFile, xmlrs)
```

If you run the package now, it will validate without any errors. But if you change the CityWeather_include.xsd and change the maxLength to 10 instead of 200, you will see the following error:

```
Error: 0xFFFFFFFF at SCR_GetCityWeather_CSharp, Validate XML: Validation error: The
'Location' element is invalid - The value 'Le Touquet, France (LFAT) 50-31N 001-37E 14M' is
invalid according to its datatype 'LimitedString' - The actual length is greater than the
MaxLength value.
```

The complete code and all the files for this chapter are available in the Chapter 7 book solution.

Summary

In this chapter, you saw how to use Script Tasks in situations where the Web Service Task cannot help. You also walked through how to validate XML in ways that XML Task cannot. Furthermore, you explored which kind of .config files are needed and generated, and found a way to avoid that. Please keep this in mind the next time you are working with XML and web services in SSIS.

CHAPTER 8

Advanced Solutions with Script Task

This chapter is about common real-world scenarios that happen in ETL—scenarios such as compressing and decompressing files, or encrypting and decrypting files. Using .NET scripting would make these scenarios much easier to achieve. And what about using regular expressions to filter in a Foreach Loop?

Regular Expressions

Regular expressions are very useful for validating or cleaning data, which is hard or nearly impossible to do with SSIS expressions. You probably would expect them in the Data Flow Task (and in Chapter 13 you will see some very helpful examples of this), but they can be very useful in the Control Flow too. Let's compare these expression types using a very simplified filter example; first with a regular expression, and then with an SSIS expression. They both filter with actual*.csv and budget*.csv:

```
^(actuals|budget).*\.csv$
```

```
LOWER(LEFT(@[User::FilePath], 7)) == "actuals" || LOWER(LEFT(@[User::FilePath], 6))
== "budget"
```

But what if the next four characters must be numeric (a year)? That SSIS expression would be quite complex and hard to read/maintain, but it is much easier with a regular expression:

```
^(actuals|budget)[0-9]{4}.*\.csv$
```

So what about filtering with regular expressions in the Foreach Loop Container? The Foreach File Enumerator only supports simple wildcards, such as a *.csv, but filtering on both actuals*.csv and budget*.csv, or *.csv and *.txt, isn't possible with a single Foreach Loop Container. In this example, you add a Script Task within the Foreach Loop to validate the variable filled by the Foreach Loop. (Figure 8-1 shows this workflow). You need all budget[year]*.csv and actuals[year]*.csv files, but none of the other .csv files. The [year] in the filter means that the text should be followed by four numbers: actuals2016.csv or budget2017.csv. Set the filter in the Foreach Loop to *.csv to filter as much as possible. This provides better performance when there are a lot of files.

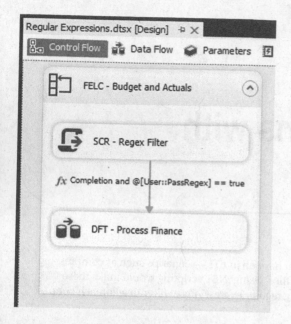

Figure 8-1. *Regex filter in loop*

Variables

The Foreach Loop File Enumerator fills the string variable FilePath with the file path of the current file, but for the regular expression filter, you need two extra variables:

- RegexFilter: A string variable containing the regular expression used for filtering: ^(actuals|budget)[0-9]{4}.*\.csv$

- PassRegex: A Boolean variable filled with True if the current file name passes the regular expression

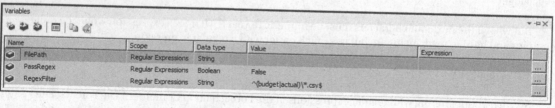

Figure 8-2. *Variables for the regular expression filter*

Script Task

Add a Script Task within your Foreach Loop Container as the first task. In the Script Task Editor, add two string variables: FilePath and RegexFilter in ReadOnlyVariables, and the Boolean variable PassRegex in ReadWriteVariables (see Figure 8-3).

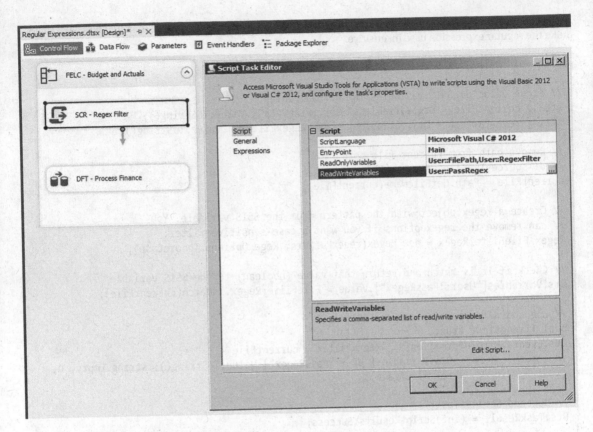

Figure 8-3. *ReadOnly and ReadWrite variables*

The Script

Go to the VSTA environment and add the following namespaces to shorten the code:

```
#region customNamespaces
using System.Text.RegularExpressions;
using System.IO;
#endregion
```

And here is the VB.NET code:

```
#Region "customNamespaces"
Imports System.Text.RegularExpressions
Imports System.IO
#End Region
```

Then add the following code to your `Main` method. Note the optional `RegexOptions` that you can use to make the regular expression case insensitive.

```csharp
public void Main()
{
  // Store value of SSIS variables in .NET variables
  string currentFile = Dts.Variables["User::FilePath"].Value.ToString();
  string regexPattern = Dts.Variables["User::RegexFilter"].Value.ToString();

  // Remove path from current file path
  // d:\sources\myFile.csv => myFile.csv
  currentFile = Path.GetFileName(currentFile);

  // Create a regex object with the pattern from the SSIS variable. You
  // can remove the regexoptions if you want a case-sensitive filter.
  Regex FileFilterRegex = new Regex(regexPattern, RegexOptions.IgnoreCase);

  // Check if it is match and return that value (boolean) to the SSIS variable
  Dts.Variables["User::PassRegex"].Value = FileFilterRegex.IsMatch(currentFile);

  // Log added for testing purpose only
  bool fireAgain = true;
  Dts.Events.FireInformation(0, "RegexFilter", currentFile + " " +
                    Dts.Variables["User::PassRegex"].Value.ToString(), string.Empty, 0,
                    ref fireAgain);

  // Succeed Script Task
  Dts.TaskResult = (int)ScriptResults.Success;
}
```

And this is the VB.NET code:

```vbnet
Public Sub Main()
  ' Store value of SSIS variables in .NET variables
  Dim currentFile As String = Dts.Variables("User::FilePath").Value.ToString()
  Dim regexPattern As String = Dts.Variables("User::RegexFilter").Value.ToString()

  ' Remove path from current file path
  ' d:\sources\myFile.csv => myFile.csv
  currentFile = Path.GetFileName(currentFile)

  ' Create a regex object with the pattern from the SSIS variable. You
  ' can remove the regexoptions if you want a case-sensitive filter.
  Dim FileFilterRegex As New Regex(regexPattern, RegexOptions.IgnoreCase)

  ' Check if it is match and return that value (boolean) to the SSIS variable
  Dts.Variables("User::PassRegex").Value = FileFilterRegex.IsMatch(currentFile)
```

```
' Log added for testing purpose only
Dim fireAgain As Boolean = True
Dts.Events.FireInformation(0, "RegexFilter", currentFile + " " + _
                Dts.Variables("User::PassRegex").Value.ToString(), String.Empty, 0,
                fireAgain)

' Succeed Script Task
Dts.TaskResult = ScriptResults.Success
End Sub
```

Precedence Constraint

The Script Task fills the PassRegex variable with True or False. You can use this variable in an expression on a *precedence constraint* to either stop or continue after the Script Task. Connect the Script Task with the regular expression to the next task in the Foreach Loop. Then, in the Precedence Constraint Editor (see Figure 8-4), change the "Evaluation operation" to Expression, and set the Expression to the following: @[User::PassRegex] == true. Or, make it even shorter, like this: @[User::PassRegex].

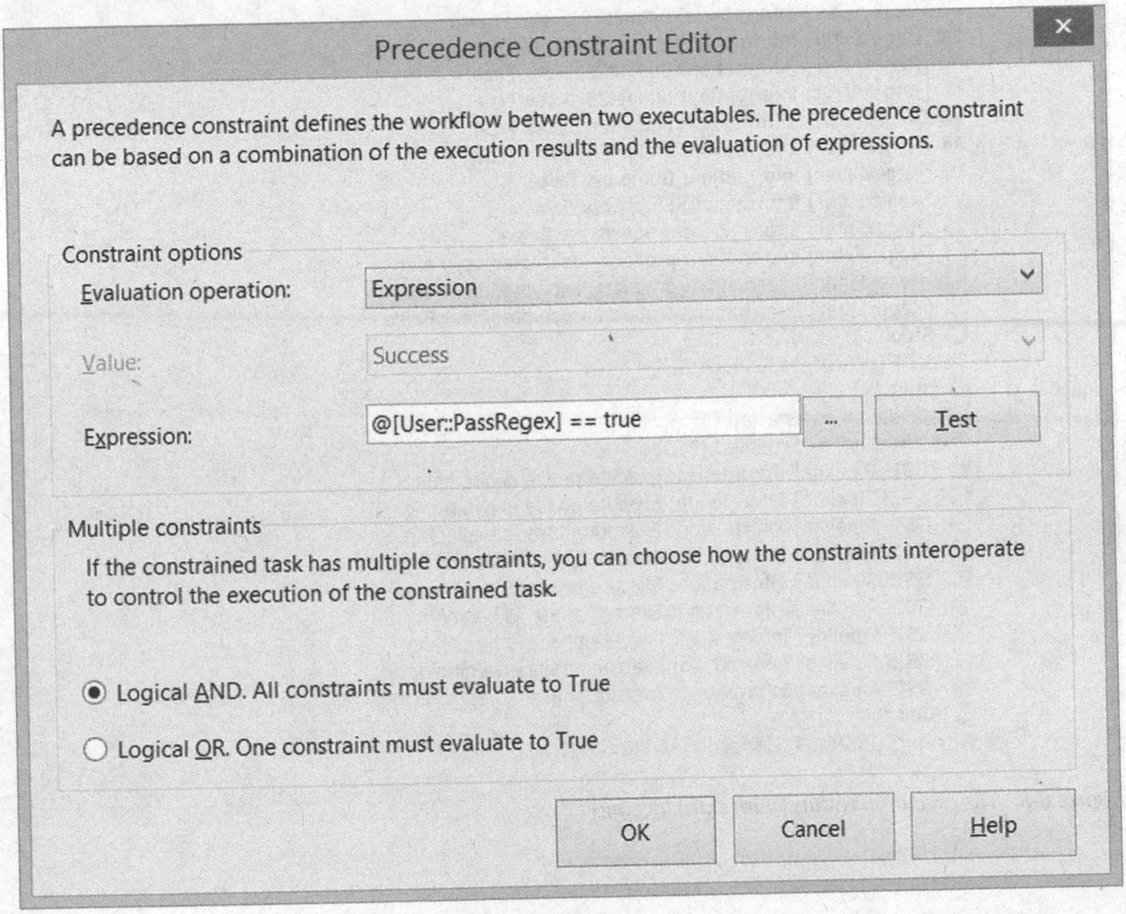

Figure 8-4. Adding an expression in the Precedence Constraint Editor

Testing

Now execute the package and watch the Execution Results tab. You will see that the Script Task is executed more times than the Data Flow Task. For testing purposes, you add some code (see Chapter 4) in the Script Task to log which files pass the regular expression, and which do not.

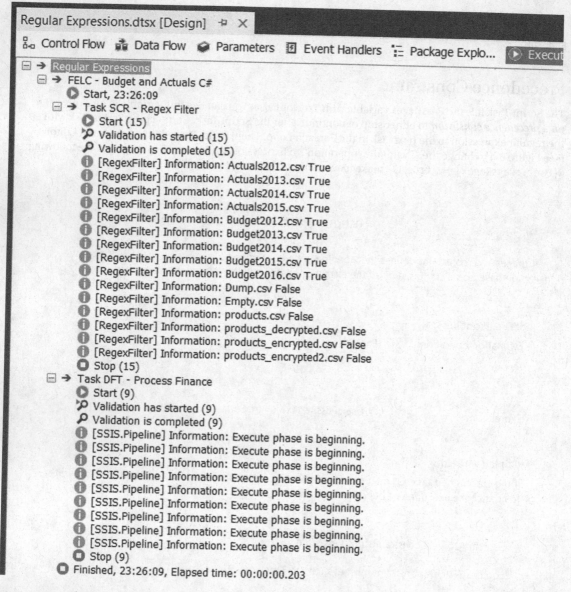

Figure 8-5. *The execution results (with extra logging)*

Zip/Unzip

For zipping and unzipping files prior to .NET Framework 4.5.3, you need a third-party assembly, because zip files weren't supported "out of the box." In the 4.5.3 Framework, Microsoft finally added support for zip files; but at the time this book was written, SSIS 2014 only supports 4.5.1. If you can switch to 4.5.3, then this would be the preferred way.

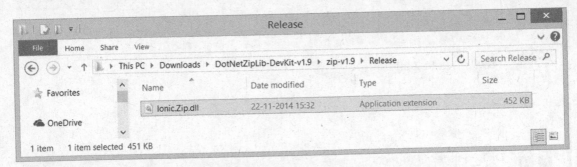

Figure 8-6. In zip file, use zip-v1.9/Release folder to install Ionic.Zip.dll

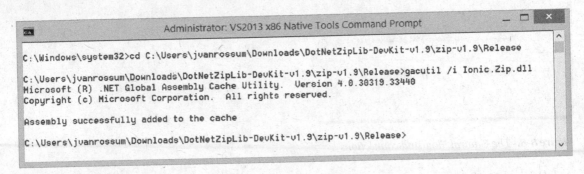

Figure 8-7. gacutil /i Ionic.Zip.dll

Downloading the Library

There are various free and open source libraries available for zipping and unzipping; for example, SharpZipLib and DotNetZip. This example uses DotNetZip, which you can download from CodePlex at http://dotnetzip.codeplex.com.

Search for Ionic.Zip.dll in the downloaded files. Find the file as shown in Figure 8-6. Depending on the version, it is probably in the \DotNetZipLib-DevKit-vX.X\zip-vX.X\ subfolder. To register this assembly in the Global Assembly Cache (GAC), open the Visual Studio Command prompt in Administrator mode (see Chapter 4). Go to the assembly location and execute gacutil /i Ionic.Zip.dll as shown in Figure 8-7.

Unzipping

For this unzip example, you have a File Connection Manager pointing to a zip file, and a Flat File Connection Manager pointing to the unzipped .csv file. Products.zip will be unzipped and then deleted. The unzipped .csv file is processed by a Data Flow Task. The Control Flow looks something like Figure 8-8.

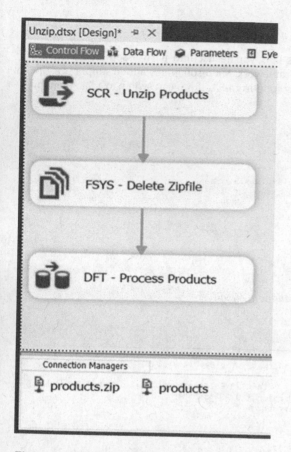

Figure 8-8. *The Control Flow and connections*

Adding a Reference

Edit the Script Task and then open the VSTA environment as shown in Figure 8-9 to add the reference to the new assembly, which is now located in the GAC. For more information about adding references, see Chapter 4.

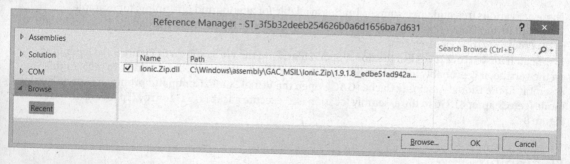

Figure 8-9. *Reference to Ionic.Zip*

The Unzip Script

For this unzip example, you will use the File Connection Manager pointing to the zip file. The unzip location is derived from the zip file location, but you can make that configurable if necessary.

This script extracts the zipped files, one by one, and filters on .csv files. But if you need all the files, you can also extract all the zipped files at once. That code is included as a comment in the script and should replace the Foreach Loop. Choose which one works for you. You can also check the properties in myZipFile to set zip file properties such as the password, and zip64 for large files (>4GB), but these options are not included in the example script.

Go to the VSTA environment and add the following namespaces to shorten the code:

```
#region customNamespaces
using Ionic.Zip;
using System.IO;
#endregion
```

And here is the VB.NET code:

```
#Region "customNamespaces"
Imports Ionic.Zip
Imports System.IO
#End Region
```

Next, add the following code to your Main method. In this example, all .csv files are unzipped and they will overwrite any existing files.

```
public void Main()
{
  // Get filepath of zipfile and unzipfolder
  string myZipFilePath = Dts.Connections["products.zip"].AcquireConnection(null).ToString();

  // Determine unzip location. In this case the folder where the
  // zipfile is located. You can replace this by a variable or
  // Connection Manager
  string myUnzipfolder = new FileInfo(myZipFilePath).Directory.FullName;

  // Create zipfile object that points to the actual zipfile
  using (ZipFile myZipFile = ZipFile.Read(myZipFilePath))
  {
    // Extract all files at once (instead of foreach loop)
    //myZipFile.ExtractAll(myUnzipfolder, ExtractExistingFileAction.OverwriteSilently);
```

```
      // Loop through all entries in the zipfile one by one
      foreach (ZipEntry myZipEntry in myZipFile)
      {
        // Filter: only extract CSV files
        if (myZipEntry.FileName.EndsWith(".csv"))
        {
          // Extract the file and overwrite existing files
          myZipEntry.Extract(myUnzipfolder, ExtractExistingFileAction.OverwriteSilently);
        }
      }
    }

  // Succeed Script Task
  Dts.TaskResult = (int)ScriptResults.Success;
}
```

This is the VB.NET code:

```
Public Sub Main()
  ' Get filepath of zipfile and unzipfolder
  Dim myZipFilePath As String = _
                  Dts.Connections("products.zip").AcquireConnection(Nothing).ToString()

  ' Determine unzip location. In this case ' the folder where the
  ' zipfile is located. You can replace this by a variable or
  ' Connection Manager
  Dim myUnzipfolder As String = New FileInfo(myZipFilePath).Directory.FullName

  ' Create zipfile object that points to the actual zipfile
  Using myZipFile As ZipFile = ZipFile.Read(myZipFilePath)
    ' Extract all files at once (instead of foreach loop)
    'myZipFile.ExtractAll(myUnzipfolder, ExtractExistingFileAction.OverwriteSilently);

    ' Loop through all entries in the zipfile one by one
    For Each myZipEntry As ZipEntry In myZipFile
      ' Filter: only extract CSV files
      If myZipEntry.FileName.ToLower().EndsWith(".csv") Then
        ' Extract the file and overwrite existing files
        myZipEntry.Extract(myUnzipfolder, ExtractExistingFileAction.OverwriteSilently)
      End If
    Next
  End Using

  ' Succeed Script Task
  Dts.TaskResult = ScriptResults.Success
End Sub
```

■ **Tip**   You could also use regular expressions to filter.

Zipping

For this zipping example, you are zipping the Flat File Designation from a Data Flow Task. For this you will use the Flat File Connection Manager from the Flat File Destination. To specify the name and path of the zip file, you will use a File Connection Manager pointing to a (nonexistent) zip file. After the Data Flow Task is ready, you will zip the created .csv file so that it can be archived, uploaded, or emailed. The simplified control flow could look something like Figure 8-10.

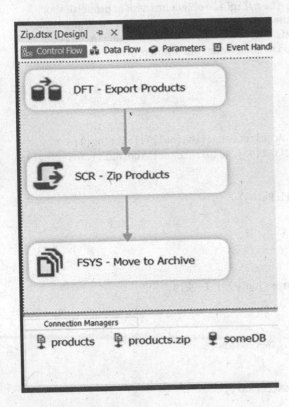

Figure 8-10. Zipping files

Reference

Edit the Script Task and then open the VSTA environment to add the reference to new Ionic.Zip assembly. For more information about adding references, see Chapter 4. Also see the unzip example that uses the same reference.

The Zip Script

As mentioned, you use the connection managers for the source file (Flat File: products) and zip file (File: products.zip) locations. First, add the following namespaces to shorten the code:

```
#region customNamespaces
using Ionic.Zip;
using System.IO;
#endregion
```

And this is the VB.NET code:

```
#Region "customNamespaces"
Imports Ionic.Zip
Imports System.IO
#End Region
```

Next, copy the following code to your Main method. The myZipFile object has a lot of properties to tune the zip file. In the following script, you only show the most common properties, but there are more. Use IntelliSense to explore all the properties and methods. You could also add some logging in the code (see Chapter 4) and a try-catch around the save method to make your code more robust.

```
public void Main()
{
  // Get source and zipfilename from
  // the Connection Managers
  string mySource = Dts.Connections["products"].AcquireConnection(null).ToString();
  string myZipFilePath = Dts.Connections["products.zip"].AcquireConnection(null).ToString();

  // Create a new zipfile
  using (ZipFile myZipFile = new ZipFile(myZipFilePath))
  {
    // Protect your zipfile with a password
    myZipFile.Password = "53cr3t!";

    // Set the compression level
    myZipFile.CompressionLevel = Ionic.Zlib.CompressionLevel.Level9;

    // Necessary for special chars in filenames
    myZipFile.AlternateEncoding = Encoding.UTF8;
    myZipFile.AlternateEncodingUsage = ZipOption.AsNecessary;

    // Necessary for very large files
    myZipFile.UseZip64WhenSaving = Zip64Option.AsNecessary;

    // Add file in root of zipfile
    myZipFile.AddFile(mySource, "\\");

    // Save the zipfile
    myZipFile.Save();
  }
  // Succeed Script Task
  Dts.TaskResult = (int)ScriptResults.Success;
}
```

And this is the VB.NET code:

```vb
Public Sub Main()
    ' Get source and zipfilename from
    ' the Connection Managers
    Dim mySource As String = _Dts.Connections("products").AcquireConnection(Nothing).
    ToString()
    Dim myZipFilePath As String = _Dts.Connections("products.zip").AcquireConnection(Nothing).
    ToString()

    ' Create a new zipfile
    Using myZipFile As New ZipFile(myZipFilePath)
        ' Protect your zipfile with a password
        myZipFile.Password = "53cr3t!"

        ' Set the compression level
        myZipFile.CompressionLevel = Ionic.Zlib.CompressionLevel.Level9

        ' Necessary for special chars in filenames
        myZipFile.AlternateEncoding = Encoding.UTF8
        myZipFile.AlternateEncodingUsage = ZipOption.AsNecessary

        ' Necessary for very large files
        myZipFile.UseZip64WhenSaving = Zip64Option.AsNecessary

        ' Add file in root of zipfile
        myZipFile.AddFile(mySource, "\")

        ' Save the zipfile
        myZipFile.Save()
    End Using
    ' Succeed Script Task
    Dts.TaskResult = ScriptResults.Success
End Sub
```

Encrypt/Decrypt Files

Sometimes you want to encrypt your files to store or send them securely. There are several encryption possibilities available in the System.Security.Cryptography namespace, but one of the best (at the time of writing) is RijnDael. In this example, you encrypt and decrypt a file via a connection manager. We'll use a flow like that in Figure 8-11.

■ **Caution**   Before implementing encryption for highly sensitive data, study all the possibilities, strengths, and weaknesses of the various encryption methods; do not just take this code for granted. Also, encryption and security develops rapidly. What was secure at the time of this book's writing could be outdated when you read this book.

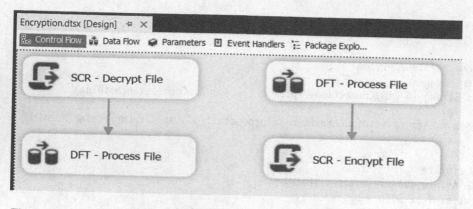

Figure 8-11. *Encrypting and decrypting files*

Connection Managers

For encrypting a flat file that was created by a Data Flow Task, you use the Flat File Connection Manager named MyProducts as a source for the Script Task. A File Connection Manager named MyProducts_encrypted is used as a destination. It contains the file path of the encrypted file.

For decrypting, it is vice versa. The File Connection Manager named MyProducts_encrypted is used as a source, and a Flat File Connection Manager named MyProducts_decrypted is used as a destination. After decrypting the file, this connection manager can be used as a source for the Data Flow Task.

Variable

For storing the password, you need a variable such as the MyPassword variable in Figure 8-12. Make sure to remove that default value from your package when you go to production; otherwise, it won't be very secure. Use configurations or parameters instead.

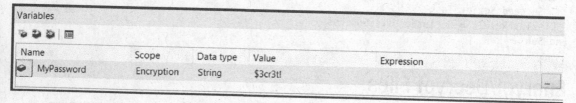

Figure 8-12. *Your secret password*

Script Task

For encrypting, add a Script Task after your Data Flow; for decrypting, add it before your Data Flow. In the Script Task Editor, add the password variable in ReadOnlyVariables (see Figure 8-13).

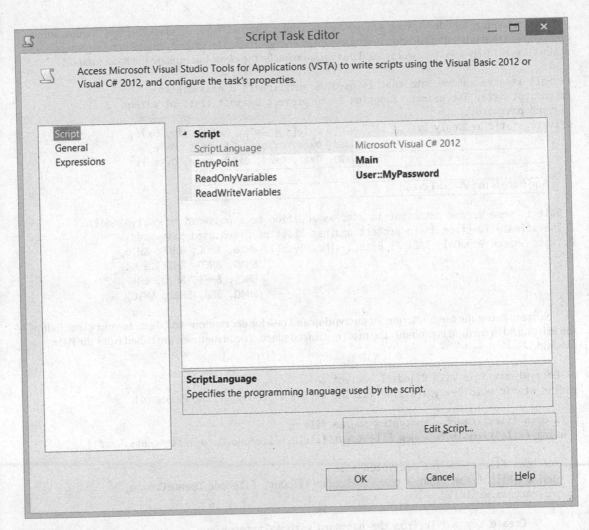

Figure 8-13. Your secret password in ReadOnlyVariables

The Script

Go to the VSTA environment and add the following namespaces to shorten the code:

```
#region customNamespaces
using System.Security.Cryptography;
using System.IO;
#endregion
```

This is the VB.NET code:

```
#Region "customNamespaces"
Imports System.Security.Cryptography
Imports System.IO
#End Region
```

For encrypting and decrypting, you need a *salt*, which is stored in a static class variable. A salt is some random data that is used in addition to a password to encrypt data. The primary function is to protect against lists of often-used passwords. Add this variable inside the class, but outside the Main method.

```
// Salt is some random data that is used as addition to a password to
// encrypt data. The primary function is to protect against lists of often
// used passwords.
private static readonly byte[] SALT = new byte[] { 0x26, 0xdc, 0xff, 0x76,
                              0xad, 0xed, 0x7a, 0x64, 0xc5, 0xfe,
                              0x20, 0xaf, 0x4d, 0x08, 0x22, 0x3c };
```

And here is the VB.NET code:

```
' Salt is some random data that is used as addition to a password to encrypt data.
' The primary function is to protect against lists of often used passwords.
Private Shared ReadOnly SALT As Byte() = New Byte() {&H26, &HDC, &HFF, &H76,_
                              &HAD, &HED, &H7A, &H64,_
                              &HC5, &HFE, &H20, &HAF,_
                              &H4D, &H8, &H22, &H3C}
```

Next are two static methods: one for encryption and one for decryption. Add these to your class. Below the existing Main method is probably the most organized place. These methods are called from the Main method.

```
// Decrypt textfile with Rijndael encryption
public static void Decrypt(string fileIn, string fileOut, string Password)
{
  // Open filestream for encrypted source file
  using (FileStream fsIn = new FileStream(fileIn, FileMode.Open, FileAccess.Read))
  {
    // Open filestream for decrypted file
    using (FileStream fsOut = new FileStream(fileOut, FileMode.OpenOrCreate,
    FileAccess.Write))
    {
      // Create Key and IV from the password with salt technique
      Rfc2898DeriveBytes pdb = new Rfc2898DeriveBytes(Password, SALT);

      // Create a symmetric algorithm with Rijndael
      Rijndael alg = Rijndael.Create();

      // Set Key and IV
      alg.Key = pdb.GetBytes(32);
      alg.IV = pdb.GetBytes(16);

      // Create a CryptoStream
      using (CryptoStream cs = new CryptoStream(fsOut, alg.CreateDecryptor(),
                                    CryptoStreamMode.Write))
      {
        // Initialize a buffer and process the input file in chunks.
        // This is done to avoid reading the whole file (which can be huge) into memory.
```

```
        int bufferLen = 4096;
        byte[] buffer = new byte[bufferLen];
        int bytesRead;

        do
        {
          // read a chunk of data from the input file
          bytesRead = fsIn.Read(buffer, 0, bufferLen);

          // Decrypt it
          cs.Write(buffer, 0, bytesRead);
        } while (bytesRead != 0);

        // close everything
        cs.Close();
        fsOut.Close();
        fsIn.Close();
      }
    }
  }
}


// Encrypt textfile with Rijndael encryption
public static void Encrypt(string fileIn, string fileOut, string Password)
{
  // Open filestream for source file
  using (FileStream fsIn = new FileStream(fileIn, FileMode.Open,
                                        FileAccess.Read))

  {

    // Open filestream for encrypted file
    using (FileStream fsOut = new FileStream(fileOut, FileMode.OpenOrCreate,
                                        FileAccess.Write))

    {

      // Create Key and IV from the password with salt technique
      Rfc2898DeriveBytes pdb = new Rfc2898DeriveBytes(Password, SALT);

      // Create a symmetric algorithm with Rijndael
      Rijndael alg = Rijndael.Create();

      // Set Key and IV
      alg.Key = pdb.GetBytes(32);
      alg.IV = pdb.GetBytes(16);

      // Create a CryptoStream
      using (CryptoStream cs = new CryptoStream(fsOut, alg.CreateEncryptor(),
                                        CryptoStreamMode.Write))

      {

        // Initialize a buffer and process the input file in chunks.
        // This is done to avoid reading the whole file (which can be huge) into memory.
```

```csharp
      int bufferLen = 4096;
      byte[] buffer = new byte[bufferLen];
      int bytesRead;

      do
      {
        // read a chunk of data from the input file
        bytesRead = fsIn.Read(buffer, 0, bufferLen);

        // encrypt it
        cs.Write(buffer, 0, bytesRead);
      } while (bytesRead != 0);

      // close everything
      cs.Close();
      fsOut.Close();
      fsIn.Close();
    }
  }
 }
}
```

This is the VB.NET code:

```vbnet
' Decrypt textfile with Rijndael encryption
Public Shared Sub Decrypt(fileIn As String, fileOut As String, Password As String)
  ' Open filestream for encrypted source file
  Using fsIn As New FileStream(fileIn, FileMode.Open, FileAccess.Read)

    ' Open filestream for decrypted file
    Using fsOut As New FileStream(fileOut, FileMode.OpenOrCreate, FileAccess.Write)

      ' Create Key and IV from the password with salt technique
      Dim pdb As New Rfc2898DeriveBytes(Password, SALT)

      ' Create a symmetric algorithm with Rijndael
      Dim alg As Rijndael = Rijndael.Create()

      ' Set Key and IV
      alg.Key = pdb.GetBytes(32)
      alg.IV = pdb.GetBytes(16)

      ' Create a CryptoStream
      Using cs As New CryptoStream(fsOut, alg.CreateDecryptor(), CryptoStreamMode.Write)

        ' Initialize a buffer and process the input file in chunks.
        ' This is done to avoid reading the whole file (which can be huge) into memory.
        Dim bufferLen As Integer = 4096
        Dim buffer As Byte() = New Byte(bufferLen - 1) {}
        Dim bytesRead As Integer
```

```vbnet
        Do
            ' read a chunk of data from the input file
            bytesRead = fsIn.Read(buffer, 0, bufferLen)

            ' Decrypt it
            cs.Write(buffer, 0, bytesRead)
        Loop While bytesRead <> 0

            ' close everything
            cs.Close()
            fsOut.Close()
            fsIn.Close()
        End Using
      End Using
  End Using
End Sub


' Encrypt textfile with Rijndael encryption
Public Shared Sub Encrypt(fileIn As String, fileOut As String, Password As String)
    ' Open filestream for source file
    Using fsIn As New FileStream(fileIn, FileMode.Open, FileAccess.Read)

        ' Open filestream for encrypted file
        Using fsOut As New FileStream(fileOut, FileMode.OpenOrCreate, FileAccess.Write)

            ' Create Key and IV from the password with salt technique
            Dim pdb As New Rfc2898DeriveBytes(Password, SALT)

            ' Create a symmetric algorithm with Rijndael
            Dim alg As Rijndael = Rijndael.Create()

            ' Set Key and IV
            alg.Key = pdb.GetBytes(32)
            alg.IV = pdb.GetBytes(16)

            ' Create a CryptoStream
            Using cs As New CryptoStream(fsOut, alg.CreateEncryptor(), CryptoStreamMode.Write)

                ' Initialize a buffer and process the input file in chunks.
                ' This is done to avoid reading the whole file (which can be huge) into memory.
                Dim bufferLen As Integer = 4096
                Dim buffer As Byte() = New Byte(bufferLen - 1) {}
                Dim bytesRead As Integer

                Do
                    ' read a chunk of data from the input file
                    bytesRead = fsIn.Read(buffer, 0, bufferLen)

                    ' encrypt it
                    cs.Write(buffer, 0, bytesRead)
                Loop While bytesRead <> 0
```

```
            ' close everything
            cs.Close()
            fsOut.Close()
            fsIn.Close()
        End Using
      End Using
    End Using
End Sub
```

And finally, the Main method code, in which you call the decrypt and encrypt methods. There are two examples: the first decrypts a file and the second encrypts a file.

```
' Decrypt
Public Sub Main()
  ' Get filepath of encrypted file
  Dim filepathEncrypted As String = Dts.Connections("MyProducts_encrypted").
                          AcquireConnection(Nothing).ToString()

  ' Get the filepath of the decrypted file.
  Dim filepathDecrypted As String = Dts.Connections("MyProducts").
                          AcquireConnection(Nothing).ToString()

  ' Get password from SSIS variable
  Dim encryptionKey As String = Dts.Variables("MyPassword").ToString()

  ' Create a decrypted copy of the encrypted file
  Decrypt(filepathEncrypted, filepathDecrypted, encryptionKey)

  ' Succeed Script Task
  Dts.TaskResult = ScriptResults.Success
End Sub

' Encrypt
Public Sub Main()
  ' Get filepath of the file that needs to be encrypted.
  Dim filepathSource As String = Dts.Connections("MyProducts").AcquireConnection(Nothing).
                          ToString()

  ' Get filepath of encrypted file
  Dim filepathEncrypted As String = Dts.Connections("MyProducts_encrypted").
                          AcquireConnection(Nothing).ToString()

  ' Get password from SSIS variable
  Dim encryptionKey As String = Dts.Variables("MyPassword").ToString()

  ' Create an encrypted copy of the file
  Encrypt(filepathSource, filepathEncrypted, encryptionKey)

  ' Succeed Script Task
  Dts.TaskResult = ScriptResults.Success
End Sub
```

And here is the VB.NET code:

```
// Decrypt
public void Main()
{
  // Get filepath of encrypted file
  string filepathEncrypted = Dts.Connections["MyProducts_encrypted"].
                       AcquireConnection(null).ToString();

  // Get the filepath of the decrypted file.
  string filepathDecrypted = Dts.Connections["MyProducts"].AcquireConnection(null).
                       ToString();

  // Get password from SSIS variable
  string encryptionKey = Dts.Variables["MyPassword"].ToString();

  // Create a decrypted copy of the encrypted file
  Decrypt(filepathEncrypted, filepathDecrypted, encryptionKey);

  // Succeed Script Task
  Dts.TaskResult = (int)ScriptResults.Success;
}

// Encrypt
public void Main()
{
  // Get filepath of the file that needs to be encrypted.
  string filepathSource = Dts.Connections["MyProducts"].AcquireConnection(null).ToString();

  // Get filepath of encrypted file
  string filepathEncrypted = Dts.Connections["MyProducts_encrypted"].
                       AcquireConnection(null).ToString();

  // Get password from SSIS variable
  string encryptionKey = Dts.Variables["MyPassword"].ToString();

  // Create an encrypted copy of the file
  Encrypt(filepathSource, filepathEncrypted, encryptionKey);

  // Succeed Script Task
  Dts.TaskResult = (int)ScriptResults.Success;
}
```

Summary

In this chapter, you saw some more-advanced coding examples, such as zipping and regular expressions. Although the examples are ready to use, you are encouraged to explore other properties from the various objects, to add logging, to add error handling, to change connection managers to variables or parameters, and to combine examples (using regular expressions to filter when unzipping files).

PART III

■■■

Script Component

CHAPTER 9

■ ■ ■

Script Component Foundation

If you have an abnormal flat file format, or you want to use regular expressions to clean your data, or you need an XML destination, then the Script Component is one of your best choices. The Script Component is part of the data flow in SSIS; it provides a scripting editor for you. It can be used as a source, a transformation, or a destination. In this chapter, you deep-dive into the Script Component and some of the most common usages of this component. You will learn how to use variables, connection managers, logging methods, and error handling in a Script Component.

Editor

Because the Script Component can be used for a variety of purposes, you first have to choose the script type (Source, Destination, or Transformation) when you add it to the surface of the Data Flow Task (see Figure 9-1). This is a "choose once" option, which means it can only be chosen when the component is created. If you want to change it, you have to delete and re-create the component. Depending on the type that you choose, the default code generated for the component will change, but also other features (like the ability to add input columns or output columns) are changed.

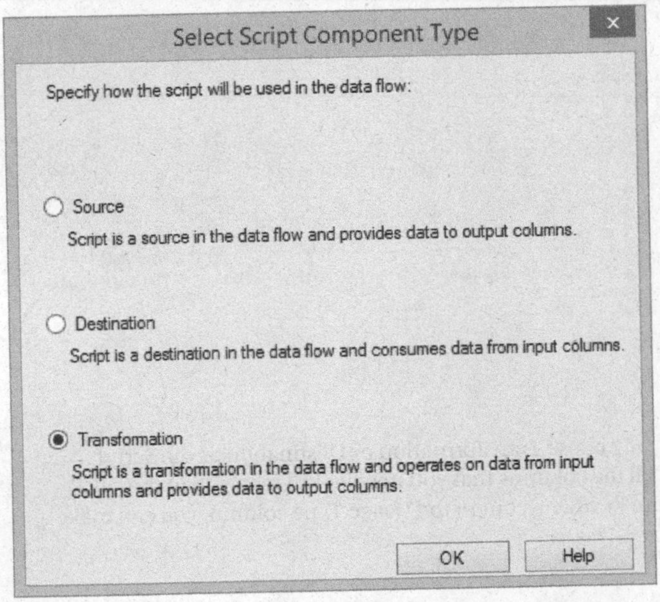

Figure 9-1. Script Component Type

219

The Script Component Editor is similar to the Script Task Editor, but it has more options and pages (see Figure 9-2). On the first page, you can add ReadOnly and ReadWrite variables to avoid hard-coded values in your code. You can also choose the Script Language: C# or VB.NET. If you still work with SSIS 2005, then the only possibility is VB.NET. This language option is "write once." After hitting the Edit Script... button, this option is grayed-out and you can no longer change the Script Language. The only way to change it is by deleting the entire Script Component, adding a new one to your data flow, and then starting over again.

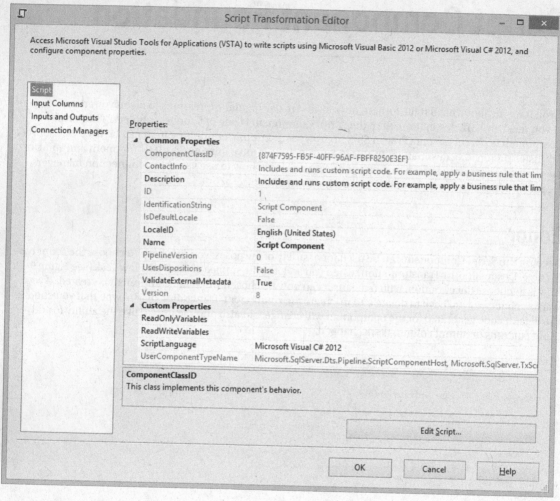

Figure 9-2. *Script Component Editor*

Input Columns

The Input Columns page is only visible when you choose Transformation or Destination as the Script Component type. On this page, you can select all the columns that you need to interact with in the .NET code (see Figure 9-3). By default, all columns are ReadOnly, but in the Usage Type column, you can make a column ReadWrite.

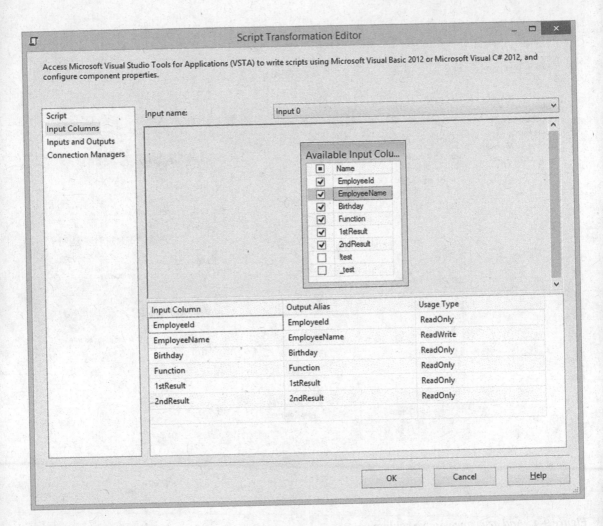

Figure 9-3. *Input Columns*

The Script Component can't handle names that don't start with a letter. When a column name starts with a number or a punctuation mark, it removes it in the internal names. So 1stResult becomes Row.stResult in the code. This could be a problem when you have two equal names with a different numeric prefix. In the Output Alias column, you can rename columns. This rename action is not only for the script, but also for the rest of the data flow.

Inputs and Outputs

On the third page, you can add new columns that can be filled by the .NET script. You could, for example, add a RowNumber column with datatype DT_I4 and fill it within the script with a sequence number (see Figure 9-4). And it is also possible to add an extra output that allows you to divide your rows to multiple outputs, for example; but more about that later in this chapter.

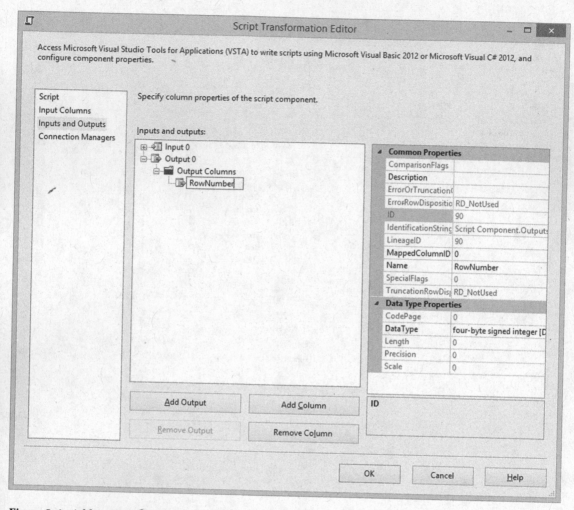

Figure 9-4. *Add new RowNumber column*

Connection Managers

On the last page, you can add the connection managers, which you want to use in the script code (see Figure 9-5). You can use connection managers to prevent hard-coded paths in your code. Before you can use a connection manager in the code, you first have to add it to this list. This is different than the Script Task Editor, where you can add connection managers in the code itself. In the Name column, you can add an alias for it that will be used in the script code. Spaces are removed, just like a prefix with numbers or punctuation marks.

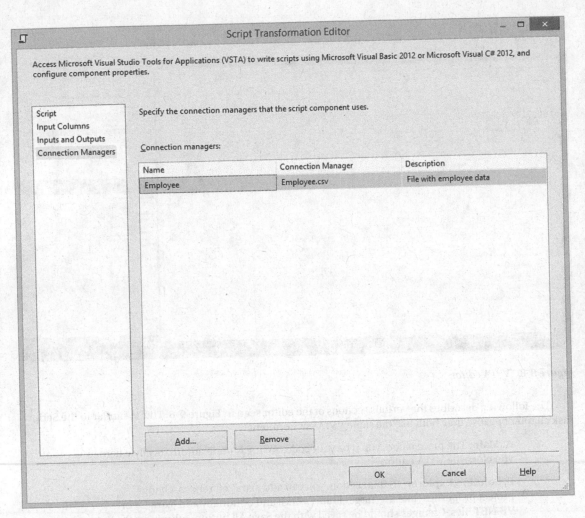

Figure 9-5. *Select Connnection Manager*

To store a file or folder path, you will most likely use the File Connection Manager, but you can use all connection managers. However, be cautious with the use of database connection mangers in a Script Component to execute queries, because there are probably easier solutions that don't require coding; for example, with an Execute SQL Task or even an OLE DB command.

Script Layout

When you are finished with the variables, columns, and connection managers, you can click the Edit Script... button to open the VSTA editor (see Figure 9-6). This editor is a new instance of Visual Studio, with a VSTA project with either C# or VB.NET code. VSTA stands for Visual Studio Tools for Applications. Depending on the script type (source, transformation, or destination), the VSTA editor adds default code with different methods. SSIS 2005 uses Visual Studio for Applications (VSA). The biggest difference compared to VSTA is that it doesn't support C# as language.

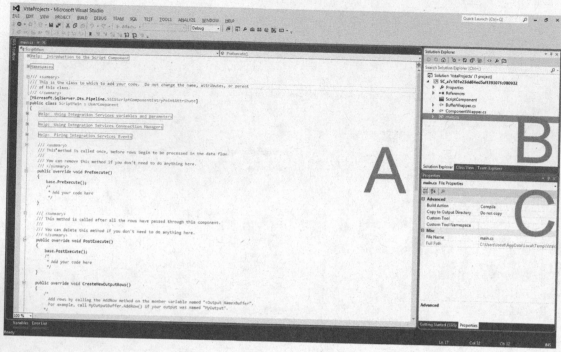

Figure 9-6. *VSTA editor*

The following describes the various sections of the editor seen in Figure 9-6. This is similar to the Script Task chapter because they both use the same VSTA environment.

A. **Main**: The place where you type your code. Saving is done automatically when you close the VSTA editor.

B. **Solution Explorer**: In this section, you can add extra references, change project properties (like the Target Framework), and optionally add extra C# or VB.NET files. Changes should be saved with the Save All button; otherwise, they will be lost when you close the VSTA editor.

C. **Properties**: Here you can see the properties of the item you selected in Solution Explorer; for example, you can see where the (temporary) VSTA project is stored on disk.

The script in section A is generated and the code varies per script type, per SSIS version, and of course, per Scripting Language. The Script Component always starts with a general comment. The text changes between SSIS versions. Remove these, or even better, replace them with a useful comment about the file/ script. Why did you use a Script Component and what is your code doing? In 2012, regions were added to make the code more orderly. You could also add them manually to SSIS 2008 script.

```
#region Help:  Introduction to the Script Component
/* The Script Component allows you to perform virtually any operation that can
 * be accomplished in a .Net application within the context of an Integration
 * Services data flow.
 *
 * Expand the other regions which have "Help" prefixes for examples of specific
 * ways to use Integration Services features within this script component. */
#endregion
```

This is the VB.NET code:

```
#Region "Help:  Introduction to the Script Component"
' The Script Component allows you to perform virtually any operation that can
' be accomplished in a .Net application within the context of an Integration
' Services data flow.

' Expand the other regions which have "Help" prefixes for examples of specific
' ways to use Integration Services features within this script component.
#End Region
```

Next are the using directives or import statements. In C# they are called using directives; for example:

```
#region Namespaces
using System;
using System.Data;
using Microsoft.SqlServer.Dts.Pipeline.Wrapper;
using Microsoft.SqlServer.Dts.Runtime.Wrapper;
#endregion
```

In VB.NET, they are called Import statements; for example:

```
#Region "Imports"
Imports System
Imports System.Data
Imports System.Math
Imports Microsoft.SqlServer.Dts.Pipeline.Wrapper
Imports Microsoft.SqlServer.Dts.Runtime.Wrapper
#End Region
```

Which namespaces are included varies per SSIS version and even per scripting language. You can add extra usings/imports to make your code more compact. They enable/allow the use of types in a given namespace without having to fully reference them (see Chapter 3 regarding .NET fundamentals).

The third part is the namespace and class declaration. These are generated. Don't change these unless you are an experienced .NET developer and have a good reason to change it.

```
/// <summary>
/// This is the class to which to add your code.  Do not change the name,
/// attributes, or parent of this class.
/// </summary>
[Microsoft.SqlServer.Dts.Pipeline.SSISScriptComponentEntryPointAttribute]
public class ScriptMain : UserComponent
{
```

This is the VB.NET code:

```
' This is the class to which to add your code.  Do not change the name,
' attributes, or parent of this class.
<Microsoft.SqlServer.Dts.Pipeline.SSISScriptComponentEntryPointAttribute> _
<CLSCompliant(False)> _
Public Class ScriptMain
    Inherits UserComponent
```

Next is a lot of help text about variables, connection managers, and events enclosed by regions. You can remove these to get clearer code because they aren't needed for the actual code. After all the help text, you reach the actual methods. The following sections describe the six most used/overridden methods: AcquireConnections, ReleaseConnections, PreExecute, PostExecute, CreateNewOutputRows, and InputO_ ProcessInputRow. They are not all included by default, but you can add them manually. Or if you don't want that many methods in your code, you can combine the code—for example, the AcquireConnections and PreExecute methods, and only use the PreExecute method. You see that in a lot of code examples on the Internet.

If you override a method, you automatically get some default code that executes the base code from the overridden method. The line starts with base. and then the name of the method. You could remove this since it's not doing anything in SSIS. Most MSDN examples don't include them either. Or you can leave it, since it doesn't hurt the code.

AcquireConnections

This method is not in the default code. As the name suggests, the AcquireConnections method is used to acquire connections from connection managers. In this example, you are getting the connection from an ADO.NET connection manager and you store it in a class variable so that you can use it in other methods.

```
// Create class variables so that they can be used in all methods.
// Added System.Data.SqlClient to usings.
IDTSConnectionManager100 myAdoConnectionManager;
System.Data.SqlClient.SqlConnection myDbConnection;

public override void AcquireConnections(object Transaction)
{
  // Fill connection manager object with a Package connection manager
  myAdoConnectionManager = this.Connections.myADOConn;

  // Fill connection object with connection from the
  // ADO.NET connection manager object.
  myDbConnection = (System.Data.SqlClient.SqlConnection)myAdoConnectionManager
                    .AcquireConnection(Transaction);
}
```

And this is the VB.NET code:

```
' Create class variables so that they can be used in all
' Added System.Data.SqlClient to imports.
Private myAdoConnectionManager As IDTSConnectionManager100
Private myDbConnection As System.Data.SqlClient.SqlConnection
```

```
Public Overrides Sub AcquireConnections(Transaction As Object)
    ' Fill connection manager object with a Package connection manager
    myAdoConnectionManager = Me.Connections.myADOConn

    ' Fill connection object woth connection from the
    ' ADO.NET connection manager object.
    myDbConnection = DirectCast(myAdoConnectionManager _
            .AcquireConnection(Transaction), System.Data.SqlClient.SqlConnection)
End Sub
```

ReleaseConnections

ReleaseConnections is the counterpart of the Acquire method. In this method, you release the connection when you don't need it any more. This code uses the same class variables as the Acquire method code.

```
public override void ReleaseConnections()
{
  // Release the connection when finished
  myAdoConnectionManager.ReleaseConnection(myDbConnection);
}
```

This is the VB.NET code:

```
Public Overrides Sub ReleaseConnections()
    ' Release the connection when finished
    myAdoConnectionManager.ReleaseConnection(myDbConnection)
End Sub
```

PreExecute

The PreExecute method is executed before any of the rows pass through the component. It is often used to get variables or connection managers, or to execute some initial code, like in the following example, where a new XML document is started.

```
// Variable that contains the XML document
// Added System.Xml to usings
XmlTextWriter textWriter;

// Start of XML document
public override void PreExecute()
{
  // Create a new XML document and use the filepath
  // from a FILE connection manager named xmldocument as XML-file
  textWriter = new XmlTextWriter(
              this.Connections.xmldocument.ConnectionString.ToString(), null);

  // Start writing the XML document:
  textWriter.WriteStartDocument();

  // Create root element <root>
  textWriter.WriteStartElement("ROOT");
}
```

227

And this is the VB.NET code:

```vb
' Variable that contains the XML document
' Added System.Xml to imports
Dim textWriter As XmlTextWriter

Public Overrides Sub PreExecute()
  MyBase.PreExecute()
   ' Create a new XML document and use the filepath
   ' from a file connection manager named xmldocument as XML-file
  textWriter = New XmlTextWriter( _
              Me.Connections.xmldocument.ConnectionString.ToString(), _
              System.Text.Encoding.Default)

   'Start writing the XML document:
  textWriter.WriteStartDocument()

   'Create root element <root>
  textWriter.WriteStartElement("ROOT")
End Sub
```

PostExecute

The PostExecute method is executed after all the rows pass through the component. It is often used to set variables or release connection managers, or to execute some final code. In this example, you are closing the XML document that was opened in the PreExecute method. In Chapter 12, you will see the complete example of this XML destination.

```csharp
// Close of XML document
public override void PostExecute()
{
  // Close root element: </root>
  textWriter.WriteEndElement();

  // Stop writing the XML document
  textWriter.WriteEndDocument();

  // Close document
  textWriter.Close();
}
```

And this is the VB.NET code:

```vb
Public Overrides Sub PostExecute()
   'Close root element: </root>
  textWriter.WriteEndElement()

   'Stop writing the XML document
  textWriter.WriteEndDocument()

   'Close document
  textWriter.Close()
End Sub
```

Input()_ProcessInputRow

The Input0_ProcessInputRow method is only available in the Script Component transformation and destination. It executes once for each record entering the Script Component. In this method, you are working with the column values in each row. In this example, you are filling a new output column called RowNumber with a sequence number. You can find the complete example in Chapter 11.

```
// New internal variable to store the rownumber
private int sequenceNumber = 0;

// Method that will be started for each record in your dataflow
public override void Input0_ProcessInputRow(InputOBuffer Row)
{
  // Seed counter
  sequenceNumber++;

  // Fill the new column
  Row.RowNumber = sequenceNumber;
}
```

And this is the VB.NET code:

```
' New internal variable to store the rownumber
Private sequenceNumber As Integer = 0

' Method that will be started for each record in your dataflow
Public Overrides Sub Input0_ProcessInputRow(ByVal Row As InputOBuffer)
  'Seed counter
  sequenceNumber = sequenceNumber + 1

  ' Fill the new column
  Row.RowNumber = sequenceNumber
End Sub
```

CreateNewOutputRows

The CreateNewOutputRows method is the Script Component source equivalent of Input0_ProcessInputRow, but it is also available for transformations with asynchronous outputs. With this method you can create new rows, but it is executed only once. So you need to add a loop construction to add multiple rows. In this very basic example, you are adding 10 rows with an integer column containing the numbers 1 to 10, and a string column containing the words *even* or *uneven*, depending on the value. In Chapter 10 you can find multiple examples of this method.

```
public override void CreateNewOutputRows()
{
  // Add 10 rows
  for (int i = 1; i <= 10; i++)
  {
    // Add a new row
    OutputOBuffer.AddRow();

    // Fill two columns with data
    OutputOBuffer.myIntegerColumn = i;
    OutputOBuffer.myStringColumn = (i % 2) == 1 ? "uneven" : "even";
  }
}
```

And this is the VB.NET code:

```
Public Overrides Sub CreateNewOutputRows()
  ' Add 10 rows
  For i As Integer = 1 To 10
    ' Add a new row
    OutputOBuffer.AddRow()

    ' Fill two columns with data
    OutputOBuffer.myIntegerColumn = i
    OutputOBuffer.myStringColumn = If((i Mod 2) = 1, "uneven", "even")
  Next
End Sub
```

Variables and Parameters

Like the Script Task, you can use variables (and parameters) in the Script Component, but there are some differences. First of all, getting variable values can only be done in the PreExecute method and setting a variable value can only be done in the PostExecute method; otherwise, you get a runtime error. If you need variable values in the Input0_ProcessInputRow or CreateNewOutputRows methods, for example, then you must create a class variable to store the value from the SSIS variable and then use that class variable in the other methods.

There are two different methods. In this example, you are filling a new RowNumber column (see the "Inputs and Outputs" section), but the starting sequence is coming from an SSIS integer variable (see Figure 9-7). This variable could be filled by configurations or by an Execute SQL Task with a query like this:

```
SELECT ISNULL(MAX(rownumber),0) + 1 as NextRowNumber FROM myTable
```

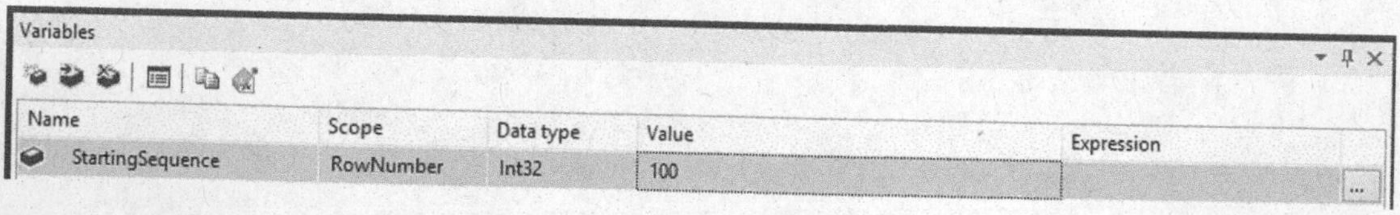

Figure 9-7. *Integer variable called StartingSequence*

Method 1: ReadOnlyVariables and ReadWriteVariables

This example is available to download. Add a Script Component of type Transformation after your source. Add a new output column called RowNumber on the Inputs and Outputs page. On the first page of the editor, you need to add the StartingSequence variable as a ReadWrite variable (see Figure 9-8). In this example, you are first reading the starting sequence, and when you are finished, you are filling it with the last row number.

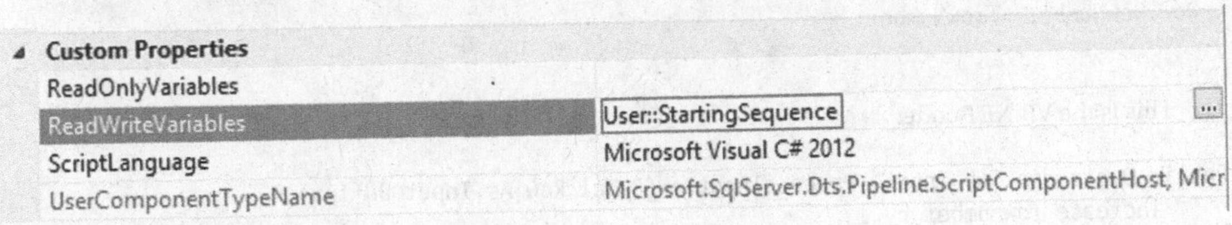

▲ **Custom Properties**	
ReadOnlyVariables	
ReadWriteVariables	User::StartingSequence
ScriptLanguage	Microsoft Visual C# 2012
UserComponentTypeName	Microsoft.SqlServer.Dts.Pipeline.ScriptComponentHost, Micr

Figure 9-8. *ReadWriteVariables*

Now click the Edit Script... button and create an integer Class variable, which is a variable within the class but not in one of the methods. The most appropriate location is right after the class declaration; but that is not a requirement.

```
// Class variable to store a rownumber
// that can only be used in all methods
private int rowNumber = 0;
```

And this is the VB.NET code:

```
' Class variable to store a rownumber
' that can only be used in all methods
Private rowNumber as Int32 = 0
```

In the PreExecute method, you can fill this class variable with the SSIS integer variable value. If you type **Variables**, then IntelliSense will show you a complete list of the available variables. These are the variables that you either selected as the ReadOnly or ReadWrite variable. You may have noticed that this differs from the Script Task.

```
public override void PreExecute()
{
  // Fill the class variable with the
  // value from the SSIS integer variable
  rowNumber = Variables.StartingSequence;
}
```

And this is the VB.NET code:

```
Public Overrides Sub PreExecute()
  ' Fill the class variable with the
  ' value from the SSIS integer variable
  rowNumber = Variables.StartingSequence
End Sub
```

In the Input0_ProcessInputRow method, you raise the value and then fill the new output row number column for each row passing through.

```csharp
public override void Input0_ProcessInputRow(InputOBuffer Row)
{
  // Increase rownumber by 1
  rowNumber++;
  // Fill new column with the rownumber
  Row.RowNumber = rowNumber;
}
```

This is the VB.NET code:

```vbnet
Public Overrides Sub Input0_ProcessInputRow(ByVal Row As InputOBuffer)
    ' Increase rownumber by 1
  rowNumber = rowNumber + 1
    ' Fill new column with the rownumber
  Row.RowNumber = rowNumber
End Sub
```

And in the PostExecute method, which executes after all rows have passed through, you could set the SSIS integer variable with the last row number for the next data flow or for logging purposes.

```csharp
public override void PostExecute()
{
  // Fill SSIS variable with final rownumber
  Variables.StartingSequence = rowNumber;
}
```

This is the VB.NET code:

```vbnet
Public Overrides Sub PostExecute()
    ' Fill SSIS variable with final rownumber
  Variables.StartingSequence = rowNumber
End Sub
```

Method 2: Variable Dispenser

The second method is very similar to the second variable method for Script Tasks. Instead of using the ReadOnly and ReadWrite variables fields in the editor, you are locking the variables in code. For this example, you are only changing the PreExecute and the PostExecute methods. The rest of the code is exactly the same. In the PreExecute method, you are locking the SSIS integer variable for reading, and after you have filled the class variable with the value from the SSIS variable, you are releasing the lock. There is also an explicit conversion (Convert.ToInt32) added because a conversion from object to integer isn't safe and data could get lost. An alternative to Convert.ToInt32 is Int32.TryParse, which is safer if you're not sure what the data type is. In this case, you are sure that it's an integer.

```
public override void PreExecute()
{
  // Lock the variable for read
  VariableDispenser variableDispenser = (VariableDispenser)VariableDispenser;
  variableDispenser.LockForRead("User::StartingSequence");

  // Create a variable 'container' to store the variable(s)
  IDTSVariables100 vars;
  variableDispenser.GetVariables(out vars);

  // Fill the class variable with the value from the SSIS integer variable
  // Because the datatype is always Object if you use this method you
  // first need to convert it to the appropriate Data Type with a convert.
  rowNumber = Convert.ToInt32(vars["User::StartingSequence"].Value);

  // Unlock the variable
  vars.Unlock();
}
```

And this is the VB.NET code:

```
Public Overrides Sub PreExecute()
  ' Lock the variable for read
  Dim variableDispenser As VariableDispenser = _
                          CType(Me.VariableDispenser, VariableDispenser)
  variableDispenser.LockForRead("User::StartingSequence")

  ' Create a variable 'container' to store the variable(s)
  Dim vars As IDTSVariables100
  variableDispenser.GetVariables(vars)

  ' Fill the class variable with the value from the SSIS integer variable
  ' Because the datatype is always Object if you use this method you
  ' first need to convert it to the appropriate Data Type with a convert.
  rowNumber = Convert.ToInt32(vars("User::StartingSequence").Value)

  ' Unlock the variable
  vars.Unlock()
End Sub
```

In the PostExecute method, you need to lock the variable for write to fill it with the final row number. Adding an extra convert is not necessary because the conversion from integer to object is an implicit conversion where no data will get lost.

```
public override void PostExecute()
{
  // Lock the variable for write
  VariableDispenser variableDispenser = (VariableDispenser)VariableDispenser;
  variableDispenser.LockForWrite("User::StartingSequence");
```

```
  // Create a variable 'container' to store the variable(s)
  IDTSVariables100 vars;
  variableDispenser.GetVariables(out vars);

  // Fill SSIS variable with final rownumber
  vars["User::StartingSequence"].Value = rowNumber;

  // Unlock the variable
  vars.Unlock();
}
```

This is the VB.NET code:

```
Public Overrides Sub PostExecute()
  ' Lock the variable for write
  Dim variableDispenser As VariableDispenser = _
                          CType(Me.VariableDispenser, VariableDispenser)
  variableDispenser.LockForWrite("User::StartingSequence")

  ' Create a variable 'container' to store the variable(s)
  Dim vars As IDTSVariables100
  variableDispenser.GetVariables(vars)

  ' Fill SSIS variable with final rownumber
  vars("User::StartingSequence").Value = rowNumber

  ' Unlock the variable
  vars.Unlock()

End Sub
```

■ **Note** If you set a variable value in the Script Component, then the new value will only be available after the Data Flow Task is finished.

If you are still using SSIS 2005, then IDTSVariables100 should be IDTSVariables90.

You can't read sensitive parameters in the Script Component; that is only possible in the Script Task.

Conclusion

In the second example that used the variable dispenser, you seem to have a little more control when you lock and unlock your variables. The big downside is that you cannot quickly see which variables you are using; you have to check the entire code. The other disadvantages are that you need much more code to accomplish the same thing, you have to convert the Object data type to something useful, and you can't use IntelliSense to get the name of the variables. Therefore, the first method should be your preferred method.

Connection Managers

Integration Services uses connection managers to provide access to various data sources, such as flat files and databases, but also to web servers and message queues. You can use these connection managers in a Script Component to avoid hard-coded paths and connection strings. But be conservative with the use of database connection managers because there are probably out-of-the-box alternatives, such as Execute SQL Task, OLE DB Source, OLE DB Command, and OLE DB Destination. If you really need a database connection manager in your script, then ADO.NET is the preferred connection manager type because connection managers like OLE DB, ADO, and ODBC don't return .NET managed objects. Instead, they return COM objects, making them hard to use.

In destination scripts, you can use either the PreExecute method or the AcquireConnections method to acquire a connection, but in a source script, you could also use the CreateNewOutputRows method since it's only executed once. However, it is best to use the AcquireConnections method since it is the only place where you can start a transaction.

Before you start coding, you first need to add your connection manager to the list of connection managers in the Script Component Editor. Once you have done that, you can use the alias (name column) in your Script Component. If you type **This.Connections.**, you can use IntelliSense to get the connection manager name.

The first example is simply getting the connection string property to extract a file path from, and using that in a StreamReader, for example.

```
using (StreamReader sr = new StreamReader(
                       this.Connections.MyProducts.ConnectionString))
{
  String line;
  // Read lines from the file until the end of the file is reached.
  while ((line = sr.ReadLine()) != null)
  {
    // do something with the line variable
  }
}
```

And this is the VB.NET code:

```
Using sr As New StreamReader(Me.Connections.MyProducts.ConnectionString)
  Dim line As String = sr.ReadLine
  ' Read lines from the file until the end of the file is reached.
  Do While (Not line Is Nothing)
    ' do something with the line variable
    ' And end the loop with a Read next line
    line = sr.ReadLine
  Loop
End Using
```

Instead of using the connection string property, it's even better to use the AcquireConnection. This will process expressions on the connection manager, if there are any.

```
this.Connections.MyProducts.AcquireConnection(null).ToString()
```

This is the VB.NET code:

```
Me.Connections.MyProducts.AcquireConnection(Nothing).ToString()
```

The return value differs depending on the connection manager type. For example, the Flat File Connection Manager returns a string containing the file path, but the ADO.NET Connection Manager returns an SqlConnection object. Search for "Working with Connection Managers Programmatically" or go to the BOL page at https://msdn.microsoft.com/en-us/library/cc645942.aspx to get a complete overview.

```
// Store the connection manager in a local Connection Manager object
IDTSConnectionManager100 myADONETConnectionManager =
                                        this.Connections.AdvantureWorks;

// Acquire the connection
SqlConnection myADONETConnection = (SqlConnection)myADONETConnectionManager.
                                        AcquireConnection(null);

// Create string with query
string QueryString = "SELECT count(*) as NumberOfStores FROM [Sales].[Store]";

// Create a command with the query and the connection
SqlCommand myCommand = new SqlCommand(QueryString, myADONETConnection);

// Execute the query and loop through record(s)
SqlDataReader dr = myCommand.ExecuteReader();
while (dr.Read())
{
  // do something with dr.GetValue(x)
}
```

A better alternative for creating all of those variables/objects is to use a using to ensure that all objects are disposed when you are ready.

```
using (SqlConnection myADONETConnection = (SqlConnection)
                    myADONETConnectionManager.AcquireConnection(null))
{
  // Do something with myADONETConnection
}
// myADONETConnection is now disposed
```

This is the VB.NET code:

```
' Store the connection manager in a local Connection Manager object
Dim myADONETConnectionManager As IDTSConnectionManager100 = Me.Connections.AdvantureWorks

' Acquire the connection
Dim myADONETConnection As SqlConnection = CType(myADONETConnectionManager.
AcquireConnection(Nothing), SqlConnection)
```

```
' Create string with query
Dim QueryString As String = "SELECT count(*) as NumberOfStores FROM [Sales].[Store]"

' Create a command with the query and the connection
Dim myCommand As New SqlCommand(QueryString, myADONETConnection)

' Execute the query and loop through record(s)
Dim dr As SqlDataReader = myCommand.ExecuteReader()
While dr.Read()
        ' do something with dr.GetValue(x)
        MessageBox.Show(dr.GetValue(0).ToString())
End While
```

And this is the same example in VB.NET:

```
Using myADONETConnection As SqlConnection = CType(myADONETConnectionManager. _
                                AcquireConnection(Nothing), SqlConnection)
    ' Do something with myADONETConnection
End Using
' myADONETConnection is now disposed
```

Logging Events

Within the Script Component you can raise/fire events for logging purposes. But firing an information event, for example, does not automatically log the message. You still have to capture those events in your package logging. Firing events work similarly to Script Task events, but there are fewer events to fire:

- FireCustomEvent
- FireError
- FireInformation
- FireProgress
- FireWarning

Next are a couple of fire event examples. Don't fire too many events because that pollutes the logging, making it worthless, and it worsens the performance of your Script Component. All methods (except for the FireProgress) have a similar structure.

The first integer is error/warning/information code. You can keep it zero, unless you want to keep up a complete list of all codes. The second parameter is a string containing the (sub)name of your transformation. In most cases, this can be the name of your Script Component, unless you have quite a large piece of code with multiple log entries; then you could use the name of the section of your code, for example. The third parameter is the actual message that you want to log. For the other parameters, you could use the value as shown. In most cases, they are less useful.

In the Script Component you can fire an error with the following code, which will result in a log line in the Progress/Execution Results tab (see Figure 9-9).

❌ [MyTransformation] Error: Something went wrong!

Figure 9-9. *FireError result (from Progress/Execution Results tab)*

The last parameters are `string.Empty` and 0 because you don't have a help file reference available.

```
// Cancel the component on error
bool bpCancel = true;
// Firing an error
ComponentMetaData.FireError(0, "MyTransformation", "Something went wrong!",
                                string.Empty, 0, out bpCancel);
```

This is the VB.NET code:

```
' Cancel the component on error
Dim bpCancel As Boolean = True
' Firing an error
ComponentMetaData.FireError(0, "MyTransformation", "Something went wrong!", _
                                String.Empty, 0, bpCancel)
```

You can combine the `FireError` method with a `try-catch` statement to handle your unexpected errors.

```
//C# code
try
{
    // your code
}
catch(Exception ex)
{
  bool pbCancel = True;
  this.ComponentMetaData.FireError(0, "MyTransformation",
                            "An error occurred: " + ex.Message,
                                string.Empty, 0, out pbCancel);
}
```

And this is the VB.NET code:

```
Try
    ' your code
Catch ex As Exception
  Dim bpCancel As Boolean = True
  ComponentMetaData.FireError(0, "MyTransformation", _
                        "An error occurred: " + ex.Message, _
                        String.Empty, 0, bpCancel)
End Try
```

Firing a warning has no cancel option; it results in an exclamation mark icon and the warning text in the Progress/Execution Results tab, as shown in Figure 9-10.

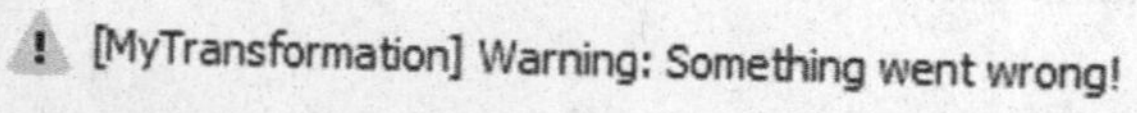

⚠ [MyTransformation] Warning: Something went wrong!

Figure 9-10. FireWarning result (from Progress/Execution Results tab)

```
// Firing a warning
ComponentMetaData.FireWarning(0, "MyTransformation", "Something went wrong!",
                                    string.Empty, 0);
```

This is the VB.NET code:

```
' Firing a warning
ComponentMetaData.FireWarning(0, "MyTransformation", "Something went wrong!", _
                                    String.Empty, 0)
```

Firing an information event has a FireAgain option to prevent multiple log rows in the Progress/ Execution Results tab, as shown in Figure 9-11.

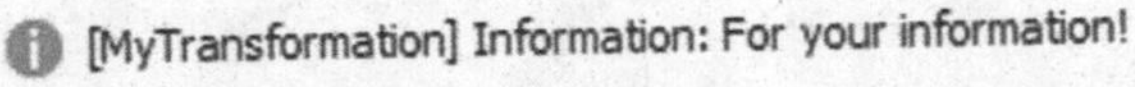

ℹ️ [MyTransformation] Information: For your information!

Figure 9-11. *FireInformation result (from Progress/Execution Results tab)*

```
// Specifies whether the event should be raised again in the future
bool pbFireAgain = true;
// Firing information
ComponentMetaData.FireInformation(0, "MyTransformation", "For your info!",
                                        string.Empty, 0, ref pbFireAgain);
```

And this is the VB.NET code:

```
'  Specifies whether the event should be raised again in the future
Dim pbFireAgain As Boolean = True
'  Firing information
ComponentMetaData.FireInformation(0, "MyTransformation", "For your info!", _
                                        String.Empty, 0, pbFireAgain)
```

If you have a loop construction or a method that executes for each row, then you could use the FireProgress event to keep you informed on the progress percentage (see Figure 9-12). This is probably only useful for processes that could take a while. In this example, 0 is the lower bound, 100 is the upper bound, and 25 the actual value.

```
// Specifies whether the event should be raised again in the future
bool pbFireAgain = false;
// Firing progress
ComponentMetaData.FireProgress("Doing something", 25, 0, 100,
                                    "MyTransformation", ref pbFireAgain);
```

This is the VB.NET code:

```
' Specifies whether the event should be raised again in the future
Dim pbFireAgain2 As Boolean = True
' Firing progress
ComponentMetaData.FireProgress("Doing something", 25, 0, 100, _
                                    "MyTransformation", pbFireAgain)
```

➔ [MyTransformation] Progress: Doing something - 25 percent complete
➔ [MyTransformation] Progress: Doing something - 50 percent complete
➔ [MyTransformation] Progress: Doing something - 75 percent complete
➔ [MyTransformation] Progress: Doing something - 100 percent complete

Figure 9-12. FireProgress result

Changing .NET Versions

Each version of SSIS has its own range of supported .NET Frameworks (see Table 9-1). This means that you can't use a .NET 3.5 feature like LINQ (Language-Integrated Query) in SSIS 2005 because it only supports .NET 2.0. In SSIS 2008, Microsoft added support up to .NET 3.5; however, the default Target Framework for SSIS 2008 is .NET 2.0, but you can change that in the VSTA editor.

Table 9-1. SSIS Versions and Supported Frameworks

SSIS Version	Supported Framework
2005	2.0
2008 (R2)	2.0 => 3.5
2012	2.0 => 4.0
2014	2.0 => 4.5.1
2016	2.0 => 4.5.2

To change the Target Framework, go to the VSTA editor and right-click the project in Solution Explorer. Then choose the properties. In a C# project, you can find the Target Framework on the first page (Application, as seen in Figure 9-13).

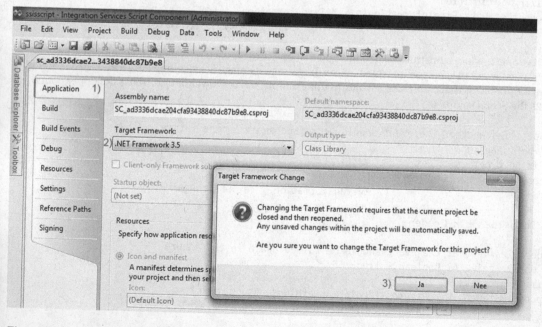

Figure 9-13. Changing Target Framework for C#

In VB.NET, the Target Framework is in different locations, depending on the version of SSIS or Visual Studio (see Figure 9-14). In older versions, you can find it on the Compile page in the Advanced options. And in newer versions, Microsoft aligned the location with C# projects and moved it to the Application page.

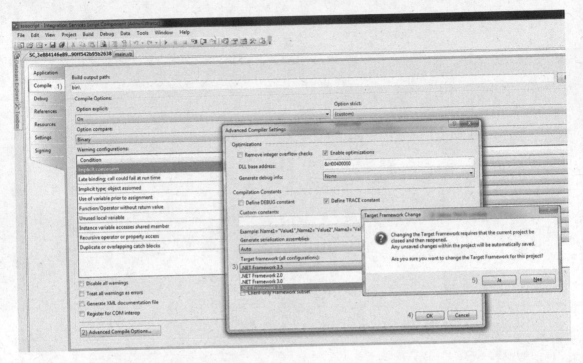

Figure 9-14. *Changing Target Framework for VB.NET*

Summary

In this chapter, you learned the Script Component basics, such as how to use variables or connection managers. In the following chapters, you will learn more about how they are used in various examples.

■ ■ ■

CHAPTER 10

Script Component As Source

This chapter focuses on the Script Component as a source. There are a lot of different sources available in the Data Flow Task, but sometimes you get, for example, files that are not properly formatted to make them readable for the Flat File Source. And what about using the Script Component to generate random test data if you don't have data to test your data flow?

Flat File with an Uneven Number of Columns

Some .csv files have rows where not all the columns at the end are filled. Instead of having empty columns, the columns have been omitted. This causes some strange behavior in the Flat File Connection Manager, where some rows and columns will be merged. This is the sample data used for this example:

```
"test1";"abc";"xyz";"123"
"test2";"cba";"zyx";"321"
"test3";"abc"
"test4";"efg";"zyx"
"test5";"cba";"zyx";"321"
```

If you show a preview in the Flat File Connection Manager, it merges the short row with the next row and shows an error. Figure 10-1 shows how that looks. You can see how "test4" is adjacent to the "abc" form the "test3" row. Figure 10-2 shows the error message that you'll receive.

Column 0	Column 1	Column 2	Column 3
"test1"	"abc"	"xyz"	"123"
"test2"	"cba"	"zyx"	"321"
"test3"	"abc""test4"	"efg"	"zyx"
"test5"	"cba"	"zyx"	"321"

Figure 10-1. Merged columns and rows

243

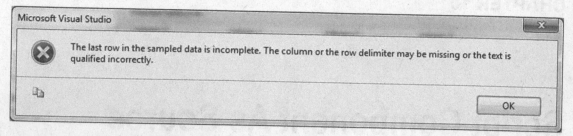

Figure 10-2. Error in the Flat File Connection Manager editor

Script Component Source

This issue was fixed in SSIS 2012 by adding a new Flat File Connection Manager property named AlwaysCheckForRowDelimiters; but for older versions, you get an error in the Flat File Connection Manager editor when you try to read a file with such data. A Script Component as a source could help you to read this file. Instead of using a Flat File Connection Manager, you will use a File Connection Manager that points to the same CSV file with the variable column numbers, but without defining the columns.

Go to the Data Flow Task and add a Script Component to the surface. You will be asked to choose between Source, Transformation, and Destination. Choose Source as shown in Figure 10-3, and give the task a useful name. Adding a description or an annotation about the reason for using the Script Component is recommended.

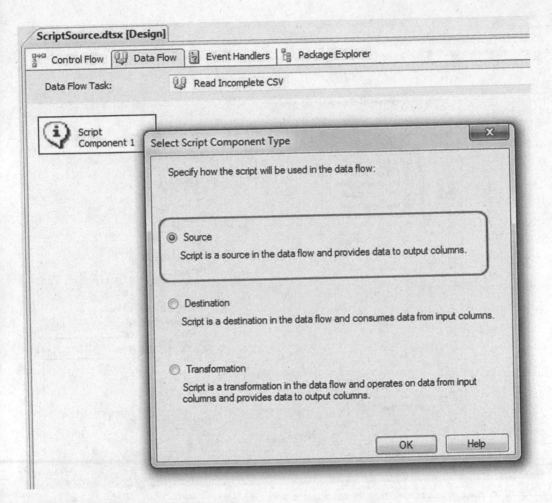

Figure 10-3. Script Component Source

Creating Output Columns

Open the Script Transformation Editor and go to the Inputs and Outputs page. Add four string columns to Output 0. Before you click the Add Column button to add a second column, you should first click Output Columns; otherwise, the new column will be added on top instead of at the bottom.

You may need to convert the data in the script from string to integer. It is a best practice to use correct data types; otherwise, you need to cast the values downstream of your data flow. Figure 10-4 highlights the data type dropdown list field.

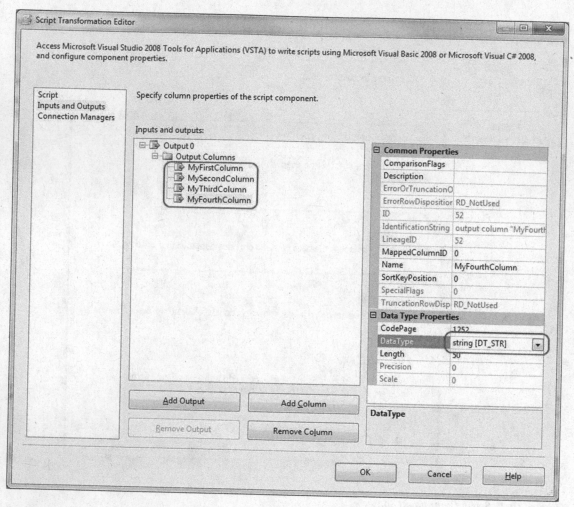

Figure 10-4. *Add new output columns*

Creating a File Connection Manager

To avoid hard-coded connection strings in the script, you need a connection manager. For this example, you are creating a new connection manager from within the Script Component Editor, but you could also do that upfront and then use that one in the editor. Go to the Connection Managers page and add a new connection (1). The Connection Manager Type (2) should be FILE and the Usage type (3) should be "Existing file". Next, change the default name from Connection to myFile in the Name column. These steps are shown in Figure 10-5.

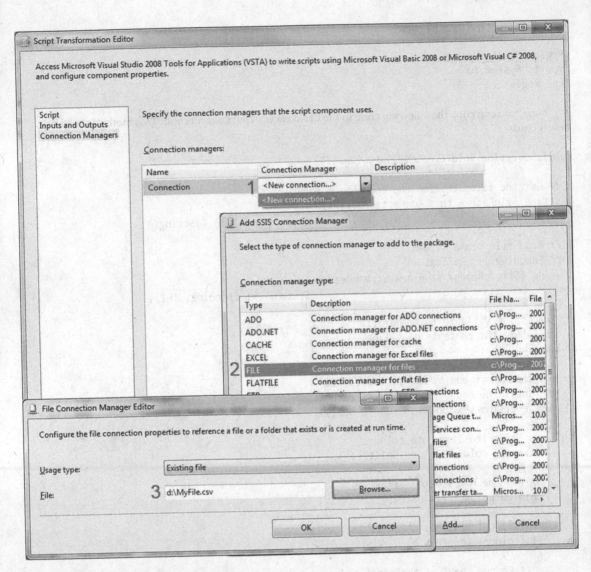

Figure 10-5. *Add new connection manager*

The Code

Now you can go back to the Script page, and choose Edit Script... to open the VSTA environment. First you need to add an extra namespace to shorten the code.

```
#region CustomNamespace
using System.IO;
#endregion
```

And here is the VB.NET code:

```
#Region "CustomNamespace"
Imports System.IO
#End Region
```

Next, you can copy the following code to the CreateNewOutputRows method. This method creates new records.

```
public override void CreateNewOutputRows()
{
  // Get the filepath from the connection manager
  string filePath = this.Connections.myFile
                              .AcquireConnection(null).ToString();

  // Read file via a stream
  // Encoding is optional
  using (StreamReader sr = new StreamReader(filePath,
                                  System.Text.Encoding.UTF7))
  {
    // string variable to temporarly
    // store the contents of 1 line.
    string line;

    // Read lines one by one from the file
    // until the end of the file is reached.
    while ((line = sr.ReadLine()) != null)
    {
      // Split the line into columns
      string[] columns = line.Split(';');

      // Add one new row to buffer
      this.OutputOBuffer.AddRow();

      // Fill columns, but check if they exist
      if (columns.Length > 0)
      {
        // Remove the " at the start and end of the string
        // with a trim or use a substring.
        OutputOBuffer.MyFirstColumn =
                    columns[0].TrimStart('"').TrimEnd('"');
      }
      if (columns.Length > 1)
      {
        OutputOBuffer.MySecondColumn =
                    columns[1].TrimStart('"').TrimEnd('"');
      }
      if (columns.Length > 2)
      {
        OutputOBuffer.MyThirdColumn =
                    columns[2].TrimStart('"').TrimEnd('"');
      }
```

```csharp
      if (columns.Length > 3)
      {
        OutputOBuffer.MyFourthColumn =
                    columns[3].TrimStart('"').TrimEnd('"');
        // If you choose integer as datatype then you
        // need to add a convert around columns:
        // OutputOBuffer.MyIntColumn =
        // Convert.ToInt32(columns[3].TrimStart('"').TrimEnd('"'));
      }
    }
  }
}
```

And this is the VB.NET code, where the while loop is slightly different from the C# example.

```vbnet
Public Overrides Sub CreateNewOutputRows()
  ' Get the filepath from the connection manager
  Dim filePath As String = Me.Connections.myFile _
                          .AcquireConnection(Nothing).ToString()

  ' Read file via a stream
  ' Encoding is optional
  Using sr As New StreamReader(filePath, System.Text.Encoding.UTF7)
    ' string variable to temporarly
    ' store the contents of 1 line.
    Dim line As String = ""

    ' Read first line before loop (unlike C#)
    line = sr.ReadLine()

    ' Read lines one by one from the file
    ' until the end of the file is reached.
    While (line <> Nothing)
      ' Split the line into columns
      Dim columns As String() = line.Split(";"c)

      ' Add one new row to buffer
      Me.OutputOBuffer.AddRow()

      ' Fill columns, but check if they exist
      If columns.Length > 0 Then
        ' Remove the " at the start and end of the string
        ' with a trim or use a substring.
        OutputOBuffer.MyFirstColumn = _
                    columns(0).TrimStart(""""c).TrimEnd(""""c)
      End If
      If columns.Length > 1 Then
        OutputOBuffer.MySecondColumn = _
                    columns(1).TrimStart(""""c).TrimEnd(""""c)
      End If
```

```
      If columns.Length > 2 Then
        OutputOBuffer.MyThirdColumn = _
                    columns(2).TrimStart("""""c).TrimEnd("""""c)
      End If
      If columns.Length > 3 Then
        OutputOBuffer.MyFourthColumn = _
                    columns(3).TrimStart("""""c).TrimEnd("""""c)
        ' If you choose integer as datatype then you
        ' need to add a convert around columns:
        ' OutputOBuffer.MyIntColumn =
        ' Convert.ToInt32(columns(3).TrimStart("""""C).TrimEnd("""""C))
      End If

      ' Read next line at bottom of loop (unlike C#)
      line = sr.ReadLine()
    End While
  End Using
End Sub
```

You have removed the overridden pre- and post- execute methods since you don't need them. You could use the pre-execute to for example check if the file is filed with data. The Script Component Editor will check whether the file in the connection manager exists before the code is executed.

The Results

When you execute the Data Flow Task, you can add a data viewer to check the results. Figure 10-6 shows an example.

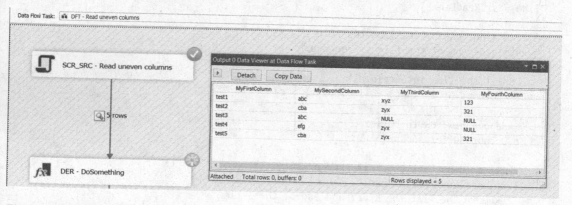

Figure 10-6. *The results*

Flat File with Records Split over Multiple Rows

Another good use of the Script Component as a source is when the records are divided over multiple lines. In this case, each line has one column.

```
id,1
name,Joost
address,Street 2
id,2
name,Regis
address,Avenue 4b
id,3
name,William
address,Plaza 5
```

Script Component Source

Go to the Data Flow Task and add a Script Component to the surface. You will be asked to choose between Source, Transformation, and Destination. Choose Source as in Figure 10-7, and give the component a useful name.

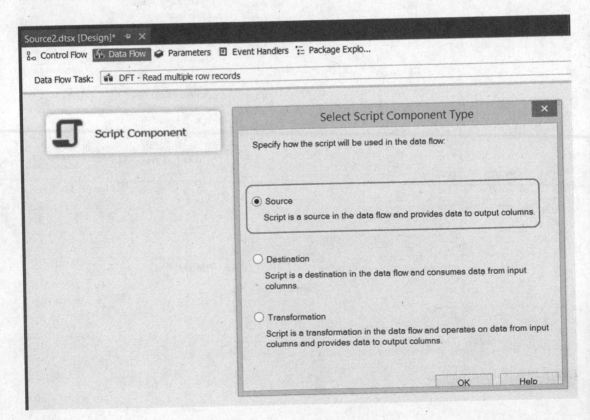

Figure 10-7. Script Component as source

Output Columns

Edit the Script Component and go to the Inputs and Outputs page (see Figure 10-8). Add three columns at the output section:

- **ID** (four-byte signed integer, DT_I4)

- **Name** (string 50, DT_STR 1252)

- **Address** (string 50, DT_STR 1252)

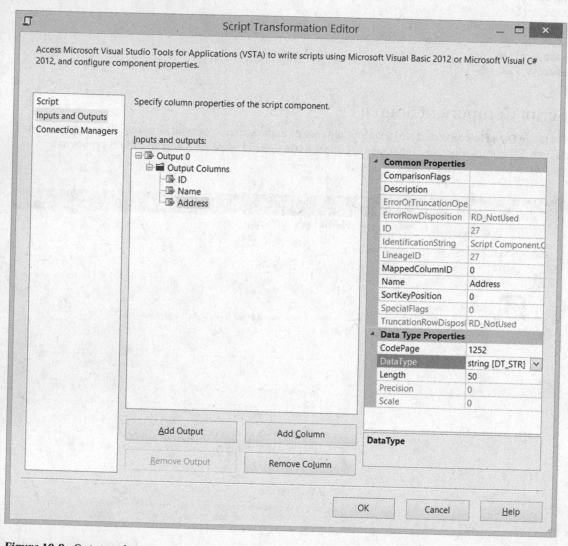

Figure 10-8. Output columns

Create a Connection Manager

In this example, you are creating a new connection manager from within the Script Component Editor, but you could also do that upfront and then use that one in this editor. Go to the Connection Managers tab and add a new connection (1) to avoid a hard-coded connection string in your Script. The Connection Manager Type (2) should be FILE and the Usage type (3) should be "Existing file". Next, change the default name from Connection to myFile. These steps are shown in Figure 10-9.

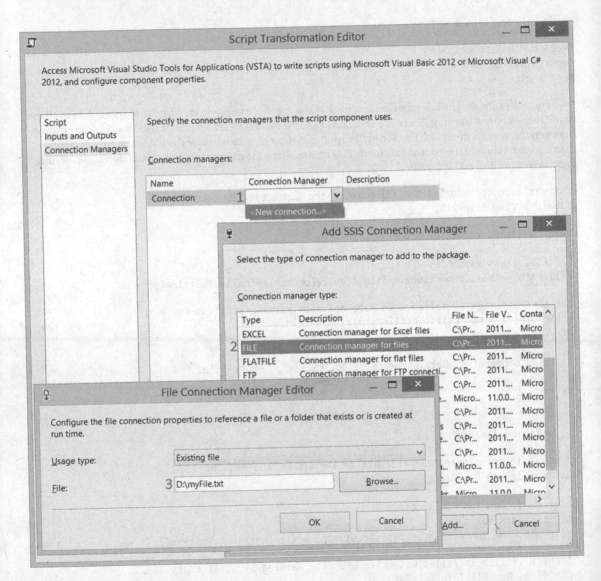

Figure 10-9. *Add a new connection manager*

The Code

Now you can go back to the Script page, and choose Edit Script... to open the VSTA environment. First you need to add an extra namespace to shorten the code.

```
#region CustomNamespace
using System.IO;
#endregion
```

And here is the VB.NET code:

```
#Region "CustomNamespace"
Imports System.IO
#End Region
```

For this example, you added a file size check in the PreExecute method. When there is no data available in the file, you fire a warning. There is also a class variable named filePath that is used for communication between the various methods. The Script Component Editor checks whether the file in the connection manager exists before the code is executed. This means that a file existence check would duplicate existing logic, so it wouldn't add any value.

```
// A variable for storing the filepath of the Connection Manager
private string filePath;

public override void PreExecute()
{
  // Fill class variable
  filePath = this.Connections.myFile.AcquireConnection(null).ToString();

  // Check if file is filled with data and fire warning if it is empty.
  FileInfo fi = new FileInfo(filePath);
  if (fi.Length == 0)
  {
    this.ComponentMetaData.FireWarning(0, "myFile", "Empty file: " +
                                  filePath, "", 0);
  }
}
```

And here is the VB.NET code:

```
' A variable for storing the filepath of the Connection Manager
Private filePath As String

Public Overrides Sub PreExecute()
  ' Fill class variable
  filePath = Me.Connections.myFile.AcquireConnection(Nothing).ToString()

  ' Check if file is filled with data and fire warning if it is empty.
  Dim fi As New FileInfo(filePath)
  If fi.Length = 0 Then
    Me.ComponentMetaData.FireWarning(0, "myFile", "Empty file: " & _
                                  filePath, "", 0)
  End If
End Sub
```

Next, you can copy the following code to the CreateNewOutputRows method. This method creates new records. It loops through all the rows in the file and keeps count of the number of columns. If it reaches the total number of columns, it creates a new record in SSIS and then resets the counter.

```
public override void CreateNewOutputRows()
{
  // Variables to store column values
  int ID = 0;                  // Column 1
  string Name = "";            // Column 2
  string Address = "";         // Column 3
  int NumberOfColumns = 3;

  // Counter to keep track of the current row/column
  int rowCounter = 0;

  // Read file via a stream. Encoding is optional
  using (StreamReader sr = new StreamReader(filePath,
                                   System.Text.Encoding.UTF7))

  {
    String line;
    // Read lines from the file until the end of the file is reached.
    while ((line = sr.ReadLine()) != null)
    {
      // Raising the counter
      rowCounter++;

      // Split the line into column and value
      string[] columns = line.Split(',');

      // Fill the right variable
      // Line 1: ID, Line 2: Name, Line 3: Address
      switch (rowCounter)
      {
        case 1:
          // Column 1
          ID = System.Convert.ToInt32(columns[1]);
          break;
        case 2:
          // Column 2
          Name = columns[1];
          break;
        case 3:
          // Column 3
          Address = columns[1];
          break;
        default:
          // Incorrect
          break;
      }
```

```csharp
    // Add a new row if the last column has been reached
    if (rowCounter.Equals(NumberOfColumns))
    {
      // Add one new row and fill columns
      this.OutputoBuffer.AddRow();
      OutputoBuffer.ID = ID;
      OutputoBuffer.Name = Name;
      OutputoBuffer.Address = Address;

      // Last column, reset counter and start with
      // the next set of rows
      rowCounter = 0;
    }
  }
 }
}
```

Here is the VB.NET code:

```vbnet
Public Overrides Sub CreateNewOutputRows()
  ' Variables to store column values
  Dim ID As Integer = 0
  ' Column 1
  Dim Name As String = ""
  ' Column 2
  Dim Address As String = ""
  ' Column 3
  Dim NumberOfColumns As Integer = 3

  ' Counter to keep track of the current row/column
  Dim rowCounter As Integer = 0

  ' Read file via a stream. Encoding is optional
  Using sr As New StreamReader(filePath, System.Text.Encoding.UTF7)
    Dim line As String

    ' Read first line
    line = sr.ReadLine()

    ' Read lines one by one from the file
    ' until the end of the file is reached.
    While (line <> Nothing)

      ' Raising the counter
      rowCounter += 1

      ' Split the line into column and value
      Dim columns As String() = line.Split(","c)

      ' Fill the right variable
      ' Line 1: ID, Line 2: Name, Line 3: Address
```

```vbnet
    Select Case rowCounter
      Case 1
        ' Column 1
        ID = System.Convert.ToInt32(columns(1))
      Case 2
        ' Column 2
        Name = columns(1)
      Case 3
        ' Column 3
        Address = columns(1)
      Case Else
        ' Incorrect
    End Select

    ' Add a new row if the last column has been reached
    If rowCounter.Equals(NumberOfColumns) Then
      ' Add one new row and fill columns
      Me.OutputOBuffer.AddRow()
      OutputOBuffer.ID = ID
      OutputOBuffer.Name = Name
      OutputOBuffer.Address = Address

      ' Last column, reset counter and start with
      ' the next set of rows
      rowCounter = 0
    End If

      ' Read one line from file
      line = sr.ReadLine()
    End While
  End Using
End Sub
```

The Results

When you execute the Data Flow Task, you can add a data viewer such as in Figure 10-10 to check the results. If you have more columns, just extent the switch statement and raise the NumberOfColumns integer variable.

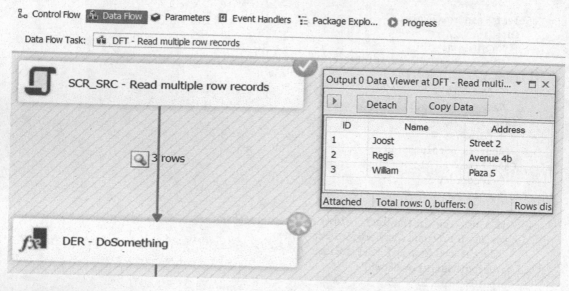

Figure 10-10. The results

Generate Random Data with the Script Component As a Source

What if you know the format of a source, but you don't have actual data to test? With the Script Component as a source, you can easily generate random data, such as numbers between a minimum and maximum value, or dates between a start and an end date, or text with random chars, or text picked randomly from a list. You can use this Script Component example to replace the source or to generate data and fill the source.

Script Component Source

Go to the Data Flow Task and add a Script Component to the surface. You will be asked to choose between Source, Transformation, and Destination. Choose Source and give it a useful name. See Figure 10-11 for an example.

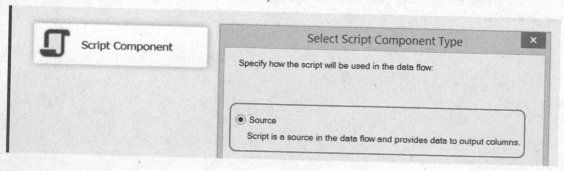

Figure 10-11. Script Component as source

Output Columns

Edit the Script Component and go to the Inputs and Outputs page (see Figure 10-12). Add the columns you need and set the appropriate data types. In this example you used string, int, date, currency, and numeric, but other data types are possible. You might have to add an extra cast/convert in your code.

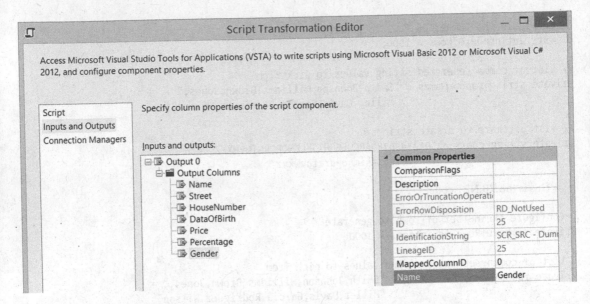

Figure 10-12. Output columns

The columns for the example are as follows:

- **Name** (string [DT_STR] 50)

- **Street** (string [DT_STR] 50)

- **HouseNumber** (four-byte signed integer [DT_I4])

- **DateOfBirth** (date [DT_DATE])

- **Price** (currency [DT_CY])

- **Percentage** (numeric [DT_NUMERIC] 5,2)

- **Gender** (string [DT_STR] 1)

Figure 10-12 shows the columns in the Script Transformation Editor.

The Code

In this example, you didn't have to use any extra namespaces, but you used three class variables. The first integer is to specify the number of rows that you want to generate. The two string variables are for random words or random chars. You could create multiple versions of these strings, each with a different set of words or chars.

```
// Configure the number of rows to generate
private int numberOfRows = 1000;

// List of comma seperated string values to pick from
private string randomNames = "Smith,Johnson,Williams,Brown,Jones," +
                            "Miller,Davis,Garcia,Rodriguez,Wilson";

// List of chars to create strings
private string chars = "0123456789ABCDEFGHIJKLMNOPQRSTUVWXYZ" +
                       "abcdefghijklmnopqrstuvwxyz";
```

This is the VB.NET code:

```
' Configure the number of rows to generate
Private numberOfRows As Integer = 1000

' List of comma seperated string values to pick from
Private randomNames As String = "Smith,Johnson,Williams,Brown,Jones," + _
                            "Miller,Davis,Garcia,Rodriguez,Wilson"

' List of chars to create strings
Private chars As String = "0123456789ABCDEFGHIJKLMNOPQRSTUVWXYZ" + _
                          "abcdefghijklmnopqrstuvwxyz"
```

Next are a couple of new methods that you have enclosed in a region called RandomMethods. These extra methods are called from the CreateNewOutputRows method and they generate the random data. The clearest place is probably below the CreateNewOutputRows method.

```
#region RandomMethods
// Pass a string and pick one randomly
private string pickRandomString(string stringlist, Random rndNumber)
{
  // Split string in array of strings
  string[] strings = stringlist.Split(',');

  // Pick one randomly and return it
  return strings[rndNumber.Next(strings.Length)];
}

// Create string with random chars from charcollection
private string createRandomString(string chars, int max, Random rndNumber)
{
  // Comment out this row to create
  // string with the same length
  max = rndNumber.Next(1, max);
```

```csharp
// Create an array of chars with a certain length
char[] stringChars = new char[max];

// Fill each array item with a random char
for (int i = 0; i < stringChars.Length; i++)
{
    stringChars[i] = chars[rndNumber.Next(chars.Length)];
}

// Convert the array of chars to string and return it
return new String(stringChars);
}

// Pick a random number between min and max value
private int pickRandomNumber(int min, int max, Random rndNumber)
{
    // Pick a random number/integer
    return rndNumber.Next(min, max);
}

// Pick a random number between min and max value
public double pickRandomNumber(double min, double max, Random rndNumber)
{
    // Pick a random number/double
    return rndNumber.NextDouble() * (max - min) + min;
}

// Pick a random date between min and max date
public static DateTime pickRandomDate(DateTime from, DateTime to,
                                      Random rndNumber)
{
    // Calculate difference between to and from
    TimeSpan range = to - from;

    // Determine random increment
    TimeSpan randTimeSpan = new TimeSpan((long)(rndNumber.NextDouble() *
                                         range.Ticks));

    // Return sum of from + random increment
    return (from + randTimeSpan).Date;
}
#endregion
```

Here is the VB.NET code:

```vbnet
#Region "RandomMethods"
' Pass a string and pick one randomly
Private Function pickRandomString(stringlist As String, _
                                  rndNumber As Random) As String

    ' Split string in array of strings
    Dim strings As String() = stringlist.Split(","c)
```

```vbnet
    ' Pick one randomly and return it
    Return strings(rndNumber.[Next](strings.Length))
End Function


' Create string with random chars from charcollection
Private Function createRandomString(chars As String, max As Integer, _
                                    rndNumber As Random) As String
    ' Comment out this row to create
    ' string with the same length
    max = rndNumber.[Next](1, max)

    ' Create an array of chars with a certain length
    Dim stringChars As Char() = New Char(max - 1) {}

    ' Fill each array item with a random char
    For i As Integer = 0 To stringChars.Length - 1
        stringChars(i) = chars(rndNumber.[Next](chars.Length))
    Next

    ' Convert the array of chars to string and return it
    Return New [String](stringChars)
End Function


' Pick a random number between min and max value
Private Function pickRandomNumber(min As Integer, max As Integer, _
                                  rndNumber As Random) As Integer
    ' Pick a random number/integer
    Return rndNumber.[Next](min, max)
End Function


' Pick a random number between min and max value
Public Function pickRandomNumber(min As Double, max As Double, _
                                 rndNumber As Random) As Double
    ' Pick a random number/double
    Return rndNumber.NextDouble() * (max - min) + min
End Function


' Pick a random date between min and max date
Public Shared Function pickRandomDate(from As DateTime, [to] As DateTime, _
                                      rndNumber As Random) As DateTime
    ' Calculate difference between to and from
    Dim range As TimeSpan = [to] - from

    ' Determine random increment
    Dim randTimeSpan As New TimeSpan(CLng(rndNumber.NextDouble() * range.Ticks))

    ' Return sum of from + random increment
    Return (from + randTimeSpan).[Date]
End Function
#End Region
```

Now it is time to add the code to the CreateNewOutputRows method. There is a for loop that loops until the requested number of records has been reached. Within the loop, the columns are filled with random data.

```csharp
// Standard method to generate new rows
public override void CreateNewOutputRows()
{
  // Loop until numberOfRows has been reached. The i will also
  // be used to generate a different random value per row.
  for (int i = 0; i < numberOfRows; i++)
  {
    // Add a new row
    OutputOBuffer.AddRow();
    // Datatype: string [DT_STR]
    OutputOBuffer.Name = pickRandomString(randomNames, new Random(i));
    // Datatype: string [DT_STR]
    OutputOBuffer.Street = createRandomString(chars, 10, new Random(i));
    // Datatype: four-byte signed integer [DT_I4]
    OutputOBuffer.HouseNumber = pickRandomNumber(1, 10, new Random(i));
    // Datatype: date [DT_DATE]
    OutputOBuffer.DateOfBirth = pickRandomDate(new DateTime(1974, 01, 01),
                                 new DateTime(1999, 12, 31), new Random(i));

    // Datatype: currency [DT_CY]
    OutputOBuffer.Price = Convert.ToDecimal(pickRandomNumber(
                          Convert.ToDouble(0), Convert.ToDouble(10000),
                          new Random(i)));
    // Datatype: numeric [DT_NUMERIC]
    OutputOBuffer.Percentage = Convert.ToDecimal(pickRandomNumber(
                               Convert.ToDouble(0), Convert.ToDouble(100),
                               new Random(i)));
    // Datatype: string [DT_STR]
    OutputOBuffer.Gender = pickRandomString("M,F", new Random(i));
  }
}
```

This is the VB.NET code:

```vbnet
' Standard method to generate new rows
Public Overrides Sub CreateNewOutputRows()
  ' Loop until numberOfRows has been reached. The i will also
  ' be used to generate a different random value per row.
  For i As Integer = 0 To numberOfRows - 1
    ' Add a new row
    OutputOBuffer.AddRow()
    ' Datatype: string [DT_STR]
    OutputOBuffer.Name = pickRandomString(randomNames, New Random(i))
    ' Datatype: string [DT_STR]
    OutputOBuffer.Street = createRandomString(chars, 10, New Random(i))
    ' Datatype: four-byte signed integer [DT_I4]
    OutputOBuffer.HouseNumber = pickRandomNumber(1, 10, New Random(i))
    ' Datatype: date [DT_DATE]
```

```
    OutputoBuffer.DateOfBirth = pickRandomDate(New DateTime(1974, 1, 1),
                            New DateTime(1999, 12, 31), New Random(i))
    ' Datatype: currency [DT_CY]
    OutputoBuffer.Price = Convert.ToDecimal(pickRandomNumber( _
                    Convert.ToDouble(0), Convert.ToDouble(10000), _
                    New Random(i)))
    ' Datatype: numeric [DT_NUMERIC]
    OutputoBuffer.Percentage = Convert.ToDecimal(pickRandomNumber( _
                        Convert.ToDouble(0), Convert.ToDouble(100), _
                        New Random(i)))
    ' Datatype: string [DT_STR]
    OutputoBuffer.Gender = pickRandomString("M,F", New Random(i))
  Next
End Sub
```

Note that if you rerun the data flow, you get the same random data. This is because you are using row number i as seed to calculate something random: New Random(i). If you don't want that, you could change the behavior by adding something like milliseconds to the seed:

```
new Random(i + DateTime.Now.Millisecond)
```

The Results

When you execute the Data Flow Task, you can add a data viewer to check the results. You can see such a viewer in Figure 10-13. You can move the data to a table or flat file and use it as a source in another data flow to test it. It's easy to extend with extra columns or other sets of strings.

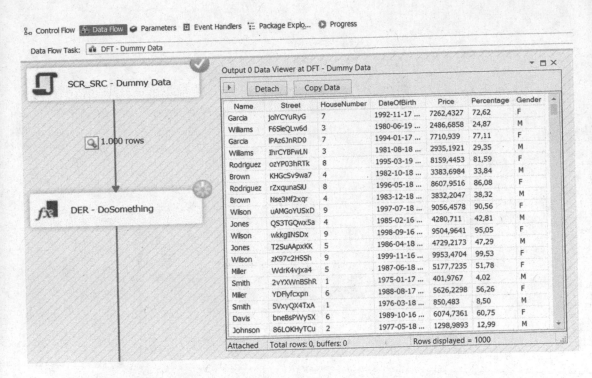

Figure 10-13. *The results*

Summary

In this chapter you learned how to use the Script Component as a source for differently formatted text files. As long as you can come up with a rule, the possibilities are endless. The second thing you saw was how to generate random data for testing purposes. Handy if you don't have data. In chapter 15 you will see that you can even use a web service as a source.

CHAPTER 11

■ ■ ■

Script Component Transformation

You can accomplish a lot with standard transformations, but sometimes the Script Component provides an easier solution. For example, a nested if construction is very possible in a derived column, but it becomes unreadable and unmaintainable if you have a lot of levels or conditions. And some features are just not available in the out-of-the-box components. This chapter shows some of the situations where a Script Component is useful.

Script Component Transformation

The basic structure of the Script Component transformation is to give you row-by-row access to the data coming from upstream. The transformation for the output is applied to every row from the input. The transformation can also happen non-synchronously, meaning that every row in the input doesn't require a match in the outgoing row (they can yield zero or more than one row in the output). For example, one folder name input row can return many output rows with the file names from this folder. Controlling the output settings is set up in the Inputs and Outputs pane of the Script Component, as shown in Figure 11-1.

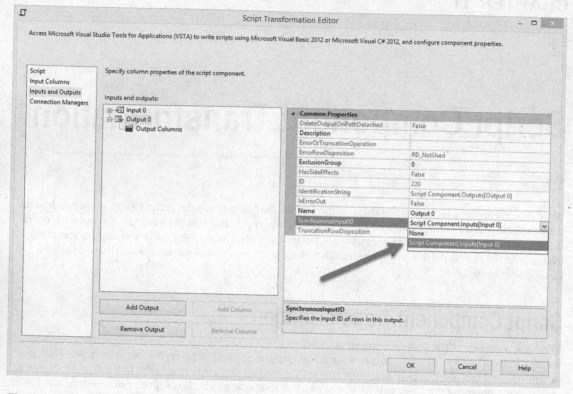

Figure 11-1. *Script Component synchronous input*

If you have several inputs to one component, you can create several outputs and match inputs and outputs or even add some asynchronous outputs.

ProperCase

Sometimes you get data that is really badly formatted and you don't have the opportunity to access the data source to reformat it. You might want to apply proper casing to it. In the following example, you have a customer table where the FirstName and LastName columns are uppercase. You want to reformat them to the proper case.

There is a VB.NET function called StrConv that can convert the case for you. In C# it is a bit more difficult. You start by adding a Data Flow Task to your package and then use the source assistant to fetch data.

The Source

To keep things simple, create a table in the APRESS_SSIS_Scripting database called Chapter_11 with the following definition:

```
CREATE TABLE [dbo].[Chapter11](
        [ID] [int] IDENTITY(1,1) NOT NULL,
        [FirstName] [nvarchar](50) NULL,
        [LastName] [nvarchar](50) NULL,
        [YearlyIncome] [int] NULL,
        [TeamName] [varchar](6) NULL
) ON [PRIMARY]
```

The table has to be populated with some first and last names, all in uppercase. This is the data source.

```
INSERT INTO [dbo].[Chapter11] ([FirstName], [LastName]) VALUES (N'JON', N'YANG')
INSERT INTO [dbo].[Chapter11] ([FirstName], [LastName]) VALUES (N'EUGENE', N'HUANG')
INSERT INTO [dbo].[Chapter11] ([FirstName], [LastName]) VALUES (N'RUBEN', N'TORRES')
INSERT INTO [dbo].[Chapter11] ([FirstName], [LastName]) VALUES (N'CHRISTY', N'ZHU')
INSERT INTO [dbo].[Chapter11] ([FirstName], [LastName]) VALUES (N'ELIZABETH', N'JOHNSON')
INSERT INTO [dbo].[Chapter11] ([FirstName], [LastName]) VALUES (N'JULIO', N'RUIZ')
INSERT INTO [dbo].[Chapter11] ([FirstName], [LastName]) VALUES (N'JANET', N'ALVAREZ')
```

■ **Note** The source code for Chapter 11 contains the table schema and a script to populate the table.

The Script Transformation

You start by adding a Data Flow Task to the surface of the package. In this Data Flow Task, add an OLE DB source component pointing to the table that you just created: "Chapter_11".

Add a Script Component named SCR_TRA_ProperCasing, as shown in Figure 11-2. In the Input pane, check the columns that you want to change, and change their usage type to ReadWrite (ReadOnly being the default). Connect the Script Component to the output of the OLE DB source component.

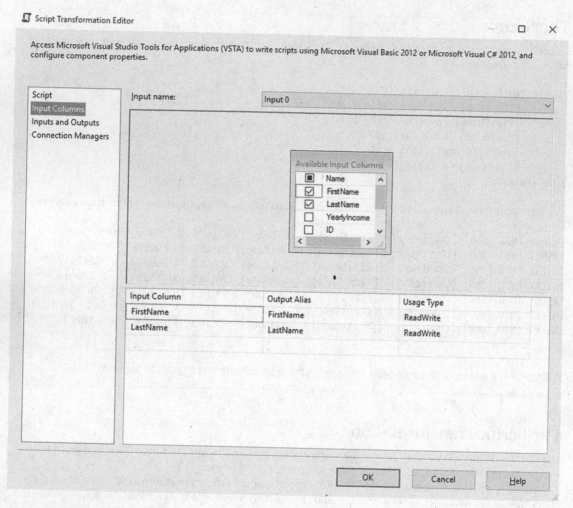

Figure 11-2. ReadWrite variables

In the VSTA script that you create, you need to locate the Input0_ProcessInputRow method and perform some string transformations.

C# doesn't have a built-in method for transforming strings to ProperCase, so you need to find a way to do that in C#. The simplest way may be to convert everything to lowercase and then apply the TitleCase method on the lowercase strings.

```
//Apply lower case first
string firstName = Row.FirstName.ToLower();
string lastName = Row.LastName.ToLower();

// The actual Proper Casing
Row.FirstName = new System.Globalization.CultureInfo("en").TextInfo.ToTitleCase(firstName);
Row.LastName = new System.Globalization.CultureInfo("en").TextInfo.ToTitleCase(lastName);
```

■ **Note** Another way to do this is to add a reference to the Visual Basic DLL in the custom namespaces and call the VBScript method from C#. Mixing programming languages is not really an elegant way in our opinion.

The solution in VB.NET is similar to that in C#:

```
Row.FirstName = StrConv(Row.FirstName, VbStrConv.ProperCase)
Row.LastName = StrConv(Row.LastName, VbStrConv.ProperCase)
```

Now that you've written the script, you can add a multicast to the data flow and connect it to the Script Component output. Add a data viewer to the connection between the two; Figure 11-3 shows the results.

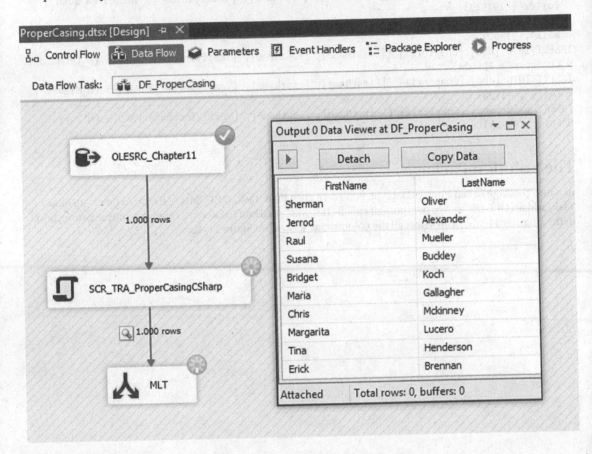

Figure 11-3. Proper casing

Encrypting and Decrypting Data

Sometimes you want to extract data from a table or a file, but you wish to encrypt the data before exporting it so that sensitive information is present but not exposed. For example, Social Security numbers, passwords, or salaries. At a later point, you might want to decrypt the data to show the original value.

For this purpose, use the YearlyIncome column from the table that you created in the previous example, which you need to encrypt, and at some point, decrypt.

Then you add some data to the table:

```
INSERT INTO [dbo].[Chapter11] ([FirstName], [LastName], [YearlyIncome]) VALUES (N'Leonardo',
N'Mc Cormick', 145872)
INSERT INTO [dbo].[Chapter11] ([FirstName], [LastName], [YearlyIncome]) VALUES (N'Josh',
N'Cortez', 292927)
INSERT INTO [dbo].[Chapter11] ([FirstName], [LastName], [YearlyIncome]) VALUES (N'Andres',
N'Wall', 318002)
INSERT INTO [dbo].[Chapter11] ([FirstName], [LastName], [YearlyIncome]) VALUES (N'Leonard',
N'Chambers', 255004)
INSERT INTO [dbo].[Chapter11] ([FirstName], [LastName], [YearlyIncome]) VALUES (N'Miguel',
N'Kelly', 71128)
INSERT INTO [dbo].[Chapter11] ([FirstName], [LastName], [YearlyIncome]) VALUES (N'Jerry',
N'Fox', 180525)
```

The Solution Package

In a new package called EncryptDecrypt, you add a Data Flow Task, DFT_EncryptData. In this Data Flow Task, add an OLE DB source component called OLE_SRC_GetDataToEncrypt. Point the source connection to the Chapter 11 table and select all the columns, as shown on Figure 11-4.

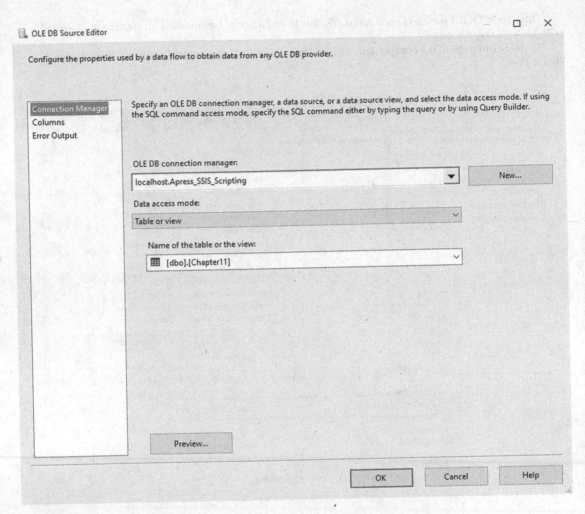

Figure 11-4. *OLE DB source connection window*

There are two kinds of encryption that you can perform with the .NET Framework: *symmetric encryption* and *asymmetric encryption*.

They are performed using different processes. Symmetric encryption is performed on streams and is therefore useful to encrypt large amounts of data. Asymmetric encryption is performed on a small number of bytes and is therefore useful only for small amounts of data. Since you are dealing with single columns, row by row, you will use asymmetric encryption.

Symmetric encryption is typically used for encrypting an entire file.

Chapter 8 has some considerations about encrypting and decrypting entire files using Script Tasks.

Variables

The first thing you need to do encryption is an encryption key. Create a string variable called EncryptionKey and assign its value to a top-secret encryption key using a classic pangram: "The quick fox jumps over the lazy dog."

Once the OLE DB source is configured, it's time to add a Script Component for transformation; call it SCR_TRA_EncryptIncome.

In the Script page of the component, add the User::EncryptionKey variable as Read-only, as shown in Figure 11-5.

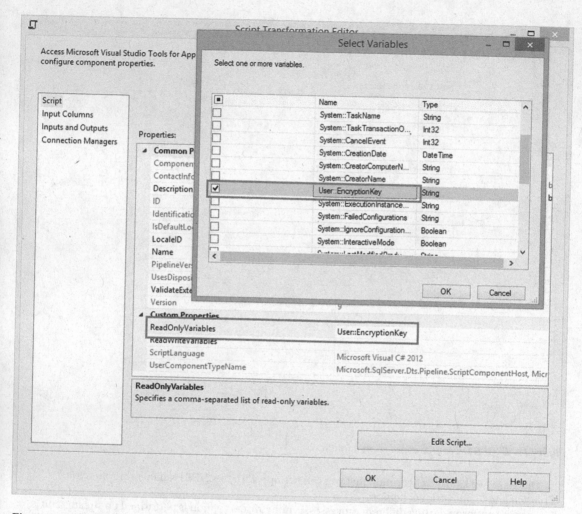

Figure 11-5. *ReadOnly variable*

In the Input Columns page of the component, select YearlyIncome, the column that you want to encrypt (see Figure 11-6).

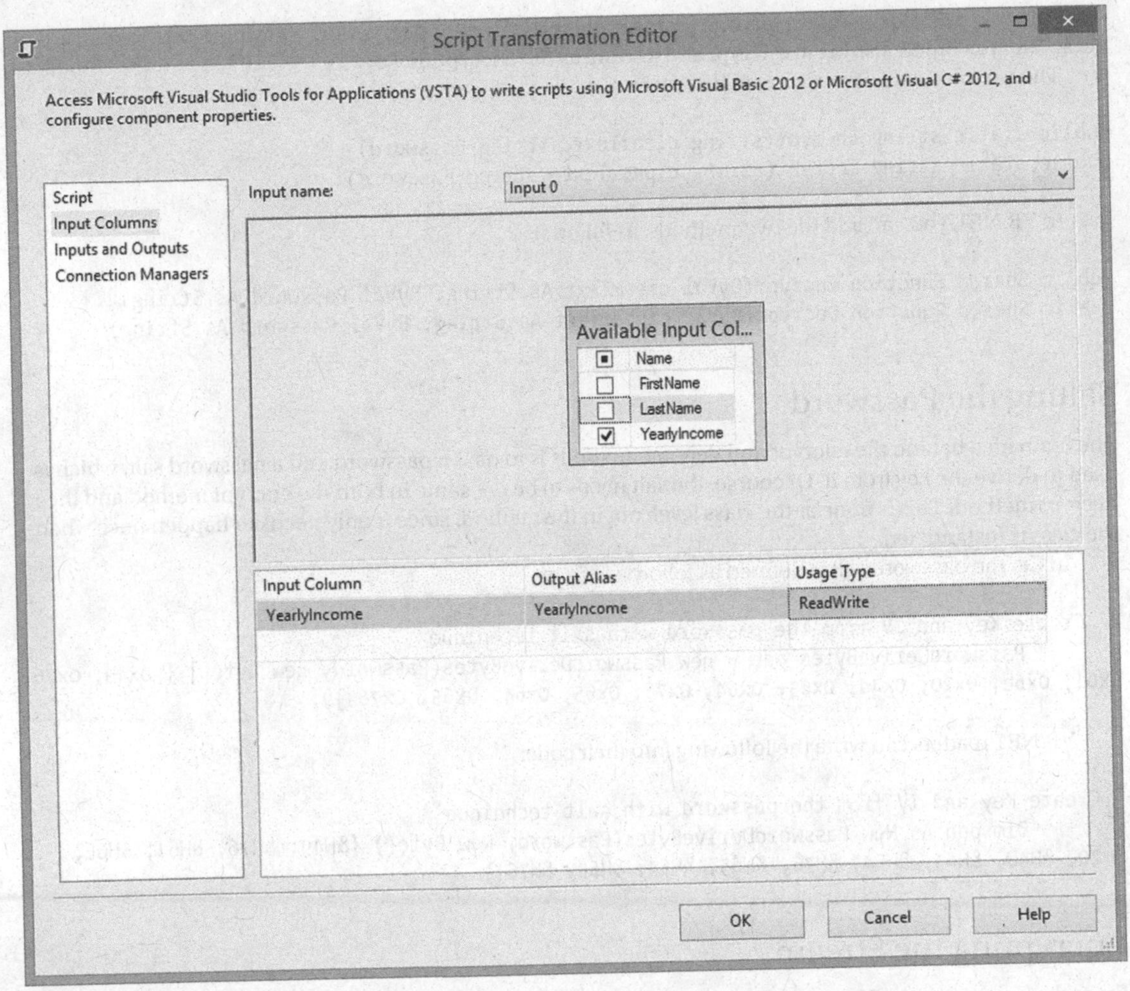

Figure 11-6. Script Transformation Editor input page

The Script

Click the Edit Script… button and start VSTA. First of all, you can remove the methods that you don't need in the autogenerated class: PreExecute and PostExecute.

Let's add the namespaces that you need for encrypting and decrypting text. Here is the beginning of the script in C#:

```
#region CustomNamespaces
using System.IO;
using System.Security.Cryptography;
#endregion
```

And here is the VB.NET version:

```
Imports System.IO
Imports System.Security.Cryptography
```

Add two methods to the script: one for encryption and one for decryption. They both take two parameters as input: a string to encrypt and a string as the encryption key.

The two methods have the same interface:

```
public static string Encrypt(string clearText, string Password)
public static string Decrypt(string cipherText, string Password)
```

In VB.NET, you can add the two methods, as follows:

```
Public Shared Function Encrypt(ByVal clearText As String, ByVal Password As String)
Public Shared Function Decrypt(ByVal cipherText As String, ByVal Password As String)
```

Salting the Password

The main idea behind the encrypt and decrypt methods is to pass a password and a password salt, which is used to derive the key from it. Of course, the salt needs to be the same in both the encrypt method and the decrypt method. This is done at the class level, not in the method, since it only needs to happen once when the class is instantiated.

In C#, the password salt is defined as follows:

```
// Create Key and IV from the password with salt technique
        PasswordDeriveBytes pdb = new PasswordDeriveBytes(Password, new byte[] { 0x49, 0x76,
0x61, 0x6e, 0x20, 0x4d, 0x65, 0x64, 0x76, 0x65, 0x64, 0x65, 0x76 });
```

VB.NET readers can write the following into their code:

```
' Create Key and IV from the password with salt technique
        Dim pdb As New PasswordDeriveBytes(Password, New Byte() {&H49, &H76, &H61, &H6E,
&H20, &H4D, &H65, &H64, &H76, &H65, &H64, &H65, &H76})
```

Encrypting the Stream

From there you create a CryptoStream with a target stream (MemoryStream), an encryption algorithm (for simplicity, you are using the Rijndael algorithm, but others are available), and the mode of the stream. The CryptoStreamMode is set to Write for both encrypting and decrypting the values.

Here is the C# code to create the stream:

```
// Create a CryptoStream
        CryptoStream cs = new CryptoStream(ms, alg.CreateDecryptor(), CryptoStreamMode.Write);
```

The VB.NET implementation is as follows:

```
' Create a CryptoStream
        Dim cs As CryptoStream = New CryptoStream(ms, alg.CreateEncryptor(),
                            CryptoStreamMode.Write)
```

The only difference between encryption and decryption happens once you have written to the MemoryStream.

Encrypting Data

For encryption, you need to convert the byte array to a Base64 string. Do that from C# as follows:

```
// return the Encypted data as a String
        return Convert.ToBase64String(encryptedData);
Perform the same conversion from VB.NET using the following: ' return the Encypted data as a String
        Encrypt = Convert.ToBase64String(encryptedData)
```

Decrypting Data

For decryption, you need to convert your content back to a regular human-readable string. In C#, write this:

```
// return the Decypted data as a String
        return System.Text.Encoding.Unicode.GetString(decryptedData);
```

Whereas in VB.NET, you can write this:

```
' return the Decypted data as a String
        Decrypt = System.Text.Encoding.Unicode.GetString(decryptedData)
```

■ **Note**   The whole script is available in the downloadable code for Chapter 11.

If you add a multicast to the output of the Script Component transformation, you are able to add a data viewer and inspect the returned data to ensure that everything is decrypted as it should. Figure 11-7 shows the results of the script.

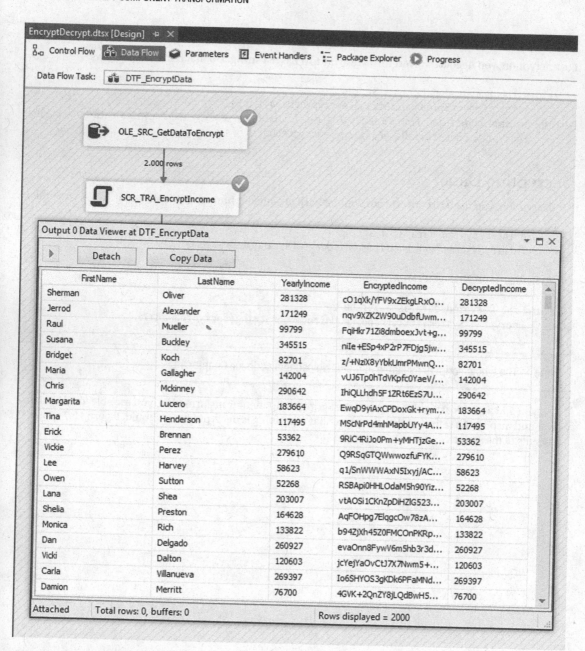

Figure 11-7. Encrypted and decrypted income

Encryption and decryption can be performed in many different ways. You have only scratched the surface of the subject, and one single example is far from enough to do it justice.

If you are interested in more information about the cryptographic capabilities in .NET, we encourage you to have a greater look at the system cryptography namespace on MSDN at https://msdn.microsoft.com/en-us/library/System.Security.Cryptography(v=vs.110).aspx.

Comparing Rows

Continuing with the employee income example, let's say that each employee is part of a team and you want to be able to check who gets the highest income in the team and also what the income difference is between the highest paid member and the other members of the team.

Let's distribute the employees into ten different teams.

```
UPDATE dbo.Chapter11 SET TeamName = 'Team ' + CAST(RIGHT(ID,1) AS VARCHAR(1))
```

On the design surface of a blank package, add a DFT_CompareRows data flow. In this data flow, add an OLE DB source connection and connect to the APRESS_SSIS_Scripting database. To do a row-by-row comparison, you need to sort the input first by TeamName and then by Income, so you need to have the Data Access mode set to SQL Command and the command text set as follows:

```
SELECT [FirstName]
      ,[LastName]
      ,[YearlyIncome]
      ,[ID]
      ,[TeamName]

  FROM [dbo].[Chapter11]
ORDER BY TeamName, YearlyIncome DESC
```

On the Columns page, select all columns, as shown in Figure 11-8.

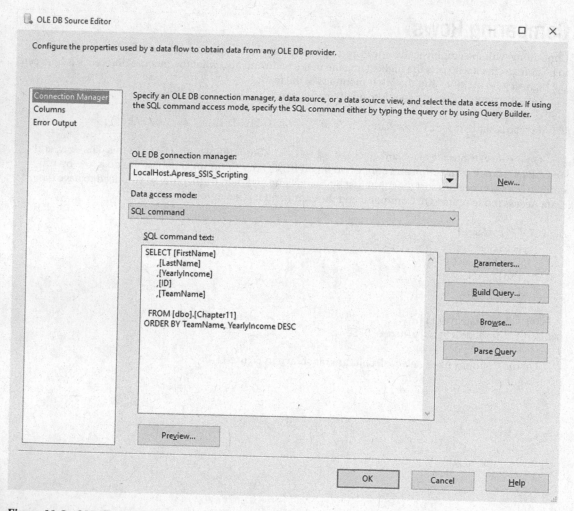

Figure 11-8. OLE DB Source Editor

You then add a Script Component for transformation (renamed to SCR_TRA_CompareRows) to the data flow and connect it to the OLE DB Source output.

On the Script Component Inputs Columns page, you need to add the YearlyIncome and TeamName as ReadOnly input columns, because you will need them in the script itself.

Next, add two columns of type DT_I4 (four-bytes signed integer) called HighestIncome and IncomeDifference to Output0. These are the columns you are going to write to in the script.

Click Edit Script... in the Script page of the component and then start VSTA. First, remove the methods you don't use: PostExecute and PreExecute. The important method in this case is Input0_ProcessInputRow, where you can compare the data, row by row, that passes through.

Because the input is sorted, you can rest assured that comparing row-wise will work. This is a very important point in this sort of script. It is crucial to the success of the comparison that the input be sorted.

The following is the C# version of the script to compare rows:

```
// Compare current row with previous row
        if (Row.TeamName == teamname)
        {
            //match compare Income with previous income
            Row.IncomeDifference = Row.YearlyIncome - highestincome;
        }
        else
        {
            //TeamName don't match, this is the first row of a new team
            highestincome = Row.YearlyIncome;
        }
        //Store current row values in variables for the next row.
        teamname = Row.TeamName;
        Row.HighestIncome = highestincome;
```

Whereas in VB.NET the code is as follows:

```
' Compare current row with previous row
If Row.TeamName = teamname Then
        'match compare Income with previous income
        Row.IncomeDifference = Row.YearlyIncome - highestincome
Else
        'TeamName don't match, this is the first row of a new team
        highestincome = Row.YearlyIncome
End If
'Store current row values in variables for the next row.
teamname = Row.TeamName
Row.HighestIncome = highestincome
```

By adding a multicast and a data viewer to the data flow, you are able to check that the script is working. Figure 11-9 is an illustration of the result from a much larger sample of data than the one in the chapter's source code.

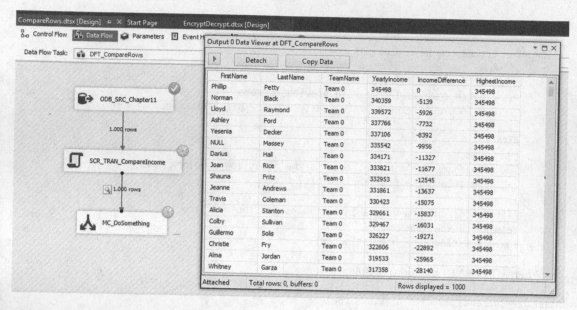

Figure 11-9. *Data viewer with result*

IsNumeric

The .NET Framework has many capabilities for testing values for datatypes, null values, and such. Although SQL Server 2012 gives you the ability to use some of these features, such as TryCast and the like, but because you don't always work with the most recent versions of SQL Server, you don't always have the opportunity to use this method. This is where the ability to use a Script Component comes in handy.

For demonstration purposes, let's use a simple text file with a single column as input. Here's the data:

```
TextNumber
1
42
3
4
Hello world!
7
I love SSIS
```

As you can see, a few of these rows are not numeric.

The testing implementation for numeric values is simple. Add a new package and a data flow to the surface.

In this data flow, add Flat File Source: FFS_TextNumbers and a connection manager pointing to the preceding text document. Leave all the configurations at their default values. Click the Columns page to confirm the values. Figure 11-10 shows the Flat File Connection Manager setup.

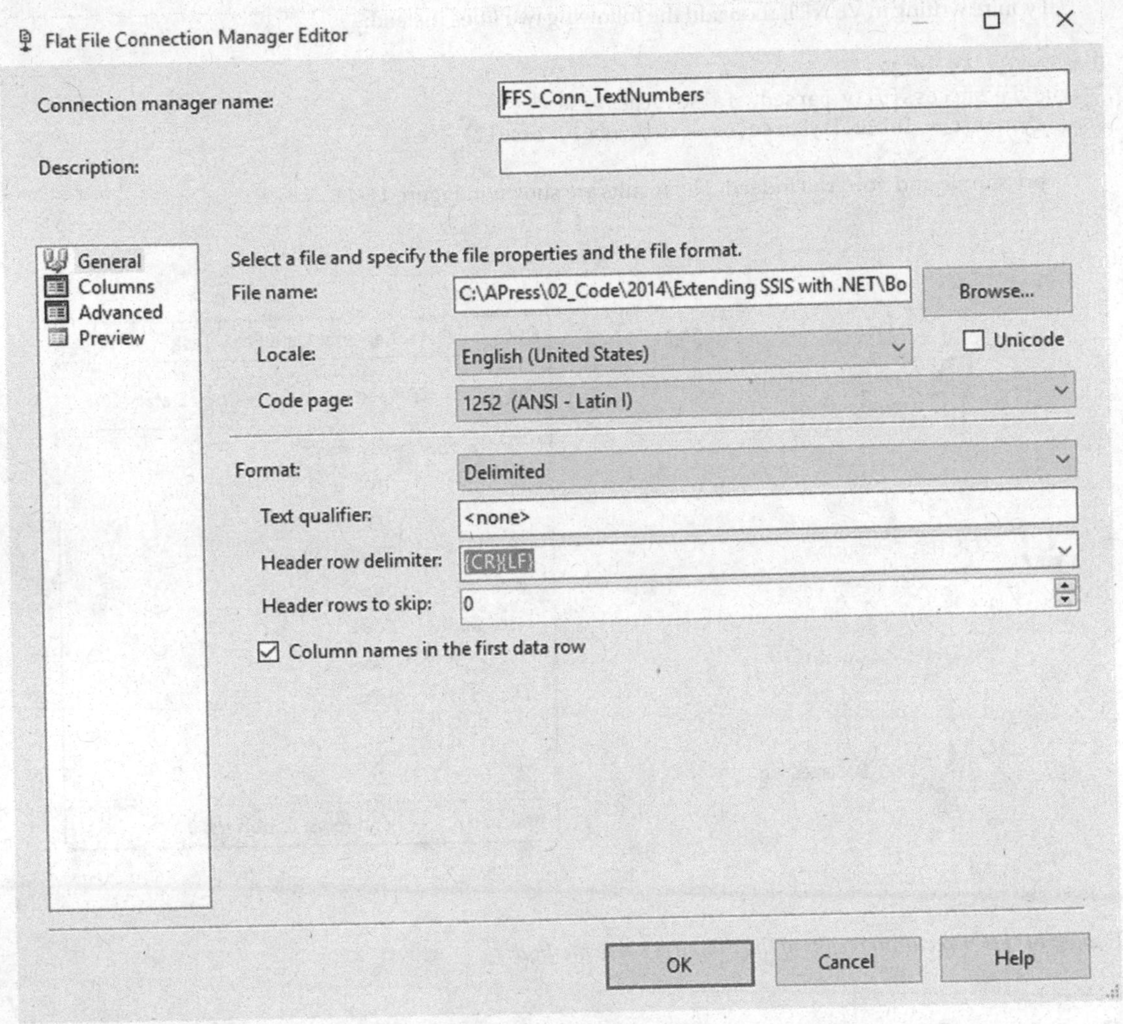

Figure 11-10. *Flat File Connection Manager Editor*

Once you have the flat file source, you add a Script Component for transformation called
SCR_TRA_TextNumber.

On the Inputs page of the component, make the TextNumber column ReadOnly.

On the Inputs and Outputs Columns page, add an output column called isNumeric of type Boolean
(DT_BOOL) to store the result.

After clicking the Edit Script… button on the Script page, remove the unnecessary PreExecute and
PostExecute methods, and add the following two lines of code to the Input0_ProcessInputRow method:

```
//Check if the value is numeric
int result;
Row.isNumeric = Int32.TryParse(Row.TextNumber, out result);
```

If you're writing in VB.NET, then add the following two lines instead:

```
Dim result As Int32
' true if successfully parsed, false otherwise
Row.isNumeric = Int32.TryParse(Row.TextNumber, result)
```

Very simple and powerful indeed. The results are shown in Figure 11-11.

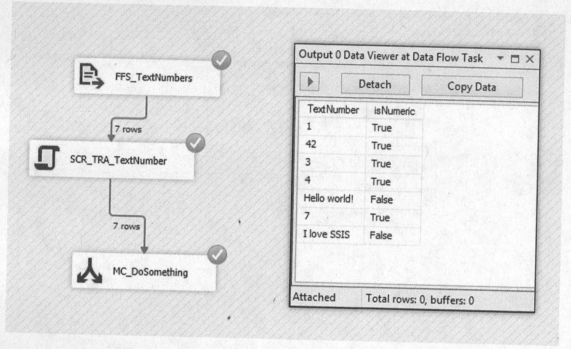

Figure 11-11. Execution results of the int32.TryParse method

Creating Surrogate Keys

There are situations where you need to generate a unique consecutive number as a key of some sort in the data flow. It can also be used for ranking, eliminating duplicates, and so forth. A script transformation is the ideal solution in situations where data comes from a semistructured source or, for example, from a text file with no knowledge of consecutive identities or row numbers.

Let's build further on the example from the previous section, where you checked for a numeric value. Let's suppose that you want to make sure that all the numeric values that you get have a row number added to the row.

■ **Note**   If you haven't seen the solution for the previous section, the code is available for download on this book's web site.

On the Input and Output Columns page, in the Script Component called SCR_TRA_TextNumber, add an output column of type four-byte signed integer [DT_I4] called RowNumber.

Open the script by clicking the Edit Script… button. In a C# solution, add the following lines of code right under the class declaration:

```
int rownumber = 0; //at class level it will retain its value for each row
```

VB.NET readers, do this:

```
Dim rownumber As Integer = 0
```

Replace the existing code in the Input0_ProcessInputrow method with the following:

```
int result;
bool isNumeric = Int32.TryParse(Row.TextNumber, out result);
if (isNumeric)
{
    Row.isNumeric = isNumeric;
    rownumber++;
    Row.RowNumber = rownumber;
}
```

If using VB.NET, write the following lines:

```
Dim result As Integer
Dim isNumeric As Boolean = Int32.TryParse(Row.TextNumber, result)
If isNumeric Then
        Row.isNumeric = isNumeric
        rownumber += 1
        Row.RowNumber = rownumber
End If
```

When running the package, you can see that a consecutive row number has been added to all the rows that are numeric. All the non-numeric rows have a 0 value for the RowNumber column. The result is shown in Figure 11-12.

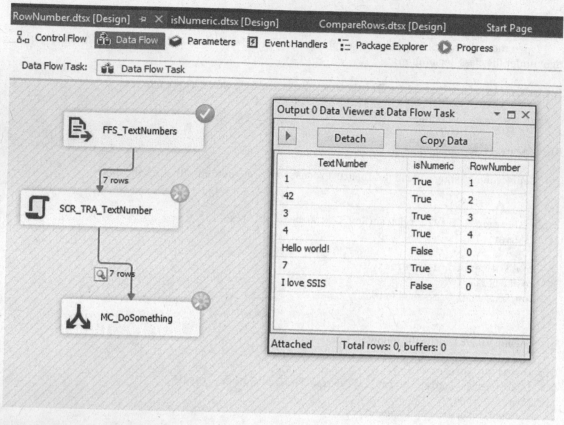

Figure 11-12. RowNumber appended to the numeric rows

Once again, a Script Component can help you perform tasks on data that is not straightforward or that is not available in SSIS.

Creating GUIDS

There are no built-in functions or expressions in SSIS to create a new GUID. If you already have a GUID stored as a string, then you can use a cast in the derived column to convert it into a real GUID datatype, or if you have an SQL Server source, then you can use the NEWID() function in your source query.

Just like in the previous example where you created a RowNumber, you can create a GUID with a Script Component in .NET with a single line of code.

Creating the Package

Start by creating a new SSIS package and add a data flow on the surface. On this data flow, add a Flat File Source connection pointing to the file from the previous examples, as shown in Figure 11-13.

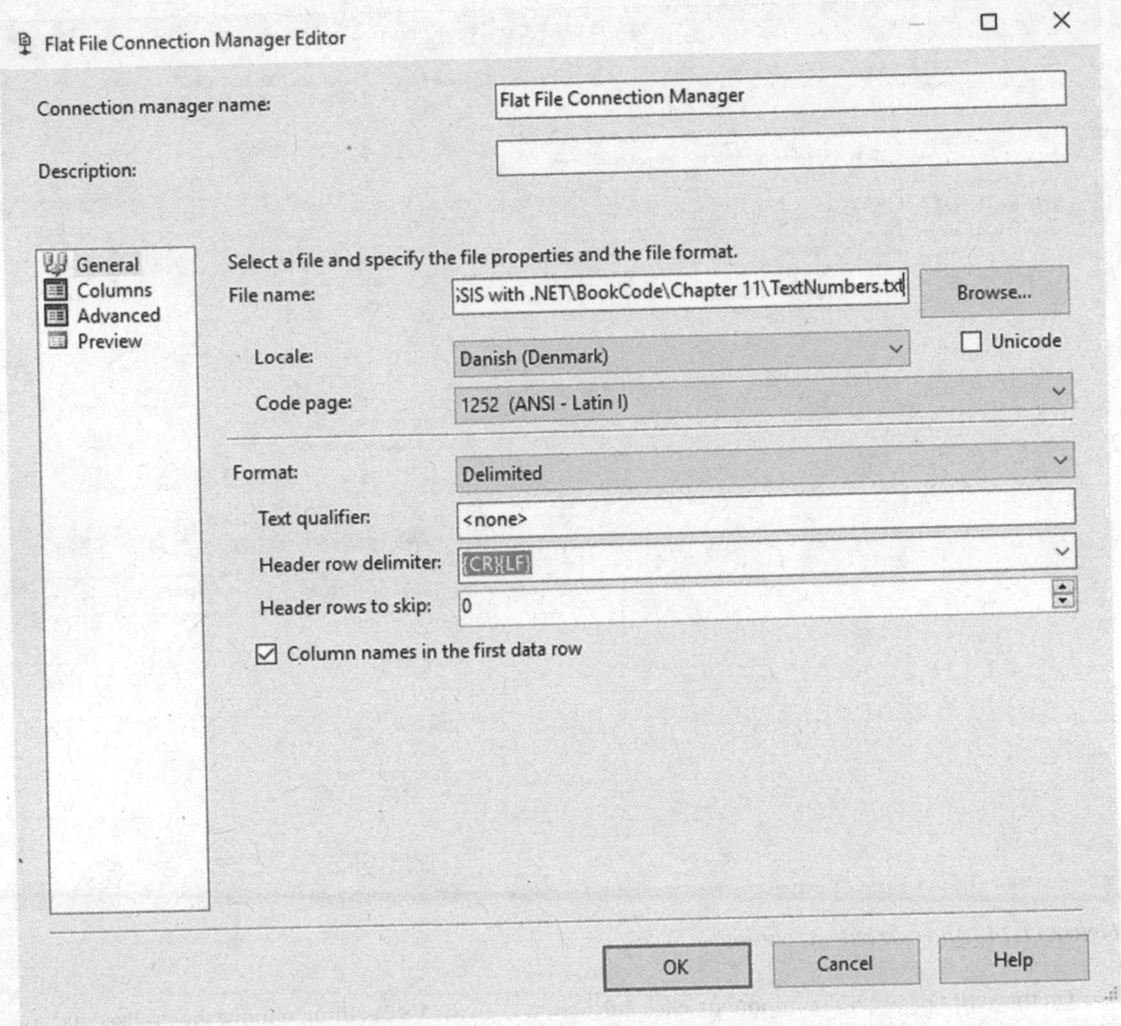

Figure 11-13. *Flat File Connection Manager configuration*

Add Script Component

Add a Script Component after the source and select Transformation as the script type. Connect it to your other components and name it SCR_CreateGUID. On the Inputs and Outputs page, go to Output 0, choose Output Columns, and then add a new column called RowGUID. Change its type to DT_GUID (unique identifier), as shown in Figure 11-14.

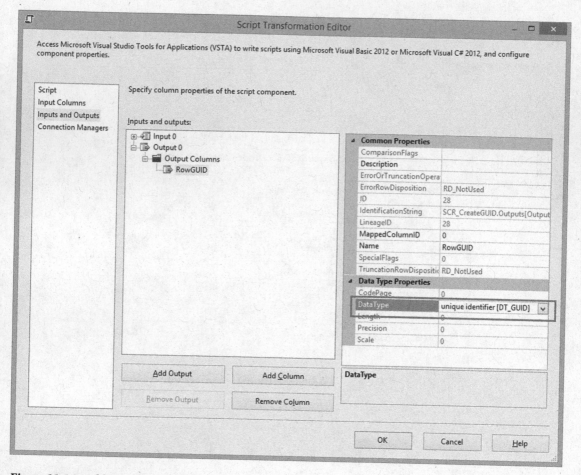

Figure 11-14. *Add new output column*

On the Script page of the component, click Edit Script…. In the VSTA editor, remove the PreExecute and PostExecute methods, which you don't need. In the Input0_ProcessInputRow method, add the single line of C# code needed to create a random GUID and assign it to the column you created previously.

```
//create and assign a GUID
    Row.RowGUID = Guid.NewGuid();
```
In VB.NET, the code is the following: ' Create a Globally Unique Identifier with SSIS
```
  Row.Guid2 = System.Guid.NewGuid()
```

The Results

Close the VSTA editor and the Script Transformation Editor. Add a multicast to the data flow and connect it to the Script Component. If you add a data viewer (by right-clicking the connection between the Script Component and the multicast), you should see the results as shown in Figure 11-15. Since a GUID is globally unique, the GUIDs generated should be different from run to run.

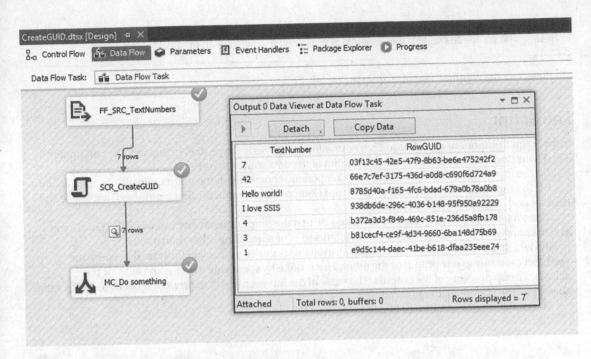

Figure 11-15. Newly added GUID column

Conditional Multicast

When dealing with fact tables in SSIS packages, you might need to handle null values. Furthermore, one of the requirements might be to log the rows that are null for auditing purposes. This is achievable with the built-in components, but it is really cumbersome because it involves Conditional Splits, several multicasts, and a Union All.

This is a situation in which the possibility of the Script Component having several outputs is really practical. There are two benefits to this approach. The first benefit is that you can handle complicated if statements in a more elegant way than with using a lot of conditional transformations; handling all the conditions in one piece of script is more readable than several conditional SSIS expressions. And the second benefit is that a single row can be redirected to multiple outputs, without the need for multicast.

In the following example, you are going through all the rows from a table and redirecting some of them to an output for auditing purposes, because the value of some of the columns have the wrong values (you could also check whether the values exceed a threshold, or have bad quality, or any other particular reason where you want to save some particular rows of data; but this is not part pf the example).

The Data Source

For the data source, you are getting the Chapter 11 data that you used previously. In this table you have the income information for some employees. Since it has been a really good year for the company, management has decided that it wants to increase everyone's income by 20% and at the same time point out everyone whose annual income was less than $200,000.

Start by adding a data flow to a blank package. In this data flow, add an OLE DB source connected to the Chapter 11 table from the book code.

Select all the columns available from the table.

The Script

Add a Script Component and choose Transformation on the Script Type dialog. Rename the component SCR_EnsureIncomeRaise and connect the output of the data source to its input.

On the Input Columns page of the Script Component, choose YearlyIncome as a ReadOnly input column.

On the Inputs and Outputs page of the Script Component, rename the first Output as GiveARaise and add a second output called LessThan200K.

There a few more steps necessary to make sure that the outputs behave as you want. First of all, you need to change the ExclusionGroup of both outputs to 1 (or something other than 0).

By default, all input rows are directed to all available outputs, unless you indicate that you want to redirect each row to one output or the other. This is done by specifying a non-zero value for the ExclusionGroup property of the outputs. The value of the integer doesn't matter but it needs to be the same value for all the specified groups of outputs.

The configuration is shown in Figure 11-16.

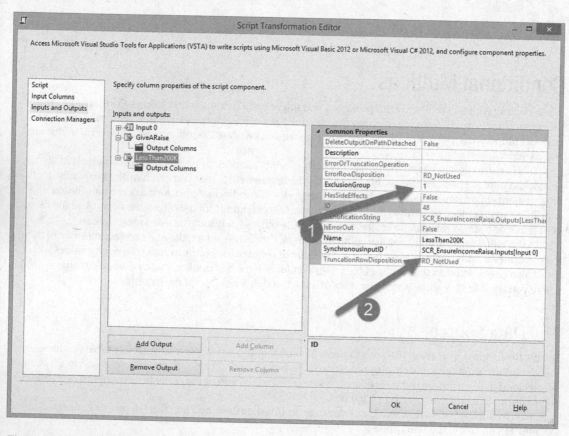

Figure 11-16. Output configuration

The following are the callouts for the configuration:

1. The ExclusionGroup is set to 1 and it needs to be the same value for all the outputs.

2. The SynchronousOuputID setting of 0 (none) creates an asynchronous output, where the output rows don't have any relationship with the input rows, thus creating new memory buffers and copying values to them. Because not all the rows from the output buffer will come to this output, this allows us to implement conditional redirect.

Once this is set up, open the script editor by clicking Edit Script... on the Script page. Remove the PreExecute and PostExecute methods. Then enter the following C# code:

In the Input0_ProcessInputRow method of the Script add these few lines:

```
if (Row.YearlyIncome < 200000)
{
    Row.DirectRowToLessThan200K();
}

    Row.DirectRowToGiveARaise();
```

Or the following VB.NET code:

```
If Row.YearlyIncome < 200000 Then
        Row.DirectRowToLessThan200K()
End If

Row.DirectRowToGiveARaise()
```

Tell the script to only use the rows where YearlyIncome is less than 200000 in one output, but use all the rows in the other output. As you can see, the logic is really easy to implement and much more readable than when using the SSIS Conditional Split.

Close the Script Component and add a derived column DER_GiveARaise to the data flow. The derived column is used to increase (and replace) the YearlyIncome by 20%. The configuration is shown in Figure 11-17.

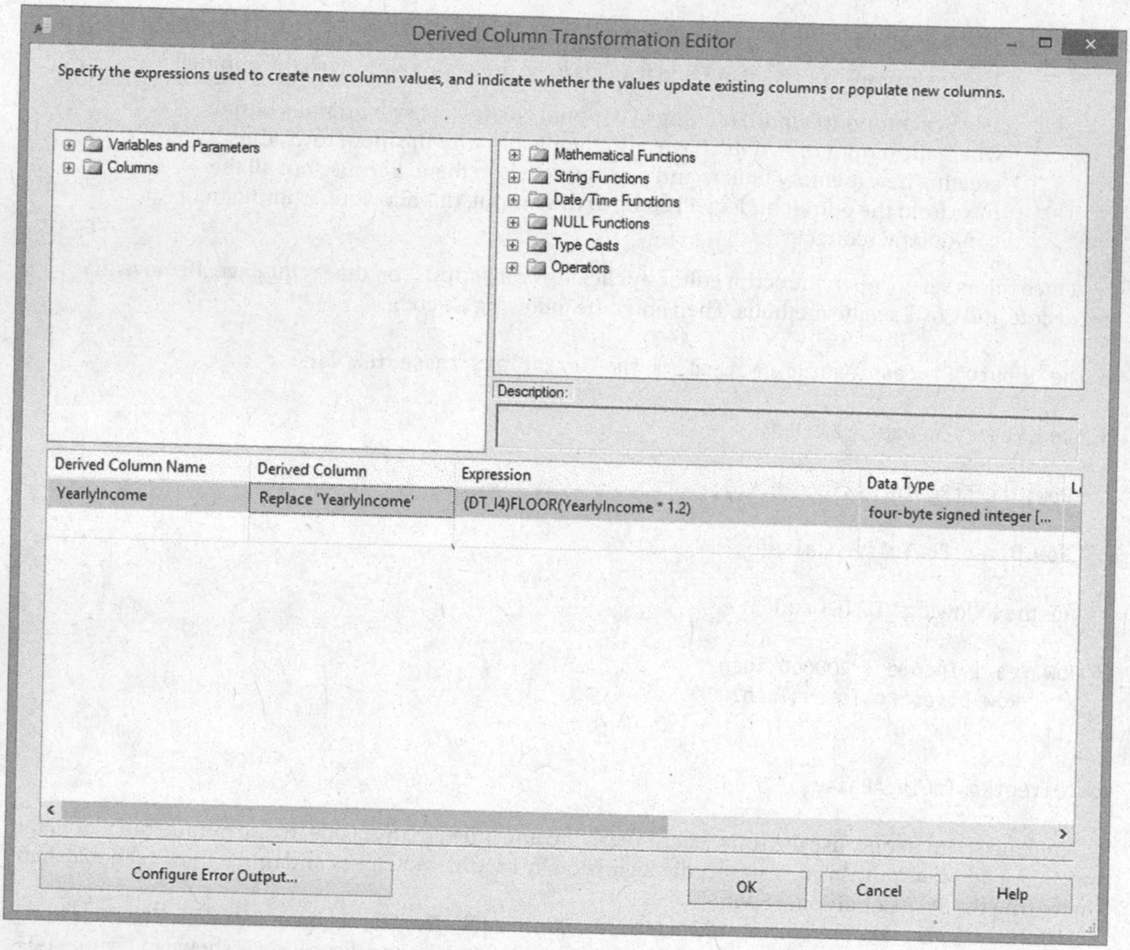

Figure 11-17. *Derived column use to increase by 20%*

Connect the derived column input to the GiveARaise output of the Script Component.

Once this is done, add a multicast to the output of the derived column and another multicast to the LessThan200K output of the Script Component. By adding data viewers to multicasts connections, you are able to see the rows with the YearlyIncome that match the condition set up in the Script Component and the rows with the increased YearlyIncome.

Figure 11-18 shows the data viewer after the income raise.

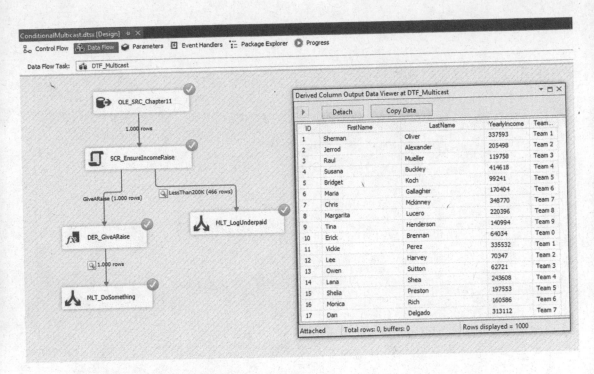

Figure 11-18. All Income raised by 20%

Summary

In this chapter you saw several examples of where a Script Component can perform tasks that were otherwise impossible in SSIS. You also saw examples of how Script Components are more flexible and simpler to use and understand than the built-in tasks.

■ ■ ■

CHAPTER 12

Script Component As Destination

This chapter focuses on the Script Component as a destination. There are a lot of out-of-the-box destinations available, but sometimes you need something special—a custom flat file with extra headers and footers, a record divided over multiple rows, and an XML destination.

But be careful when using the Script Component as a destination. Because records are processed row by row, it is probably not a good idea to insert a lot of data into a database with stored procedure calls or a lot of single query commands. The OLE DB destination with the fast load on is likely a lot faster; and if you really need stored procedure calls, then the OLE DB command it a lot easier to understand and maintain. But for custom text files, the Script Component as a destination is very useful. Web services also have a practical use for the Script Component destination. There are some web service examples in Chapter 15.

Basic Flat File Destination with Header and Footer

The first example is a basic Flat File Destination. It is quite similar to the regular Flat File Destination, but has extra headers and footers. You can extend this example easily to your own needs.

Create a File Connection Manager

Since you don't want to hard-code the file path of the flat file in the script, you will use a File Connection Manager. Create a File Connection Manager to an existing or non-existing file. See Figure 12-1 for an example.

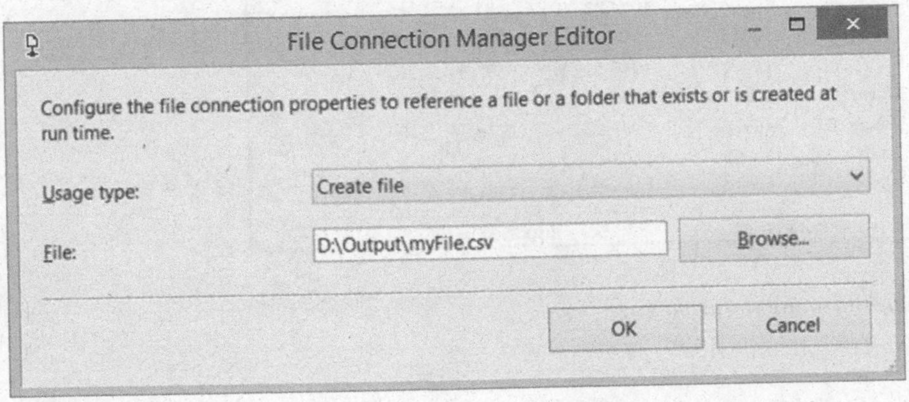

Figure 12-1. *File Connection Manager pointing to CSV file*

Source

For this example, you are using the random test data example from Chapter 10 as a source. You can use the starter package or use your own data as source. The following are the output columns:

- **FirstName** (DT_STR, 1252, 50)
- **LastName** (DT_STR, 1252, 50)
- **EmployeeId** (DT_I4)
- **DateOfBirth** (DT_DATE)
- **Salary** (DT_NUMERIC, 6, 2)
- **Gender** (DT_STR, 1252, 1)

Figure 12-2 shows the random data source starter package for the example in this chapter.

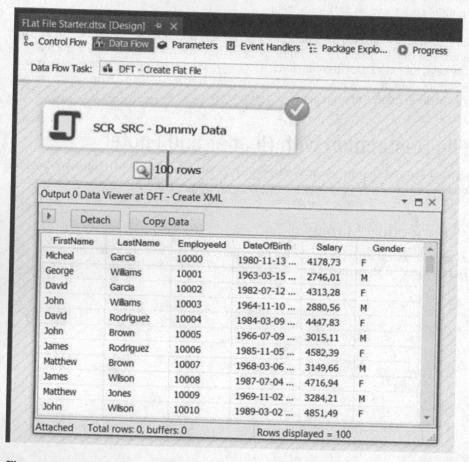

Figure 12-2. Random data source starter package

Script Component

Drag a Script Component to the canvas of the data flow and choose Destination as type as shown in Figure 12-3. Give it a suitable name and connect it to the last transformation in your data flow.

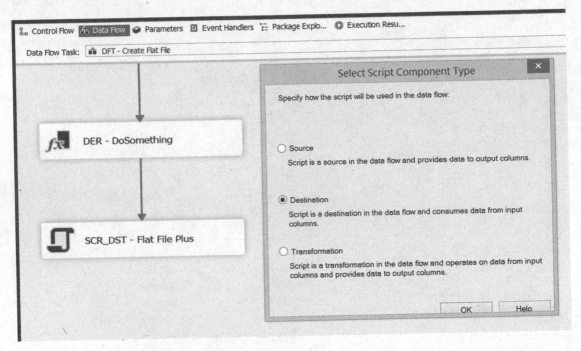

Figure 12-3. *Script Component Type: Destination*

Adding Input Columns

Edit the Script Component and go to the Input Columns page. Select all the columns that you need in your .csv file as shown in Figure 12-4. Columns that start with a number or a punctuation mark should be renamed in the Output Alias column because they are removed with in the script code.

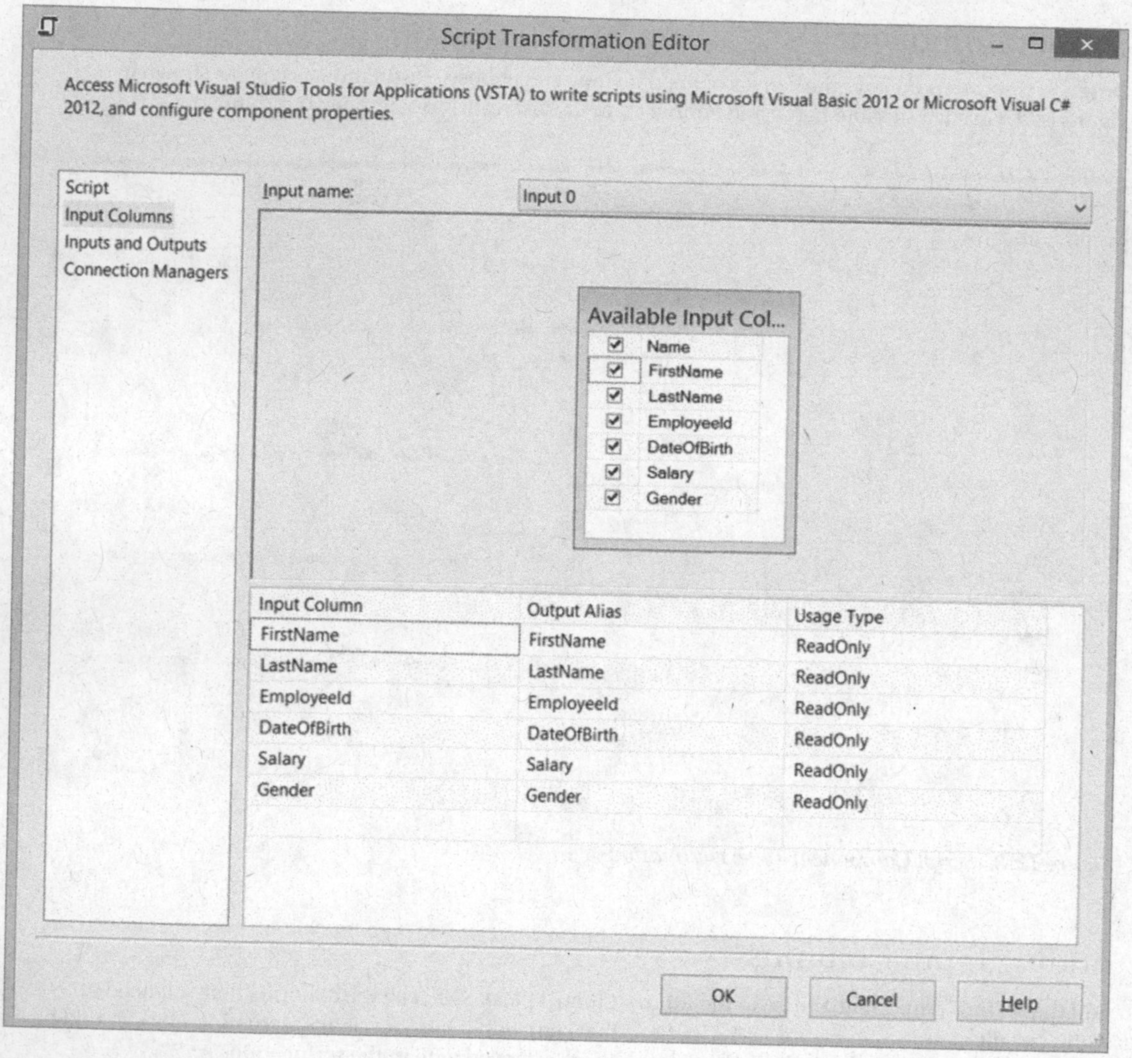

Figure 12-4. *Select the needed Input Column*

The following are the input columns:

- FirstName
- LastName
- EmployeeId
- DateOfBirth
- Salary
- Gender

Selecting Connection Manager

Go to the Connection Manager page and select the newly created File Connection Manager. After adding it as shown in Figure 12-5, name it myFile. You can also add a new Connection Manager via the drop-down list.

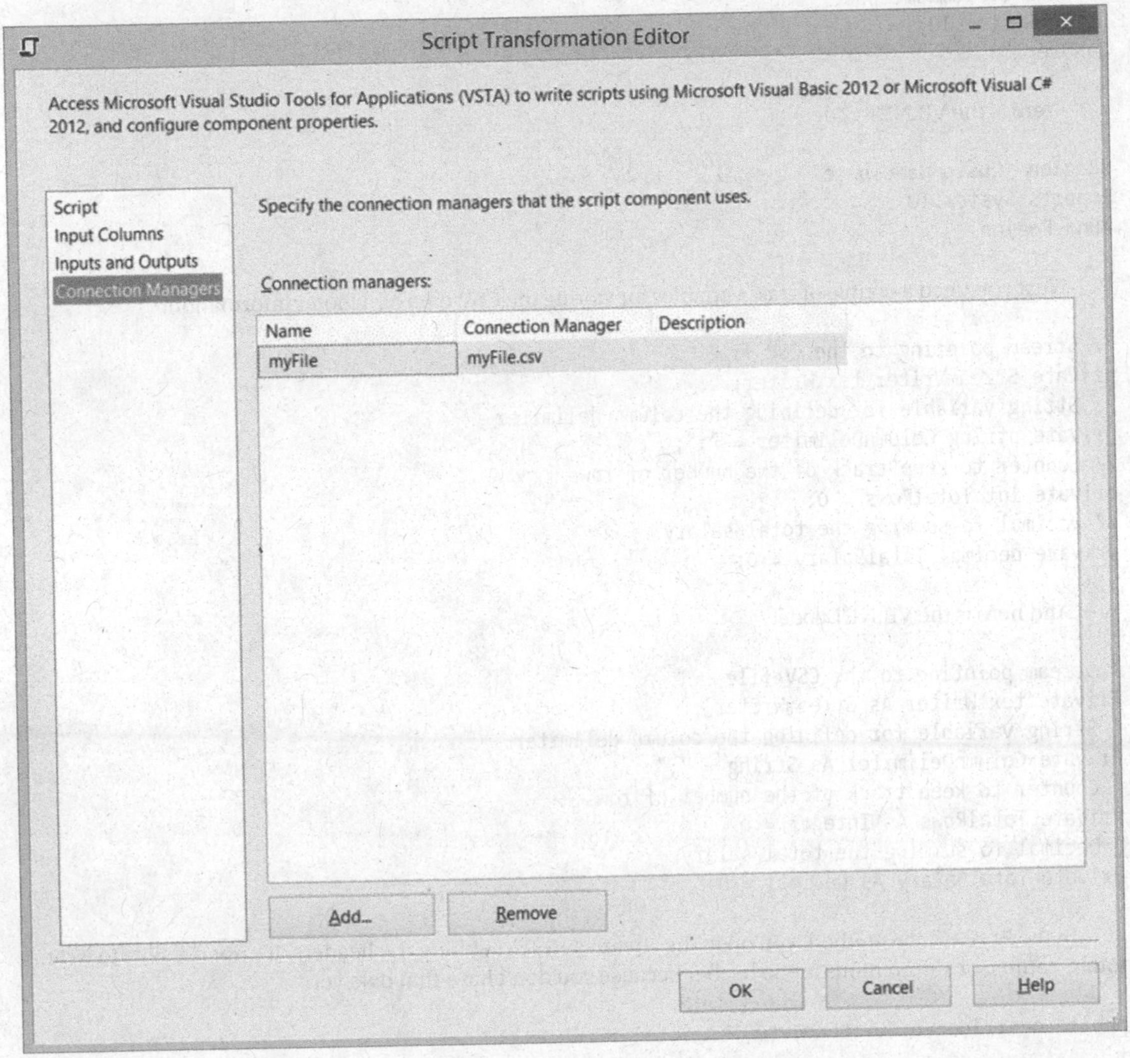

Figure 12-5. *Add Connection Manager*

The Code

Now you can go back to the Script page, and click the Edit Script. . . button to open the VSTA environment. First, you need to add an extra namespace to shorten the code.

```
#region CustomNamespace
using System.IO;
#endregion
```

Here is the VB.NET code:

```
#Region "CustomNamespace"
Imports System.IO
#End Region
```

Next you need a couple of class variables for storing the CSV data and footer information.

```
// Stream pointing to the CSV file
private StreamWriter textWriter;
// String variable for defining the column delimiter
private string ColumnDelimiter = ";";
// Counter to keep track of the number of rows
private int TotalRows = 0;
// Decimal fo summing the total salary
private decimal TotalSalary = 0;
```

And here is the VB.NET code:

```
' Stream pointing to the CSV file
Private textWriter As StreamWriter
' String variable for defining the column delimiter
Private ColumnDelimiter As String = ";"
' Counter to keep track of the number of rows
Private TotalRows As Integer = 0
' Decimal fo summing the total salary
Private TotalSalary As Decimal = 0
```

In the PreExecute method, you open the stream and start writing the headers. It's not possible to write totals, counts, or summations in the header because you don't have that data yet.

```
public override void PreExecute()
{
  // Create a new CSV file and use the
  // filepath from the connection manager
  textWriter = new StreamWriter(
             this.Connections.myFile.AcquireConnection(null).ToString());

  // Write header with current date
  textWriter.WriteLine("ExportDate: " + DateTime.Now.ToShortDateString());
```

```
// Write header with column names
textWriter.Write("EmployeeId" + ColumnDelimiter);
textWriter.Write("FirstName" + ColumnDelimiter);
textWriter.Write("LastName" + ColumnDelimiter);
textWriter.Write("DateOfBirth" + ColumnDelimiter);
textWriter.Write("Gender" + ColumnDelimiter);
textWriter.WriteLine("Salary");
}
```

This is the VB.NET code:

```
Public Overrides Sub PreExecute()
  ' Create a new CSV file and use the
  ' filepath from the connection manager
  textWriter = New StreamWriter( _
              Me.Connections.myFile.AcquireConnection(Nothing).ToString())

  ' Write header with current date
  textWriter.WriteLine("ExportDate: " + DateTime.Now.ToShortDateString())

  ' Write header with column names
  textWriter.Write(Convert.ToString("EmployeeId") & ColumnDelimiter)
  textWriter.Write(Convert.ToString("FirstName") & ColumnDelimiter)
  textWriter.Write(Convert.ToString("LastName") & ColumnDelimiter)
  textWriter.Write(Convert.ToString("DateOfBirth") & ColumnDelimiter)
  textWriter.Write(Convert.ToString("Gender") & ColumnDelimiter)
  textWriter.WriteLine("Salary")
End Sub
```

In the PostExecute method, you are adding headers and closing the .csv file. In this stage of the script, you can use the totals and summations because the Input0_ProcessInputRow method has calculated those.

```
public override void PostExecute()
{
  // Add Footers
  textWriter.WriteLine("Rows: " + TotalRows.ToString());
  textWriter.WriteLine("Total Salary: " + TotalSalary.ToString());

  // Close file
  textWriter.Close();
}
```

And here is the VB.NET code:

```
Public Overrides Sub PostExecute()
  ' Add Footers
  textWriter.WriteLine("Rows: " + TotalRows.ToString())
  textWriter.WriteLine("Total Salary: " + TotalSalary.ToString())

  ' Close file
  textWriter.Close()
End Sub
```

In the Input0_ProcessInputRow method, you are processing all records. Each column value, combined with the column delimiter, is written to the .csv file. The Last column uses a WriteLine instead of a Write to add a row delimiter. This is also the place where you can calculate items that can be used in the header.

```
public override void Input0_ProcessInputRow(Input0Buffer Row)
{
  // Write column values with a column delimiter
  textWriter.Write(Row.EmployeeId.ToString() + ColumnDelimiter);
  textWriter.Write(Row.FirstName.ToString() + ColumnDelimiter);
  textWriter.Write(Row.LastName.ToString() + ColumnDelimiter);
  textWriter.Write(Row.DateOfBirth.ToShortDateString() + ColumnDelimiter);
  textWriter.Write(Row.Gender.ToString() + ColumnDelimiter);
  // Use WriteLine for the last column as row delimiter
  textWriter.WriteLine(Row.Salary.ToString());

  // Calculations for the header
  TotalRows++;
  TotalSalary = TotalSalary + Row.Salary;
}
```

This is the VB.NET code:

```
Public Overrides Sub Input0_ProcessInputRow(ByVal Row As Input0Buffer)
  ' Write column values with a column delimiter
  textWriter.Write(Row.EmployeeId.ToString() & ColumnDelimiter)
  textWriter.Write(Row.FirstName.ToString() & ColumnDelimiter)
  textWriter.Write(Row.LastName.ToString() & ColumnDelimiter)
  textWriter.Write(Row.DateOfBirth.ToShortDateString() & ColumnDelimiter)
  textWriter.Write(Row.Gender.ToString() & ColumnDelimiter)
  ' Use WriteLine for the last column as row delimiter
  textWriter.WriteLine(Row.Salary.ToString())

  ' Calculations for the header
  TotalRows += 1
  TotalSalary = TotalSalary + Row.Salary
End Sub
```

The Results

Now run the package and check the result of your flat file. Note that this is a very basic example, but very easy to extend to your own needs. Figure 12-6 shows our results in this chapter's example.

```
ExportDate: 8-7-2015
EmployeeId;FirstName;LastName;DateOfBirth;Gender;Salary
10000;Micheal;Garcia;13-11-1980;F;4178,73
10001;George;Williams;15-3-1963;M;2746,01
10002;David;Garcia;12-7-1982;F;4313,28
10003;John;Williams;10-11-1964;M;2880,56
...
10096;James;Rodriguez;10-7-1986;F;4637,22
10097;Matthew;Jones;8-11-1968;M;3204,50
10098;John;Wilson;7-3-1988;F;4771,77
10099;Matthew;Jones;7-7-1970;M;3339,05
Rows: 100
Total Salary: 354888,90
```

Figure 12-6. Part of the text file

Basic XML Destination

Unfortunately, there is still no out-of-the-box XML File Destination available. If your source is an SQL Server table, then you could use a FOR XML query in an OLE DB Source Component and then write the results to a headerless Flat File Destination. If you have a different source or a lot of transformations, then the FOR XML query is not usable. The Script Component could help you out here.

Creating a File Connection Manager

Since you don't want to hard-code the file path of the XML File in the script, you will use a File Connection Manager. Create a File Connection Manager to an existing or non-existing file. Figure 12-7 shows an example.

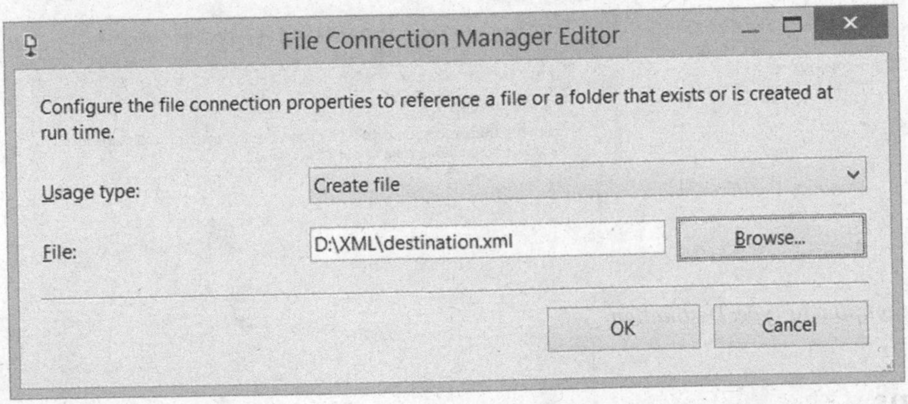

Figure 12-7. File Connection Manager pointing to XML file

Source

For this example, you are using the random test data from the previous Flat File Destination example, which came from Chapter 10. The following are the output columns:

- **FirstName** (DT_STR, 1252, 50)
- **LastName** (DT_STR, 1252, 50)
- **EmployeeId** (DT_I4)
- **DateOfBirth** (DT_DATE)
- **Salary** (DT_NUMERIC, 6, 2)
- **Gender** (DT_STR, 1252, 1)

Script Component

Drag a Script Component to the canvas of the data flow and choose Destination as the type, as shown in Figure 12-8. Give it a suitable name and connect it to the last transformation in your data flow.

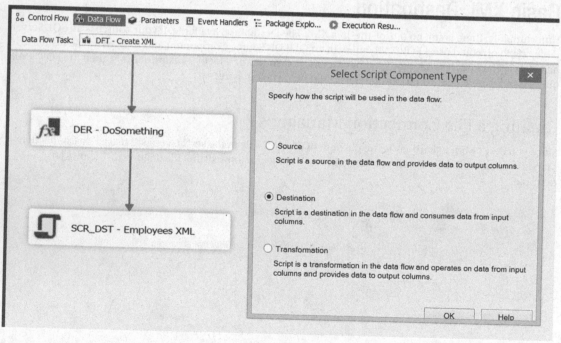

Figure 12-8. Script Component Type: Destination

Input Columns

Edit the Script Component and go to the Input Columns page. Select all the columns you need in your XML, as shown in Figure 12-9. Columns that start with a number or a punctuation mark should be renamed in the Output Alias column because they are removed with in the script code.

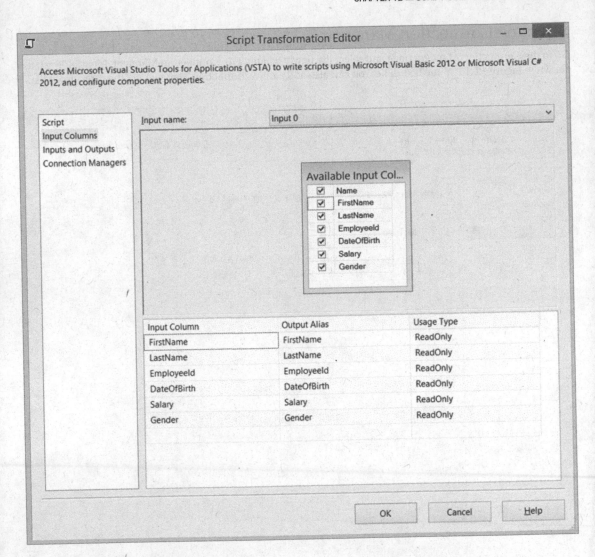

Figure 12-9. Select needed Input Column

The following are the input columns:

- FirstName

- LastName

- EmployeeId

- DateOfBirth

- Salary

- Gender

Selecting Connection Manager

Go to the Connection Manager page and select the newly created File Connection Manager. After adding it as shown in Figure 12-10, name it xmlFile. You can also add a new Connection Manager via the drop-down list.

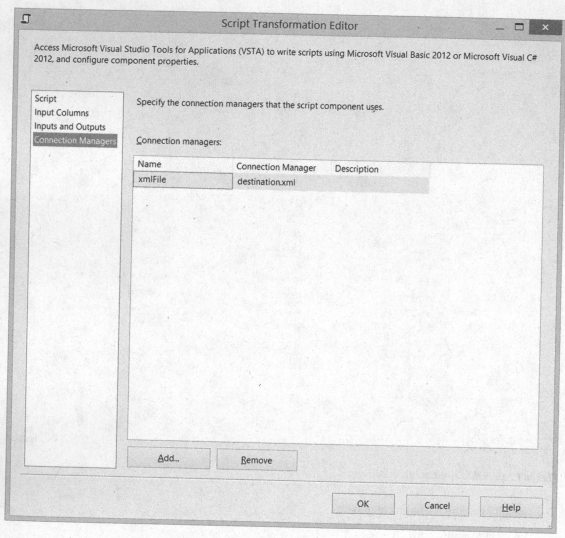

Figure 12-10. *Add connection manager*

The Code

Now you can go back to the Script page, and click the Edit Script. . . button to open the VSTA environment. First, you need to add an extra namespace to shorten the code.

```
#region CustomNamespace
using System.Xml;
#endregion
```

And here is the VB.NET code:

```
#Region "CustomNamespace"
Imports System.Xml
#End Region
```

Next you need a class variable for storing the XML data. For this example, you use the XmlTextWriter namespace.

```
// XmlTextWriter (stream) object to write the XML
XmlTextWriter textWriter;
```

And this is the VB.NET code:

```
' File stream object to write the XML
Private xmlFile As StreamWriter
```

In the PreExecute method, you open the stream and start writing the opening tags for the XML structure.

```csharp
public override void PreExecute()
{
  // Create a new XML document and use the
  // filepath in the connection as XML-file
  textWriter = new XmlTextWriter(this.Connections.
                xmlFile.AcquireConnection(null).ToString(), null);

  // Start writing the XML document:
  textWriter.WriteStartDocument();

  // Create root element <Employees>
  textWriter.WriteStartElement("Employees");
}
```

And here is the VB.NET code:

```vbnet
Public Overrides Sub PreExecute()
   ' Create a new XML document and use the
   ' filepath in the connection as XML-file
   textWriter = New XmlTextWriter(Me.Connections. _
                xmlFile.AcquireConnection(Nothing).ToString(), _
                System.Text.Encoding.Default)

   ' Start writing the XML document:
   textWriter.WriteStartDocument()

   ' Create root element <Employees>
   textWriter.WriteStartElement("Employees")
 End Sub
```

307

And in the PostExecute method, you close the XML tags and clean up the resources.

```
public override void PostExecute()
{
  // Close root element: </Employees>
  textWriter.WriteEndElement();

  // Stop writing the XML document
  textWriter.WriteEndDocument();

  // Close document and clean up resources
  textWriter.Close();
}
```

This is the VB.NET code:

```
Public Overrides Sub PostExecute()
  'Close root element: </Employees>
  textWriter.WriteEndElement()

  'Stop writing the XML document
  textWriter.WriteEndDocument()

  'Close document and clean up resources
  textWriter.Close()
End Sub
```

In the Input0_ProcessInputRow method, you process all records. Each column is mentioned as an element of Employee, but the ID column is used as an attribute of Employee.

```
public override void Input0_ProcessInputRow(Input0Buffer Row)
{
  // Opening tag employee with ID as attribute
  textWriter.WriteStartElement("Employee");
  textWriter.WriteStartAttribute("id");
  textWriter.WriteString(Row.EmployeeId.ToString());
  textWriter.WriteEndAttribute();

  // Writing elements within the Employee tag
  textWriter.WriteStartElement("FirstName");
  textWriter.WriteString(Row.FirstName.ToString());
  textWriter.WriteEndElement();

  textWriter.WriteStartElement("LastName");
  textWriter.WriteString(Row.LastName.ToString());
  textWriter.WriteEndElement();
```

```
textWriter.WriteStartElement("DateOfBirth");
textWriter.WriteString(Row.DateOfBirth.ToShortDateString());
textWriter.WriteEndElement();

textWriter.WriteStartElement("Gender");
textWriter.WriteString(Row.Gender.ToString());
textWriter.WriteEndElement();

textWriter.WriteStartElement("Salary");
textWriter.WriteString(Row.Salary.ToString());
textWriter.WriteEndElement();

// Closing tag employee
textWriter.WriteEndElement();
}
```

And this is the VB.NET code:

```
Public Overrides Sub Input0_ProcessInputRow(ByVal Row As Input0Buffer)
    ' Write opening tag for row with id property
    xmlFile.WriteLine("<Employee id=""" & Row.EmployeeId.ToString() & """>")

    ' Extra columns
    xmlFile.WriteLine("<FirstName>" & Row.FirstName.ToString() _
                    & "</FirstName>")
    xmlFile.WriteLine("<LastName>" & Row.LastName.ToString() & "</LastName>")
    xmlFile.WriteLine("<DateOfBirth>" & Row.DateOfBirth.ToShortDateString() _
                    & "</DateOfBirth>")
    xmlFile.WriteLine("<Gender>" & Row.Gender.ToString() & "</Gender>")
    xmlFile.WriteLine("<Salary>" & Row.Salary.ToString() & "</Salary>")

    ' Closing tag for row
    xmlFile.WriteLine("</Employee>")
End Sub
```

The Results

Now run the package and check the result of your XML file. (Figure 12-11 shows our results). This is a very basic example without error handling or escaping restricted characters like < and >. And it could be very time-consuming if you have a lot of columns. Chapter 14 shows a more flexible example that loops through the collection of columns.

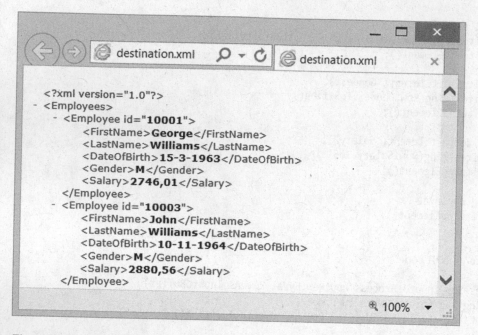

Figure 12-11. Your XML file viewed in Internet Explorer

Summary

In this chapter you learned how to create your own text files (.csv and .xml) with the Script Component. Very basic, but easy to extend. Both are perhaps a little time-consuming if you have a lot of columns, but in Chapter 14 you will learn how to use reflection to loop through all columns.

CHAPTER 13

■■■

Regular Expressions

Many ETL applications and processes usually deal with strings or have to parse large amounts of text; it is not unusual to be in a situation where you want to strip some elements from a block of text or to validate that an email address is in a valid format.

Regular expressions provide a flexible, powerful, and efficient method for processing text. The regular expression pattern-matching engine enables you to

- Parse large amount of texts to find specific character patterns

- Validate text to ensure that it matches a predefined pattern

- Extract, edit, or delete text substrings and to add these substrings in a collection to generate a report

In the heart of the regular expression is its engine, which is represented by the System.Text. RegularExpression.Regex object in the .NET Framework.

Processing text using regular expressions requires that the regular expression engine has at least two parameters:

- The regular expression pattern to find in the text

- The text to parse for the regular expression pattern

More information about the regular expression object model is on MSDN at https://msdn.microsoft.com/en-us/library/30wbz966(v=vs.110).aspx.

As mentioned, a regular expression is a pattern that the engine tries to match. A pattern consists of one or more of these three parts:

- character literals

- operators

- constructs

A complete list of the regular expression syntax with character escapes, character classes, anchors, grouping constructs, quantifiers, backreference constructs, alternation constructs, substitutions, regular expression options, and other constructs is available for reference on MSDN at https://msdn.microsoft.com/en-us/library/az24scfc(v=vs.110).aspx.

The following is a list of some great sites for finding Regex samples and resources:

- http://www.regexr.com

- http://www.regular-expressions.info/

- http://rubular.com

- http://regexone.com

The Regex class has methods that let you perform the operations mentioned earlier.

- The IsMatch method is used for determining whether the regular expression occurs in the input text; for example, when validating that an email address is in the correct format.

- The Match or Matches methods that retrieve an object or a collection of objects with all the occurrences of text that match the regular expression pattern.

- The Replace method is used to replace the text that matches the regular expression pattern.

This chapter looks at three examples, where you will parse, validate, and then extract substrings.

Prerequisites

All the examples in this chapter are based on a sample file, ProductList.csv, which can be found in the source code for this chapter.

The following are the six columns in which to keep information:

- Product ID

- Product name, which is simply the name of the product

- Date created

- The country in which the product is produced

- The email address (with some formatting errors) of the person responsible for the product

- An HTML description of the product (the HTML description is taken from Wikipedia)

Figure 13-1 is an extract of the .csv file opened in Excel.

	A	B	C	D	E	F	G
1	ProductID	Date	ProductName	Productio	Email	Summary	
2	1	12-02-2015	Goat cheese	France	regis!bacc	<h3><span class=	
3	2	13/05/2015	Fast red car	Italy	enzo@fer	<p><b>Ferrari S.	
4	3	######	Rye bread	Denmark	ryebread(	<p><b>Rye brea(	
5	4	######	Running shoes	USA	nikuma@	<p>Athletic shoe	

Figure 13-1. Product list .csv document

Validating Email Addresses

A large part of the work done with regular expressions is to ensure greater data quality. According to the International Data Corporation (IDC), it is estimated that bad data quality costs businesses $6.5 billion every year. An invalid email address is the kind of error that can be caught with regular expressions.

Start by creating a new package and add a Data Flow Task to the surface. Inside the Data Flow Task, add a Flat File Source and a new Flat File Connection Manager pointing to the .csv document mentioned earlier (ProductList.csv, which is in the source code for this chapter). Leave all the settings from the General page at the default, as shown in Figure 13-2.

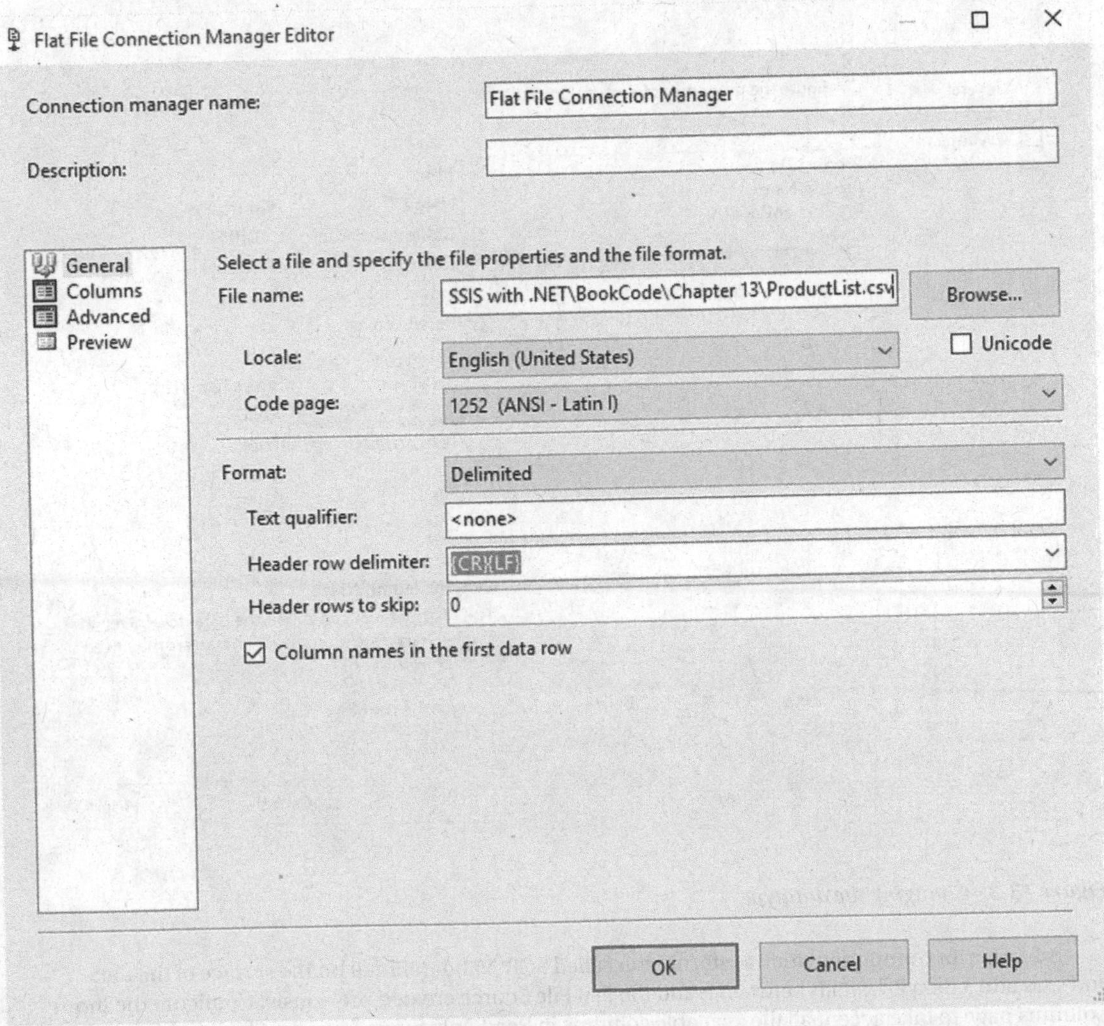

Figure 13-2. Flat File Connection Manager Editor

Visit the Columns page to ensure that the metadata is fetched and that the columns are parsed correctly.

In the Advanced page of the Flat File Connection Manager, change the length of the Summary column since truncation will occur if the data is more than 50 chars long, which triggers an error when running the package. Change the datatype to string [DT_STR] with a width of 4000, as shown in Figure 13-3. The width should be large enough so that truncation doesn't occur.

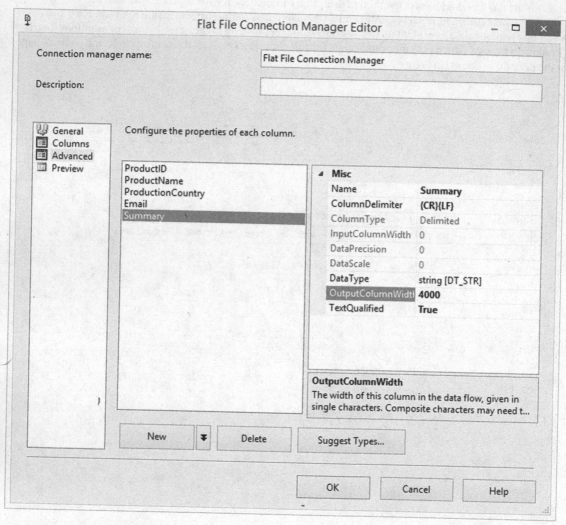

Figure 13-3. Changing the datatype

Add a Script Component for transformation called SCR_ValidateEmail on the surface of the data flow and add a data flow path between it and the Flat File Source created previously. Configure the Input Columns page to take accept all the available columns in ReadOnly mode from the Flat File Source, as shown in Figure 13-4. In this example, you are only using the Email column, so best practice would be to only fetch the column you need, but since you will use some of the other columns in other examples, take all the available columns.

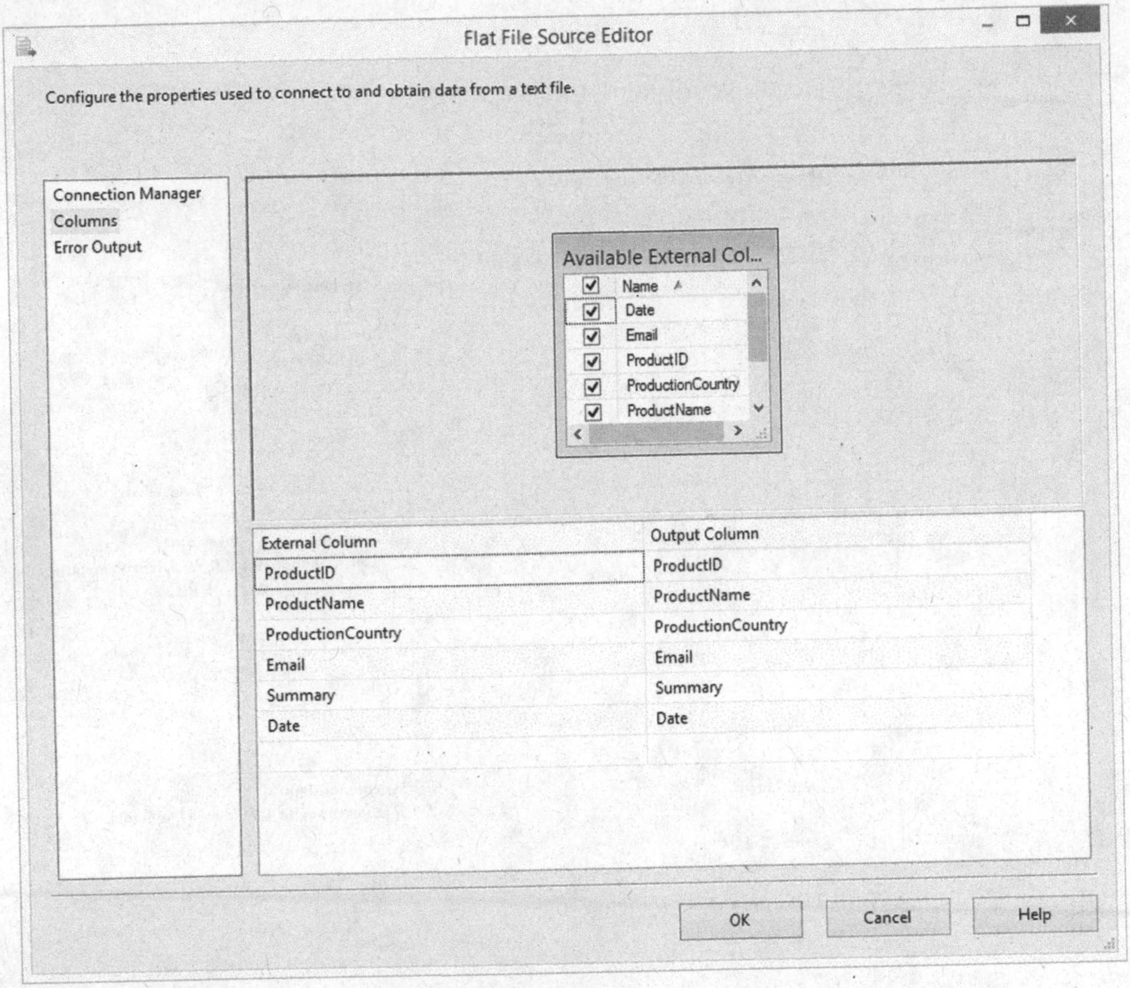

Figure 13-4. *Input page of the Script Task Transformation Editor*

On the Inputs and Outputs page of the editor, you basically need two outputs: ValidEmail and InvalidEmail. The first is for the valid email addresses and the second is for the invalid email addresses. Start by renaming Output 0 to ValidEmail. For both outputs, you need to set the ExclusionGroup to 1 and the SynchronousInputID to Input 0 (since you have exactly one output per input). Output 1 is renamed InvalidEmail. The two outputs are shown in Figure 13-5.

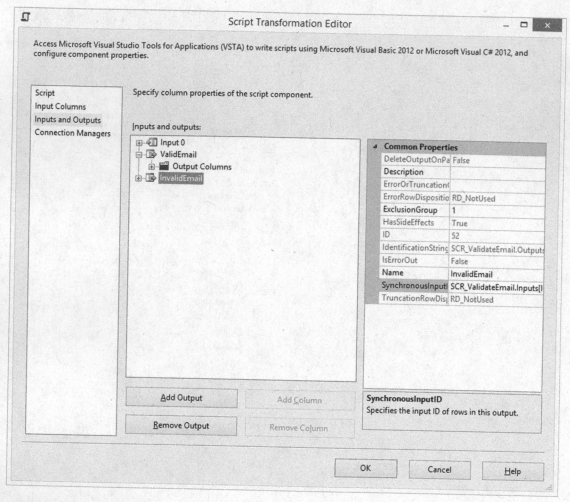

Figure 13-5. Output columns

The Script

Clicking the Edit Script... button on the Script page brings up the VSTA editor; you can begin to add code to perform the validation to keep the row data. First, you can safely remove the PreExecute and PostExecute methods since you don't need them. Then you need to add a reference to the Regular Expression namespace.

```
#region CustomNamespace
using System.Text.RegularExpressions;
#endregion
```

By packing all the validations steps in functions, you can keep a clean interface. The first function that you implement is for validating a given email address.

Here is the C# implementation:

```csharp
// A boolean method that validates an email address
// with a regex pattern.
public bool IsCorrectEmail(String emailAddress)
{
    // The pattern for email
    string emailAddressPattern = @"^(([^<>()[\]\\.,;:\s@\""]+"
                    + @"(\.[^<>()[\]\\.,;:\s@\""]+)*)|(\"".+\""))@"
                    + @"((\[[0-9]{1,3}\.[0-9]{1,3}\.[0-9]{1,3}"
                    + @"\.[0-9]{1,3}\])|(([a-zA-Z\-0-9]+\.)+"
                    + @"[a-zA-Z]{2,}))$";

    // Check if it is match and return that value (boolean)
    return Regex.IsMatch(emailAddress,emailAddressPattern,RegexOptions.IgnoreCase);
}
```

And here is the VB.NET implementation:

```vbnet
' A boolean method that validates an email address
' with a regex pattern.
Public Function IsCorrectEmail(emailAddress As [String]) As Boolean

    ' The pattern for email
    Dim emailAddressPattern As String = "^(([^<>()[\]\\.,;:\s@\""]+" + _
        "(\.[^<>()[\]\\.,;:\s@\""]+)*)|(\"".+\""))@" + _
        "((\[[0-9]{1,3}\.[0-9]{1,3}\.[0-9]{1,3}" + _
        "\.[0-9]{1,3}\])|(([a-zA-Z\-0-9]+\.)+" + _
        "[a-zA-Z]{2,}))$"

    ' Check if it is match and return that value (boolean)
    Return Regex.IsMatch(emailAddress, emailAddressPattern, RegexOptions.IgnoreCase)
End Function
```

This is not a very complicated pattern, but it matches most valid email addresses according to the email address standard definition. Note that the pattern doesn't determine if an email address exists, only if it is in a valid format. Furthermore, the pattern doesn't check if the top-level domain name is an existing domain.

■ **Note** Patterns can get very complicated, especially if you've never seen a regular expression before. For validating email addresses, there is an easier way to do it—by using the System.Net.Mail.MailAddress class. To determine whether an email address is valid, pass the email address to the MailAddress.MailAddress(String) class constructor. We really encourage you to have a look at the Regex resources and samples available on the Internet.

Calling the Method

Once you add the method, you need to call it for each row with an email address that passes through the script. If the method returns true, the email is valid, and you direct it to the ValidEmail output; otherwise, it's not valid and it has to go to the InvalidEmail output.

Here is how to invoke the method in C#:

```csharp
public override void Input0_ProcessInputRow(Input0Buffer Row)
{
    bool isEmailValid = false;

    //If no email is provided consider it invalid
    if (!Row.Email_IsNull)
    {
        isEmailValid = IsCorrectEmail(Row.Email);
    }

    if (isEmailValid)
    {
        Row.DirectRowToValidEmail();
    }
    else
    {
        Row.DirectRowToInvalidEmail();
    }
}
```

In VB.NET, you can invoke the method as follows:

```vbnet
Public Overrides Sub Input0_ProcessInputRow(Row As Input0Buffer)
        Dim isEmailValid As Boolean = False

        'If no email is provided consider it invalid
        If Not Row.Email_IsNull Then
                isEmailValid = IsCorrectEmail(Row.Email)
        End If

        If isEmailValid Then
                Row.DirectRowToValidEmail()
        Else
                Row.DirectRowToInvalidEmail()
        End If
End Sub
```

Close the script editor and add two multicasts to the package: one connected to the ValidEmail output and one connected to the InvalidEmail output. In a real-life scenario, you would probably want to log the invalid emails rows and stop processing the row.

If you add data viewers to both precedence constraints and run the package with the input file provided in the code example for this chapter, you can see that the invalid emails are caught by the validation method, as shown in Figure 13-6.

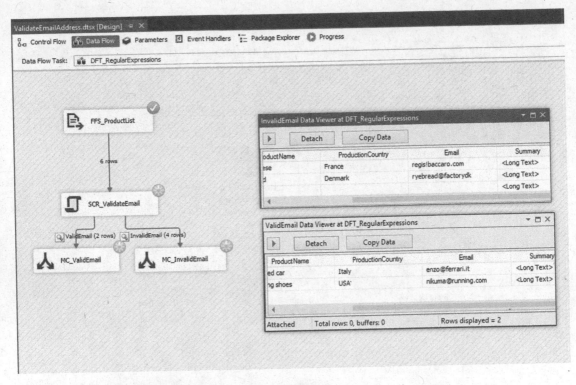

Figure 13-6. *Successfully running the package showing data viewers*

Removing HTML Tags

When working with text in SSIS, you sometimes encounter HTML formatted text with a lot of markup that you are not interested in keeping. Stripping markup from text is a well-known problem that can easily be achieved using regular expressions. What you need to do is specify the pattern for an HTML tag, which is quite simple:

It starts with < and has to match any single character, and even a new line, one or more times. This pattern of one or more characters can be repeated once or not at all, thus yielding an expression like this:

```
<(.|\n)+?>
```

The Package

Starting from the previous example (or from the sample code for Chapter 13), add a Data Flow Task to the surface of the package and name it DFT_RemoveHTML.

Inside the Data Flow Task, add a Flat File Source as described in the previous example (Validate Email address) and configure it to take all the columns from the source file.

Add a Script Component called Scr_RemoveHTML to the surface, choose Transformation as the type, and connect its input to the output of the Flat File Source. Double-click the Script Component and choose only the Summary column to be ReadWrite, as shown in Figure 13-7.

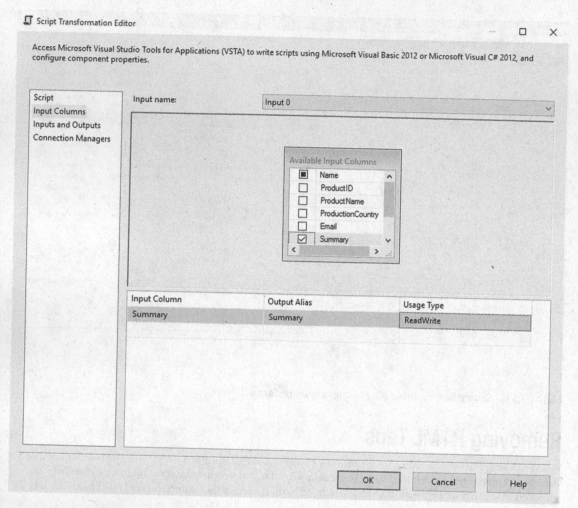

Figure 13-7. Configuring Input columns

On the Script page, click Edit Script... to open VSTA. Remove the PreExecute and PostExecute methods from the script.

The Script

Before you can use regular expressions in the code, you need to add a reference to the namespace with a Using or Imports directive. Write the following code if using C#:

```
#region CustomNamespace
using System.Text.RegularExpressions;
#endregion
```

You need a method that can use the pattern described earlier to remove HTML code.

```csharp
//Created at class level for better performance
// The pattern for a html tag
public static String htmlTagPattern = "<(.|\n)+?>";
// Create a regex object with the pattern
public Regex objRegExp = new Regex(htmlTagPattern);

// A boolean method that strips HTML
// with a regex pattern.
public String RemoveHtml(String message)
{

    // Replace html tag by an empty string
    message = objRegExp.Replace(message, String.Empty);
    // Return the message without html tags
    return message;
}
```

Here is the code to use in VB.NET:

```vbnet
'Created at class level for better performance
' The pattern for a html tag
Public Shared htmlTagPattern As [String] = "<(.|" & vbLf & ")+?>"
' Create a regex object with the pattern
Public objRegExp As New Regex(htmlTagPattern)

' A boolean method that strips HTML
' with a regex pattern.
Public Function RemoveHtml(message As [String]) As [String]

        ' Replace html tag by an empty string
        message = objRegExp.Replace(message, [String].Empty)
        ' Return the message without html tags
        Return message
End Function
```

In the preceding function, you use the regular expression Replace method to remove the HTML markup and replace it with an empty string whereas in the first example you were only interested in matching.

Then you can call the method in the Input0_ProcessInputRow method, as shown here for C#:

```csharp
public override void Input0_ProcessInputRow(Input0Buffer Row)
{
    Row.Summary = RemoveHtml(Row.Summary);
}
```

And the VB.NET invocation is as follows:

```vbnet
Public Overrides Sub Input0_ProcessInputRow(Row As Input0Buffer)
        Row.Summary = RemoveHtml(Row.Summary)
End Sub
```

Close the VSTA editor and add a multicast to the output of the Script Component, enabling the data viewer on the precedence constraint. When running the package you should be able to see the summary with no HTML markup, as shown in Figure 13-8.

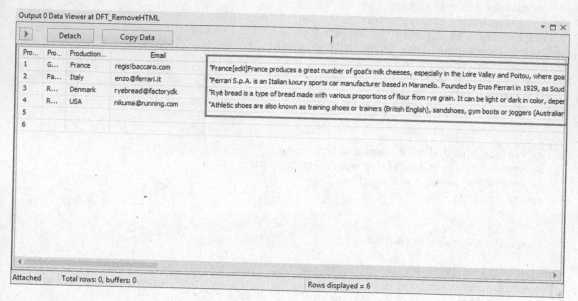

Figure 13-8. *Data viewer showing the result*

In this example, you saw how to use the regular expressions Replace method to strip the HTML code from text. In the next example, you are shown how to validate and replace dates with a default value if the date doesn't match the required format.

Cleaning/Validating

Regular expressions are also a great tool for ensuring data quality. Implementing patterns based on cleaning and validating rules is quite straightforward. In the preceding example code, there is a date column. The only issue with this column is the data quality. Sometimes parts of the date are separated with a forward slash (/), and other times with a dash (-). In other situations, there is no date at all, only a series of # symbols. Let's implement a script to ensure that the date is always represented in the correct way, so that it eventually can be converted to a datetime format. Furthermore, let's agree that empty or invalid date strings will be replaced by 9999-12-31.

The Package

Starting from the previous example (or from the sample code for Chapter 13), add a Data Flow Task to the surface of the package and name it DFT_CleanseDate.

Inside the Data Flow Task, add a Flat File Source as described in the previous example (Validate Email address) and configure it to take all the columns from the source file.

Add a Script Component called SCR_CleanseDate to the surface, choose the transformation type, and connect its input to the output of the Flat File Source. Double-click the Script Component and choose only the columns needed for better performance—in this case, the Date column, and mark it as ReadWrite, as shown on Figure 13-9. Click the Edit Script... button on the Script page to open VSTA.

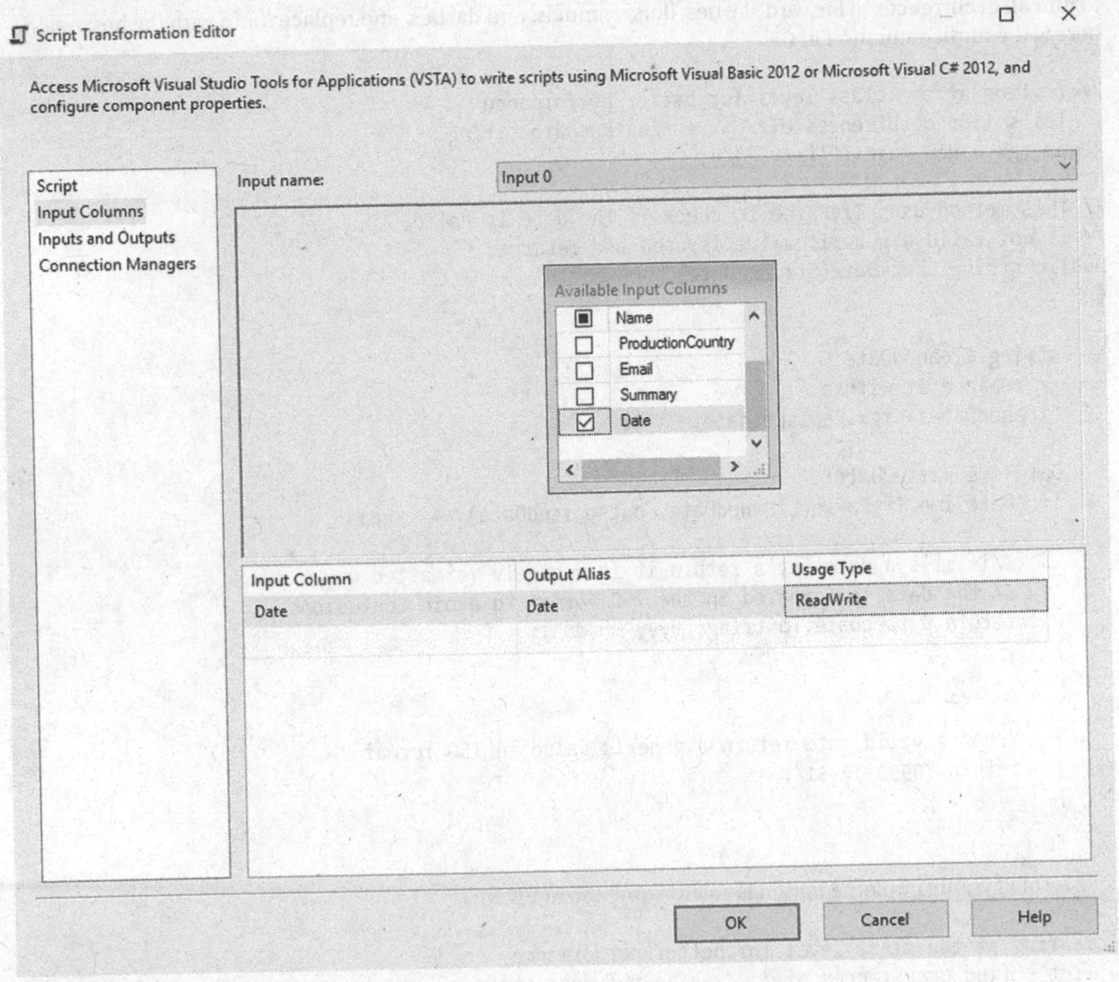

Figure 13-9. Date column changed to ReadWrite

The Script

Start by removing the unnecessary PreExecute and PostExecute methods. Before you can use regular expressions in the code, you need to add a reference to the namespace with a Using or Imports directive. Here is the C# code for that:

```
#region CustomNamespace
using System.Text.RegularExpressions;
#endregion
```

You need a method that can validate whether the input string is in the correct format. This what the DateTime.TryParse method does. TryParse converts the specified string representation of a date and time to its DateTime equivalent, and returns a value that indicates whether the conversion succeeded, which is more easily handled than returning an error. The regular expression used is quite straightforward; you want

323

to find all occurrences of forward slashes, dots, commas, and dashes, and replace them with dashes. Again, here is the implementation in C#:

```csharp
//creating at the class level for better performance
// let's find occurrences of / , . - in the date string
Regex rgx = new Regex("([-/,.])");

// This method uses TryParse to check if the date is valid,
// if not valid a generic value is used and returned.
public string CheckDate(String date)
{

    string CleanedDate;
    // replace it with a -
    CleanedDate = rgx.Replace(date, "-");

    DateTime parsedDate;
    if (DateTime.TryParse(CleanedDate, out parsedDate) == true)
    {
        //if it's a date let's return it in a nicely formatted way
        // the date is formated in the ISO format to avoid confusion
        return parsedDate.ToString("yyyy-MM-dd");
    }
    else
    {
        //not a valid date return a generic value in ISO format
        return "9999-12-31";
    }
}
```

As always, the implementation is easily expressed in VB.NET:

```vbnet
'creating at the class level for better performance
' let's find occurrences of / , . - in the date string
Private rgx As New Regex("([-/,.])")

' This method uses TryParse to check if the date is valid,
' if not valid a generic value is used and returned.
Public Function CheckDate([date] As [String]) As String

    Dim CleanedDate As String
    ' replace it with a -
    CleanedDate = rgx.Replace([date], "-")

    Dim parsedDate As DateTime
    If DateTime.TryParse(CleanedDate, parsedDate) = True Then
        'if it's a date let's return it in a nicely formatted way
        ' the date is formated in the ISO format to avoid confusion
        Return parsedDate.ToString("yyyy-MM-dd")
```

```
    Else
        'not a valid date return a generic value in ISO format
        Return "9999-12-31"
    End If
End Function
```

Now from the Main method it is easy to call the help method for every row passing through. In C#, write this:

```
public override void Input0_ProcessInputRow(Input0Buffer Row)
{
        if (!Row.Date_IsNull)
    {
        Row.Date = CheckDate(Row.Date);
    }
    else
    {
        Row.Date = "9999-12-31";
    }
}
```

And in VB.NET, write this:

```
Public Overrides Sub Input0_ProcessInputRow(Row As Input0Buffer)
        If Not Row.Date_IsNull Then
        Row.Date = CheckDate(Row.Date)
        Else
        Row.Date = "9999-12-31"
        End If
End Sub
```

Close the VSTA editor and add a multicast to the output of the Script Component, enabling the data viewer on the precedence constraint. When running the package, you should be able to see the validated and cleansed date, as shown in Figure 13-10.

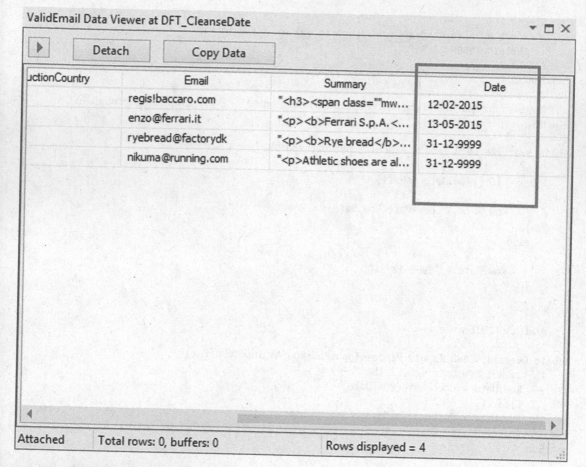

Figure 13-10. *Data viewer with cleansed date*

Summary

Using regular expressions, you have matched, formatted, cleansed, and validated data in a nicely straightforward way. These examples demonstrated some of the basic features of regular expressions. By composing more complicated patterns, you can unleash the true power of the highly performant regular expression engine.

There are also tools out there to help you build expressions, so that you don't have to struggle with it yourself. One of the best tools available, RegExr, is at http://regexr.com.

If you prefer offline tools, RegexMagic is also a nice tool; it's available at www.regular-expressions.info/regexmagic.html.

■ ■ ■

CHAPTER 14

Script Component Reflection

This chapter focuses on flexibility within the Script Component, because sometimes you have to do the same transformation for a lot of columns, which could be a little tiresome. Or what about Chapter 12's XML destination with a lot of columns? You don't want to code a couple dozen column names. On reflection, you can loop through all input columns on runtime. So you don't have to hard-code all of those columns. Another great opportunity to use reflection is calculating a hash value for all the columns.

However, this flexibility comes with a price because reflection is not the best technique if performance is your top concern. In this case, you need to enumerate through the columns multiple times, which is a COM bases object. At the end of this chapter, you will refer to a solution for this.

There are two points of attention before you start. First, the script loops through the collection of input columns in the order that you selected in the editor. And second, when you change column names, data types, or even the order of columns, you have to edit the script and let SSIS change the generated scripts.

Flexible XML Destination

This first example continues with the basic XML destination example from Chapter 12 (see Figure 14-1). The only difference is the script itself. You can either continue with that package or use the starter package called XML Starter.dtsx from the example project. Make sure that you have selected all the input columns you need in your XML file, in the right order, and then click the Edit Script... button.

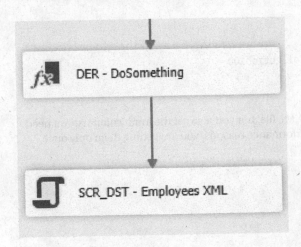

Figure 14-1. XML destination

The Script

For this example, you are using all the default methods, including `PreExecute` and `PostExecute`, but first you need to add System.XML to the namespaces to shorten the code.

```
#region customNamespaces
using System.Xml;
#endregion
```

This is the VB.NET code:

```
#Region "customNamespaces"
Imports System.Xml
#End Region
```

You also need a couple of class variables to use in the various methods.

```
// XmlTextWriter (stream) object to write the XML
XmlTextWriter textWriter;
// Boolean variable to do something only onces
Boolean FirstRow = true;
// Variable to store the row type
Type rowType;
// Variable to store the input columns
IDTSInputColumnCollection100 InputColumnCollection;
// Variable to store the value of the column
String columnValue = "";
```

And this is the VB.NET code:

```
' XmlTextWriter (stream) object to write the XML
Dim textWriter As XmlTextWriter
' Boolean variable to do something only onces
Dim FirstRow As Boolean = True
' Variable to store the row type
Dim rowType As Type
' Variable to store the input columns
Dim InputColumnCollection As IDTSInputColumnCollection100
' Variable to store the value of the column
Dim columnValue As String = ""
```

In the `PreExecute` method, you are creating the XML file, but you also get the input columns. You need those later on to loop through all the columns. For performance reasons, you are getting them only once here in the `PreExecute`.

```csharp
public override void PreExecute()
{
  // Get collection of input columns
  InputColumnCollection = this.ComponentMetaData
                        .InputCollection[0].InputColumnCollection;

  // Create a new XML document and use the filepath
  //in the connection as XML-file
  textWriter = new XmlTextWriter(this.Connections.xmlFile
                .AcquireConnection(null).ToString(), null);

  // Start writing the XML document:
  textWriter.WriteStartDocument();

  // Create root element <Employees>
  textWriter.WriteStartElement("Employees");
}
```

And this is the VB.NET code:

```vbnet
Public Overrides Sub PreExecute()
    ' Get collection of input columns
    InputColumnCollection = Me.ComponentMetaData _
                        .InputCollection(0).InputColumnCollection

    ' Create a new XML document and use the
    ' filepath in the connection as XML-file
    textWriter = New XmlTextWriter(Me.Connections.xmlFile _
                    .AcquireConnection(Nothing).ToString(), _
                    System.Text.Encoding.Default)

    ' Start writing the XML document:
    textWriter.WriteStartDocument()

    ' Create root element <Employees>
    textWriter.WriteStartElement("Employees")
End Sub
```

The PreExecute method closes the XML document.

```csharp
public override void PostExecute()
{
  // Close root element: </Employees>
  textWriter.WriteEndElement();

  // Stop writing the XML document
  textWriter.WriteEndDocument();

  // Close document and clean up resources
  textWriter.Close();
}
```

This is the VB.NET code:

```
Public Overrides Sub PostExecute()
  'Close root element: </Employees>
  textWriter.WriteEndElement()

  'Stop writing the XML document
  textWriter.WriteEndDocument()

  'Close document and clean up resources
  textWriter.Close()
End Sub
```

Next is the `ProcessInputRow` method that adds XML tags for each row. It has a `foreach` loop in it that loops through all the columns from the input column collection. It then tries to get the value from each column and adds an XML tag to the XML document. Within the `try-catch`, you find the "reflection" code: `.GetProperty(____)`. Also notice the extra helper method that removes "forbidden" chars from the XML document. These chars mess up your XML tags, making it impossible to read the document.

```
public override void Input0_ProcessInputRow(Input0Buffer Row)
{
  // Do only onces
  if (FirstRow)
  {
    // Row type to get the value of a column
    rowType = Row.GetType();
  }
  FirstRow = false;

  // Create row element: <Employee>
  textWriter.WriteStartElement("Employee");

  // Loop through all columns and create a column element:
  // <col1>value</col1><col2>value</col2>
  foreach (IDTSInputColumn100 column in InputColumnCollection)
  {
    // Use the SSIS column name as element name: <col1>
    textWriter.WriteStartElement(column.Name);

    // Get column value, will fail if null
    try
    {
      columnValue = rowType.GetProperty(column.Name)
                           .GetValue(Row, null).ToString();
    }
    catch
    {
      // Default value for null values: "null", "" or string.Empty
      columnValue = string.Empty;
    }
```

```
    finally
    {
      textWriter.WriteString(removeForbiddenXmlChars(columnValue));
    }
    // Close column element: </col1>
    textWriter.WriteEndElement();
  }
  // Close row element: </Employee>
  textWriter.WriteEndElement();

  // Extra: output the number of processed rows. 103 = RowsWritten
  this.ComponentMetaData.IncrementPipelinePerfCounter(103, 1);
}

private string removeForbiddenXmlChars(string columnValue)
{
  // Remove forbidden chars that could damage your XML document
  return columnValue.Replace("&", "&amp;")
                    .Replace("<", "&lt;")
                    .Replace(">", "&gt;");

}
```

And this is the VB.NET code:

```
Public Overrides Sub Input0_ProcessInputRow(Row As Input0Buffer)
  ' Do only onces
  If FirstRow Then
      ' Row type to get the value of a column
      rowType = Row.GetType()
  End If
  FirstRow = False

  ' Create row element: <Employee>
  textWriter.WriteStartElement("Employee")

  ' Loop through all columns and create a column element:
  ' <col1>value</col1><col2>value</col2>
  For Each column As IDTSInputColumn100 In InputColumnCollection
    ' Use the SSIS column name as element name: <col1>
    textWriter.WriteStartElement(column.Name)

    ' Get column value, will fail if null
    Try
      columnValue = rowType.GetProperty(column.Name) _
                  .GetValue(Row, Nothing).ToString()
    Catch
      ' Default value for null values: "null", "" or string.Empty
      columnValue = String.Empty
    Finally
      textWriter.WriteString(removeForbiddenXmlChars(columnValue))
    End Try
```

```
    ' Close column element: </col1>
    textWriter.WriteEndElement()
  Next
  ' Close row element: </Employee>
  textWriter.WriteEndElement()

  ' Extra: output the number of processed rows. 103 = RowsWritten
  Me.ComponentMetaData.IncrementPipelinePerfCounter(103, 1)
End Sub

Private Function removeForbiddenXmlChars(columnValue As String) As String
  ' Remove forbidden chars that could damage your XML document
  Return columnValue.Replace("&", "&amp;") _
                    .Replace("<", "&lt;") _
                    .Replace(">", "&gt;")

End Function
```

The Results

Now run the package and check the results of your XML file. It should look like Figure 14-2. This is a bit more sophisticated script that doesn't require a lot of manual labor, but it does require a very basic XML structure. For deviating requirements, you will probably have to add a lot of if statements in the column loop. In that case, you are likely better off with the example in Chapter 12.

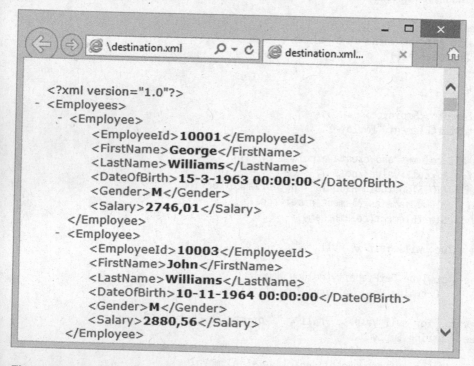

Figure 14-2. *Your XML file viewed in Internet Explorer*

Transformation of All Columns

Another good use of reflection in a Script Component is to do "something" on all columns. For example, trim all the columns or replace all the null values. Of course, you can do that with the derived column, but if there are a lot of columns, then it could be tiresome and error prone. In this example, you will convert all the string columns to uppercase. You can use the same source as in the previous example, or you can use the "Upper all Starter.dtsx" starter package or your own source file.

Script Component Type

Add a Script Component as a transformation to your data flow and connect it to another component (see Figure 14-3). Make sure to give it a suitable name; for example, SCR – Uppercase.

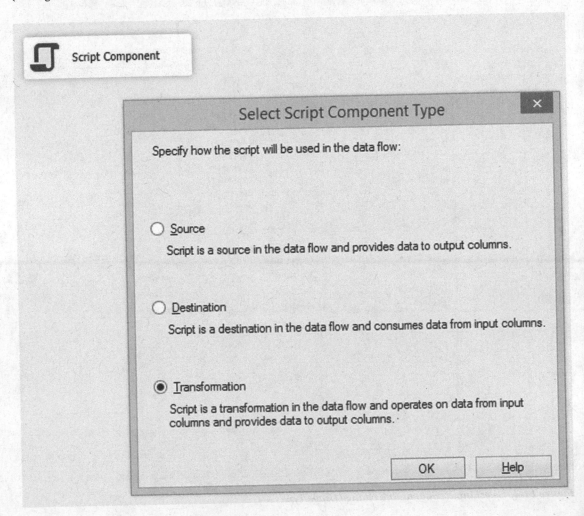

Figure 14-3. *Script Component type transformation*

Script Component Input Columns

Go to the Input Columns page and select all (string) columns that you want to change and set the Usage Type for those columns to ReadWrite (see Figure 14-4). You can select all the columns, even those with non-string data types, because you will check the data type in the script itself. Of course, it is better for performance to only select the correct columns. There is one downside to this method: you have to change the Usage Type of all selected columns, one by one. This is a lot of work if you have many columns, but with your keyboard, you can do it pretty fast (change the first and then repeat: {tab} {tab} {tab} {down}). Tiresome, but still easier than adding dozens of expressions in a derived column.

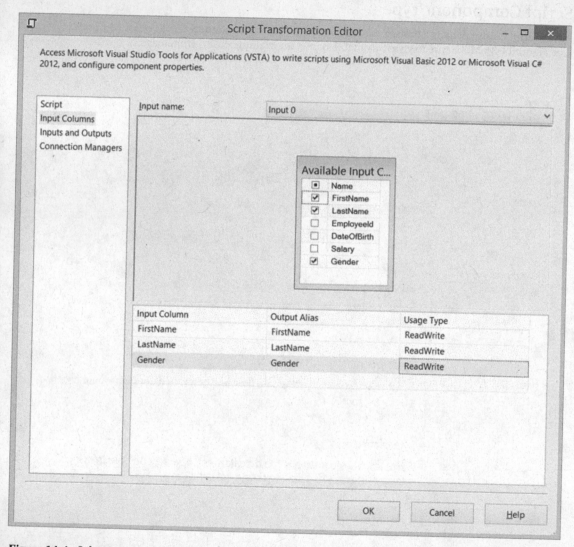

Figure 14-4. *Select input columns and change Usage Type*

The Script

For this example, you need a couple of class variables. These variables are used to prevent doing an action in the ProcessInputRow multiple times.

```
// Boolean variable to do something only onces
Boolean FirstRow = true;
// Variable to store the row type
Type rowType;
// Variable to store the input columns
IDTSInputColumnCollection100 InputColumnCollection;
// Variable to store the value of the column
String columnValue = "";
```

This is the VB.NET code:

```
' Boolean variable to do something only onces
Dim FirstRow As Boolean = True
' Variable to store the row type
Dim rowType As Type
' Variable to store the input columns
Dim InputColumnCollection As IDTSInputColumnCollection100
' Variable to store the value of the column
Dim columnValue As String = ""
```

In the PreExecute method, you are filling a variable with the input column collection. This variable is used in the ProcessInputRow method.

```
public override void PreExecute()
{
  // Get collection of input columns
  InputColumnCollection = this.ComponentMetaData
                    .InputCollection[0].InputColumnCollection;
}
```

And this is the VB.NET code:

```
Public Overrides Sub PreExecute()
  ' Get collection of input columns
  InputColumnCollection = Me.ComponentMetaData _
                    .InputCollection(0).InputColumnCollection

End Sub
```

The Input0_ProcessInputRow method executes for each row, and then loops through the column collection and changes the value of the ReadWrite string columns. Changing the value is done with a separate method, which you can adjust to your own needs.

If you are changing the size of a text or a number, then you should make sure that you don't exceed the length or precision, which would cause a truncation error. The variable column has various properties, such as column.Precision or column.Length, which you can use to add extra checks. For this uppercase example, it is not necessary to add extra checks.

```csharp
public override void Input0_ProcessInputRow(Input0Buffer Row)
{
  // Do only onces
  if (FirstRow)
  {
    // Row type to get the value of a column
    rowType = Row.GetType();
  }
  FirstRow = false;

  foreach (IDTSInputColumn100 column in InputColumnCollection)
  {
    // Only change columns of datatype string
    // and make sure the column is READWRITE
    if ((column.DataType.ToString().Equals("DT_WSTR") ||
         column.DataType.ToString().Equals("DT_STR")) &&
         column.UsageType.ToString().Equals("UT_READWRITE"))
    {
      // Get column value, will fail if null
      try
      {
        // Get current column value
        columnValue = rowType.GetProperty(column.Name).GetValue(Row,
                                          null).ToString();

        // Change the column value with a method. Make sure you comply
        // to the data type incl. size(/precision/scale). The variable
        // column has properties to get the size of the column.
        rowType.GetProperty(column.Name).SetValue(Row,
                                    UpperColumnValue(columnValue), null);
      }
      catch
      {
        // Do nothing when value is null
      }
    }
  }
}


// New function that you can adjust to suit your needs
public string UpperColumnValue(string ValueOfProperty)
{
  // Uppercase the value
  ValueOfProperty = ValueOfProperty.ToUpper();
  return ValueOfProperty;
}
```

And this is the VB.NET code:

```vbnet
Public Overrides Sub Input0_ProcessInputRow(ByVal Row As Input0Buffer)
    ' Do only onces
    If FirstRow Then
        ' Row type to get the value of a column
        rowType = Row.GetType()
    End If
    FirstRow = False

    For Each column As IDTSInputColumn100 In InputColumnCollection
        ' Only change columns of datatype string
        ' and make sure the column is READWRITE
        If ((column.DataType = DataType.DT_WSTR Or _
             column.DataType = DataType.DT_STR) And _
             column.UsageType = DTSUsageType.UT_READWRITE) Then

            ' Get column value, will fail if null
            Try
                ' Get current column value
                columnValue = rowType.GetProperty(column.Name).GetValue(Row, _
                                            Nothing).ToString()

                ' Change the column value with a method. Make sure you comply
                ' to the data type incl. size(/precision/scale). The variable
                ' column has properties to get the size of the column.
                rowType.GetProperty(column.Name).SetValue(Row, _
                        UpperColumnValue(columnValue), Nothing)

            Catch ex As Exception
                ' Do nothing when value is null
            End Try
        End If
    Next
End Sub

' New function that you can adjust to suit your needs
Private Function UpperColumnValue(ValueOfProperty As String) As String
    ' Uppercase the value
    ValueOfProperty = ValueOfProperty.ToUpper()
    Return ValueOfProperty
End Function
```

The Results

Add data viewers to test your script and run the package. You should see a lot of capitals (see Figure 14-5).

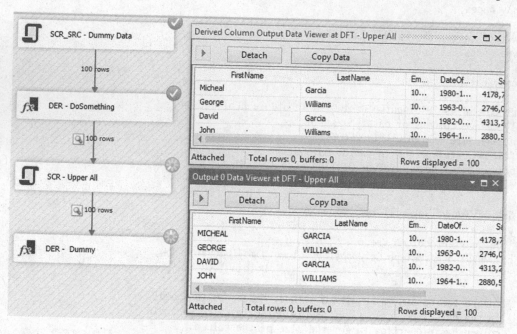

Figure 14-5. The results of upper all text columns

Calculating a Hash for a Row

Hashing can be used to store your passwords and other sensitive data more securely, but it can also be used to detect changes in your records. For example, if you want to check whether you should update the record in your destination table with data from your source, then you could compare all column values, one by one. That's OK if you have a four or five columns, but tiring if you have 20 columns. The trick is to calculate and store a hash value (also called a *checksum*) of all of your column values. The next time you want to check for changes, then you only have to check that hash column.

Note that calculating a hash costs extra time in SSIS and it costs extra space and time to populate the hash in your destination table, but in most cases, that extra time and space is worth it. There are various hashing algorithms. For example, MD5 (Message Digest 5 Algorithm) takes less time and costs less space than SHA512 (Secure-Hash Algorithm, 512 bytes), but it is also less secure and there is a (negligibly) small possibility that two different strings will result in the same hash value. That is called *hash collision*. So take the time to research which algorithm is best for your situation, and choose wisely. For comparison, the MD5 is OK for securing sensitive data, but you should consider a more secure algorithm. And be careful with very large (n)text columns. Hashing them could take too much time.

Variables

If you are using this script to calculate a secure hash instead of a checksum only, then you need to add a string variable to store the salt value. For the checksum, you can skip this part. Make sure to use configurations to avoid hard-coded values in the package. The name of the string variable is saltValue. Make sure to add a dummy/test value (see Figure 14-6).

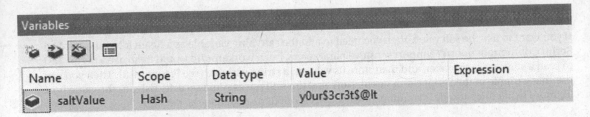

Figure 14-6. *Variable to store the salt*

Script Component

For this example, you will reuse the source of the previous examples. You can use the starter package or use your own source. Add a Script Component (type transformation) in your data flow (see Figure 14-7). Give it a suitable name, like SCR – Hash All, and connect it to your other components.

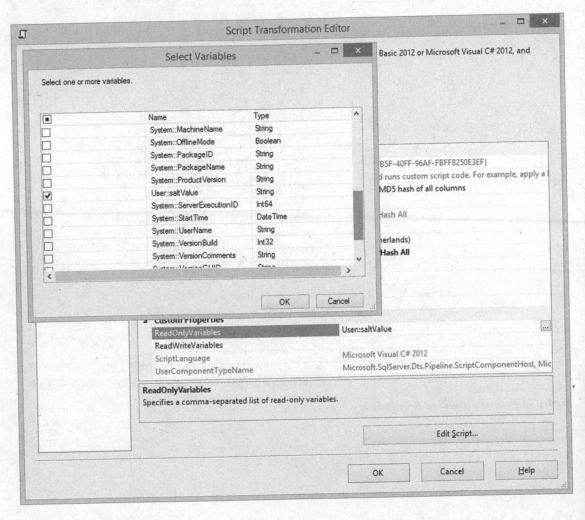

Figure 14-7. *The data flow*

ReadOnly Variable

If you want to use the salt value, then you need to add the saltValue variable as a ReadOnly variable. The Script Component doesn't support sensitive parameters, but a workaround would be to use a Script Task to read a sensitive parameter, and then store its value in a string variable (see Figure 14-8). Then you can use that variable in the Script Component. Note that this still poses some security risks, as the value is in memory while the package is running. But at least it is not hard-coded in the package.

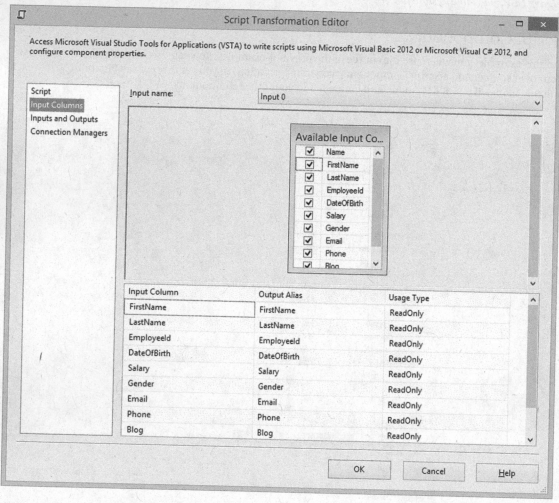

Figure 14-8. *Salt variable as ReadOnly*

Input Columns

Go to the Input Columns tab and select all the columns you need as ReadOnly (the default); but it is not useful to select the key column(s), since they won't change. If this package isn't the only place where you calculate the hash, then make sure to always use the same order of columns. Otherwise, the hashes won't be the same. For this example, you select all the columns except EmployeeId, since this is the unique key (see Figure 14-9).

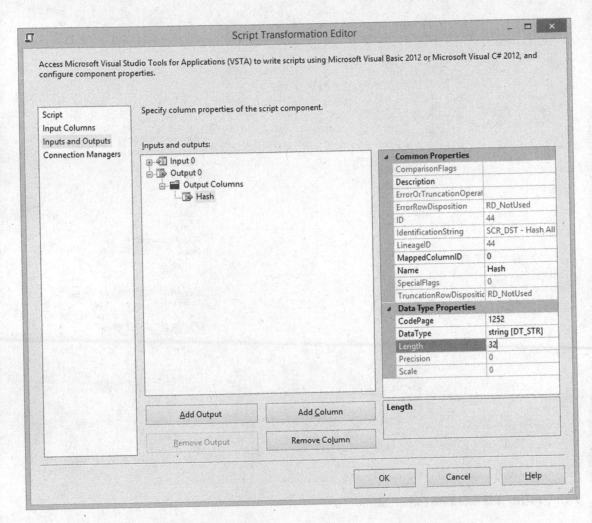

Figure 14-9. Select input columns as ReadOnly

Output Columns

You need a new string column to store the calculated hash value. The length could vary between 32 for MD5 and 128 for SHA512. In this example, you will use an MD5 hash, which is 32 chars. Go to the Inputs and Outputs page. Expand Output 0 and then select Output Columns. Click the Add Column button to add the new string column (see Figure 14-10).

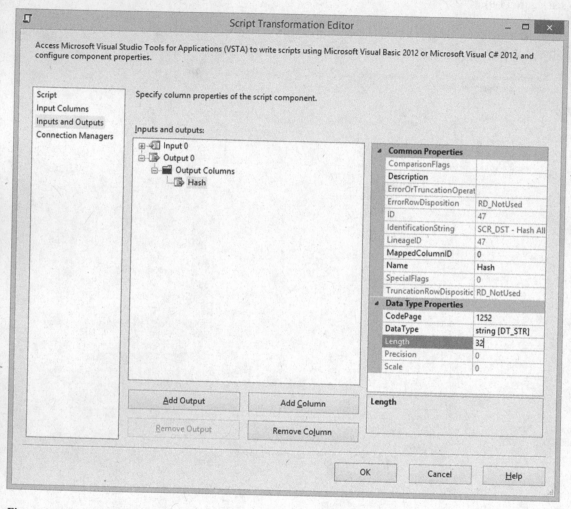

Figure 14-10. *Add new hash output column*

The Script

For this example, you are using all the default methods, including PreExecute and PostExecute, but first you need to add System.Security.Cryptography to the namespaces to shorten the code.

```
#region customNamespaces
using System.Security.Cryptography;
#endregion
```

This is the VB.NET code:

```
#Region "customNamespaces"
Imports System.Security.Cryptography
#End Region
```

You also need a couple of class variables. These variables are used to prevent doing an action in the ProcessInputRow multiple times. Also note the column separator variable, which is used to make a difference between two columns with, for example, the values AB AB and ABA B. It is best to use a separator that won't appear in the data. You could use multiple chars.

```
// Boolean variable to do something only onces
Boolean FirstRow = true;
// Variable to store the row type
Type rowType;
// Variable to store the input columns
IDTSInputColumnCollection100 InputColumnCollection;
// Variable to store the value of the column
String columnValue = "";
// Create hashing object. Choose
// the type in the PreExecute
HMAC hashingObject = null;
// Column seperator to make a difference
// between values AB AB and ABA B
String columnSeparator = "|";
```

This is the VB.NET code:

```
' Boolean variable to do something only onces
Dim FirstRow As Boolean = True
' Variable to store the row type
Dim rowType As Type
' Variable to store the input columns
Dim InputColumnCollection As IDTSInputColumnCollection100
' Variable to store the value of the column
Dim columnValue As String = ""
' Create hashing object. Choose
' the type in the PreExecute
Private hashingObject As HMAC = Nothing
' Column seperator to make a difference
' between values AB AB and ABA B
Private columnSeparator As String = "|"
```

In the PreExecute method, you need to choose the hashing type. In this example, you will use MD5, but other algorithms are also possible. If you don't want to use a salt, then you leave out the first two code rows and remove the word saltByteArray in the third row of code.

```csharp
public override void PreExecute()
{
    // Define salt to make hashing more secure.
    String salt = Variables.saltValue.ToString();

    // Create the ByteArray from the Salt string
    byte[] saltByteArray = Encoding.Unicode.GetBytes(salt);

    // Choose hashtype by replacing HMACMD5 with
    // HMACSHA1, HMACSHA256, HMACSHA384, HMACSHA512
    // or HMACRIPEMD160. These are more secure but
    // also take more time to generate.
    hashingObject = new HMACMD5(saltByteArray);

    // Get collection of input columns
    InputColumnCollection = ComponentMetaData.InputCollection[0]
                            .InputColumnCollection;
}
```

This is the VB.NET code:

```vbnet
Public Overrides Sub PreExecute()
    ' Define salt to make hashing more secure.
    Dim salt As String = Variables.saltValue.ToString()

    ' Create the ByteArray from the Salt string
    Dim saltByteArray As Byte() = Encoding.Unicode.GetBytes(salt)

    ' Choose hashtype by replacing HMACMD5 with
    ' HMACSHA1, HMACSHA256, HMACSHA384, HMACSHA512
    ' or HMACRIPEMD160. These are more secure but
    ' also take more time to generate.
    hashingObject = New HMACMD5(saltByteArray)

    ' Get collection of input columns
    InputColumnCollection = Me.ComponentMetaData _
                            .InputCollection(0).InputColumnCollection
End Sub
```

In the PostExecute method, you are only cleaning up the hashing object.

```csharp
public override void PostExecute()
{
    // Clean up hashing object
    if (hashingObject != null)
    {
        hashingObject.Clear();
        hashingObject = null;
    }
}
```

This is the VB.NET code:

```vbnet
Public Overrides Sub PostExecute()
    ' Clean up hashing object
    If (IsNothing(hashingObject)) Then
        hashingObject.Clear()
        hashingObject = Nothing
    End If
End Sub
```

In the Input0_ProcessInputRow method, you are looping through all selected columns to concatenate all column values to one big string, including column separators. This string will be hashed by a separate method and the returned hash value will be saved in the new output column.

```csharp
public override void Input0_ProcessInputRow(Input0Buffer Row)
{
    // Do only onces
    if (FirstRow)
    {
        // Row type to get the value of a column
        rowType = Row.GetType();
    }
    FirstRow = false;

    // string builder to concatenate all column values
    StringBuilder columnConcatenation = new StringBuilder();

    // Used to indicate the first column
    Boolean FirstColumn = true;

    foreach (IDTSInputColumn100 column in InputColumnCollection)
    {
        // Get column value, will fail if null
        try
        {
            // Get current column value
            columnValue = rowType.GetProperty(column.Name).GetValue(Row,
                                                  null).ToString();
        }
        catch
        {
            // Do nothing when value is null
            columnValue = null;
        }

        // Add separator except for the first column
        if (!FirstColumn)
        {
            columnConcatenation.Append(columnSeparator);
        }
        FirstColumn = false;
```

```
    // Concatenate column value to string
    columnConcatenation.Append(columnValue);
  }
  // Call hash method to calculate the hash
  // and store hash in new output column
  Row.Hash = GetHash(columnConcatenation.ToString());
}


// Hash method to convert a string to bytes
public string GetHash(string text)
{
  byte[] bytes = Encoding.Unicode.GetBytes(text);
  return GetHash(bytes);
}


// Hash method to calculate the hash and create
// a hash string
public string GetHash(byte[] bytes)
{
  // Hashing the bytes
  byte[] hash = hashingObject.ComputeHash(bytes);

  // Format the bytes as string
  string hashString = string.Empty;
  foreach (byte x in hash)
  {
    // Format the byte as a hexadecimal byte
    // X = Hexadecimal format
    // 2 = 2 characters
    hashString += String.Format("{0:x2}", x);
  }
  return hashString;
}
```

And this is the VB.NET code:

```
Public Overrides Sub Input0_ProcessInputRow(ByVal Row As Input0Buffer)
  ' Do only onces
  If FirstRow Then
    ' Row type to get the value of a column
    rowType = Row.GetType()
  End If
  FirstRow = False

  ' String builder to concatenate all column values
  Dim columnConcatenation As New StringBuilder()

  ' Used to indicate the first column
  Dim FirstColumn As Boolean = True
```

```vb
For Each column As IDTSInputColumn100 In InputColumnCollection
    ' Get column value, will fail if null
    Try
        ' Get current column value
        columnValue = rowType.GetProperty(column.Name).GetValue(Row, _
                                                    Nothing).ToString()

    Catch
        ' If fail then make value null/nothing
        columnValue = Nothing
    End Try

    ' Add separator except for the first column
    If (Not FirstColumn) Then
        columnConcatenation.Append(columnSeparator)
    End If
    FirstColumn = False

    ' Concatenate column value to string
    columnConcatenation.Append(columnValue)
  Next
  ' Call hash method to calculate the hash
  ' and store hash in new output column
  Row.Hash = GetHash(columnConcatenation.ToString())
End Sub

' Hash method to convert a string to bytes
Public Function GetHash(text As String) As String
    Dim bytes As Byte() = Encoding.Unicode.GetBytes(text)
    Return GetHash(bytes)
End Function

' Hash method to calculate the hash and create
' a hash string
Public Function GetHash(bytes As Byte()) As String
    ' Hashing the bytes
    Dim hash As Byte() = hashingObject.ComputeHash(bytes)

    ' Format the bytes as string
    Dim hashString As String = String.Empty
    For Each x As Byte In hash
        ' Format the byte as a hexadecimal byte
        ' X = Hexadecimal format
        ' 2 = 2 characters
        hashString += [String].Format("{0:x2}", x)
    Next
    Return hashString
End Function
```

The Results

Now run your data flow and check the results. If you add a data viewer after the Script Component, you can see the newly created and filled hash column (see Figure 14-11).

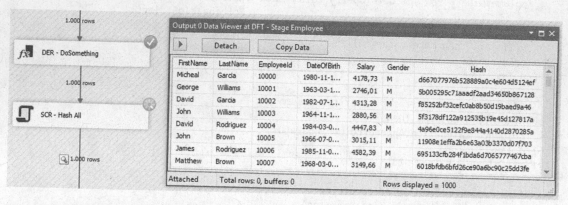

Figure 14-11. *The new Hash column*

You could add a lookup behind this Script Component to check whether the EmployeeId exists in the destination table. If you also retrieve the hash in that same lookup, then you can compare that to the freshly created hash to determine if you need to update the data. Note that you shouldn't update the records with an OLE DB command because that is slow. Inserting into a temporary table and then bulk updating with an Execute SQL Task is probably faster.

Summary

In this chapter you saw the possibilities of reflection. It's handy when doing a lot of repetitive actions for a lot of columns. Adding or removing a column doesn't require a lot of work. You only have to open and close the VSTA environment to let SSIS generate the standard code.

The downside is that the code is a bit more complex and performance is a little worse than when you hard-code all column actions. You can solve some of this performance degradation by moving the columns object to a custom object in the `PreExecute` method and use that object instead of the slower COM object. In the CodePlex project for the Dimension Merge SCD component by Todd McDermid, you can find an excellent example for that, but it requires some heavy coding (see `http://dimensionmergescd.codeplex.com`). You have to consider whether this is useful for your case.

■ ■ ■

CHAPTER 15

Web Services

Chapter 7 explained how to use a web service in a Script Task, but it is also useful in the Data Flow Task for enriching your data, as a destination, and even as a source. Many products use web services as an interface. Tools like Microsoft Dynamics CRM and SharePoint store all data in an SQL Server database, but you are not allowed to edit the data directly in the database. Instead, the vendors provide web services to modify data. This chapter provides some web service examples for commonly used Microsoft products and for web services that you can find on the Internet.

Enriching with Weather

This first example uses the public weather web service seen in Chapter 7. For details and theory about web services, you should read that chapter. In this example, you will enrich the geographical data coming from a flat file with weather information from a web service. Create a package with an empty data flow. Add a Flat File Source Component named FF_SRC – Cities, and connect it to a flat file with the following data. The default 50 string size is OK for the columns in this example. The file in the example package is called Weather.csv.

```
Country,City
netherlands,amsterdam
netherlands,maastricht
belgium,antwerp
france,le touquet
france,agen
germany,hamburg
germany,munich
denmark,alborg
```

Variables

Add a string variable named WebserviceUrl to the package and fill it with the following web service URL: http://www.webservicex.net/globalweather.asmx. This makes it easier to configure the URL, as shown in Figure 15-1.

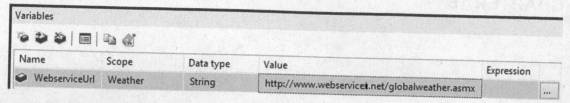

Figure 15-1. String variable to configure the web service

Script Component

Add a Script Component, type transformation, to the data flow and connect it to the source, as shown in Figure 15-2. Give it a useful name, like SCR - Get weather. Then edit the Script Component and add the variable from the previous step to the ReadOnlyVariables property.

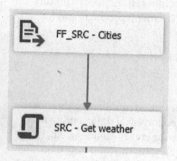

Figure 15-2. Script Component Transformation

Input Columns

In the Script Component Editor, go to the Input Columns tab and add the Country and City columns as ReadOnly input columns for the script; Figure 15-3 shows an example.

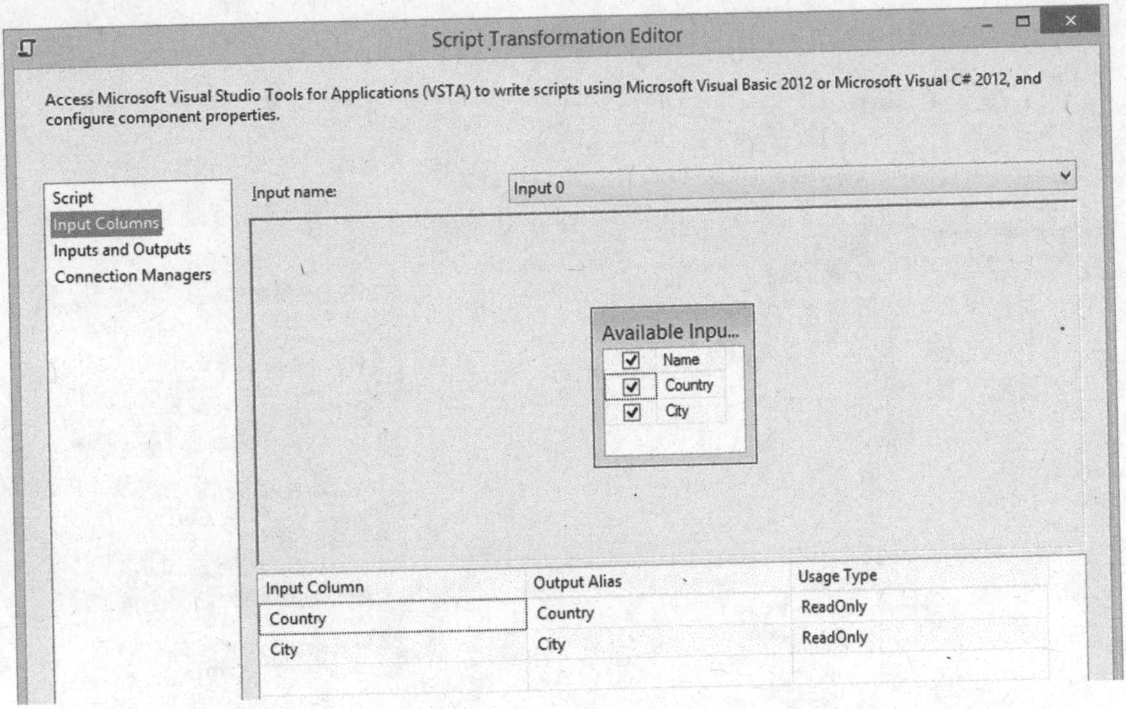

Figure 15-3. Input columns

Inputs and Outputs

You need to create a new string column in which to store the weather information. The web service returns an XML document that you will store in the string column. You could also split the XML in separate columns to make it even nicer. Go to the Inputs and Outputs tab and add a new string column named Weather with date type string 1000. It should be added in Output 0, as shown in Figure 15-4.

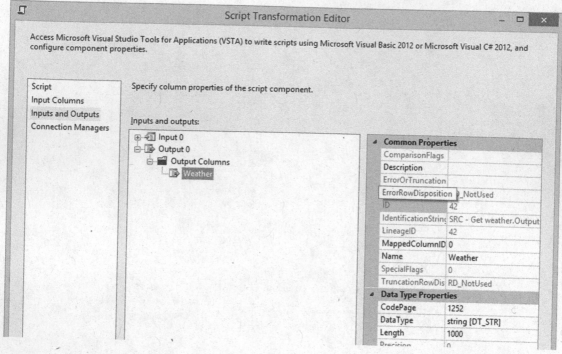

Figure 15-4. *New output column*

Add References

Click the Edit Script... button to open the VSTA environment in Figure 15-5. In the Solution Explorer, right-click the References and add a new Reference named System.ServiceModel. You can find it in the .NET/Framework page. If you use VB.NET, then right-click the VSTA project to add the new reference.

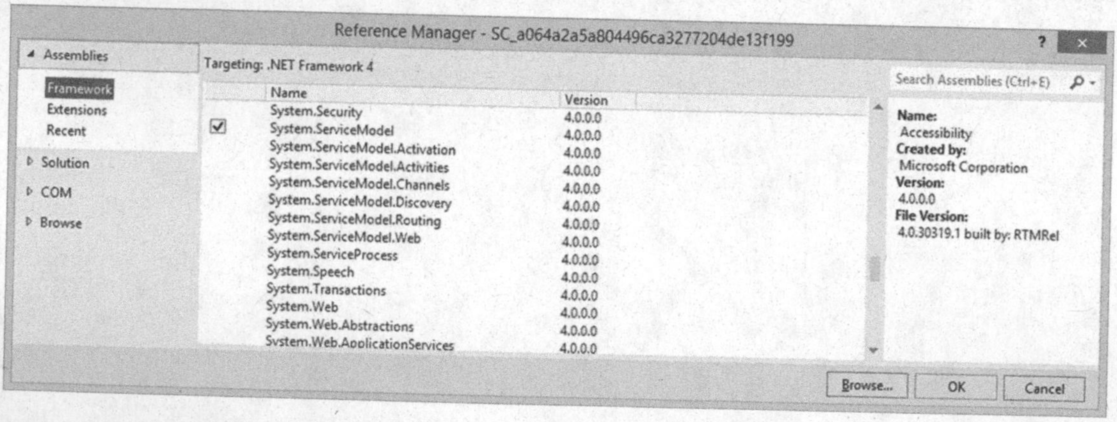

Figure 15-5. *System.ServiceModel*

Add Service Reference

The next step is to add a new Service Reference by right-clicking References, and then choosing Add Service Reference.... In the address bar, paste the URL (http://www.webservicex.net/globalweather.asmx) of the web service, and then click Go to find the web service. Figure 15-6 shows an example.

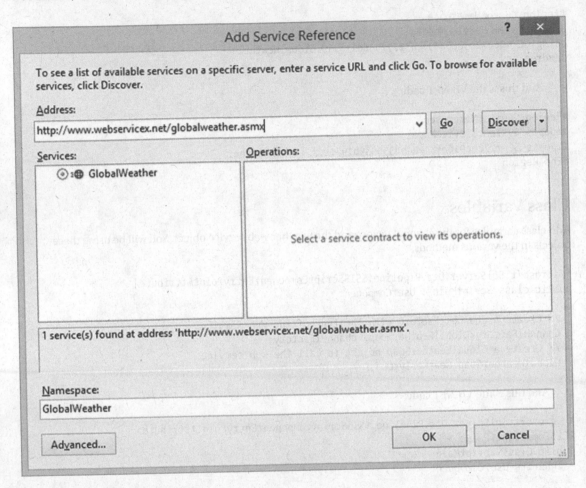

Figure 15-6. *Add Service Reference*

In the NameSpace field, type **GlobalWeather** and then click OK. Now you have added a web service as reference for the design-time code. Make sure to press the Save All button in older versions of Visual Studio.

Namespaces

To shorten the code, add the following namespaces. The prefix of the second namespace named GlobalWeather is coming from the internal VSTA project name. It will be different for each Script Component, but start typing **SC_** and IntelliSense will do the rest.

```
#region CustomNamespace
using System.ServiceModel;
using SC_a064a2a5a804496ca3277204de13f199.GlobalWeather;
#endregion
```

And this is the VB.NET code:

```
#Region "CustomNamespace"
Imports System.ServiceModel
Imports SC_f27cac918ef84ea4bd35b959b1971ecf.GlobalWeather
#End Region
```

Class Variables

Add class variables for the channel factory and the weather web service object. You will be using these objects in the various methods.

```
[Microsoft.SqlServer.Dts.Pipeline.SSISScriptComponentEntryPointAttribute]
public class ScriptMain : UserComponent
{
  // Create a Channel Factory with the type of the Web Service.
  ChannelFactory<GlobalWeatherSoap> channelFactory;
  // Create a GlobalWeatherSoap object to call the web service
  GlobalWeatherSoap weatherSvcObj;
```

And this is the VB.NET code:

```
<Microsoft.SqlServer.Dts.Pipeline.SSISScriptComponentEntryPointAttribute> _
<CLSCompliant(False)> _
Public Class ScriptMain
  Inherits UserComponent

  ' Create a Channel Factory with the type of the Web Service.
  Dim channelFactory As ChannelFactory(Of GlobalWeatherSoap)
  ' Create a GlobalWeatherSoap object to call the web service
  Dim weatherSvcObj As GlobalWeatherSoap
```

PreExecute

In the PreExecute method, you are getting the web service URL from the SSIS string variable. This URL is used in runtime.

```
public override void PreExecute()
{
  // Get the right binding: basicHttp
  BasicHttpBinding httpb = new BasicHttpBinding();
  // And initiate the channelFactory with this binding
  channelFactory = new ChannelFactory<GlobalWeatherSoap>(httpb);

  // The necessary endpoint with our address from the variable
  EndpointAddress ep = new EndpointAddress(Variables.WebserviceUrl.ToString());

  // Create the representation of the web service
  weatherSvcObj = channelFactory.CreateChannel(ep);
}
```

And this is the VB.NET code:

```
Public Overrides Sub PreExecute()
    ' Get the right binding: basicHttp
    Dim httpb As New BasicHttpBinding()
    ' And initiate the channelFactory with this binding
    channelFactory = New ChannelFactory(Of GlobalWeatherSoap)(httpb)

    ' The necessary endpoint with our address from the variable
    Dim ep As New EndpointAddress(Variables.WebserviceUrl.ToString())

    ' Create the representation of the webservice
    weatherSvcObj = channelFactory.CreateChannel(ep)
End Sub
```

Input0_ProcessInputRow

In the ProcessInputRow method, you are calling the web service with the two input columns as parameters to the GetWeather method. The result is stored in the new output column. If you want to split the XML document in separate columns, this is the place. You also might want to add a try-catch construction to catch unexpected errors that this public web service might cause. The example package has an extra try-catch included.

```
public override void Input0_ProcessInputRow(Input0Buffer Row)
{
    // Call Web service with city and country parameters
    Row.Weather = weatherSvcObj.GetWeather(Row.City, Row.Country);
}
```

And this is the VB.NET code:

```vbnet
Public Overrides Sub Input0_ProcessInputRow(ByVal Row As InputOBuffer)
  ' Call Web service with city and country parameters
  Row.Weather = weatherSvcObj.GetWeather(Row.City, Row.Country)
End Sub
```

PostExecute

When you are done, you can close the communication in the PostExecute method.

```
public override void PostExecute()
{
  // Close the communication
  channelFactory.Close();
}
```

And this is the VB.NET code:

```vbnet
Public Overrides Sub PostExecute()
  ' Close the communication
  channelFactory.Close()
End Sub
```

The Results

Now add a dummy derived column and connect it to the Script Component. Add a data viewer, as shown in Figure 15-7, to see the result of our web service call.

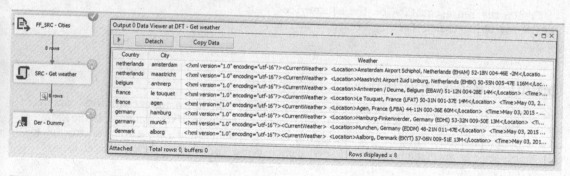

Figure 15-7. Data viewer

Dynamics CRM

This part of the chapter shows how to insert or update data in Microsoft Dynamics CRM 2013, but other versions have a similar web service with similar code. If you don't have Microsoft Dynamics CRM, you can skip this part of the chapter. As stated in the introduction, you are not allowed to edit CRM data directly in the database. Updates are done through web services. But for reading data, you can use the views in the CRM database.

Because each CRM solution uses different entities with a different set of attributes, you don't have a step-by-step example to follow. Instead, you have a set of guidelines and some code examples for all different field types, like regular text fields, option sets, and lookups. The data flow varies per person and per solution, but the script design with the web service is roughly the same. First, a couple of guidelines:

- You want to avoid inserting duplicate data. Therefore, you have to check whether you have a unique key in the source that you can compare to a key in CRM. If there isn't, then you could store the business key from the source in a (hidden) column of CRM. This makes it easy to compare data in the next run.

- To update or delete data in CRM, you need the GUID of the record (the unique key or entity id). So you want to get this data via a lookup transformation on the CRM view (data flow example 2) or with a join to an OLE DB source (data flow example 1) that uses that same CRM view.

- You don't want to unnecessarily update records in CRM. This worsens the performance and it pollutes the CRM history information. So, you want to check for changes in the data. This can be done by getting all columns from CRM that you want to compare, joining it to the source database using the business key, and then using a big expression to compare each column. Another trick is to hash all the columns of both the source and the CRM view. Then you only have to compare one hash column. You can find an example of this in the previous chapter.

Next are two possible data flow designs that you could use to move data from your source to CRM. The bottom part of both solutions (with the Script Components) is the same. If you have multiple sources inserting and updating records in the same CRM identity, then you have to figure out a way to determine which source, or even which record, is leading before moving the data to CRM.

Data Flow Example 1

Example 1 uses a merge-join to compare data from the source to CRM. Figure 15-8 shows the entire data flow for the example.

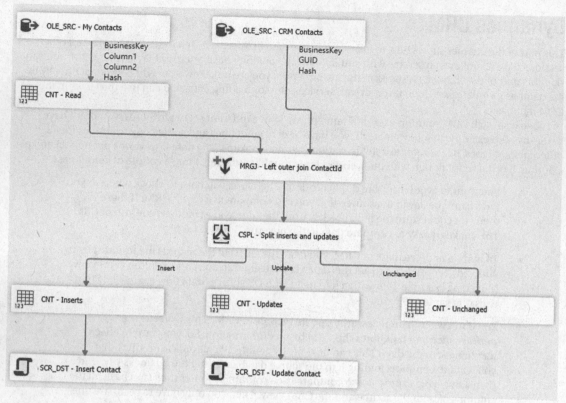

Figure 15-8. *Data flow example 1*

In this first example, you are getting all columns from your source (My Contacts), including the business key. And you add a hash to compare all the columns at once. Instead of using hashbytes, you could also use the Script Component example from Chapter 14 to calculate the hash for all columns or use one of the third-party checksum transformations. The query should look something like this:

```
SELECT      ContactId as SourceContactId
,           Column1
,           Column2
,           HASHBYTES('MD5', Column1 + '|' + Column2) as hash
FROM        myTable
ORDER BY    ContactId        -- For join in SSIS
```

Any data transformations should be added before the merge-join and before calculating the hash. Otherwise, you will compare two different things and always update all existing records. This example doesn't have transformations; therefore, you can calculate the hash in the source query.

In the CRM source (CRM Contacts), select the GUID from CRM (for update/deletes), the source id (for joining), and the hash (for comparing). Only select contacts that have a source id.

```
SELECT      ContactId            -- GUID (entity ID)
,           SourceContactId -- ID from source
,           HASHBYTES('MD5', Column1 + '|' + Column2) as hash
FROM        myCrmContactsView
WHERE       SourceContactId is not null    -- Only contacts from this source
ORDER BY    SourceContactId                -- For join in SSIS
```

In the merge-join, you do a left outer join on the source id between the source and CRM (getting all rows from the source and only those rows from CRM that have a matching sourceid). In the next conditional split, you check which rows should be inserted, updated, or ignored. If the source id from the CRM side is empty, then you need to insert the record. And if the hashes are different, you need to update the record in CRM. All other rows are ignored because they are already in CRM and nothing has changed.

Data Flow Example 2

The second example uses a lookup transformation to compare data from the source to CRM. Figure 15-9 shows this example's flow.

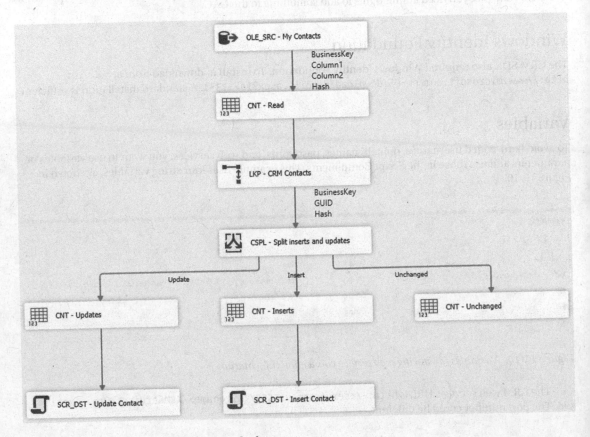

Figure 15-9. *Data flow example 2 using a lookup*

In this second example, you are getting the CRM data with a lookup transformation instead of using an OLE DB source and merge-join. The queries will be the same as in the first example, except without the sorting what was only needed for the merge-join. Which solution you choose depends on the number of records that you get from CRM (preferably, it should fit into memory if you use a lookup) and on the record length of the CRM record because the hashbytes input is limited to 8000 bytes. Any larger and you have to calculate the hash with a different method; for example, with a Script Component. And if you also want to delete or inactivate records in CRM because they don't exist in the source any more, then you need a full outer join, which is only possible with the merge-join.

Download CRM SDK

Before you go to the Script Component, you first have to download the Microsoft CRM 2013 Software Development Kit (SDK), which can be found at http://www.microsoft.com/en-us/download/details.aspx?id=40321 (for 2011, change the ID value in the URL to 24004, 2015 ID=44567). Execute the downloaded file to extract all the files. You only need the Microsoft.Xrm.Sdk.dll assembly, which is found in the SDK\Bin folder.

The next step is to add that assembly to the GAC on the SSIS machine and copy it to the SSIS Binn folder at C:\Program Files (x86)\Microsoft SQL Server\110\DTS\Binn\. (The folder name 110 refers to the SQL Server version: 100 for 2008, 110 for 2012, and 120 for 2014). On a development machine, you can use gacutil to add the assembly to the GAC. On a production server, you need to create an installer or disable UAC and use Windows Explorer to drag the assembly to the GAC, or use a PowerShell script to add them to the GAC. Note that you need admin rights to add something to the GAC.

Windows Identity Foundation

The CRM SDK also required Windows Identity Foundation. To install it, download from at http://www.microsoft.com/en-US/download/details.aspx?id=17331. A standard installation is sufficient.

Variables

To avoid hard-coded usernames, domain names, passwords, and web services, you want to use variables or parameters and use those in the Script Components. This example uses four string variables, as shown in Figure 15-10.

Name	Scope	Data type	Value
CrmWebservice	CRM	String	http://crmserver:5555/CRMDev/XRMServices/2011/Organization.svc
CrmUser	CRM	String	crm_systemuser
CrmPassword	CRM	String	53cr3t!
CrmDomain	CRM	String	yourdomain

Figure 15-10. Variables for storing web service connection information

The CRM web services URL is http://<servername>:5555/<sitename>/XRMServices/Organization. svc. The port number could be different.

Add Script Component

Add a Script Component (type destination) for insert or update, and add the four string variables from the previous step as ReadOnlyVariables. This step is the same for all scripts, as illustrated in Figure 15-11.

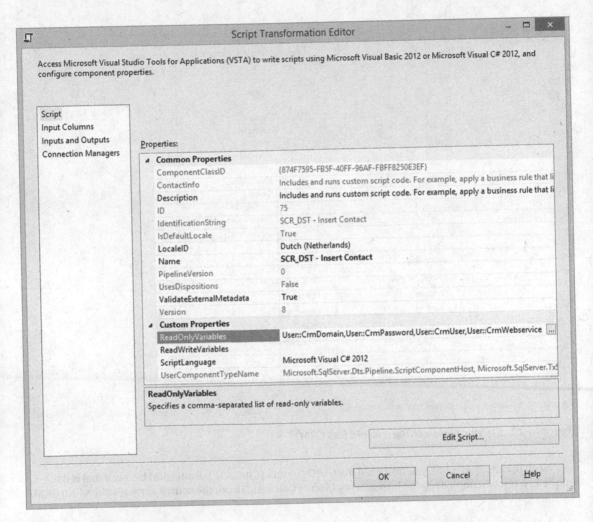

Figure 15-11. ReadOnlyVariables

Input Columns

When inserting a record into CRM, you need the unique id from the source to store it in a (hidden) CRM column, and you need all the data columns from the source (see Figure 15-12) that you want to insert into CRM. For this script, you don't need the hashes or the columns coming from CRM (they are empty anyway).

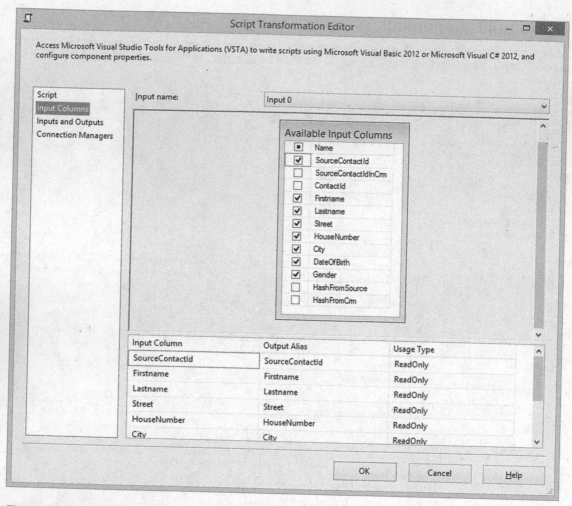

Figure 15-12. *Columns for inserting a record into CRM*

When updating a record, you also need the GUID column (ContactId) from CRM because that is the unique key, but you don't need the business key (SourceContactId) from the source since it's already in CRM.

Add References

Click the Edit Script... button to open the VSTA environment. In the Solution Explorer, you need to add three references, as shown in Figure 15-13:

- microsoft.xrm.sdk.dll (from the SSIS bin folder, use browse)
- System.Runtime.Serialization.dll (from the .NET/Assemblies tab)
- System.ServiceModel.dll (from the .NET/Assemblies tab)

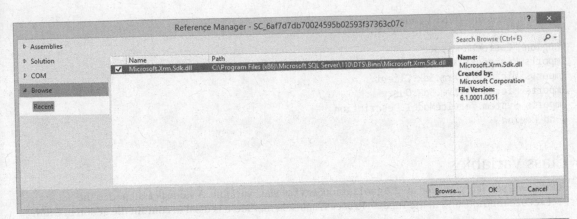

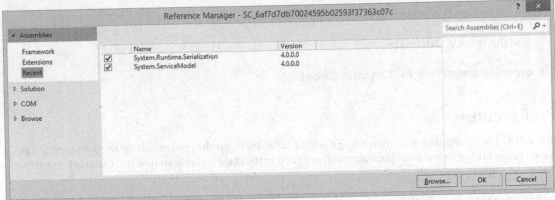

Figure 15-13. Add references

For older versions of Visual Studio (< 2013), it is now time to press the Save All button to save the entire internal VSTA project (including the new references).

Add Namespaces

For shortening the code, add extra using/imports statements on top of the CRM SDK namespaces and to the ServiceModel.Description for the ClientCredentials.

```
#region customNamespaces
using Microsoft.Xrm.Sdk;
using Microsoft.Xrm.Sdk.Client;
using Microsoft.Xrm.Sdk.Query;
using System.ServiceModel.Description;
#endregion
```

And this is the VB.NET code:

```vb
#Region "CustomNamespace"
Imports Microsoft.Xrm.Sdk
Imports Microsoft.Xrm.Sdk.Client
Imports Microsoft.Xrm.Sdk.Query
Imports System.ServiceModel.Description
#End Region
```

Class Variables

For the web service, you need an IOrganizationService class variable. A value is assigned in the PreExecute method; and in the Input0_ProcessInputRow method it is used to commit the action in CRM.

```csharp
IOrganizationService organizationservice;
```

And this is the VB.NET code:

```vb
Dim organizationservice As IOrganizationService
```

PreExecute

In the PreExecute method, you are reading the SSIS variables to get the credentials for the web service call. A new proxy for the web service is created and assigned to the class variable so that you can use it to submit inserts and updates later on.

```csharp
public override void PreExecute()
{
  // Fill the string variables with values from package variables
  string CrmUrl = this.Variables.CrmWebservice.ToString();
  string CrmDomainName = this.Variables.CrmDomain.ToString();
  string CrmUserName = this.Variables.CrmUser.ToString();
  string CrmPassWord = this.Variables.CrmPassword.ToString();

  // Connect to web service with credentials
  ClientCredentials credentials = new ClientCredentials();
  credentials.UserName.UserName = string.Format("{0}\\{1}", CrmDomainName
                                                  , CrmUserName);
  credentials.UserName.Password = CrmPassWord;
  organizationservice = new OrganizationServiceProxy(new Uri(CrmUrl), null
                                          , credentials, null);
}
```

And this is the VB.NET code:

```vbnet
Public Overrides Sub PreExecute()
    ' Fill the string variables with values from package variables
    Dim CrmUrl As String = Me.Variables.CrmWebservice.ToString()
    Dim CrmDomainName As String = Me.Variables.CrmDomain.ToString()
    Dim CrmUserName As String = Me.Variables.CrmUser.ToString()
    Dim CrmPassWord As String = Me.Variables.CrmPassword.ToString()

    ' Connect to web service with credentials
    Dim credentials As New ClientCredentials()
    credentials.UserName.UserName = String.Format("{0}\{1}", CrmDomainName, _
                                                            CrmUserName)

    credentials.UserName.Password = CrmPassWord
    organizationservice = New OrganizationServiceProxy(New Uri(CrmUrl), Nothing _
                                                    , credentials, Nothing)

End Sub
```

Input0_ProcessInputRow

In this method, you are feeding each row in SSIS to the web service. You will use the late binding method because it's faster than early binding, but the end result is the same. A disadvantage of late binding is that you cannot verify names and data types at compile time. In the following are the differences between early and late binding.

```csharp
// Early binding
Contact newContact = new Contact();
newContact.Name = "Joost van Rossum";
organizationservice.Create(newContact);

// Late binding
Entity newContact = new Entity("contact");
newContact["name"] = "Régis Baccaro";
organizationservice.Create(newContact);
```

And this is the VB.NET code:

```vbnet
' Early binding
Dim newContact As New Contact()
newContact.Name = "Joost van Rossum"
organizationservice.Create(newContact)

' Late binding
Dim newContact As New Entity("contact")
newContact("name") = "Régis Baccaro"
organizationservice.Create(newContact)
```

Input0_ProcessInputRow - Insert

The insert code starts with creating an entity object with the name of the CRM entity as parameter.

```
// Create an Entity object of type 'contact'
Entity newContact = new Entity("contact");
```

And this is the VB.NET code:

```
' Create an Entity object of type 'contact'
Dim newContact As New Entity("contact")
```

After that, you can start filling the CRM columns. If you're sure that the SSIS columns are filled with data, then you can assign the value directly.

```
// Store the business key of the source in CRM
// This makes it easier to compare and filter records for update
newContact["SourceContactId"] = Row.SourceContactId;

// Fill crm fields. Note fieldnames are case sensitive!
newContact["firstname"] = Row.Firstname;
newContact["lastname"] = Row.Lastname;
```

And this is the VB.NET code:

```
' Store the business key of the source in CRM
' This makes it easier to compare and filter records for update
newContact("SourceContactId") = Row.SourceContactId

' Fill crm fields. Note fieldnames are case sensitive!
newContact("firstname") = Row.Firstname
newContact("lastname") = Row.Lastname
```

You can also add null checks to the assignment to leave the CRM field untouched in case of a null value. In that case, the value in CRM is null or a default value is used.

```
// Address, but check if the columns are filled
if (!Row.Street_IsNull)
{
  newContact["address1_line1"] = Row.Street;
}
if (!Row.HouseNumber_IsNull)
{
  newContact["address1_line2"] = Row.HouseNumber;
}
if (!Row.City_IsNull)
{
  newContact["address1_city"] = Row.City;
}
```

And this is the VB.NET code:

```
' Address, but check if the columns are filled
If Not Row.Street_IsNull Then
        newContact("address1_line1") = Row.Street
End If
If Not Row.HouseNumber_IsNull Then
        newContact("address1_line2") = Row.HouseNumber
End If
If Not Row.City_IsNull Then
        newContact("address1_city") = Row.City
End If
```

Filling an OptionSet (a drop-down list with defined values) is a little different. Instead of assigning a string, you need to assign the associated id. You need some CRM knowledge to find that id in CRM, so it's probably easier to consult the CRM consultant for this.

```
OptionSetValue contactType = new OptionSetValue();
if (!Row.ContactType_IsNull)
{
    switch (Row.ContactType)
    {
        case "Client":
            contactType.Value = 1;
            break;
        case "Partner":
            contactType.Value = 2;
            break;
        case "Personal":
            contactType.Value = 3;
            break;
        default:
            contactType.Value = 2;
            break;
    }
    newContact.Attributes.Add("contacttype", (OptionSetValue)contactType);
}
```

And this is the VB.NET code:

```
Dim contactType As New OptionSetValue()
If Not Row.ContactType_IsNull Then
  Select Case Row.ContactType
    Case "Client"
      contactType.Value = 1
      Exit Select
    Case "Partner"
      contactType.Value = 2
      Exit Select
    Case "Personal"
      contactType.Value = 3
      Exit Select
```

```
     Case Else
       contactType.Value = 2
     Exit Select
   End Select
   newContact.Attributes.Add("contacttype", DirectCast(contactType, _
                             OptionSetValue))
End If
```

Linking our new contact to an account (a lookup), for example, is done via EntityReference, but you need the GUID of the concerning account. This should be done with a query on CRM in a lookup transformation.

```
// Reference to another entity (lookup)
EntityReference Account = new EntityReference("account", Row.AccountGuid);
newContact["accountid"] = Account;
```

And this is the VB.NET code:

```
' Reference to another entity (lookup)
Dim Account As New EntityReference("account", Row.AccountGuid)
newContact("accountid") = Account
```

And finally, actually adding the contact to CRM is only one line of code.

```
// Create new contact
organizationservice.Create(newContact);
```

And this is the VB.NET code:

```
' Create new contact
organizationservice.Create(newContact)
```

Input0_ProcessInputRow - Update

Updating a contact is very similar to inserting one, but you need the GUID of the contact.

```
// Create an Entity object of type 'contact'
Entity existingContact = new Entity("contact");

// Most important attribute to fill is the entity id
// This is a GUID column from CRM. Without this
// column you can't update records in CRM.
existingContact["contactid"] = Row.ContactId;
```

And this is the VB.NET code:

```
' Create an Entity object of type 'contact'
Dim existingContact As New Entity("contact")
```

```
' Most important attribute to fill is the entity id
' This is a GUID column from CRM. Without this
' column you can't update records in CRM.
existingContact("contactid") = Row.ContactId
```

Next, you can start filling all the CRM columns as in the insert.

```
// Fill crm fields. Note fieldnames are case sensitive!
existingContact["firstname"] = Row.Firstname;
existingContact["lastname"] = Row.Lastname;
```

And this is the VB.NET code:

```
' Fill crm fields. Note fieldnames are case sensitive!
existingContact("firstname") = Row.Firstname
existingContact("lastname") = Row.Lastname
```

But when you add an if statement to check for nulls, you also need to add an else; otherwise, the column won't get updated.

```
// Address, but check if the columns are filled
if (!Row.Street_IsNull)
{
    existingContact["address1_line1"] = Row.Street;
}
else
{
    existingContact["address1_line1"] = "";
}
```

And this is the VB.NET code:

```
' Address, but check if the columns are filled
If Not Row.Street_IsNull Then
    existingContact("address1_line1") = Row.Street
Else
    existingContact("address1_line1") = ""
End If
```

And the last step is the actual update code.

```
// Update contact
organizationservice.Update(existingContact);
```

And this is the VB.NET code:

```
' Update contact
organizationservice.Update(existingContact)
```

Input0_ProcessInputRow - Hard Delete

You can also delete a record from CRM if it's not in your source anymore. In your data flow (merge-join), you should change the left outer join to a full outer join. After that you need to change the expressions in the conditional split. The first "insert" output expression checks whether the sourceContactId on the CRM side is empty. The second "delete" output expression checks whether the sourceContactId on the source side is empty. The last "update" output expression checks whether the hashes are different.

For the input columns in the Script Component, you only need the GUID column from CRM. Note that this will be a physical delete from CRM that can't be undone!

```
// Delete account. First pararameter is the entityname, second parameter
// is the entity id from the CRM source.
organizationservice.Delete("contact", Row.ContactId);
```

And this is the VB.NET code:

```
' Delete account. First pararameter is the entityname, second parameter
' is the entity id from the CRM source.
organizationservice.Delete("contact", Row.ContactId)
```

Input0_ProcessInputRow - Soft Delete

If a physical delete is too much, then you can also inactivate the record, but you need to add an additional assembly from the SDK to the GAC and to the Binn folder: Microsoft.Crm.Sdk.Proxy.dll. And then you also need to reference this assembly in the VSTA environment. In the Add Reference window, browse to the SSIS Binn folder. After that you need to add one more extra namespace for the inactivation.

```
using Microsoft.Crm.Sdk.Messages;
```

And this is the VB.NET code:

```
Import Microsoft.Crm.Sdk.Messages
```

Then the actual inactivate code. Note that this is a request that is added to the queue. So when it's busy in CRM, the script may already be finished, while the request is still in the queue.

```
// Create CRM request to (de)activate record
SetStateRequest setStateRequest = new SetStateRequest();

// Which entity/record should be (de)activate?
// First part in the entityname, second is the entity id from the CRM source.
setStateRequest.EntityMoniker = new EntityReference("contact", Row.ContactId);

// Setting 'State' (0 - Active ; 1 - InActive)
setStateRequest.State = new OptionSetValue(1);

// Setting 'Status' (1 - Active ; 2 - InActive)
setStateRequest.Status = new OptionSetValue(2);
```

```
// Execute the request
SetStateResponse response =
                  (SetStateResponse)organizationservice.Execute(setStateRequest);
```

And this is the VB.NET code:

```
' Create CRM request to (de)activate record
Dim setStateRequest As New SetStateRequest()

' Which entity/record should be (de)activate?
' First part in the entityname, second is the entity id from the CRM source.
setStateRequest.EntityMoniker = New EntityReference("contact", Row.ContactId)

' Setting 'State' (0 - Active ; 1 - InActive)
setStateRequest.State = New OptionSetValue(1)

' Setting 'Status' (1 - Active ; 2 - InActive)
setStateRequest.Status = New OptionSetValue(2)

' Execute the request
Dim response As SetStateResponse = _
    DirectCast(organizationservice.Execute(setStateRequest), SetStateResponse)
```

SharePoint

Calling a SharePoint web service from a Script Component is sometimes necessary. In some cases, you can use a Web Service Task but in other cases, for example where you only have the data available inside the rows of a Data Flow Task, you have to use a Script Component.

In the following example, you are going to get all the documents from all Document libraries in a SharePoint site and get the Excel documents from each library.

You are using SharePoint 2013, but this will also work in SharePoint 2010.

Variables

Figure 15-14 shows the Variables window. Two variables are defined: SiteURL specifies the address of the SharePoint site, and fileType specifies the type of document that is of interest. The document type in the figure is xsls, denoting Microsoft Excel's Open XML spreadsheet format.

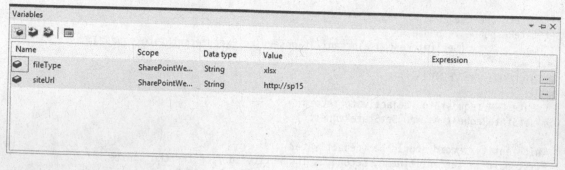

Figure 15-14. The Variables window

Start by creating two string variables that you need for the execution of the package.

Script Component

Add a Data Flow Task to the surface and inside the data flow, add a Script Component called SCR_SRC-GetSharePointLists. Specify the type as Source, as shown in Figure 15-15.

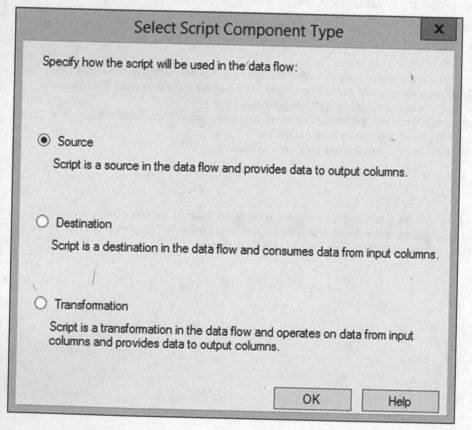

Figure 15-15. Script Component

Inside the Script Transformation Editor, on the Script page, add the SiteUrl variable as ReadOnlyVariable. On the Inputs and Outputs page, add three output columns: ListName, ListID, and webID. Make all three of type string. Figure 15-16 shows the three columns in the example.

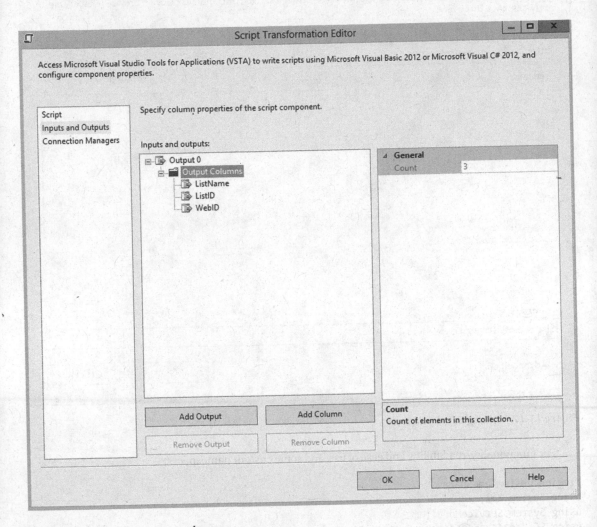

Figure 15-16. *Adding output columns*

The Script

Now it is time to edit the script. First, because you are working with web services, you want to add a Service Reference to your SharePoint list web service. It has the address http://<sitename>/_vti_bin/lists.asmx, where <sitename> is the name of the site. You can see this in Figure 15-17. For the Namespace, choose SharePointListWebService.

The address in Figure 15-17 is for generating the service interface and contracts. The address itself will be dynamic and specified at runtime with the help of the variable SiteURL.

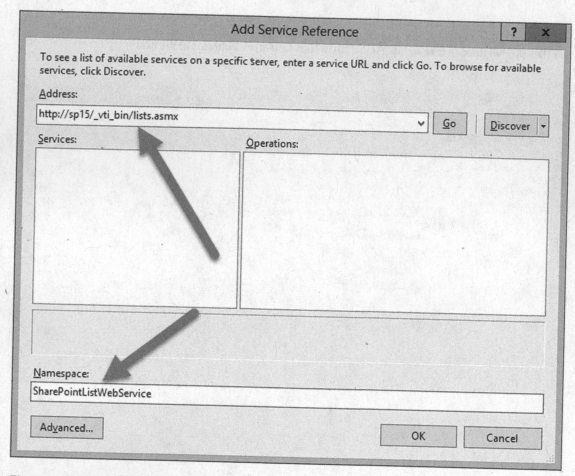

Figure 15-17. Adding Service Reference

For functionality, readability, and ease of use, add some custom namespaces.

```
#region CustomNameSpace
using System.Xml;
using System.ServiceModel;
using SC_3ed715c2a09541348a1ee539d02fd266.SharePointListWebService;
#endregion
```

And this is the VB.NET code:

```
#Region "CustomNamespace"
Imports System.Xml
Imports System.ServiceModel
Imports SC_3ed715c2a09541348a1ee539d02fd266.SharePointListWebService
#End Region
```

If you read Chapter 7, you already know the struggle that it is to get all the right values in all the right config files for web service configuration. This time you've created a method to implement the security needed by SharePoint web service (NTLM). The following method is a C#/VB.NET version of what is in the app.config. The method needs to be added after the last method declaration but inside the C# or VB.NET class in VSTA.

```csharp
internal static ListsSoapClient CreateWebServiceInstance(string siteUrl)
{
    BasicHttpBinding binding = new BasicHttpBinding();
    // These are defaults and reflect  app.config:
    binding.SendTimeout = TimeSpan.FromMinutes(1);
    binding.OpenTimeout = TimeSpan.FromMinutes(1);
    binding.CloseTimeout = TimeSpan.FromMinutes(1);
    binding.ReceiveTimeout = TimeSpan.FromMinutes(10);
    binding.AllowCookies = false;
    binding.BypassProxyOnLocal = false;
    binding.HostNameComparisonMode = HostNameComparisonMode.StrongWildcard;
    binding.MessageEncoding = WSMessageEncoding.Text;
    binding.TextEncoding = System.Text.Encoding.UTF8;
    binding.TransferMode = TransferMode.Buffered;
    binding.UseDefaultWebProxy = true;
    binding.Security.Mode = BasicHttpSecurityMode.TransportCredentialOnly;
    binding.Security.Transport.ClientCredentialType =
                            HttpClientCredentialType.Ntlm;
    binding.Security.Message.ClientCredentialType =
                            BasicHttpMessageCredentialType.UserName;

    return new ListsSoapClient(binding, new EndpointAddress(siteUrl + @"/_vti_bin/lists.asmx"));
}
```

And this is the VB.NET code:

```vbnet
Friend Shared Function CreateWebServiceInstance(siteUrl As String) As ListsSoapClient
    Dim binding As New BasicHttpBinding()
        ' These are defaults and reflectapp.config:
    binding.SendTimeout = TimeSpan.FromMinutes(1)
    binding.OpenTimeout = TimeSpan.FromMinutes(1)
    binding.CloseTimeout = TimeSpan.FromMinutes(1)
    binding.ReceiveTimeout = TimeSpan.FromMinutes(10)
    binding.AllowCookies = False
    binding.BypassProxyOnLocal = False
    binding.HostNameComparisonMode = HostNameComparisonMode.StrongWildcard
    binding.MessageEncoding = WSMessageEncoding.Text
    binding.TextEncoding = System.Text.Encoding.UTF8
    binding.TransferMode = TransferMode.Buffered
    binding.UseDefaultWebProxy = True
    binding.Security.Mode = BasicHttpSecurityMode.TransportCredentialOnly
    binding.Security.Transport.ClientCredentialType = _
                            HttpClientCredentialType.Ntlm
    binding.Security.Message.ClientCredentialType = _
                            BasicHttpMessageCredentialType.UserName
```

```
        Return New ListsSoapClient(binding, New EndpointAddress(siteUrl & _
                                 Convert.ToString("/_vti_bin/lists.asmx")))
End Function
```

As you can see, everything you need for the configuration is in there. The important part though is the ClientCredentialType. SharePoint requires NTLM. If you are calling from within, you don't need to pass credentials in. Instantiate the client in the PreExecute method of the script:

```
//Create the client with all the bindings set
ListsSoapClient client = CreateWebServiceInstance(siteUrl);
//Programatically sets the credentials
client.ClientCredentials.Windows.ClientCredential = new System.Net.NetworkCredential();
client.ClientCredentials.Windows.AllowedImpersonationLevel = System.Security.Principal.
TokenImpersonationLevel.Impersonation;

client.Open();

//Call the method to get all the lists
result = client.GetListCollection();
//Tidy up
client.Close();
```

And this is the VB.NET code:

```
'Create the client with all the bindings set
Dim client As ListsSoapClient = CreateWebServiceInstance(siteUrl)
'Programatically sets the credentials
client.ClientCredentials.Windows.ClientCredential = New System.Net.NetworkCredential()
client.ClientCredentials.Windows.AllowedImpersonationLevel = System.Security.Principal.
TokenImpersonationLevel.Impersonation

client.Open()

'Call the method to get all the lists
result = client.GetListCollection()
'Tidy up
client.Close()
```

The result is stored in a variable called result, and after that in the CreateNewOutputRows method, you can loop over it and add one row with the information for each result.

```
foreach (XmlNode node in result)
{
    if (node.Name == "List")
    {
        OutputOBuffer.AddRow();
        OutputOBuffer.ListID = node.Attributes["ID"].Value;
        OutputOBuffer.ListName = node.Attributes["Title"].Value;
    }
}
```

And this is the VB.NET code:

```
For Each node As XmlNode In result
        If node.Name = "List" Then
                OutputoBuffer.AddRow()
                OutputoBuffer.ListID = node.Attributes("ID").Value

                OutputoBuffer.ListName = node.Attributes("Title").Value
        End If
Next
```

Extracting Excel Files from the Libraries

Now that you have the output rows, you need to add another Script Component called SRC_TRA-GetExcelDocuments to the Data Flow Task. This time, you choose the Transformation type because you will take every list and get the items you need from it.

On its Script page, add fileType and siteURL to the list of ReadOnlyVariables.

On the Input columns page, check all available columns: ListName, ListID, and WebID.

In the Inputs and Outputs page, it is important to remember to set the SynchronousInputID to None, because you want the Script Component to generate more rows in its output than it received. Obviously, there can be more than one Excel file per document library.

■ **Note**   The difference between synchronous and asynchronous outputs is explained in more detail in Chapter 11.

You also add two columns to the output: FileFullPath of type string and length 250, and a listName of type string with a default length for returning the name of the library where the file is stored (see Figure 15-18).

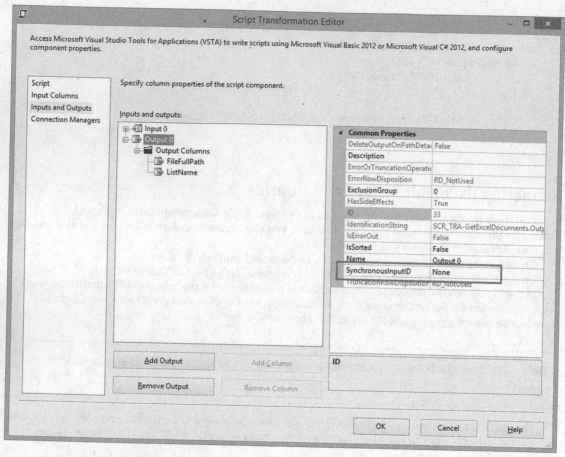

Figure 15-18. *Adding output to the Script Component*

You need to add a reference to the SharePoint web service once more, exactly as before. You also add the help method to set the bindings.

Again, you need some custom namespaces:

```
#region CustomNameSpace
using System.Xml;
using System.Windows.Forms;
using System.ServiceModel;
using SC_3ed715c2a09541348a1ee539d02fd266.SharePointListWebService;
using System.Text;
using System.ServiceModel.Description;
#endregion
```

And this is the VB.NET code:

```
#Region "CustomNameSpace"
Imports System.Xml
Imports System.Windows.Forms
```

```
Imports System.ServiceModel
Imports SC_3ed715c2a09541348a1ee539d02fd266.SharePointListWebService
Imports System.Text
Imports System.ServiceModel.Description
#End Region
```

PreExecute

In the PreExecute method of the script, instantiate and open the web service. You don't want it to get instantiated for each row that you go through.

```
//Assign the package variables to some local variables
string siteUrl = Variables.siteUrl;
fileType = Variables.fileType;
//Create the client with all the bindings set
client = CreateWebServiceInstance(siteUrl);
//Programatically sets the credentials
client.ClientCredentials.Windows.ClientCredential = new
                                         System.Net.NetworkCredential();
client.ClientCredentials.Windows.AllowedImpersonationLevel =
            System.Security.Principal.TokenImpersonationLevel.Impersonation;
client.Open();
```

And this is the VB.NET code:

```
'Assign the package variables to some local variables
Dim siteUrl As String = Variables.siteUrl
fileType = Variables.fileType
'Create the client with all the bindings set
client = CreateWebServiceInstance(siteUrl)
'Programatically sets the credentials
client.ClientCredentials.Windows.ClientCredential = New System.Net.NetworkCredential()
client.ClientCredentials.Windows.AllowedImpersonationLevel = System.Security.Principal.
TokenImpersonationLevel.Impersonation
client.Open()
```

Input0_ProcessInputRow

The Input0_ProcessInputRow method is where the work happens. You call another SharePoint web service method there. The GetListItems method returns all elements from a list. More information about this method is available at https://msdn.microsoft.com/en-us/library/lists.lists.getlistitems.

Basically, you need to define a query element containing the query that determines which records are returned and in what order, as well as a viewFields element that specifies which fields to return in the query and in what order. To keep things tidy, there are some helping methods to create the XML nodes and elements. The complete script for the chapter is available for download, so only the relevant parts are listed here.

The call to the web service looks like the following:

```
XmlNode listContent = client.GetListItems(listName, null, null,
          (XmlElement)ViewFields, null, (XmlElement)QueryOptions, webID);
```

And this is the VB.NET code:

```vbnet
Dim listContent As XmlNode = client.GetListItems(listName, Nothing, Nothing,
DirectCast(ViewFields, XmlElement), Nothing, DirectCast(QueryOptions, XmlElement), _webID)
```

After calling the web service and doing some work with the schema and namespace, you are able to loop over the result to extract the file types that you need.

```csharp
foreach (XmlNode row in rows)
{
    if (row.Attributes["ows_ContentType"].Value == "Document" &&
        row.Attributes["ows_DocIcon"].Value == fileType)
    {
        //more than one excel file per library - add one row per file to the output
        OutputOBuffer.AddRow();
        OutputOBuffer.FileFullPath = row.Attributes["ows_EncodedAbsUrl"].Value;
        OutputOBuffer.ListName = listName;
        //xmlResultsDoc.Save(@"c:\listContent.xml"); // for debug
    }
}
```

And this is the VB.NET code:

```vbnet
For Each row As XmlNode In rows
        If row.Attributes("ows_ContentType").Value = "Document" AndAlso row.Attributes
        ("ows_DocIcon").Value = fileType Then
                'more than one excel file per library - add one row per file to the output
                OutputOBuffer.AddRow()
                OutputOBuffer.FileFullPath = row.Attributes("ows_EncodedAbsUrl").Value
                OutputOBuffer.ListName = listName
        End If
Next
```

Finally, add a Multicast and a data viewer to the data flow to be able to see the data. The result is in Figure 15-19.

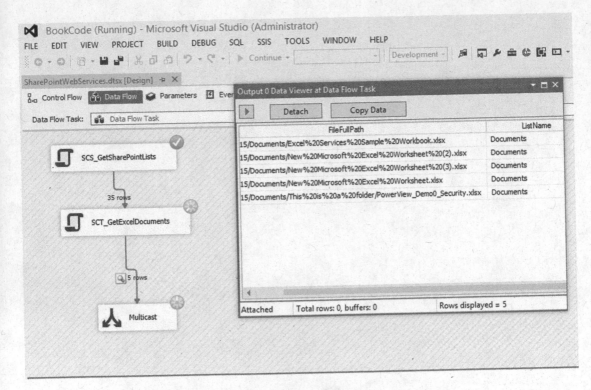

Figure 15-19. The result of the call to SharePoint web service

Summary

In this chapter you learned how to use web services in the Script Component, especially for Microsoft products like Dynamics CRM and SharePoint. Note that web services in general are slower than accessing APIs directly. But it has a lot of advantages, such as being the industry standard, the vendor agnostics, and it's decoupled. Furthermore, the nature of web services allows you to add some extreme flexibility to your SSIS solutions.

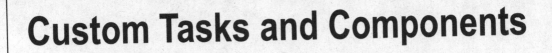

PART IV

Custom Tasks and Components

■ ■ ■

CHAPTER 16

Create a Custom Task

In the previous chapters, you created some very useful Script Tasks to help you with all kinds of tasks. The downside of using a Script Task is that the code is stored in the package itself. If you have multiple packages using the same Script Task, then you end up with a whole bunch of Script Tasks—each using its own copy of the code. When you need to fix a bug or add some extra functionality, you first have to find all the packages that use that particular Script Task and then change them all, one by one.

Another problem with the Script Task is that it requires some .NET knowledge. No problem for you, but most SSIS developers don't have .NET programming skills. If they want to use your handy Script Task code, then simple things like using another variable or connection manager will require you to edit the script. When you create a custom task, you add a user interface so that people who use your task don't need particular programming skills (see Figure 16-1).

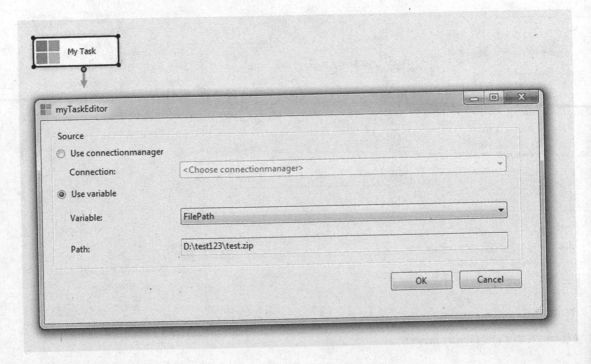

Figure 16-1. Custom task for the control flow

There is one downside for using custom tasks in SSIS. You need to install your task on all the servers and all the development stations that use it. In some organizations that can be a huge challenge, because some server administrators don't like adding assemblies to the Global Assembly Cache.

Custom Task Preparations

For this example, you will create a task that checks whether a file exists. It uses either a connection manager or a variable to get the file path that it will check. For this you need a Visual Studio version that supports C# and VB.NET projects. BIDS or SSDT is not enough because they only support BI projects. We used Visual Studio Professional 2013 for this example, but there are less expensive versions that also support C# and VB.NET; for example, Visual Studio Community or Visual Studio Express.

And, of course, you need to install all SSIS versions that you want to support with your custom task. You need to recompile your code with different references if you want your task to work with multiple versions of SSIS.

Creating Visual Studio Projects

For this custom task you use two Class Library projects: one for the actual task and one for the user interface. Make sure that you choose the appropriate .NET version for the task (SSIS 2005: 2.0, SSIS 2008: 3.5, SSIS 2012: 4.0, and SSIS 2014 also 4.0). First, create a new project called myTask (see Figure 16-2) and then add a second Class Library project, called myTaskUI, to the same solution.

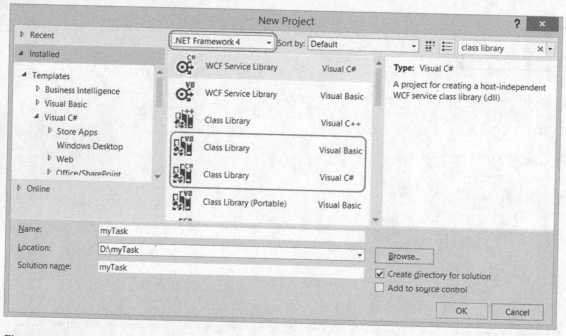

Figure 16-2. *Class Library projects*

Before you start coding, you have to address a lot of other things, like references, strong names, build events, and icons.

Adding SSIS References

To communicate with SSIS, you need to add SSIS references to the projects. Both projects need a reference to Microsoft.SqlServer.ManagedDTS. The second UI project also needs a reference to Microsoft.SqlServer.Dts. Design. For SSIS 2012 and above, you can find these assemblies (.dll files) in the Global Assembly Cache (GAC): `C:\Windows\Microsoft.NET\assembly\GAC_MSIL\`.

```
Microsoft.SqlServer.Dts.Design\v4.0_11.0.0.0__89845dcd8080cc91\Microsoft.SqlServer.Dts.
Design.dll
Microsoft.SqlServer.ManagedDTS\v4.0_11.0.0.0__89845dcd8080cc91\Microsoft.SqlServer.
ManagedDTS.dll
```

If you have installed multiple versions of SSIS 2012 and above then it is version 4.0_11.0.0.0 for 2012, v4.0_12.0.0.0 for 2014 and for 2016 it is version 4.0_13.0.0.0 For older SSIS versions you can find these dll files in the assemblies folder of SQL Server: C:\Program Files (x86)\Microsoft SQL Server\100\SDK\Assemblies (replace 100 with 90 for SSIS 2005).

Default Namespace and Assembly Name

Go to the properties of your project. In the Application page, you need to change the Assembly name and Default namespace in both projects. The Default namespace will be ScriptingBook.myTask and the Assembly name will be the default namespace plus the project name: ScriptingBook.myTask.myTask and ScriptingBook.myTask.myTaskUI (see Figure 16-3).

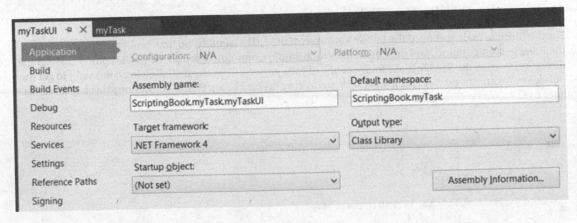

Figure 16-3. *Setting the namespace and the assembly name*

Creating a Key for a Strong Name

An SSIS runtime requirement for assemblies is that they be located in the GAC. The GAC requires that assemblies are strong named. This provides a unique identity as well as a guaranteed location (the GAC) in which the SSIS runtime can find the executables it needs. So you need to strong name your assemblies. Go to the properties of one of the projects and then to the Signing page. Check the "Sign the assembly" check box and then add a new key file in the drop-down list. The name for this example is myTask.snk, with sha256RSA as signature algorithm and no password (see Figure 16-4). After clicking the OK button, the new key file will be visible in the Solution Explorer. Next, copy the same .snk file to the other project and then sign that project with the same key.

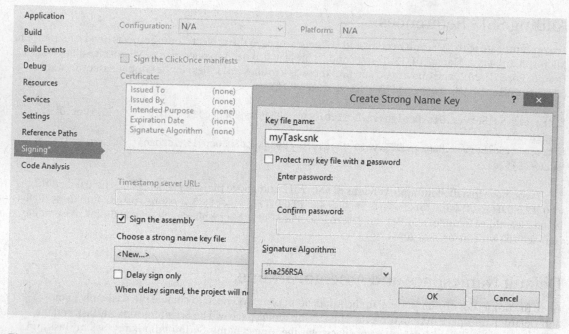

Figure 16-4. Add key file (C# project, but VB.NET looks similar)

Getting the Public Key Token

For the runtime code you need the Public KeyToken of the GUI assembly. So first, build the projects using the Release configuration, and then open the Visual Studio Command Prompt. Use a CD command (change directory) to go to the Bin\Release folder of one of your projects. Execute the following command to get the publicKeyToken: sn.exe -t ScriptingBook.myTask.myTask.dll (see Figure 16-5). Copy this key token for later use.

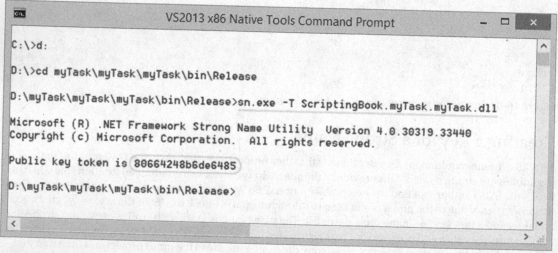

Figure 16-5. Strong name utility to get the public key token

Icons

Of course you need a good icon for the task. There are plenty of free icons available online and there are also tools to create new icons. Add an icon file to both projects via the Solution Explorer. After adding the icon file, make sure to change the Build Action property to Embedded Resource, as shown in Figure 16-6; otherwise, the icon won't show up. Later on you can use this icon in the Windows Form of the UI project. Then it will show when you edit the task.

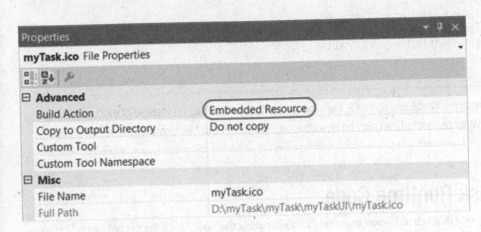

Figure 16-6. *Setting the Build Action of the icon*

In the runtime project, you can use this file to give your task a custom icon instead of the default. This will show in the SSIS Toolbox and in the control flow. The code is explained later on.

Build Events

To use the assemblies in SSIS, you need to install them in the GAC for runtime and copy them to the task folder of SSIS for design-time. With the Build Events page, you can do that automatically when you build the Visual Studio project. But because you are adding assemblies to the GAC, you need to run Visual Studio as administrator. Go to the properties of your projects and then to the Build Events page. C# projects have a separate tab named Build Events, but VB.NET projects have a Build Events button on the Compile tab. Add the following command to the post-build events. Note that the number in the SQL Server folder is different for each SSIS version: 2005: 90, 2008: 100, 2012, 110, 2014: 120, and 2016: 130.

SSIS 2008
```
cd $(ProjectDir)
@SET TASKDIR="C:\Program Files (x86)\Microsoft SQL Server\100\DTS\Tasks\"
@SET GACUTIL="C:\Program Files (x86)\Microsoft SDKs\Windows\v7.0A\bin\gacutil.exe"
Echo Installing dll in GAC
Echo $(OutDir)
Echo $(TargetFileName)
%GACUTIL% -if "$(OutDir)$(TargetFileName)"
Echo Copying files to Tasks
copy "$(OutDir)$(TargetFileName)" %TASKDIR%
```

SSIS 2012 with SSDT 2010

```
cd $(ProjectDir)
@SET TASKDIR="C:\Program Files (x86)\Microsoft SQL Server\110\DTS\Tasks\"
@SET GACUTIL="C:\Program Files (x86)\Microsoft SDKs\Windows\v7.0A\Bin\NETFX 4.0 Tools\
gacutil.exe"
Echo Installing dll in GAC
Echo $(OutDir)
Echo $(TargetFileName)
%GACUTIL% -if "$(OutDir)$(TargetFileName)"
Echo Copying files to Tasks
copy "$(OutDir)$(TargetFileName)" %TASKDIR%
```

■ **Note** If you are using Visual Studio 2012, then the gacutil is located in v8.0a instead of v7.0a. This could also vary for other versions. gactuil can also be downloaded. It is part of the Microsoft Windows SDK.

Custom Task Runtime Code

You first start with code that is used when executing and validating the task. Since the complete code is too big to show it in a book, you are focusing on the most important SSIS stuff. But the code is available with this book, so you can copy the myTask.cs file from example code and add it to your project.

First, you need to add the Microsoft.SqlServer.Dts.Runtime to the namespaces to shorten the code. The following is the complete list used for this project:

```
using System;
using System.ComponentModel;
using System.IO;
using System.Xml;
using Microsoft.SqlServer.Dts.Runtime;
```

Now the most important code of your task: where you name it, add an icon for it, and connect it to the editor assembly: DtsTask. The following is the code; note that the UITypeName assignment has been wrapped for readability, but should be one long line in your code.

```
namespace ScriptingBook.myTask
{
    // Connection Dir to the editor assembly. Copy the PublicKeyToken from the previous step.
    [DtsTask(
    DisplayName = "My Task",
    TaskType = "myTask",
    TaskContact = "ScriptingBook Example",
    IconResource = "ScriptingBook.myTask.myTask.ico",
    UITypeName = "ScriptingBook.myTask.myTaskInterface,
                  ScriptingBook.myTask.myTaskUI,
                  Version=1.0.0.0,
                  Culture=Neutral,
                  PublicKeyToken=80664248b6de6485",
```

```
RequiredProductLevel = DTSProductLevel.None)]
public class myTask : Task, IDTSComponentPersist
}
```

The DtsTask tag has a couple of properties that can change:

- **DisplayName**: The name you see in the toolbox; it is the default name when you drag the task to the control flow.

- **TaskType**: The technical name of your task.

- **TaskContact**: Your name and contact information. This information will be shown in case of fatal errors. The users are then able to contact you.

- **IconResource**: The fully qualified name of your embedded icon. This is shown in the toolbox and when you drag the task to the control flow. Try to find an icon that describes your task and fits the rest of the icons. Quite a daunting task.

- **UITypeName**: This is the connection to the editor where you name the interface class and UI class. In this string you also need to paste the Public key token that you retrieved via the sn command.

- **RequiredProductLevel**: It is best to keep this at the default, but you can choose another product level (Enterprise, Standard, Workgroup), after which your tasks only work for that edition of SQL Server.

Also notice the interface and base class names that follow the class name. IDTSComponentPersist is an interface declaring methods that you implement as part of your class that implements that interface. Task is a base class implementing certain default methods that you are able to override and implement somewhat differently in your own code.

Task Properties

Next are the properties of the task (see Figure 16-7). These properties are for storing the chosen values from your task editor. Besides the name and datatype of each task property, you can add extra metadata, like a description to clarify the use of the property, a default value, or a category to order all properties.

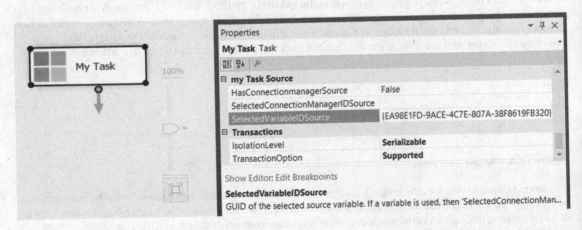

Figure 16-7. Custom Task properties

The following code shows the three properties that you are using for this task:

```
private bool _hasConnectionmanagerSource = true;
[CategoryAttribute("my Task Source")]
[Description("True if a connectionmanager is used for the task as source.")]
[DefaultValue(true)]
public bool HasConnectionmanagerSource
{
  get { return this._hasConnectionmanagerSource; }
  set {this._hasConnectionmanagerSource = value; }
}

private string _selectedConnectionManagerIDSource = "";
[CategoryAttribute("my Task Source")]
[Description("GUID of the selected source connectionmanager.")]
public string SelectedConnectionManagerIDSource
{
  get { return this._selectedConnectionManagerIDSource; }
  set { this._selectedConnectionManagerIDSource = value; }
}

private string _selectedVariableIDSource = "";
[CategoryAttribute("my Task Source")]
[Description("GUID of the selected source variable.")]
public string SelectedVariableIDSource
{
  get { return this._selectedVariableIDSource; }
  set { this._selectedVariableIDSource = value; }
}
```

Validating Task

To validate the custom task, you need to override the Validate method. Basically, you need to check the values of the properties from the previous paragraph. When they don't match your expectations, you can fire an error or warning and return Failure as a result. The validation method is executed at design-time when you close the editor, and twice in runtime: when the package is initialized and when the task is executed.

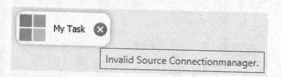

Figure 16-8. Design-time error

In this example you are checking if a connection manager or variable has been selected by the user. If not, you fire an error. You are also checking if the selected variable or connection manager still exists. This is done by looping through all variables or connection managers to verify that the GUID exists.

It is also possible to add checks. For example, checking whether the file path in the variable or connection manager exists.

```csharp
public override DTSExecResult Validate(Connections connections,
                                       VariableDispenser variableDispenser,
                                       IDTSComponentEvents componentEvents,
                                       IDTSLogging log)

{

    // If you have used a ConnectionManager then
    // you check if you have a valid one !
    if (HasConnectionmanagerSource)
    {
        // Check if a connection manager is selected in the combobox
        if (String.IsNullOrEmpty(_selectedConnectionManagerIDSource))
        {
            componentEvents.FireError(0, "MyTask",
                                      "Connectionmanager is mandatory.",
                                      "", 0);

            return DTSExecResult.Failure;
        }

        // Check if the selected connection manager still exists
        if (FindConnectionManager(connections,
                                  _selectedConnectionManagerIDSource)
                        == null)

        {
            componentEvents.FireError(0, "MyTask",
                                      "Connectionmanager doesn't exist.",
                                      "", 0);
            return DTSExecResult.Failure;
        }
    }
    else
    {
                // Do the same checks for variables
    }
        // No errors encountered
    return DTSExecResult.Success;
}

// Method to translate a guid to an actual connection manager.
// It loops through all connection managers and compairs the guid.
private ConnectionManager FindConnectionManager(Connections connections,
                                                string connectionManagerID)

{
  ConnectionManager tempConnManager = null;
  foreach (ConnectionManager connManager in connections)
  {
    if (connManager.ID == connectionManagerID)
    {
```

```
        tempConnManager = connManager;
        return tempConnManager;
    }
  }
  return tempConnManager;
}
```

Execution Code

The actual code for the task is executed in the overridden method called Execute. In this example, you are first checking whether a connection manager or variable has been used. After that you are translating the GUID into an actual connection manager or variable to extract the file path from it. This is done with methods similar to those used in the preceding editor code.

Finally, you use a simple File.Exists to check whether the file path refers to an existing file. If it doesn't exist, you fire an error event with a descriptive error message and return Failure as the execution result, causing the task to fail.

```
// Class variable for storing the filepath
private string _filePathSource = "";

public override DTSExecResult Execute(Connections connections,
                            VariableDispenser variableDispenser,
                            IDTSComponentEvents componentEvents,
                            IDTSLogging log,
                            object transaction)
{
  // Convert the guid to an actual variable or Connection Manager
  // and get the filepath from the connection manager or variable
  if (HasConnectionmanagerSource)
  {
        _selectedConnectionManagerSource = FindConnectionManager
                                (connections,_selectedConnectionManagerIDSource);
        _filePathSource = GetFilePathSource(
                        _selectedConnectionManagerSource);
  }
  else
  {
        _selectedVariableSource = FindVariable(
                            variableDispenser,
                                _selectedVariableIDSource);
        _filePathSource = GetFilePathSource(_selectedVariableSource);
  }

  if (!File.Exists(_filePathSource))
  {
        componentEvents.FireError(0, "My Task", "File "
                            + _filePathSource
                                + " doesn't exist", "", 0);
        return DTSExecResult.Failure;
  }
```

```
    else
    {
            return DTSExecResult.Success;
    }
}
```

SaveToXML and LoadFromXml

In the class definition, you inherited from Task for executing and validating your task, but you also implemented the IDTSComponentPersist interface for saving changes from the editor into the package XML and vice versa.

```
void IDTSComponentPersist.LoadFromXML(System.Xml.XmlElement node,
                                      IDTSInfoEvents infoEvents)

{
  // This might occur when the task's XML
  // has been modified outside BIDS/SSDT
  if (node.Name != "MyTask")
  {
    throw new Exception(string.Format(
        "Unexpected task element when loading task - {0}.", "MyTask"));
  }
  else
  {
    // populate the private property variables with values from package XML.
    _hasConnectionmanagerSource = Convert.ToBoolean(
                             node.Attributes.GetNamedItem(
                             "HasConnectionmanagerSource").Value);
    _selectedConnectionManagerIDSource = node.Attributes.GetNamedItem(
                           "SelectedConnectionManagerIDSource").Value;
    _selectedVariableIDSource = node.Attributes.GetNamedItem(
                           "SelectedVariableIDSource").Value;

  }
}


void IDTSComponentPersist.SaveToXML(System.Xml.XmlDocument doc,
                                    IDTSInfoEvents infoEvents)

{
  // create node in the package XML
  XmlElement taskElement = doc.CreateElement(string.Empty, "MyTask",
                                             string.Empty);


  // create attributes in the node that represent the custom properties
  // and add each to the element

  // Boolean indicating if you are using a connection manager or variable
  XmlAttribute MyTaskXmlAttribute = doc.CreateAttribute(string.Empty,
                             "HasConnectionmanagerSource", string.Empty);
  MyTaskXmlAttribute.Value = _hasConnectionmanagerSource.ToString();
  taskElement.Attributes.Append(MyTaskXmlAttribute);
```

```
// The GUID from the connection manager
MyTaskXmlAttribute = doc.CreateAttribute(string.Empty,
                        "SelectedConnectionManagerIDSource",
                        string.Empty);
MyTaskXmlAttribute.Value = _selectedConnectionManagerIDSource.ToString();
taskElement.Attributes.Append(MyTaskXmlAttribute);

// The GUID from the variable
MyTaskXmlAttribute = doc.CreateAttribute(string.Empty,
                            "SelectedVariableIDSource", string.Empty);
MyTaskXmlAttribute.Value = _selectedVariableIDSource.ToString();
taskElement.Attributes.Append(MyTaskXmlAttribute);

//add the new element to the package document
doc.AppendChild(taskElement);
}
```

Custom Task Form

The form layout is very basic to keep things easy to explain (see Figure 16-9). To select the file that needs to be checked, the user should be able to select a File, Flat File or Excel Connection Manager, or the user should be able to select a string variable (that contains a file path). And to make it user-friendly, the user should also be able to create a new connection manager or a new variable directly in the task.

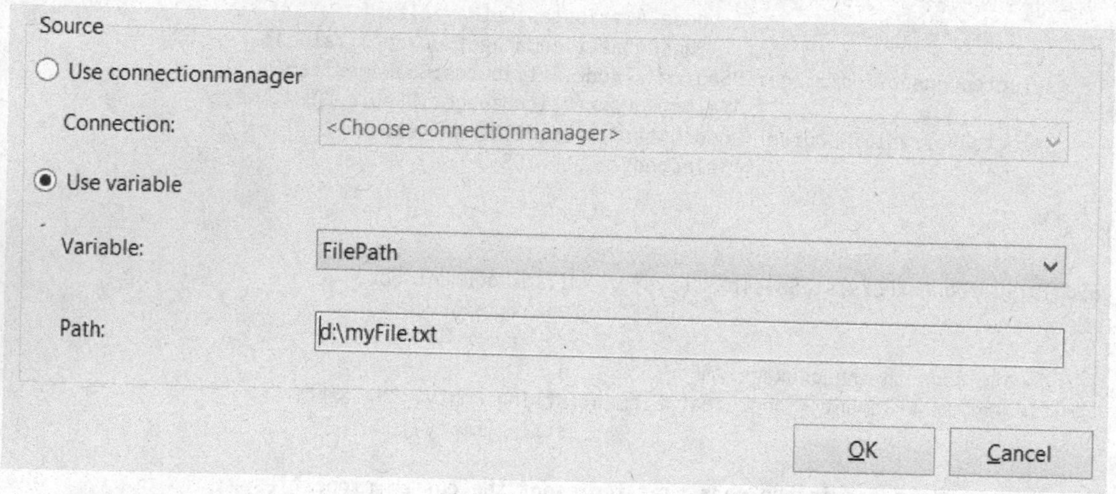

Figure 16-9. The basic form

Even a very simple task like this one has a lot of code that could easily reach over 30 pages, which probably isn't very useful in a book. Therefore, we will only show parts of the code focusing on the SSIS stuff, but the complete code is, of course, available with this book. You can add the form from the example project to your UI project in four steps:

1. Add a reference to System.Drawing and System.Windows.Forms in the UI project.

2. Copy the three form files—myTaskEditor.cs, myTaskEditor.Designer.cs, and myTaskEditor.resx—to the folder in your own UI project.

3. Right-click your UI project and choose "Add, Existing item" to add myTaskEditor.cs, myTaskEditor.Designer.cs and myTaskEditor.resx.

4. Close and reopen your solution. Then, open the form to see what you have added.

Form Code

First, the usings to shorten the code. You only need six namespaces in here. By default there are more, but you can remove them. Visual Studio even has an option to remove unused usings: right-click a using and choose Organize usings (this could vary per Visual Studio version).

```
using System;
using System.Collections;
using System.Drawing;
using System.Windows.Forms;
using Microsoft.SqlServer.Dts.Runtime;
using Microsoft.SqlServer.Dts.Runtime.Design;
```

TaskHost and ServiceProvider

The taskHost property is used to get and set the properties of the current task. By properties, we mean all things you want to save when you close the editor, such as which variable or connection manager was selected. Or if you want to extend the example with a retry feature, then you also want to store the number of retries and the pause between the retries. In the runtime code, you saw that these properties are used in the Validate and Execute methods to check the correct file path. But the TaskHost can also be used to get properties of the current package, like a list of all the variables that are available in this particular package. And the ServiceProvider property is used to add new variables or connection managers or to get a list of current connection managers. The following code is added at the top within the class code.

```
// Setting and getting taskhost
private TaskHost _taskHost;
public TaskHost TaskHost
{
  get { return _taskHost; }
  set { _taskHost = value; }
}

// Getting connections, setting is done within ServiceProvider method
private Connections _connections;
public Connections connections
{
```

```
    get { return _connections; }
}

// Gets or sets the serviceprovider. Used for getting
// f.a. the VariablesProvider and ConnectionsProvider
private IServiceProvider _serviceProvider = null;
public IServiceProvider ServiceProvider
{
  get
  {
    return _serviceProvider;
  }
  set
  {
    _serviceProvider = value;
    // Get connections from the services provider
    // The code looks difficult, but it is just a cast
    _connections = ((IDtsConnectionService)
                    (value.GetService(typeof(IDtsConnectionService))))
                    .GetConnections();
  }
}
```

In the constructor method of this class, the taskhost and serviceprovider properties are set. This is done with the code in myTaskInterface.cs, which is explained later on. Now you can use these properties in all the other methods.

```
// Constructor to set taskhost and serviceprovider
// See GetView in myTaskInterface.cs
public myTaskEditor(TaskHost taskHost,
                        IServiceProvider serviceprovider)
{
        InitializeComponent();

        this.TaskHost = taskHost;
        this.ServiceProvider = serviceprovider;
}
```

PageLoad

In the PageLoad method, you need to fill combo boxes with variables or connection managers so that users can select. For this you can use the TaskHost. The first example fills a combo box with all the string variables that are not system variables. In the combo box, the variable name property is visible, but the QualifiedName property is used as the key.

```
// Fill the combobox with string variables
cmbVariablesSource.Items.Clear();
cmbVariablesSource.DisplayMember = "Name";
cmbVariablesSource.ValueMember = "QualifiedName";
cmbVariablesSource.Items.Add("<Choose variable>");
cmbVariablesSource.Items.Add("<New variable>");  // opens new popup
```

```
// Loop through all package variables
foreach (Variable variable in _taskHost.Variables)
{
  // No system variables and only string variables
  if ((!variable.SystemVariable) && (variable.DataType == TypeCode.String))
  {
    cmbVariablesSource.Items.Add(variable);
  }
}
```

The same can be done for connection managers. In this example, you only want connection managers with a file path in it (File, Flat File, and Excel). Again, the name property is used in the list, but the id (a GUID) is used as key.

```
cmbConnectionsSource.Items.Clear();
cmbConnectionsSource.DisplayMember = "Name";
cmbConnectionsSource.ValueMember = "ID";
cmbConnectionsSource.Items.Add("<Choose connectionmanager>");
// This options will open new connection manager popup
cmbConnectionsSource.Items.Add("<New connectionmanager>");

foreach (ConnectionManager connection in this._connections)
{
    string ConnectionType = connection.CreationName;

    if (ConnectionType == "FILE" ||
        ConnectionType == "EXCEL" ||
        ConnectionType == "FLATFILE")
    {
        cmbConnectionsSource.Items.Add(connection);
    }
}
```

Translating the GUID into a Variable

Later on, in the OnClick event of the OK button, you will see that you are storing the GUID of a variable instead of the name. If you want to select the correct variable in the combo box, you have to retrieve the GUID variable from the task and then loop through all the variables and compare the GUID of each one to find the right variable. When you have found it, you can use it to select the right variable in the combo box when the form opens.

But first you need to retrieve the GUID variable from the task. The following is the code to retrieve a value of a property stored in the task, shown in Figure 16-10:

```
_taskHost.Properties["SelectedVariableIDSource].GetValue(_taskHost);
```

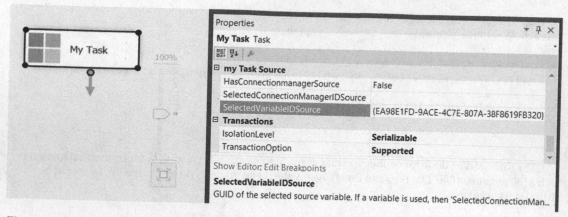

Figure 16-10. *The property you need to retrieve*

This is the complete code. The FindVariable method translates this GUID into a real variable object, which you can use to select the right item in the combo box.

```
Variable var = FindVariable(_taskHost.Properties["SelectedVariableIDSource"]
                              .GetValue(_taskHost).ToString().Trim());
if (var != null)
{
  // Variable found, now select it in combobox
  cmbVariablesSource.SelectedItem = var;
}
else
{
  // Variable not found, select first item in combobox
  cmbVariablesSource.SelectedIndex = 0;
}
```

This is the extra method that loops through all package variables to compare the GUID. If the GUID is found, it returns the correct variable; else it returns null.

```
private Variable FindVariable(string variableID)
{
  // This methods loops through all variables
  // and returns the one that matches the GUID.
  foreach (Variable var in _taskHost.Variables)
  {
    if (var.ID == variableID)
    {
      return var;
    }
  }
  return null;
}
```

The same approach can be used to find the right connection manager. You will find that code in the example task.

Adding Variables

In the onChange event of the variable combo box, you want to add a new variable when the second item in the list <New variable> is selected. If this is the case, you use the serviceProvider to open the default SSIS "Add variable" dialog (see Figure 16-11). After closing the dialog with OK, the new variable is added to the package, and then you can add the new variable to the combo box and select it. On Cancel, you close the dialog and select the default item in the combo box.

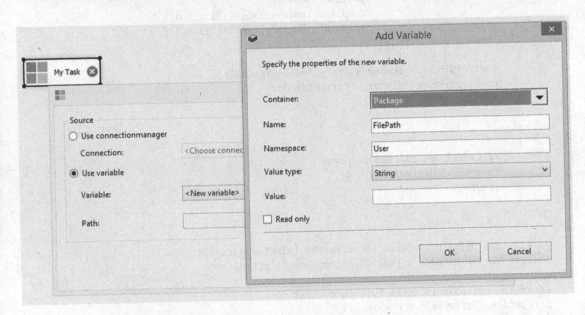

Figure 16-11. *Add Variable dialog*

```
// Class variable to store the selected variable. It will be filled by
// the SelectedIndexChange event and used by the OK button click event.
private Variable selectedVariableSource = null;

// Method to set the selected variable
private void cmbVariablesSource_SelectedIndexChanged(object sender, EventArgs e)
{
    ComboBox combobox = (ComboBox)sender;

    // If <Choose variable> is selected then empty the textbox with the path
    if (combobox.SelectedIndex == 0)
    {
        this.txtFilePathFinalSource.Text = "";
        return;
    }
```

```
    // If <New variable> is selected then popup to create a new variable
    if (combobox.SelectedIndex == 1)
    {
        int currentdIndex = -1;
        IDtsVariableService _dtsVariableService = _serviceProvider
                            .GetService(typeof(IDtsVariableService))
                            as IDtsVariableService;
        Variable newVariable = _dtsVariableService
                              .PromptAndCreateVariable(this, null,
                              "FilePath", "User", typeof(String));
        if (newVariable != null)
        {
            currentdIndex = combobox.Items.Add(newVariable);
            combobox.SelectedIndex = currentdIndex;
            return;
        }
        else
        {
            // Cancel was clicked in popup
            combobox.SelectedIndex = 0;
            return;
        }
    }


    // Fill the private variable to store the selected variable
    selectedVariableSource = (Variable)combobox.SelectedItem;

    // If the variable is still null then clear form
    if (selectedVariableSource == null)
    {
        this.cmbVariablesSource.SelectedIndex = 0;
        this.txtFilePathFinalSource.Text = "";
        return;
    }

    // Show path in textbox
    this.txtFilePathFinalSource.Text = (String)selectedVariableSource.Value;
}
```

Add Connection Managers

When adding a connection manager, you have a similar construction, but because you first want to choose between File, Flat File or Excel, you add an extra custom dialog before the standard SSIS Add Connection Manager dialog is shown (see Figure 16-12). The dialog Prompt.ShowConnectionManagerTypeDialog() returns a string with "FILE", "FLATFILE", or "EXCEL". This string is used to open the correct Add Connection Manager dialog from SSIS.

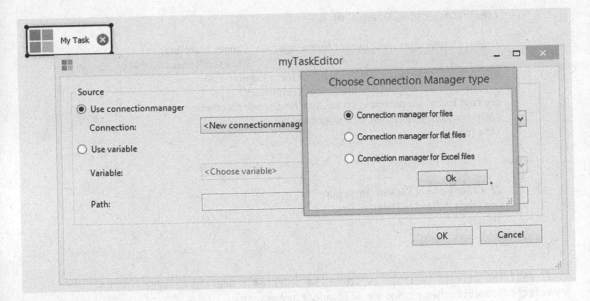

Figure 16-12. *Custom dialog before the Connection Manager dialog*

```
// Class variable to store the selected connectionmanager. It will be filled
// by the SelectedIndexChange event and used by the OK button click event.
private ConnectionManager selectedConnectionManagerSource = null;

// Method to set the selected connectionmanager
private void cmbConnectionsSource_SelectedIndexChanged(object sender,
                                                        EventArgs e)
{
    ComboBox combobox = (ComboBox)sender;

    // If <Choose connectionmanager> is selected
    // then empty the textbox with the path
    if (combobox.SelectedIndex == 0)
    {
        this.txtFilePathFinalSource.Text = "";
        return;
    }

    // If <New connectionmanager> is selected
    // then popup to create a new connection manager
    if (combobox.SelectedIndex == 1)
    {
        int currentIndex = -1;
        IDtsConnectionService _dtsConnectionService = _serviceProvider
                        .GetService(typeof(IDtsConnectionService))
                        as IDtsConnectionService;
        ArrayList createdConnection = _dtsConnectionService
                        .CreateConnection
                        (Prompt.ShowConnectionManagerTypeDialog());
```

```
        if (createdConnection.Count > 0)
        {
            ConnectionManager newConnectionManager = (ConnectionManager)
                                                    createdConnection[0];
            _dtsConnectionService.AddConnectionToPackage(
                                    newConnectionManager);
            currentIndex = combobox.Items.Add(newConnectionManager);
            combobox.SelectedIndex = currentIndex;
            return;
        }
        else
        {
            // Cancel was clicked in popup
            combobox.SelectedIndex = 0;
            return;
        }
    }


    // Fill the private variable to store the selected connectionmanager
    selectedConnectionManagerSource = (ConnectionManager)
                                        combobox.SelectedItem;
    // If the variable is still null then clear form
    if (selectedConnectionManagerSource == null)
    {
        this.cmbConnectionsSource.SelectedIndex = 0;
        this.txtFilePathFinalSource.Text = "";
        return;
    }

    // Get the path of the connectionmanager. For Excel connectionmanagers
    // you should use ExcelFilePath property instead of the connectionstring
    if (selectedConnectionManagerSource.CreationName == "EXCEL")
    {
        this.txtFilePathFinalSource.Text = selectedConnectionManagerSource
                            .Properties["ExcelFilePath"]
                            .GetValue(selectedConnectionManagerSource)
                            .ToString();
    }
    else
    {
        this.txtFilePathFinalSource.Text = selectedConnectionManagerSource
                                    .ConnectionString;
    }
}
```

Close Editor and Save Changes

When you close the editor with the OK button, you want to save the values from the form into the properties of the task so that you can use them when you reopen the editor or when you execute the task. And when you click the Cancel button, you just close the editor and return Cancel as the dialog result.

```csharp
private void btnCancel_Click(object sender, EventArgs e)
{
  // Close editor with Cancel
  this.DialogResult = DialogResult.Cancel;
  this.Close();
}

private void btnSave_Click(object sender, EventArgs e)
{
  // Save values (connectionmanager and variable guid) in tasks properties.
  if (this.cmbConnectionsSource.SelectedIndex != 0)
  {
    // Something is selected, get selected connection
    // manager from private class variable
    _taskHost.Properties["SelectedConnectionManagerIDSource"]
            .SetValue(_taskHost, selectedConnectionManagerSource.ID);
  }
  else
  {
    // Nothing selected, save empty string
    _taskHost.Properties["SelectedConnectionManagerIDSource"]
                      .SetValue(_taskHost, string.Empty);
  }

  if (this.cmbVariablesSource.SelectedIndex != 0)
  {
    // Something is selected, get selected variable
    // from private class variable
    _taskHost.Properties["SelectedVariableIDSource"]
                      .SetValue(_taskHost, selectedVariableSource.ID);
  }
  else
  {
    // Nothing selected, save empty string
    _taskHost.Properties["SelectedVariableIDSource"].SetValue(_taskHost,
                                                    string.Empty);
  }

  // Close editor with OK
  this.DialogResult = DialogResult.OK;
  this.Close();
}
```

Interface Class Code

The next class file interfaces IDtsTaskUI. The only thing it is doing is passing through the taskHost and serviceProvider to the editor. This class file is called myTaskInterface.cs and it is located in the UI project.

```csharp
using System;
using System.Windows.Forms;
```

405

```csharp
using Microsoft.SqlServer.Dts.Runtime;
using Microsoft.SqlServer.Dts.Runtime.Design;

// Class, Interfacing for task editor
namespace ScriptingBook.myTask
{
  public class myTaskInterface : IDtsTaskUI
  {
    private TaskHost _taskHost;
    private IServiceProvider _serviceProvider;

    public myTaskInterface()
    {
    }

    public void Initialize(TaskHost taskHost,
                            IServiceProvider serviceProvider)
    {
      // Get taskhost and service provider
      // and fill class variables
      taskHost = taskHost;
      serviceProvider = serviceProvider;
    }

    public ContainerControl GetView()
    {
      // Pass through taskHost and serviceProvider to editor
      myTaskEditor editor = new myTaskEditor();
      editor.TaskHost = this._taskHost;
      editor.ServiceProvider = this._serviceProvider;
      return editor;
    }

    public void Delete(IWin32Window parentWindow)
    {
    }

    public void New(IWin32Window parentWindow)
    {
    }
  }
}
```

Expression Builder

It is also possible to use the built-in Expression Builder in a custom task (see Figure 16-13). However, it is an unsupported feature, which means you have no guarantees that it will still work after the next SSIS update. The code is not included in the example task, but it is available in a separate text file.

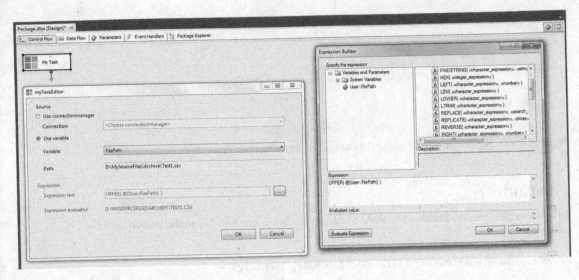

Figure 16-13. *Expression Builder in a custom task*

References

To use the Expression Builder, you need to add two references to the UI project. The first reference, which is located in the GAC, is to Microsoft.DataTransformationServices.Controls.

```
C:\Windows\Microsoft.NET\assembly\GAC_MSIL\Microsoft.DataTransformationServices.Controls\
v4.0_11.0.0.0__89845dcd8080cc91\Microsoft.DataTransformationServices.Controls.DLL
```

And the second reference is to Microsoft.SqlServer.DTSRuntimeWrap, which is also located in the GAC, however not in MSIL.

```
C:\Windows\Microsoft.NET\assembly\GAC_32\Microsoft.SqlServer.DTSRuntimeWrap\
v4.0_11.0.0.0__89845dcd8080cc91\Microsoft.SqlServer.DTSRuntimeWrap.dll
 C:\Windows\Microsoft.NET\assembly\GAC_64\Microsoft.SqlServer.DTSRuntimeWrap\
v4.0_11.0.0.0__89845dcd8080cc91\Microsoft.SqlServer.DTSRuntimeWrap.dll
```

Usings

To make the code more compact, you need to add two extra usings to the code of the UI project. Because of duplicate names in various namespaces, you see that the wrapper using is a little different.

```
usings Microsoft.DataTransformationServices.Control;
usings Wrapper = Microsoft.SqlServer.Dts.Runtime.Wrapper;
```

Form Controls

For this simplified example, you add a button (for opening the Expression Builder), a read-only text box (for showing the expression), and a label (for showing the evaluated expression).

Expression

Expression text | UPPER(@[User::FilePath]) | ...

Expression evaluated | D:\MYSOURCEFILES\ARCHIVE\TEST1.CSV

Figure 16-14. Form controls for using the Expression Builder

The Code

To open the Expression Builder, you need to add an onclick event handler to the button with the following code.

```
private void btnExpression_Click(object sender, EventArgs e)
{
 try
 {
  // Create an expression builder popup and make sure the expressions can be
  // evaluated as a string or change it to System.Boolean if you want a
  // boolean, etc. Last property is the textbox containing the expression that
  // you want to edit.
  using (var expressionBuilder = ExpressionBuilder.Instantiate(
                                         _taskHost.Variables,
                                         _taskHost.VariableDispenser,
                                         Type.GetType("System.String"),
                                         txtExpression.Text))
  {
   // Open the window / dialog with expression builder
   if (expressionBuilder.ShowDialog() == DialogResult.OK)
   {
    // If pressed OK then the textbox gets populated with the created
    // expression and the label will be emptied
    txtExpression.Text = expressionBuilder.Expression;
    lblExpressionEvaluated.Text = "";

    // Create object to evaluate the expression
    Wrapper.ExpressionEvaluator evaluator =
                             new Wrapper.ExpressionEvaluator();

    // Add the expression
    evaluator.Expression = txtExpression.Text;

    // Object for storing the evaluated expression
    object result = null;
```

```
try
{
  // Evalute the expression and store it in the result object
  evalutor.Evaluate(DtsConvert.GetExtendedInterface(
                    _taskHost.VariableDispenser),
                        out result, false);
}
catch (Exception ex)
{
  // Store error message in label
  // Perhaps a little useless in this example because the expression
  // builder window already validated the expression. But you could
  // also make the textbox readable and change the expression there
  // (without opening the expression builder window)
  lblExpressionEvaluated.Text = ex.Message;
}
// If the Expression contains some error, the "result" will be <null>.
if (result != null)
{
  // Add evaluated expression to label
  lblExpressionEvaluated.Text = result.ToString();
}
}
}
}
catch (Exception ex)
{
  MessageBox.Show(ex.Message);
}
}
```

Now you can store that expression in a property and retrieve it on runtime. On runtime, you can evaluate the expression with this same code.

Summary

In this chapter you learned the basics of generating your own custom task. We encourage you to first learn some basic .NET coding before rushing to create a whole bunch of custom tasks.

CHAPTER 17

■ ■ ■

Create Custom Transformation

This chapter shows you how to create a custom transformation for the data flow. Compared to the custom task, this is slightly more difficult because there are more methods and more points to address. To keep things comprehensible, you will be using the row number script that you saw in the Script Component chapters. A very basic transformation, but easy to extend with all the bells and whistles that you can find on the various blogs and forums.

Creating a custom transformation instead of a Script Component has the same pros and cons as the custom task vs. the Script Task (see Figure 17-1). However, because this is more difficult, the tipping point where you decide to go for the custom transformation instead of the Script Component will probably shift a little in the direction of the Script Component.

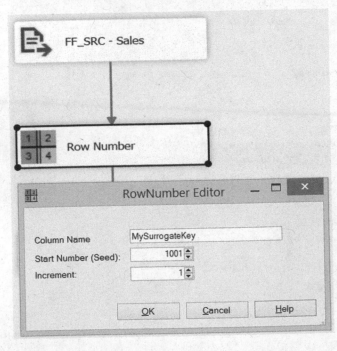

Figure 17-1. Custom transformation for the data flow

Custom Transformation Preparations

For this example, you will create a transformation that adds a new column with a surrogate key (or row number). For this you need a Visual Studio version that supports C# and VB.NET projects. BIDS or SSDT alone is not enough because they only support BI projects. For this example, you use Visual Studio Professional 2013, but there are less expensive versions that also support C# and VB.NET; for example, Visual Studio Community or Visual Studio Express. The example code contains one extra installer project. The template for this can be downloaded at https://visualstudiogallery.msdn.microsoft.com/9abe329c-9bba-44a1-be59-0fbf6151054d.

And of course you need to install all SSIS versions that you want to support with your custom transformation. You need to recompile your code with different references if you want your transformation to work with multiple versions of SSIS.

Creating Visual Studio Projects

For this custom transformation, you use two Class Library projects. One for the actual transformation and one for the user interface. Make sure that you choose the appropriate .NET version for the transformation. SSIS 2005: 2.0, SSIS 2008: 3.5, SSIS 2012: 4.0, and SSIS 2014 4.0. First create a new project called RowNumber and then add a second Class Library project to the same solution called RowNumberUI, as shown in Figure 17-2.

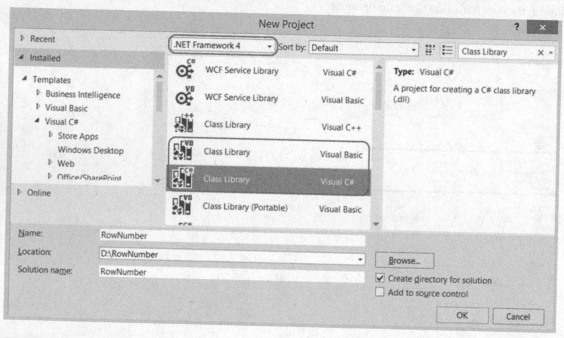

Figure 17-2. *Class Library projects*

Before you start coding, you first have to address a lot of other things, like references, strong names, build events, and, of course, icons.

Adding SSIS References

To communicate with SSIS, you need to add SSIS references to these projects. Both projects need references to

- Microsoft.SqlServer.Dts.Design
- Microsoft.SQLServer.DTSPipelineWrap
- Microsoft.SqlServer.DTSRuntimeWrap
- Microsoft.SqlServer.ManagedDTS

And the RowNumber project with the runtime code also needs a reference to

- Microsoft.SQLServer.PipelineHost

For SSIS 2012 and above, you can find these assemblies (.dll files) in the Global Assembly Cache (GAC) at C:\Windows\Microsoft.NET\assembly\GAC_MSIL\. For example:

```
Microsoft.SqlServer.Dts.Design\v4.0_11.0.0.0__89845dcd8080cc91\Microsoft.SqlServer.Dts.
Design.dll
```

If you have installed multiple versions of SSIS 2012 and above, then it is version 4.0_11.0.0.0 for 2012, v4.0_12.0.0.0 for 2014, and version 4.0_13.0.0.0 for 2016. For older SSIS versions, you can find these .dll files in the assemblies folder of SQL Server at C:\Program Files (x86)\Microsoft SQL Server\100\SDK\ Assemblies (replace 100 with 90 for SSIS 2005).

Default Namespace and Assembly Name

Go to your project's properties. In the Application page, you need to change the Assembly name and the Default namespace for both projects (see Figure 17-3). The Default namespace will be ScriptingBook. RowNumber. The Assembly name will be the default namespace plus the project name: ScriptingBook. RowNumber.RowNumber and ScriptingBook.RowNumber.RowNumberUI for the RowNumber and RowNumberUI projects, respectively.

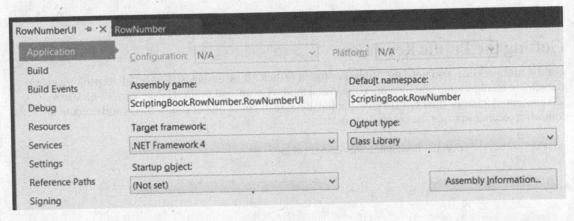

Figure 17-3. Setting the namespace and the assembly name

413

Creating a Key for the Strong Name

An SSIS runtime requirement for assemblies is that they are located in the GAC. The GAC requires that assemblies are strong-named. This provides a unique identity. So you need to strong name for the assemblies. Go to the properties of one of the projects and then to the Signing page. Check the "Sign the assembly" check box and then add a new key file in the drop-down list. The name for this example is RowNumber.snk, with sha256RSA as the signature algorithm and no password (see Figure 17-4). After clicking the OK button, the new key file will be visible in the Solution Explorer. Next, you need to copy the same .snk file to the other project and then sign that project with the same key file. You could also reuse the key file from the custom task project by copying it to the current projects.

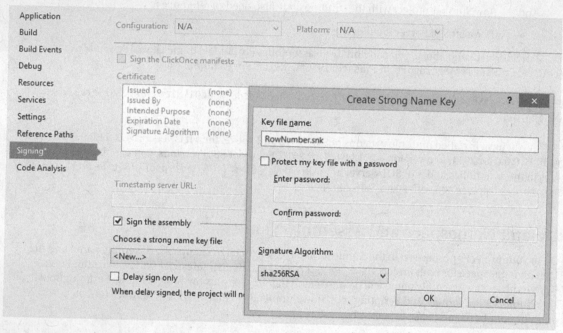

Figure 17-4. Add key file (C# project, but VB.NET looks similar)

Getting the Public Key Token

For the runtime code, you need the Public KeyToken of the GUI assembly. So first build the projects using the release configuration and then open the Visual Studio Command prompt (see Figure 17-5). Use a CD command (change directory) to go to the Bin\Release folder of one of your projects and execute the following command to get the public key token:

```
sn.exe -T ScriptingBook.RowNumber.RowNumber.dll
```

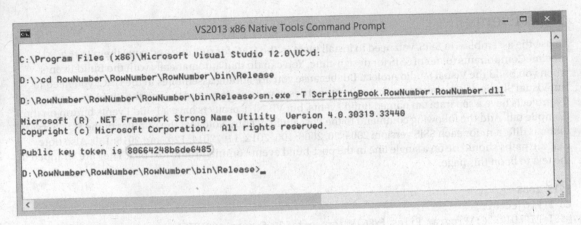

Figure 17-5. *The strong name utility to get the public key token*

Copy this key token for later use.

If you reused the key file from the custom task project, then the public key token is the same and you can skip this step.

Icons

Of course you need a good icon for our transformation. There are plenty of free icons available online and there are also tools to create new icons. Add an .ico file to both projects via the Solution Explorer. After adding the icon file, make sure to change the Build Action property to Embedded Resource; otherwise, the icon won't show up. Later on you can use this icon in the Windows Form of the UI project. Then it will show when you edit the transformation (see Figure 17-6).

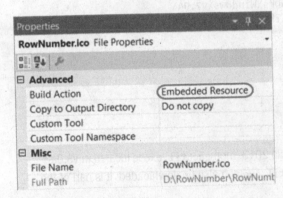

Figure 17-6. *Setting the Build Action of the icon*

In the runtime project, you can use this file to give your transformation a custom icon instead of the default. This will show in the SSIS Toolbox and in the data flow. The code to do this is explained later on.

Build Events

To use the assemblies in SSIS, you need to install them in the GAC for runtime and copy them to the PipelineComponents folder of SSIS for design-time. You can do that automatically with the Build Events when you build the Visual Studio project. But because you are adding assemblies to the GAC, you need to run Visual Studio as administrator. Go to the properties of your projects and then to the Build Events. C# projects have a separate tab named Build Events, but VB.NET projects have a Build Events button on the Compile tab. Add the following command to the Post-Build events. Note that the number in the SQL Server folder is different for each SSIS version: 2005: 90, 2008: 100, 2012: 110, 2014: 120, and 2016: 130. Also note that the paths should be on a single line in the post-build event command-line text box. They are wrapped in the text to fit on this page.

SSIS 2008
```
cd $(ProjectDir)
@SET PIPEDIR="C:\Program Files (x86)\Microsoft SQL Server\100\DTS\
                                        PipelineComponents\"
@SET GACUTIL="C:\Program Files (x86)\Microsoft SDKs\Windows\v7.0A\
                                        bin\gacutil.exe"

Echo Installing dll in GAC
Echo $(OutDir)
Echo $(TargetFileName)
%GACUTIL% -if "$(OutDir)$(TargetFileName)"
Echo Copying files to Tasks
copy "$(OutDir)$(TargetFileName)" %PIPEDIR%
```

SSIS 2012 with Visual Studio 2010
```
cd $(ProjectDir)
@SET PIPEDIR="C:\Program Files (x86)\Microsoft SQL Server\110\DTS\
                                        PipelineComponents\"
@SET GACUTIL="C:\Program Files (x86)\Microsoft SDKs\Windows\v7.0A\
                                Bin\NETFX 4.0 Tools\gacutil.exe"

Echo Installing dll in GAC
Echo $(OutDir)
Echo $(TargetFileName)
%GACUTIL% -if "$(OutDir)$(TargetFileName)"
Echo Copying files to Tasks
copy "$(OutDir)$(TargetFileName)" %PIPEDIR%
```

■ **Note** If you are using Visual Studio 2012 or Visual Studio 2013, then gacutil.exe is located in v8.0a instead of v7.0a. It could also vary for other versions. gacutil.exe can also be downloaded; it is part of the Microsoft Windows SDK.

Custom Transformation Runtime Code

You start with code that is used when executing transformation. Since the complete code is too big to show in a book, you will focus on the most important SSIS stuff. But the code is available with this book. So you can copy the RowNumber.cs file from the example code and add it to your project.

First you need to add some extra SSIS namespaces to shorten the code. This is the complete list that you'll use for this project:

```
using System;
using Microsoft.SqlServer.Dts.Pipeline;
using Microsoft.SqlServer.Dts.Pipeline.Wrapper;
using Microsoft.SqlServer.Dts.Runtime.Wrapper;
```

Now the most important code of your transformation—where you name it, give it an icon, and connect it to the editor assembly: DtsPipelineComponent. This attribute allows you to set all the metadata of your component.

```
namespace ScriptingBook.RowNumber
{
    [DtsPipelineComponent(
    DisplayName = "Row Number",
    ComponentType = ComponentType.Transform,
    Description = "Adds a rownumber to the output",
    IconResource = "ScriptingBook.RowNumber.RowNumber.ico",
    UITypeName = "ScriptingBook.RowNumber.RowNumberInterface,
                ScriptingBook.RowNumber.RowNumberUI,
                Version=1.0.0.0,
                Culture=Neutral,
                PublicKeyToken=80664248b6de6485",
    CurrentVersion = 1
    )]
    public class RowNumber : PipelineComponent
    {
```

The DtsPipelineComponent tag has properties that can change, which are as follows:

- **DisplayName**: This is the name you see in the toolbox; it is the default name when you drag the transformation to the data flow.

- **ComponentType**: With this you tell SSIS whether it is a transformation, source, or destination.

- **Description**: The text used as the default description of your transformation.

- **IconResource**: The fully qualified name of your embedded icon. This is shown in the toolbox and when you drag the transformation to the data flow. Try to find an icon that describes your task and fits the rest of the icons. Quite a daunting task.

- **UITypeName**: This is the connection to the editor in which you name the interface class and the UI class. In this string you also need to paste the public key token that you retrieved via the sn command. Note that this is one line of code, but wrapped to fit the page.

- **CurrentVersion**: This can be used in a method called PerformUpgrade to handle changes when you add extra properties that don't exist in packages that use an older version of the transformation. If you don't handle those, you get an error in the package that uses the older version. More information follows.

417

Also notice the interface after the class name: PipelineComponent. This allows you to override the methods from the interface with your own code. Each method in the code with the override modifier in it comes from this interface.

Component Properties and Input and Output Ports

The first method is ProvideComponentProperties, which is called when the component is added to the data flow surface. In this method, you initialize the component by adding an input port, output port, custom properties, and a new output column to store the row number in.

In the input port, you let the component know what is coming into the component and what should you do when that fails. In this case you don't need input columns because you don't use data from upstream and you don't want an error output.

In the output port, you let the component know whether the output is synchronous and which new output columns you added. Our example is synchronous and you need a new output column to store the new row number in.

The custom property port is where you add the properties (Increment and Seed) to the component (see Figure 17-7). This is in a totally different way than in the custom task example. Besides the name, description, and initial value, you can also indicate whether the user can use expressions in the properties.

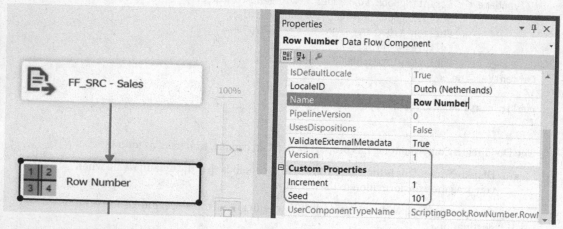

Figure 17-7. Custom Properties and the metadata version

And there is one addition. The version number of the component is stored in a property. If afterward a new version of the component is installed, this initial (metadata) version number can be compared to the current (binary) version in the PerformUpgrade method. More details will follow.

```
// Class variables to store the default
// values of the custom properties
private Int64 _seed = 1;
private int _increment = 1;
private string _newColumnName = "RowNumber";

public override void ProvideComponentProperties()
{
  // This method is called when the component
  // is initially added to the data flow task.
```

```
// Add the input
IDTSInput100 input = ComponentMetaData.InputCollection.New();
input.Name = "RowNumberInput";
// You don't use the ErrorRowDisposition.
// If you fail somewhere in the rows, you
// don't wan't it to go to an alternative output buffer.
input.ErrorRowDisposition = DTSRowDisposition.RD_NotUsed;


// Add the output (Synchronous)
// Async creates new buffers
// Sync adds columns to existing buffers
// SynchronousInputID connects the input
// and output for sync components
IDTSOutput100 output = ComponentMetaData.OutputCollection.New();
output.Name = "RowNumberOutput";
output.SynchronousInputID = input.ID;
output.ExclusionGroup = 1;


// Add Column
// Initially you start with a new output column
// with a default name. In the UI you can change
// this name. The Default datatype is DT_I8. You
// could add a combobox with datatypes to let the
// user choose which datatype to use.
IDTSOutputColumn100 outputColumn = output.OutputColumnCollection.New();
outputColumn.Name = _newColumnName;
outputColumn.Description = "Generated Rownumber";
outputColumn.SetDataTypeProperties(DataType.DT_I8, 0, 0, 0, 0);


// Define the CustomProperties of the this component
AddProperty("Seed", "Starting number.", _seed, false);
AddProperty("Increment", "Increment size.", _increment, false);


// Workaround for versioning bug by Todd McDermid
// When adding the component to the data flow the
// version number is saved in the package. When
// a new component version is installed then the
// PerformUpgrade method can handle the changes.
DtsPipelineComponentAttribute componentAttribute =
                        (DtsPipelineComponentAttribute)
                        Attribute.GetCustomAttribute(this.GetType(),
                        typeof(DtsPipelineComponentAttribute), false);
ComponentMetaData.Version = componentAttribute.CurrentVersion;
}


// Helper method to add custom properties
private void AddProperty(string name,
                        string description,
                        object value,
                        bool supportsExpression)
```

```
{
    // Add a custom property to the component
    IDTSCustomProperty100 commandProp = this.ComponentMetaData.CustomPropertyCollection.New();
    commandProp.Name = name;
    commandProp.Description = description;
    if (supportsExpression)
    {
        // Let SSIS know that you allow expressions on our property
        commandProp.ExpressionType = DTSCustomPropertyExpressionType.CPET_NOTIFY;
    }
    commandProp.Value = value;

    return;
}
```

Validating Transformation

For validating the custom transformation, you need to override the Validate method. Just like in the custom task, you can check the values of the custom properties to see if they match expectations. But you can also validate the inputs and outputs: Is the number of output columns correct? Is a certain input column read/write? Or is the number of inputs more than one? The validation method is executed at design-time when you close the editor, and twice in runtime when the package is initialized and when the data flow task is executed (see Figure 17-8).

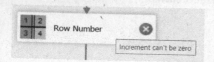

Figure 17-8. *Design-time error*

The following are the four different statuses that you can return:

- VS_ISBROKEN: Metadata of the component is not OK. The user should resolve this in the data flow. Example: the increment = 0.

- VS_ISCORRUPT: Something is broken that can't be fixed. Better to start over by removing and adding the component. Example: Incorrect number of inputs or outputs.

- VS_ISVALID: Everything is OK.

- VS_NEEDSNEWMETADATA: Something is wrong with the metadata of the columns, which needs to be fixed. Example: removed or changed a column upstream.

```
public override DTSValidationStatus Validate()
{
    // boolean used for FireError to specify whether execution is cancelled
    bool pbCancel = false;
```

```
        // If you are using an input column and input flow
        // is removed or changed then that could hurt our
        // code. Therefore check if the input columns are
        // still valid
        if (!ComponentMetaData.AreInputColumnsValid)
        {
            return DTSValidationStatus.VS_NEEDSNEWMETADATA;
        }

        // Validate that there is only 1 input
        if (ComponentMetaData.InputCollection.Count != 1)
        {
            ComponentMetaData.FireError(0, ComponentMetaData.Name,
            "Incorrect number of inputs.", "", 0, out pbCancel);
            return DTSValidationStatus.VS_ISCORRUPT;
        }

        // Validate that there are no input columns
        if (ComponentMetaData.InputCollection[0].InputColumnCollection.Count !=
            0)
        {
            ComponentMetaData.FireError(0, ComponentMetaData.Name,
            "Incorrect number of inputs columns.", "", 0, out pbCancel);
            return DTSValidationStatus.VS_ISCORRUPT;
        }

        // Validate that there is only 1 output
        if (ComponentMetaData.OutputCollection.Count != 1)
        {
            ComponentMetaData.FireError(0, ComponentMetaData.Name,
            "Incorrect number of outputs.", "", 0, out pbCancel);
            return DTSValidationStatus.VS_ISCORRUPT;
        }

        // Validate that there is 1 output column
        if (ComponentMetaData.OutputCollection[0].OutputColumnCollection.Count
            != 1)
        {
            ComponentMetaData.FireError(0, ComponentMetaData.Name,
            "Incorrect number of outputs columns", "", 0, out pbCancel);
            return DTSValidationStatus.VS_ISCORRUPT;
        }

        // Validate that the increment isn't zero
        if (_increment == 0)
        {
            ComponentMetaData.FireError(0, ComponentMetaData.Name,
            "Increment can't be zero", "", 0, out pbCancel);
            return DTSValidationStatus.VS_ISBROKEN;
        }
        return base.Validate();
    }
```

Execution Code

The actual code for this transformation is executed in the overridden method called ProcessInput. For this example, with no input columns and only one output column, it is rather simple. The method is executed for each buffer passed to the component. You loop through the rows in the current buffer, fill the new column, and then increment the row number for the next row.

There is also the possibility to validate the new values. If your new column is a DT_I4, then you want make sure that the new row number will fit. This example uses a DT_I8 with a rather large max value, which isn't reached quickly.

```
public override void ProcessInput(int inputID, PipelineBuffer buffer)
{
  // Loop through the rows in the buffer
  while (buffer.NextRow())
  {
    // Check if the new number isn't out of range. Perhaps less usefull
    // for a bigint with a max size of 9,223,372,036,854,775,807
    if (_currentRowNumber < Int64.MinValue ||
        _currentRowNumber > Int64.MaxValue)
    {
      // Throw an error, the value can't be contained
      // in the variable type chosen !
      bool pbCancel = true;
      ComponentMetaData.FireError(0, this.ComponentMetaData.Name,
      "Rownumber is not in range of the chosen variables" +
      " type DT_I8 (Int64)", string.Empty, 0, out pbCancel);
      throw new ApplicationException("Rownumber is not in range of the " +
      " chosen variables type 'DT_I8 (Int64)'.");
    }
    // Fill first (0) output column with the rownumber
    buffer.SetInt64(0, _currentRowNumber);

    // Increment when ready
    _currentRowNumber = _currentRowNumber + _increment;

    // Direct the row to the defaultOutput
    buffer.DirectRow(ComponentMetaData.OutputCollection[0].ID);
  }
}
```

PreExecute

The PreExecute method executes once, right before starting the ProcessInput method. It is a good location to do any processing that can be done upfront and cached for other methods. For this example, you only get the values from the properties so that they can be used for adding the row number in the ProcessInut method. If you also have input columns, then this is also the location to map the input and output.

```
public override void PreExecute()
{
  // Get values from the properties for use in the ProcessInput
  _currentRowNumber = Int64.Parse(this.ComponentMetaData
                    .CustomPropertyCollection["Seed"].Value.ToString());
  _increment = (int)this.ComponentMetaData
              .CustomPropertyCollection["Increment"].Value;
}
```

PerformUpgrade

This is an important method if you want to extend your custom transformation. You compare the version in the code with the version in the package (see Figure 17-9). If version 0 of the transformation didn't have a property to change the increment, and version 1 introduces that property, then you don't want existing packages that were created with version 0 to fail.

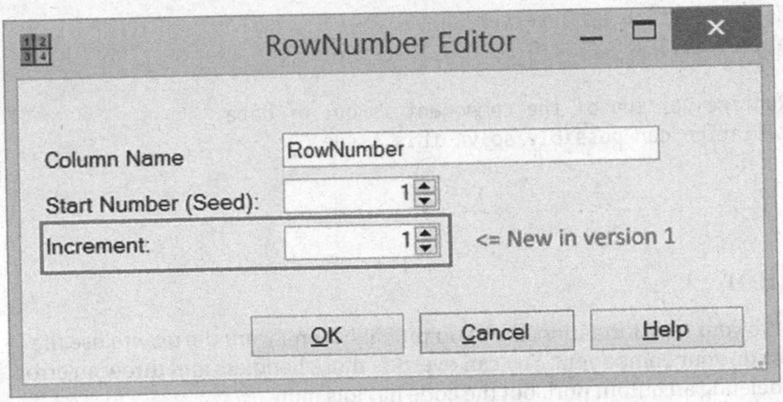

Figure 17-9. *New version with increment option*

If the metadata version is lower than the binary version, then you can add additional properties with a default value. This should prevent errors due to upgrades.

And if you, for example, forgot to upgrade the transformation on the production server, then the metadata version could be higher than the binary version. In that case you also want to throw an error.

```
public override void PerformUpgrade(int pipelineVersion)
{
  // Obtain the current component version from the attribute.
  DtsPipelineComponentAttribute componentAttribute =
      (DtsPipelineComponentAttribute)Attribute.GetCustomAttribute(
        this.GetType(), typeof(DtsPipelineComponentAttribute), false);
  int binaryVersion = componentAttribute.CurrentVersion;
  int metaDataVersion = ComponentMetaData.Version;

  // If the component version saved in the package is less than
  // the current version, Version 2, perform the upgrade.
```

```
  if (metaDataVersion < binaryVersion)
  {
    // Upgrade from version 0 to 1
    if (metaDataVersion == 0)
    {
      if (ComponentMetaData.CustomPropertyCollection["Increment"] == null)
      {
        // Add the new property with a default value
        AddProperty("Increment", "Increment size.", 1, false);
      }
    }
    // Update the metadata version otherwise the versions are still
    // different and then next time you open the package it will perform
    // the upgrade again causing errors.
    ComponentMetaData.Version = binaryVersion;
  }

  // Forgot to upgrade the transformation on a server?
  if (metaDataVersion > binaryVersion)
  {
    throw new Exception("Runtime version of the component is out of date."
    + " Upgrading the installation can possibly solve this issue.");
  }
}
```

Disable Advanced Editor

If you have added a custom editor to your transformation, then you probably don't want the user to use the advanced editor and possibly mess up your component. You can override those handlers and throw an error. The following is one example for deleting an output port, but the code has lots more.

```
public override void DeleteOutput(int outputID)
{
  throw new Exception(string.Format("Deleting output from '{0}' isn't" +
  " allowed.", ComponentMetaData.Name), null);
}
```

Custom Transformation Form

The form layout is, again, very basic in order to keep things easy to explain (see Figure 17-10). To add a row number, the user can specify the name of the new column containing the row number. And the user can change the start number and increment in the editor.

Column Name	RowNumber
Start Number (Seed):	1
Increment:	1

Figure 17-10. *The basic form*

The complete code for this editor is available with the book. You can add the form from the example project to your UI project in four steps:

1.   Add a reference to System.Drawing and System.Windows.Forms in the UI project.

2.   Copy the three form files RowNumberEditor.cs, RowNumberEditor.resx, and RowNumberEditor.Designer.cs to your UI project folder.

3.   Right-click your UI project and choose Add ä Existing item to add the following files: RowNumberEditor.cs, RowNumberEditor.Designer.cs, and RowNumberEditor.resx.

4.   Close and reopen your solution. Then open the form to see what you have added.

Form Code

First, the usings to shorten the code. You only need four namespaces in here. By default there are more, but you can remove them. Visual Studio even has an option to remove unused usings if you right-click a using and choose Organize Usings (this could vary per Visual Studio version).

```
using System;
using System.Windows.Forms;
using Microsoft.SqlServer.Dts.Pipeline.Wrapper;
using Microsoft.SqlServer.Dts.Runtime;
```

ServiceProvider, Connections, Variables, and Metadata

The component provides some objects that can be used to get variables or connection managers, or to get and set custom properties. These objects will be set by the RowNumberInterface class that implements IDtsComponentUI.

In this example, you will only use the IDTSComponentMetaData100 to get the values from the custom properties. The IServiceProvider can create variables. The Variables object can be used to loop through all variables, and Connections can be used to loop through all connection managers.

```
private Variables _vars = null;
public Variables Variables
{
  get { return _vars; }
  set { _vars = value; }
}

private Connections _conns = null;
public Connections Connections
{
  get { return _conns; }
  set { _conns = value; }
}
```

425

```
private IServiceProvider _sp = null;
public IServiceProvider ServiceProvider
{
  get { return _sp; }
  set { _sp = value; }
}


private IDTSComponentMetaData100 _cmd = null;
public IDTSComponentMetaData100 ComponentMetadata
{
  get { return _cmd; }
  set { _cmd = value; }
}
```

FormLoad

In the Form Load method RowNumberEditor_Load, you get the values from the custom properties and use them to fill the fields in the editor.

```
private void RowNumberEditor_Load(object sender, EventArgs e)
{
  // Get the name of the new column and fill the textbox
  txtColumnName.Text = _cmd.OutputCollection[0]
                          .OutputColumnCollection[0].Name;
  // Cast seed from custom property to bigint
  // and fill the spincontrol
  numSeed.Value = Int64.Parse(_cmd
                    .CustomPropertyCollection["Seed"].Value.ToString());
  // Cast increment from custom property to int
  // and fill the spincontrol
  numIncrement.Value = (int)_cmd
                          .CustomPropertyCollection["Increment"].Value;
}
```

This example doesn't use variables, but if you want a combo box with variables, then this is the location to fill that combo box. Here is some basic example code for that (this is not included in the example code):

```
// Extra namespace
using Microsoft.SqlServer.Dts.Runtime;

// Looping through all variables
foreach (Microsoft.SqlServer.Dts.Runtime.Variable variable in Variables)
{
  // Filter system variables
  if (!variable.SystemVariable)
  {
    // Fill combobox
    cmbMyVariables.Items.Add(variable);
```

```
  // Select variable from custom property in combobox
  if (variable.QualifiedName ==
                   (string)_cmd.CustomPropertyCollection["myVar"].Value)
  {
    cmbMyVariables.SelectedItem = variable;
  }
 }
}
```

And adding a variable in the editor is also possible and works similarly to the custom task example. The following code is not included in the example code:

```
// integer to store the index of the variable in the combobox
int currentdIndex = -1;

// Open new add variable screen to add an integer variable
IDtsVariableService _dtsVariableService = _sp.GetService(
                  typeof(IDtsVariableService)) as IDtsVariableService;
Variable newVariable = _dtsVariableService.PromptAndCreateVariable(this,
                  null, "StartNumber", "User", typeof(Int32));

// Check if a new variable was created
if (newVariable != null)
{
  // Add variable to combobox
  currentdIndex = combobox.Items.Add(newVariable);
  // Select new variable in combobox
  combobox.SelectedIndex = currentdIndex;
}
```

Close Editor and Save Changes

When you close the editor with the OK button, you want to save the values from the form into the custom properties of the transformation so that you can use them when you reopen the editor or when you execute the transformation. And when you click the Cancel button, you just close the editor.

```
// Wrapper around the DTSComponent
private CManagedComponentWrapper _designTimeInstance;

private void btnOK_Click(object sender, EventArgs e)
{
  // Only instantiate once. You don't want to add outputs
  // and columns each time you close the editor
  if (_designTimeInstance == null)
  {
      _designTimeInstance = _cmd.Instantiate();
  }

  // Check if the column name already exists
  // If not change the name of the output column
```

427

```
    IDTSOutputColumn100 outputColumn = _cmd.OutputCollection[0]
                                     .OutputColumnCollection[0];
    if (outputColumn.Name != txtColumnName.Text)
    {
        outputColumn.Name = txtColumnName.Text;
    }


    // Pass the Seed to the componentProperty
    _designTimeInstance.SetComponentProperty("Seed", (Int64)numSeed.Value);

    // Pass the Incremenent to the componentProperty
    _designTimeInstance.SetComponentProperty("Increment",
                                        (int)numIncrement.Value);
}

private void btnCancel_Click(object sender, EventArgs e)
{
    // Close the window and undo changes
    this.Close();
}
```

Interface Class Code

The next class file implements IDtsComponentUI. The only thing it is doing is passing through the objects, like variables and serviceProvider, to the editor. It acts as an interaction point between the SSIS logic and your custom code. This class file is called RowNumberInterface.cs, which is located in the UI project.

The empty methods are here because they are required by interface IDtsComponentUI, but for this example, you haven't implemented any custom code for them. If you leave them out, you will get a build error telling you that you forgot to implement an interface member.

```
using System;
using System.Windows.Forms;
using Microsoft.SqlServer.Dts.Pipeline.Design;
using Microsoft.SqlServer.Dts.Pipeline.Wrapper;
using Microsoft.SqlServer.Dts.Runtime;

// Class, Interfacing for transformation editor
namespace ScriptingBook.RowNumber
{
  public class RowNumberInterface : IDtsComponentUI
  {
    IDTSComponentMetaData100 _cmd;
    IServiceProvider _sp;

    public void Help(System.Windows.Forms.IWin32Window parentWindow)
    {
    }
    public void New(System.Windows.Forms.IWin32Window parentWindow)
    {
    }
```

```
public void Delete(System.Windows.Forms.IWin32Window parentWindow)
{
}
public bool Edit(System.Windows.Forms.IWin32Window parentWindow,
                 Variables variables, Connections connections)
{
  // Create and display the form for the user interface.

  RowNumberEditor componentEditor = new RowNumberEditor();

  componentEditor.Connections = connections;
  componentEditor.Variables = variables;
  componentEditor.ComponentMetadata = _cmd;
  componentEditor.ServiceProvider = _sp;

  return componentEditor.ShowDialog(parentWindow) == DialogResult.OK;
}
public void Initialize(IDTSComponentMetaData100 dtsComponentMetadata,
                       IServiceProvider serviceProvider)
{
  // Store the component metadata.
  _cmd = dtsComponentMetadata;
  _sp = serviceProvider;
}
}
}
```

When running the data flow with the new custom transformation, you can add a data viewer to see the result of your hard work, as shown in Figure 17-11.

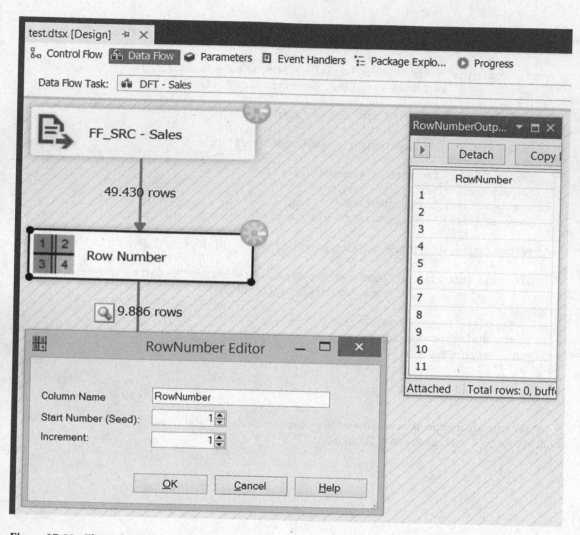

Figure 17-11. The end result

Summary

In this chapter you saw the basics for generating your own custom transformation. We encourage you to first learn some basic .NET coding before rushing to create a whole bunch of custom tasks and components. MSDN is full of example code that you can use to extend this basic example with all the bells and whistles.

■ ■ ■

PART V

Scripting from .NET Applications

■■■

CHAPTER 18

Package Creation

This chapter shows that besides using .NET within an SSIS package, you can also use .NET to create an SSIS package. Although that sounds like a lot of work, especially when you can easily do that in SSDT by using drag-and-drop, there are benefits.

Creating a couple of staging packages is not the most challenging work, but what about creating dozens of them? That could be really tiresome and error-prone if you don't pay attention. Beyond not having to do the boring part of ETL, mass-producing packages has the following benefits:

- *Speed*: Even the most experienced SSIS specialist can't create 50 or more packages in a day.

- *Extensibility*: It's easy to add additional functionality to all packages.

- *Equality*: All packages look the same and use the same naming conventions.

There are two different ways of mass-producing packages:

- Programmatically with C# or VB.NET only

- BIMLScript with XML mixed with some C# or VB.NET code

Creating an SSIS Package Programmatically

The first method programmatically creates packages using .NET assemblies. You can do this with a Class Library project in Visual Studio; but if you only have SSDT for BI without projects for C# or VB.NET, you could even use a Script Task to execute the following code (by adding it to the Main method). However, you could also obtain a free version of Visual Studio Community or Visual Studio Express to do this.

First, add a reference to Microsoft.SqlServer.ManagedDTS.dll, which is located in the Global Assembly Cache (GAC). Each version of SSIS has its own version of the assemblies in the GAC. Next, add a Using or Import for Microsoft.SqlServer.Dts.Runtime. If you are using the Script Task, you can skip the reference and namespace because it is already there by default. In this example, you will create a very basic package with an OLE DB connection manager and only one Execute SQL Task that executes a certain statement.

```
// Create new package
Package package = new Package();

// Add an OLE DB connection manager to the package
ConnectionManager OleDbCon = package.Connections.Add("OLEDB");
OleDbCon.ConnectionString = "Data Source=.;Integrated Security=SSPI;
                                          Initial Catalog=MyDB;";

OleDbCon.Name = "MyOleDbConnection";
```

```
// Add an Execute SQL Task to the package
Executable exec = package.Executables.Add("STOCK:SQLTask");
TaskHost thSqlTask = exec as TaskHost;
thSqlTask.Name = "SQL - Truncate Stage";

// Add properties to the Execute SQL Task (sample table)
thSqlTask.Properties["SqlStatementSource"].SetValue(thSqlTask,

"Truncate table ABC;");
thSqlTask.Properties["Connection"].SetValue(thSqlTask, OleDbCon.ID);

// Create an application object to save the package
Microsoft.SqlServer.Dts.Runtime.Application app = new
                                Microsoft.SqlServer.Dts.Runtime.Application();

// Save the package to XML
app.SaveToXml(@"D:\myPackage.dtsx", package, null);
```

And here is the VB.NET code:

```
' Create new package
Dim package As New Package()

' Add an OLE DB connection manager to the package
Dim OleDbCon As ConnectionManager = package.Connections.Add("OLEDB")
OleDbCon.ConnectionString = "Data Source=.;Integrated Security=SSPI;
                                            Initial Catalog=MyDB;"
OleDbCon.Name = "MyOleDbConnection"

' Add an Execute SQL Task to the package
Dim exec As Executable = package.Executables.Add("STOCK:SQLTask")
Dim thSqlTask As TaskHost = TryCast(exec, TaskHost)
thSqlTask.Name = "SQL - Truncate Stage"

' Add properties to the Execute SQL Task (sample table)
thSqlTask.Properties("SqlStatementSource").SetValue(thSqlTask, _
                    "Truncate table ABC;")
thSqlTask.Properties("Connection").SetValue(thSqlTask, OleDbCon.ID)

' Create an application object to save the package
Dim app As New Microsoft.SqlServer.Dts.Runtime.Application()

' Save the package to XML
app.SaveToXml("D:\myPackage.dtsx", package, Nothing)
```

The tasks are relatively easy to add, but the transformations are quite difficult due to the use of native COM APIs. If you really like this method and want to continue this example, go to https://msdn.microsoft.com/en-us/library/ms345167.aspx for more examples.

For most ETL consultants, this is probably too difficult. That's why some clever people at Microsoft created EzAPI, which is a powerful framework for generating packages; it is also much easier to use. Before the arrival of BIML (see the next section), this was the most popular way to generate packages. Unfortunately, this project hasn't been updated for a while; perhaps due the rise of the even more popular BIMLScript. But EzAPI is still available on CodePlex if you want to check it out at http://sqlsrvintegrationsrv.codeplex.com/releases/view/21238.

Creating an SSIS Package with BIMLScript

Business Intelligence Markup Language (BIML) is an XML dialect for creating SSIS, SSAS, and database assets; it was created by Varigence. The most interesting part of this method is that you can add .NET code to the XML to add, for example, an iteration that loops through all source tables. So you can create the package with XML and then add flexibility and repeatability with relatively easy .NET statements.

The free community version of BIMLScript is available via BIDSHelper, but there is also a commercial version, called MIST, with even more functionality. You can download a trial version from https://varigence.com/Mist. For this example, you will use BIDSHelper, which can be downloaded from CodePlex at https://bidshelper.codeplex.com. Download and install the appropriate version for your SQL Server version and check whether you have the AdventureWorks database (OLTP, 2012, or 2014) available. If you don't already have this database, you can download it from CodePlex at http://msftdbprodsamples.codeplex.com.

In this example, you will create staging packages to stage tables from AdventureWorks. The packages are very basic, but you can extend them to your own needs. There are many examples available on the Web. You can even generate the destination tables; you do that manually in the next step.

Creating Stage Database

Create a new database called StageAW to store the staging tables from AdventureWorks. The first table to stage is Person.Person; you need to create this table in the stage database. Remove all the "clutter" (constraints, defaults, schemas, etc.) to create a very basic stage table. Later on you can do that for all the tables that you want to stage. A script for the second table, Person.EmailAddress, is also included.

```
USE [StageAW]

GO

CREATE TABLE [Person](
        [BusinessEntityID] [int] NULL,
        [PersonType] [nvarchar](2) NULL,
        [NameStyle] [bit] NULL,
        [Title] [nvarchar](8) NULL,
        [FirstName] [nvarchar](50) NULL,
        [MiddleName] [nvarchar](50) NULL,
        [LastName] [nvarchar](50) NULL,
        [Suffix] [nvarchar](10) NULL,
        [EmailPromotion] [int] NULL,
        [AdditionalContactInfo] [nvarchar](max) NULL,
        [Demographics] [nvarchar](max) NULL,
        [rowguid] [uniqueidentifier] NULL,
        [ModifiedDate] [datetime] NULL
) ON [PRIMARY]

GO
```

```
CREATE TABLE [EmailAddress](
        [BusinessEntityID] [int]  NULL,
        [EmailAddressID] [int] NULL,
        [EmailAddress] [nvarchar](50) NULL,
        [rowguid] [uniqueidentifier] NULL,
        [ModifiedDate] [datetime]  NULL
) ON [PRIMARY]
```

Adding a New BIML File

Create a new SSIS project in SSDT/BIDS called StageAW. Then right-click the project or the folder called SSIS Packages and choose Add New BIML File (see Figure 18-1). If this option isn't available, make sure that the Add-in BIDSHelper is active (in the Tools menu). A new file called BimlScript.biml will be added to the Miscellaneous folder.

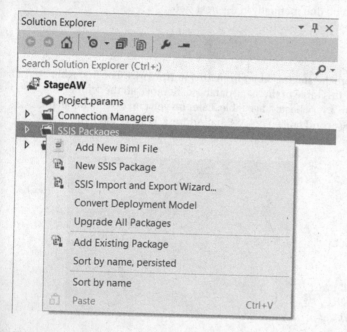

Figure 18-1. *Add a new BIML file*

Open the new BIML file. It contains the following XML start and end tags. Within these tags you will add new tags to generate a single stage package for Person.Person. Add a few empty rows between them and start adding new tags. Notice that there is no .NET code in the first part; but don't worry, you will add that later on.

```
<Biml xmlns="http://schemas.varigence.com/biml.xsd">
</Biml>
```

Start with the OLE DB connection managers. You need a source and a destination connection manager. The CreateInProject option is for the Project Deployment model only. If you type "<" within the Connections tags, IntelliSense will show you all the possible connection managers that are available. Change the connection strings if necessary.

```
<!--Package connection managers-->
<Connections>
  <OleDbConnection
    Name="Source"
    CreateInProject="true"
    ConnectionString="Data Source=.;Initial Catalog=AdventureWorks2012;
    Provider=SQLNCLI11.1;Integrated Security=SSPI;Auto Translate=False;">
  </OleDbConnection>

  <OleDbConnection
    Name="Destination"
    CreateInProject="true"
    ConnectionString="Data Source=.;Initial Catalog=StageAW;
    Provider=SQLNCLI11.1;Integrated Security=SSPI;Auto Translate=False;">
  </OleDbConnection>
</Connections>
```

The second step is to add the package tag, which is still within the BIML tags, but after the Connections tags. Again, IntelliSense will help you define all the properties of the package tag. Make sure that the protection level matches your SSIS project. A linear constraint mode automatically connects all tasks with default precedence constraints. The variable and tasks in the next steps will be added within the package tags.

```
<Packages>
  <Package
    ProtectionLevel="EncryptSensitiveWithUserKey"
    ConstraintMode="Linear"
    AutoCreateConfigurationsType="None"
    Name="stg_Person">

  </Package>
</Packages>
```

The third step is to add an integer variable, which you need for a Row Count transformation within the data flow. Add this within the package tags.

```
<Variables>
  <Variable Name="ReadCount" DataType="Int32">0</Variable>
</Variables>
```

The fourth step is to add the tasks. Add an Execute Package Task that truncates the stage table, and a Data Flow Task that transfers the data to the stage table. Add these tasks within the package tags. In the next step, you will be adding the transformations within the data flow tags. Note the ConnectionName property, which refers to the connections from the first step.

```
<!--Control Flow Tasks -->
<Tasks>
  <!--Execute SQL Task to truncate the staging table-->
  <ExecuteSQL
    Name="SQL - Truncate Person"
    ConnectionName="Destination"
    ResultSet="None">
    <DirectInput>TRUNCATE TABLE Person</DirectInput>
  </ExecuteSQL>

  <!--Data Flow Task to fill the staging table-->
  <Dataflow
    Name="DFT - Stage Person">

  </Dataflow>
</Tasks>
```

The fifth step is to add the transformations: a source, a row count, and a destination. Note the connection names that refer to the first step and the variable in the row count that refers to the third step. Since all source columns exist with the same name in the stage table, there is no column mapping required, because BIML will do that for you. However, you can add column mappings for more complex scenarios.

```
<Transformations>
  <OleDbSource
    ConnectionName="Source"
    Name="OLE_SRC - Person">
    <!-- A ugly SELECT *, but you could replace it with some .net code retrieving the
    columnnames -->
    <DirectInput>SELECT * FROM [Person].Person</DirectInput>
  </OleDbSource>

  <!-- Count the rows -->
  <RowCount
    Name="CNT - ReadCount"
    VariableName="User.ReadCount">
  </RowCount>

  <!--Destination without column mappings -->
  <OleDbDestination
    Name="OLE_DST - Person"
    ConnectionName="Destination">
    <ExternalTableOutput Table="Person" />
  </OleDbDestination>
</Transformations>
```

Now save the BIMLScript file and right-click it in Solution Explorer. Choose Check Biml for Errors to find typos and errors. If there are no errors, right-click it again and choose Generate SSIS Packages. It generates a single SSIS package within the project, as shown in Figure 18-2.

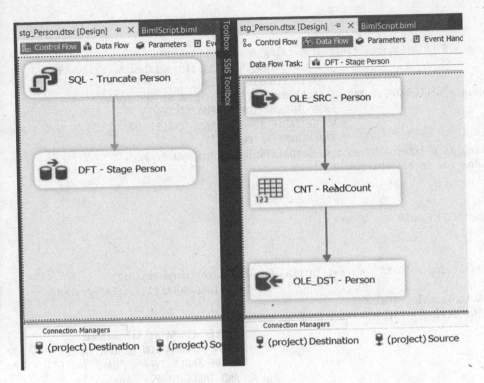

Figure 18-2. Generated stage package

Adding .NET Code

It may seem like a lot of work for a single package, but now it's time to add some .NET code and loop through all the AdventureWorks tables. All hard-coded table names will now be replaced by a piece of script, which gets the table name from the loop. The BIML engine will then generate multiple packages instead of one. But first you let BIML know which programming language you want to use and which Usings/Imports you need. You need to put these outside the BIML tags. The best place to put them is on the bottom of the BIMLScript. Putting them on top could cause you to lose IntelliSense. If you want to use VB, then replace C# with VB.

```
<!--Includes/Imports for C#-->
<#@ template language="C#" hostspecific="true"#>
<#@ import namespace="System.Data"#>
<#@ import namespace="System.Data.SqlClient"#>
```

.NET code should be added between the <# and #> tags. Between <Packages> and <Package> you are executing a query via .NET to retrieve table information from AdventureWorks. And you are also opening the Foreach Loop that loops through all the records from that query. Note that the strings are wrapped to fit on this page!

```
<Packages>
  <#
    string myConn = @"Data Source=.;Initial Catalog=AdventureWorks2012;
                                     Provider=SQLNCLI11.1;Integrated Security=SSPI;
                                     Auto Translate=False;";
    string myQuery ="SELECT TABLE_NAME as tableName, TABLE_SCHEMA as schemaName
                                     FROM INFORMATION_SCHEMA.TABLES
                                     WHERE TABLE_TYPE = 'BASE TABLE' AND
                                     TABLE_NAME = 'Person'";
  DataTable allTables = ExternalDataAccess.GetDataTable(myConn,myQuery);
  foreach (DataRow row in allTables.Rows) {
  #>
  <Package
```

And here is the VB.NET code:

```
<Packages>
  <#
    Dim myConn As String = "Data Source=.;Initial Catalog=AdventureWorks2012;
                                     Provider=SQLNCLI11.1;Integrated
Security=SSPI; Auto Translate=False;"
    Dim myQuery As String = "SELECT TABLE_NAME as tableName,
                                     TABLE_SCHEMA as schemaName
                                     FROM INFORMATION_SCHEMA.TABLES
                                     WHERE TABLE_TYPE = 'BASE TABLE'
                                     AND TABLE_NAME = 'Person'"
    Dim allTables As DataTable = ExternalDataAccess.GetDataTable(myConn, myQuery)
    For Each row As DataRow In allTables.Rows
  #>
  <Package
```

And between </Package> and </Packages> you are closing the loop. This means that everything between this code is repeated X times, depending on the number of rows in the query.

```
  </Package>
  <#}#>
</Packages>
```

And here is the VB.NET code:

```
  </Package>
  <#Next#>
</Packages>
```

Now you can replace every hard-coded table name and schema name in the BIMLScript with data from the query. If you want to write something with .NET, you can do that by adding the equal sign: <#=something#>. In this case, you can use <#=row["tableName"]#> and <#=row["schemaName"]#> like this.

```
<Package
  ProtectionLevel="EncryptSensitiveWithUserKey"
  ConstraintMode="Linear"
  AutoCreateConfigurationsType="None"
  Name="stg_<#=row["tableName"]#>">
```

```
<Variables>
  <Variable Name="ReadCount" DataType="Int32">0</Variable>
</Variables>
<!--Control Flow tasks -->
<Tasks>
  <!--Execute SQL Task to truncate the staging table-->
  <ExecuteSQL
    Name="SQL - Truncate <#=row["tableName"]#>"
    ConnectionName="Destination"
    ResultSet="None">
    <DirectInput>TRUNCATE TABLE <#=row["tableName"]#>
    </DirectInput>
```

A downside of adding .NET code to your BIMLScript is that is messes up the format and the IntelliSense (see Figure 18-3). C# comments will particularly ruin your code format.

```
  foreach (DataRow row in allTables.Rows) {
#>
<Package
  ProtectionLevel="EncryptSensitiveWithUserKey"
  ConstraintMode="Linear"
  AutoCreateConfigurationsType="None"
  Name="stg_<#=row["tableName"]#>">
  <Variables>
    <Variable Name="ReadCount" DataType="Int32">0</Variable>
  </Variables>
  <!--Control Flow tasks -->
  <Tasks>
    <!--Execute SQL Task to truncate the staging table-->
    <ExecuteSQL
      Name="SQL - Truncate <#=row["tableName"]#>"
      ConnectionName="Destination"
      ResultSet="None">
      <DirectInput>TRUNCATE TABLE <#=row["tableName"]#>
      </DirectInput>
    </ExecuteSQL>
```

Figure 18-3. A messed up format and annoying and wavy lines

After replacing all hard-coded parts (names, queries, and destination) test your code and generate the package. If there are no errors and the generated package is correct, then you can add the second table (EmailAddress) to your staging area and extend your query in the BIMLScript so that it also selects that extra table in the WHERE clause: `AND TABLE_NAME in ('Person', 'EmailAddress')`. If that also generates two working packages, you can add all the tables and adjust the WHERE clause. In a matter of seconds, you will have dozens of staging packages.

Adding a Script Component with a RowNumber

You can also add a Script Task or Component with BIMLScript; for example, the row number Script Component that you have often used in this book. To keep things easy, you will continue with the previous example, but first you need to add an extra integer column called SurrogateKey to the stage tables. You can do that manually with the designer in SSMS or by using a TSQL script (as follows), which adds a new column at the bottom of the person table.

```
ALTER TABLE dbo.Person ADD
        SurrogateKey int NULL
GO
```

Next you need to add an integer variable to store the seed (starting number). The best place to do this is immediately after the opening `<Package>` tag. If you want to expand the BIMLScript, you could fill this variable with an Execute SQL Task by retrieving the max value from a table to set the correct starting seed. Since there will already be a `<Variables>` tag, you can just add the variable line below the existing ReadCount variable and skip the variables lines.

```
<Variables>
    <Variable Name="Seed" DataType="Int32">1</Variable>
</Variables>
```

Now the Script Component. In Visual Studio, this is an internal project that is opened in the VSTA environment. In BIMLScript, this is also a separate project enclosed in the `<ScriptProjects>` tag. Add the following tags below the closing Connections tag. It contains the unique ProjectCoreName, which contains a GUID. This the same project name that you see in Solution Explorer when you edit a Script Component. The Name property is used later to reference to this project from the Data Flow Task. Within these tags you add references, input and output columns, variables, and the actual script. For VB, use the `.vbproj` extension and change the ScriptLanguage to VB.

```
<ScriptProjects>
  <ScriptComponentProject
    ScriptLanguage="CSharp"
    ProjectCoreName="sc_c253bef215bf4d6b85dbe3919c35c167.csproj"
    Name="SurrogateKeyScript">

  </ScriptComponentProject>
</ScriptProjects>
```

Next are the assembly references. You need to add the same references that you see in the Solution Explorer of the Script Component. Add these after the opening `<ScriptComponentProject>` tag. For VB you find these in the project properties, but they are equal to C#.

```
<AssemblyReferences>
  <AssemblyReference AssemblyPath="Microsoft.SqlServer.DTSPipelineWrap" />
  <AssemblyReference AssemblyPath="Microsoft.SqlServer.DTSRuntimeWrap" />
  <AssemblyReference AssemblyPath="Microsoft.SqlServer.PipelineHost" />
  <AssemblyReference AssemblyPath="Microsoft.SqlServer.TxScript" />
  <AssemblyReference AssemblyPath="System.dll" />
  <AssemblyReference AssemblyPath="System.AddIn.dll" />
  <AssemblyReference AssemblyPath="System.Data.dll" />
  <AssemblyReference AssemblyPath="System.Xml.dll" />
</AssemblyReferences>
```

The next step is to add read-only and read-write variables. In this example, you only use the Seed variable as ReadOnlyVariable. Add these after the closing `</AssemblyReferences>` tag. Note that this is not the same variable tag as before, but you have to specify nearly the same properties.

```
<ReadOnlyVariables>
  <Variable
    VariableName="Seed"
    Namespace="User"
    DataType="Int32" />
</ReadOnlyVariables>
```

Next you have to add the file content of the AssemblyInfo.cs and main.cs files. If you don't want a lot of white space in the generated code, then it is advisable to decrease the indentation to a minimum and align it to the far left. The actual file content is in the next step. For VB you should use the .vb extension.

```
<Files>
  <File Path="AssemblyInfo.cs">

  </File>
  <File Path="main.cs">

  </File>
</Files>
```

The first file is the AssemblyInfo.cs. You can just open the file in Solution Explorer and copy the content to the BIMLScript. Paste the following inside the preceding file tag.

```
using System.Reflection;
using System.Runtime.CompilerServices;

//
// General Information about an assembly is controlled through the following
// set of attributes. Change these attribute values to modify the information
// associated with an assembly.
//
[assembly: AssemblyTitle("SC_ c253bef215bf4d6b85dbe3919c35c167")]
[assembly: AssemblyDescription("")]
[assembly: AssemblyConfiguration("")]
[assembly: AssemblyCompany("Joost and Régis")]
[assembly: AssemblyProduct("SC_ c253bef215bf4d6b85dbe3919c35c167")]
[assembly: AssemblyCopyright("Copyright @ Joost and Régis 2015")]
[assembly: AssemblyTrademark("")]
[assembly: AssemblyCulture("")]
//
// Version information for an assembly consists of the following four values:
//
//      Major Version
//      Minor Version
//      Build Number
//      Revision
//
// You can specify all the values or you can default the Revision and Build Numbers
// by using the '*' as shown below:

[assembly: AssemblyVersion("1.0.*")]
```

And here is the VB.NET code:

```
Imports System
Imports System.Reflection
Imports System.Runtime.InteropServices

' General Information about an assembly is controlled through the following
' set of attributes. Change these attribute values to modify the information
' associated with an assembly.

' Review the values of the assembly attributes

&lt;Assembly: AssemblyTitle("SC_ c253bef215bf4d6b85dbe3919c35c167")&gt;
&lt;Assembly: AssemblyDescription("")&gt;
&lt;Assembly: AssemblyCompany("Joost and Régis")&gt;
&lt;Assembly: AssemblyProduct("SC_ c253bef215bf4d6b85dbe3919c35c167")&gt;
&lt;Assembly: AssemblyCopyright("Copyright @ Joost and Régis  2015")&gt;
&lt;Assembly: AssemblyTrademark("")&gt;
&lt;Assembly: CLSCompliant(True)&gt;

&lt;Assembly: ComVisible(False)&gt;

'The following GUID is for the ID of the typelib if this project is exposed to COM
&lt;Assembly: Guid("4d9b8fe7-8cfa-45ea-98e5-0eec88be0a93")&gt;

' Version information for an assembly consists of the following four values:
'
'       Major Version
'       Minor Version
'       Build Number
'       Revision
'
' You can specify all the values or you can default the Build and Revision Numbers
' by using the '*' as shown below:
' &lt;Assembly: AssemblyVersion("1.0.*")&gt;

&lt;Assembly: AssemblyVersion("1.0.0.0")&gt;
&lt;Assembly: AssemblyFileVersion("1.0.0.0")&gt;
```

The second file is the main.cs. Again, just open your example script and copy the content to the BIMLScript, but first replace < and > with > and <; otherwise, the XML tags will be messed up. Paste this in the second file tag:

```
#region Namespaces
using System;
using System.Data;
using Microsoft.SqlServer.Dts.Pipeline.Wrapper;
using Microsoft.SqlServer.Dts.Runtime.Wrapper;
#endregion
```

```
/// &lt;summary&gt;
/// Rownumber transformation to create an identity column
/// &lt;/summary&gt;
[Microsoft.SqlServer.Dts.Pipeline.SSISScriptComponentEntryPointAttribute]
public class ScriptMain : UserComponent
{
  int rownumber = 0;

  /// &lt;summary&gt;
  /// Get starting rownumber from variable
  /// &lt;/summary&gt;
  public override void PreExecute()
  {
    rownumber = this.Variables.Seed;
  }


  /// &lt;summary&gt;
  /// Fill rownumber column and then increase the rownumber
  /// &lt;/summary&gt;
  /// &lt;param name="Row"&gt;The row that is currently passing through the
  component&lt;/param&gt;
  public override void Input0_ProcessInputRow(Input0Buffer Row)
  {
    Row. SurrogateKey = rownumber;
    rownumber++;
  }
}
```

And here is the VB.NET code:

```
#Region "Imports"
Imports System
Imports System.Data
Imports System.Math
Imports Microsoft.SqlServer.Dts.Pipeline.Wrapper
Imports Microsoft.SqlServer.Dts.Runtime.Wrapper
#End Region

'Rownumber transformation to create an identity column
&lt;Microsoft.SqlServer.Dts.Pipeline.SSISScriptComponentEntryPointAttribute&gt; _
&lt;CLSCompliant(False)&gt; _
Public Class ScriptMain
    Inherits UserComponent

    Dim rownumber As Integer = 0

    'Get starting rownumber from variable
    Public Overrides Sub PreExecute()
        rownumber = Me.Variables.Seed
    End Sub
```

445

```
'Fill rownumber column and then increase the rownumber
Public Overrides Sub Input0_ProcessInputRow(ByVal Row As Input0Buffer)
  Row.SurrogateKey = rownumber
  rownumber = rownumber + 1
End Sub
End Class
```

And the last step of the "internal" project is adding input and output columns. In this example, there is only one output column, named SurrogateKey. This should also be added within the ScriptComponentProject tag.

```
<InputBuffer Name="Input0">
  <Columns>
        <!-- No input columns -->
  </Columns>
</InputBuffer>
<OutputBuffers>
  <OutputBuffer Name="Output0">
        <Columns>
          <Column Name="SurrogateKey" DataType="Int32"></Column>
        </Columns>
  </OutputBuffer>
</OutputBuffers>
```

In the Data Flow Task, you can add a reference to the project that you just created. And since the output column has the same name as the new column that was added to the destination table, you don't have to add any mappings. Add this between the Row Count transformation and the OLE DB Destination:

```
<ScriptComponentTransformation Name="SCR - Rownumber">
  <ScriptComponentProjectReference ScriptComponentProjectName="SurrogateKeyScript" />
</ScriptComponentTransformation>
```

Now regenerate the packages by right-clicking the BIMLScript in the miscellaneous folder. Replace the existing package. It is preferable that you first close those packages if they are still opened in Visual Studio; otherwise, you get reload requests.

If the BIMLScript gets too large, you can move parts (such as the ScriptProjects) to a separate BIML file and then embed this file in the main BIML file with an include tag.

```
<#@ include file="ScriptProjects.biml" #>
```

Of course, the ScriptProjects.biml file contains the exact XML that should replace the include tag when you generate the packages. This makes your BIMLScript much more compact and clear. Moreover, it also makes it easier to reuse parts in other BIML files.

BIMLScript: Master Package

Now that you have created dozens of stage packages, you also need to generate a master package; otherwise, you end up adding a lot of Execute Package Tasks by hand. Here is some basic BIML code for a simple master package. It generates a package called Master.dtsx and has one Execute Package Task.

```
<Biml xmlns="http://schemas.varigence.com/biml.xsd">
  <Packages>
    <Package
      Name="Master"
      ConstraintMode="Parallel"
      AutoCreateConfigurationsType="None"
      ProtectionLevel="EncryptSensitiveWithUserKey">
      <Tasks>
        <!--Execute Project Package-->
        <ExecutePackage Name="EPT - stg_Person">
          <ExternalProjectPackage Package="stg_Person.dtsx" />
        </ExecutePackage >
      </Tasks>
    </Package>
  </Packages>
</Biml>
```

First, specify the programming language at the bottom and add an import to System.IO. Replace C# with VB if you prefer that language.

```
<!--Includes/Imports for C#-->
<#@ template language="C#" hostspecific="true"#>
<#@ import namespace="System.IO"#>
```

Next, add a loop within the Tasks tag and around the Execute Package Task. This loop could be similar to the one in the first example, but you can also loop through files. In this example, you are looping through the project folder of the current SSIS project. Change the D:\stageAW\ path, if necessary.

```
<!-- Get all staging packages from SSIS project folder on file system -->
<#
string[] myStagingfiles = Directory.GetFiles(@"D:\stageAW\", "stg_*.dtsx");
foreach(string fileName in myStagingfiles) {
  FileInfo stagePackage = new FileInfo(fileName);
  // Remove Extension because . is not allowed in the task name
  string nameOnly = Path.GetFileNameWithoutExtension(stagePackage.Name);
#>
<!--Execute Project Package-->
<ExecutePackage Name="EPT - <#=nameOnly#>">
  <ExternalProjectPackage Package="<#=stagePackage.Name#>" />
</ExecutePackage>
<# } #>
```

And this is the VB.NET code:

```
<!-- Get all staging packages from SSIS project folder on file system -->
<#
Dim myStagingfiles As String() = Directory.GetFiles("D:\stageAW\","stg_*.dtsx")
For Each fileName As String In myStagingfiles
  Dim stagePackage As New FileInfo(fileName)
  ' Remove Extension because . is not allowed in the task name
  Dim nameOnly As String = Path.GetFileNameWithoutExtension(stagePackage.Name)
#>
```

```
<!--Execute Project Package-->
<ExecutePackage Name="EPT - <#=nameOnly#>">
  <ExternalProjectPackage Package="<#=stagePackage.Name#>" />
</ExecutePackage>
<# Next #>
```

Figure 18-4 shows the simplified master package with Execute Package Tasks.

Figure 18-4. *Simplified master package with Execute Package Tasks*

■ **Tip**   If you want to test your .NET code before adding it to BIML, you can use a tool like LINQPad
(www.linqpad.net) to test your code snippets.

Summary

In this chapter you learned how to generate packages. The first package may take a little longer than using
drag-and-drop, but if you have to create dozens of dull packages by hand, then generating is the best option.

There are two flavors: .NET assemblies and BIML. The diehard .NET developers probably prefer the
first, but BIML is increasingly getting more popular. As an ETL consultant, you should master one of these
methods. All examples in this chapter were very simple, but the purpose was to show you the absolute
basics. There are plenty of online resources available, especially for BIML (http://bimlscript.com).

CHAPTER 19

■ ■ ■

Package Execution from .NET

This chapter shows you how to execute a package from a .NET application, which could be a web application, a web service, a Windows service, or a Windows application. Since there are two deployment models, there are also two different ways to execute packages; however, there is one requirement: you need SQL Server Integration Services installed on the same machine as your application. The packages will run on this machine. If this is not possible in your situation, you could create a web service on machine A to execute packages locally and then call that web service from an application that runs on machine B. Another alternative is to let your code on machine B execute a remote SQL Server Agent job on machine A to execute a package locally. In both cases, the application runs on machine B, but the package runs on machine A.

And if you are using the Integration Services catalog (project deployment model), you can execute a stored procedure from that database remotely.

Package Deployment Model

This first example uses a Windows application running a package that is stored on the file system. Make sure that you have a dummy package available to work with. You can create a new package and add a Script Task that fires a warning event (see Chapter 4 for an example).

To create this Windows application, you need a version of Visual Studio that has C# or VB.NET templates; SSDT for BI or BIDS isn't enough (see Chapter 16 for more details).

Start Visual Studio and create a new Windows Forms Application project named MySsisApplication. Make sure to choose the appropriate .NET Framework version. For this example, you are using .NET Framework 4 to execute an SSIS 2012 package. The screenshots, starting with Figure 19-1, are from Visual Studio 2013.

449

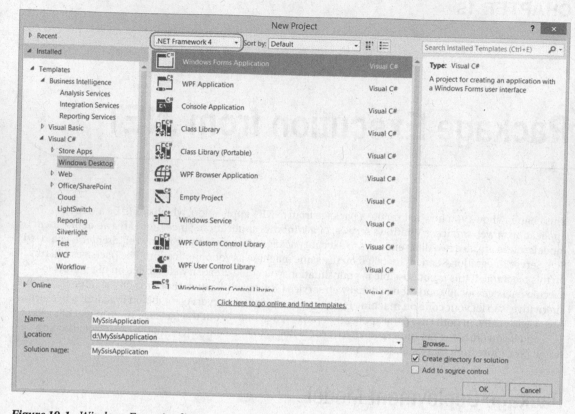

Figure 19-1. *Windows Form Application to execute an SSIS package*

Add Reference

First, you need to add a reference to SSIS, particularly to Microsoft.SqlServer.ManagedDTS.dll, which is located in the global assembly cache in Windows. Right-click References (in VB, right-click the project) in Solution Explorer and choose Add Reference.... Then browse to the correct assembly. If you have multiple versions of SSIS installed on your development machine, make sure to choose the right one. Each version of SSIS has its own folder. The X in the file path differs per version.

```
C:\Windows\Microsoft.NET\assembly\GAC_MSIL\Microsoft.SqlServer.ManagedDTS\
v4.0_1X.0.0.0__89845dcd8080cc91\Microsoft.SqlServer.ManagedDTS.dll
```

In Figure 19-2, you see three versions: v4.0_11 (SSIS 2012), v4.0_12 (SSIS 2014), and v4.0_13 (SSIS 2016).

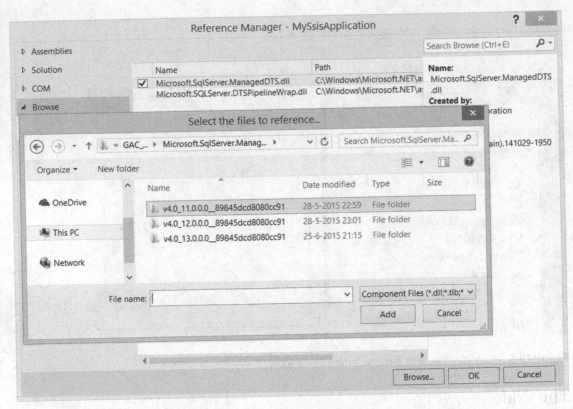

Figure 19-2. *Add a reference to Microsoft.SqlServer.ManagedDTS.dll*

Create a Form

Open the Form1 file and add a button called btnStart and a label called lblStatus. You can find them in the toolbox. When ready, your form should look something like Figure 19-3.

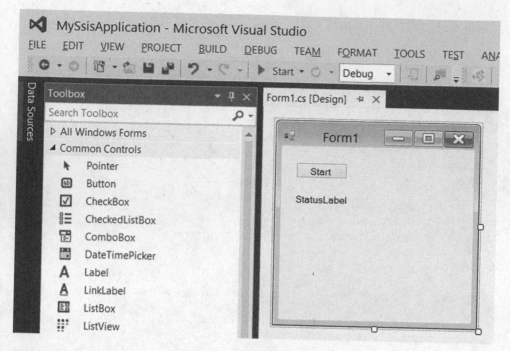

Figure 19-3. *A simple form with just one button and a label*

The Code

Now double-click the Start button (btnStart) to create an onClick event handler. The code page opens and a new method is created, called btnStart_Click.

```
private void btnStart_Click(object sender, EventArgs e)
{
}
```

And this is the VB.NET code:

```
Private Sub btnStart_Click(sender As Object, e As EventArgs) Handles _
                                                btnStart.Click

End Sub
```

You will add the code to this method, but first you need to add an extra namespace to shorten the code. For VB.NET projects, the imported namespace is a property of the project, but you can also add the imports code at the top of your code, like in a Script Task or a Script Component.

```
#region CustomNamespace
using Microsoft.SqlServer.Dts.Runtime;
#endregion
```

And this is the VB.NET code:

```
#Region "CustomNamespace"
Imports Microsoft.SqlServer.Dts.Runtime
#End Region
```

Now back to the code for the button. This example uses myApplication .LoadPackage to load a package from the file system, but you can also use LoadFromSqlServer or LoadFromDtsServer to load the package from the MSDB or the package store. If you type a dot behind myApplication, then IntelliSense will show you all the possibilities.

In this code, you need to change the reference to your own example package. On the line below that, there is code to set the value of a variable. Either remove that line or add a variable to your sample package.

```
private void btnStart_Click(object sender, EventArgs e)
{
  // Instantiate SSIS application object
  Microsoft.SqlServer.Dts.Runtime.Application myApplication =
                          new Microsoft.SqlServer.Dts.Runtime.Application();


  // Load package from file system
  //(use LoadFromSqlServer for SQL Server based packages)
  lblStatus.Text = "Loading package from file system.";
  Package myPackage = myApplication.LoadPackage(@"D:\myPackage.dtsx", null);


  // Optional set the value from one of the SSIS package variables
  myPackage.Variables["User::myVar"].Value = "test123";


  // Execute package
  lblStatus.Text = "Executing package";
  DTSExecResult myResult = myPackage.Execute();


  // Show the execution result
  lblStatus.Text = "Package result: " + myResult.ToString();
}
```

This is the VB.NET code:

```
Private Sub btnStart_Click(sender As Object, e As EventArgs) Handles btnStart.Click
  ' Instantiate SSIS application object
  Dim myApplication As Application = New Application()

  ' Load package from file system
  ' (use LoadFromSqlServer for SQL Server based packages)
  lblStatus.Text = "Loading package from file system."
  Dim myPackage As Package = _
                  myApplication.LoadPackage("D:\myPackage.dtsx", Nothing)

  ' Optional set the value from one of the SSIS package variables
  myPackage.Variables("User::myVar").Value = "test123"
```

```
' Execute package
lblStatus.Text = "Executing package"
Dim myResult As DTSExecResult = myPackage.Execute()

' Show the execution result
lblStatus.Text = "Package result: " + myResult.ToString()
End Sub
```

Logging

Since this example is for packages using the package deployment model, there isn't any default logging available like in the catalog. If you are logging to a table, text file, or so forth, and you want to show that in the Windows application, then you need to add custom code for it. However, it is also possible to get warnings and errors from the package and display these messages in a simple list box, for example. First, add a list box named lbLog to your form. It should look something like what's shown in Figure 19-4.

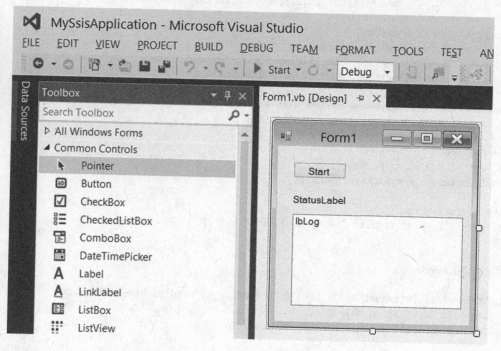

Figure 19-4. The simple form extended with a list box for log messages

Next, you need to add the warnings and errors to the list box. One drawback is that they come from two different sets. If you want to show them in order of appearance, then you have to merge and order them. For this example, you stored both errors and warnings in a temporary data table to add them sorted to the list box. You can add this code at the bottom of the btnStart_Click method. Note that this is a quick and dirty way to show the logs, which works just fine, but there are more sophisticated ways or more convenient controls to do this. Let's focus on the SSIS stuff, however.

```
// Create a temporary table to store warnings and errors
DataTable myLogTable = new DataTable("myLogTable");
myLogTable.Columns.Add("LogTime", typeof(DateTime));
myLogTable.Columns.Add("Source", typeof(string));
myLogTable.Columns.Add("Message", typeof(string));

// Loop through all warnings and add them to the table
foreach (DtsWarning packageWarning in myPackage.Warnings)
{
    myLogTable.Rows.Add(Convert.ToDateTime(packageWarning.TimeStamp), packageWarning.Source,
    packageWarning.Description);
}

// Loop through all errors and add them to the table
foreach (DtsError packageError in myPackage.Errors)
{
    myLogTable.Rows.Add(Convert.ToDateTime(packageError.TimeStamp), packageError.Source,
packageError.Description);
}

// Create a sorted view and then make a new datatable with it
myLogTable.DefaultView.Sort = "LogTime";
DataTable myLogTableSorted = myLogTable.DefaultView.ToTable();

// Cleanup resource
myLogTable.Dispose();

// Loop through the new sorted dataset and add rows to the listbox
foreach (DataRow row in myLogTableSorted.Rows)
{
    lbLog.Items.Add(row.Field<DateTime>(0).ToLongTimeString() + " - " + row.Field<string>(1)
    + " - " + row.Field<string>(2));
}

// Cleanup resource
myLogTableSorted.Dispose();
```

This is the VB.NET code:

```
' Create a temporary table to store warnings and errors
Dim myLogTable As DataTable = New DataTable("myLogTable")
myLogTable.Columns.Add("LogTime", GetType(DateTime))
myLogTable.Columns.Add("Source", GetType(String))
myLogTable.Columns.Add("Message", GetType(String))
```

```
' Loop through all warnings and add them to the table
For Each packageWarning As DtsWarning In myPackage.Warnings
    myLogTable.Rows.Add(Convert.ToDateTime(packageWarning.TimeStamp), packageWarning.Source,
    packageWarning.Description)
Next

' Loop through all errors and add them to the table
For Each packageError As DtsError In myPackage.Errors
    myLogTable.Rows.Add(Convert.ToDateTime(packageError.TimeStamp), packageError.Source,
    packageError.Description)
Next

' Create a sorted view and then make a new datatable with it
myLogTable.DefaultView.Sort = "LogTime"
Dim myLogTableSorted As DataTable = myLogTable.DefaultView.ToTable()

' Cleanup resource
myLogTable.Dispose()

' Loop through the new sorted dataset and add rows to the listbox
For Each row As DataRow In myLogTableSorted.Rows
    lbLog.Items.Add(row.Field(Of DateTime)(0).ToLongTimeString() + " - " + row.Field
    (Of String)(1) + " - " + row.Field(Of String)(2))
Next

' Cleanup resource
myLogTableSorted.Dispose()
```

The Results

Now run the application and click the Start button. Check the package log to see if the package was really executed. As explained earlier, an easy way to check if the log works is to add a Script Task to your sample package to fire some warnings and/or errors (see Chapter 4 for firing event examples).

If you get the following error, you are probably using an older version of Visual Studio (2010).

```
The Execute method on the task returned error code 0x80131621 (Mixed mode assembly is built
against version 'v2.0.50727' of the runtime and cannot be loaded in the 4.0 runtime without
additional configuration information.). The Execute method must succeed, and indicate the
result using an "out" parameter.
```

The solution is to tell Visual Studio that it is OK to use .NET Framework 2.0 code in a 4.0 application. You do this by adding the useLegacyV2RuntimeActivationPolicy="true" attribute to the startup tag in the App.config file. If you don't have an App.config file, you can add one by right-clicking the project in Solution Explorer and then selecting Add ➤ New Item ➤ Application Configuration File ➤ App.config, which should look something like Figure 19-5.

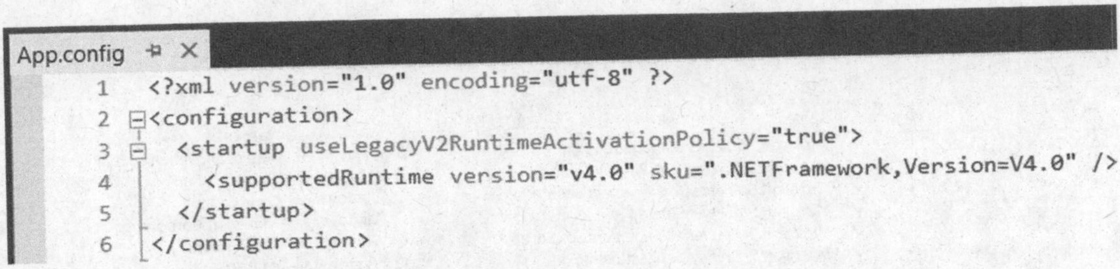

```
App.config  ⊞ ×
     1    <?xml version="1.0" encoding="utf-8" ?>
     2  ⊟<configuration>
     3  ⊟  <startup useLegacyV2RuntimeActivationPolicy="true">
     4        <supportedRuntime version="v4.0" sku=".NETFramework,Version=V4.0" />
     5      </startup>
     6  └</configuration>
```

Figure 19-5. App.config example used in a C# project

Another option is to change the target framework of your Windows application project to 2.0 or 3.5.

Project Deployment Model

This second example also uses a Windows application—this time running a package that is stored in the Integration Services Catalog. Start Visual Studio and create a new Windows Forms Application project named MySsisApplication2. Make sure to choose the appropriate .NET Framework version. For this example, you are using .NET Framework 4 to execute an SSIS 2012 package.

Add Reference

First, you need to add four references, which are located in the global assembly cache in Windows. Right-click References (in VB, right-click the project) in Solution Explorer and choose Add Reference.... Then browse to the correct assembly. If you have multiple versions of SSIS installed on your development machine, make sure to choose the right one. Each version of SSIS has its own folder. The X in the file path differs per version (see previous example; also see Figure 19-6).

C:\Windows\assembly\GAC_MSIL\Microsoft.SqlServer.ConnectionInfo\1X.0.0.0__89845dcd8080cc91\
Microsoft.SqlServer.ConnectionInfo.dll
C:\Windows\assembly\GAC_MSIL\Microsoft.SqlServer.Management.Sdk.Sfc\1X.0.0.0__89845dcd8080cc91
Microsoft.SqlServer.Management.Sdk.Sfc.dll
C:\Windows\assembly\GAC_MSIL\Microsoft.SqlServer.Smo\1X.0.0.0__89845dcd8080cc91**Microsoft.
SqlServer.Smo.dll**
C:\Windows\assembly\GAC_MSIL\Microsoft.SqlServer.Management.IntegrationServices\1X.0.0.0__
89845dcd8080cc91**Microsoft.SqlServer.Management.IntegrationServices.dll**

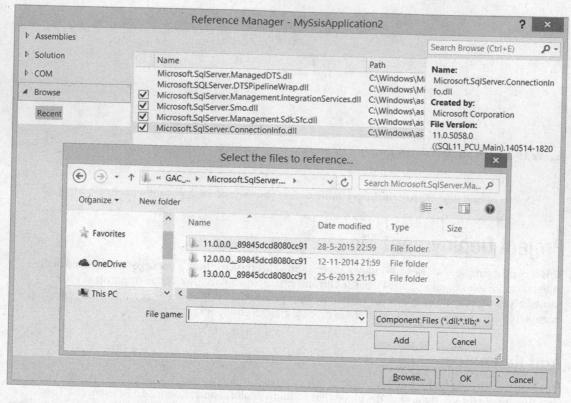

Figure 19-6. *Add multiple references to SSIS*

Create a Form

Open the Form1 file and add a button called btnStart and a label called lblStatus. You can find them in the toolbox. When ready, your form should look something like Figure 19-7.

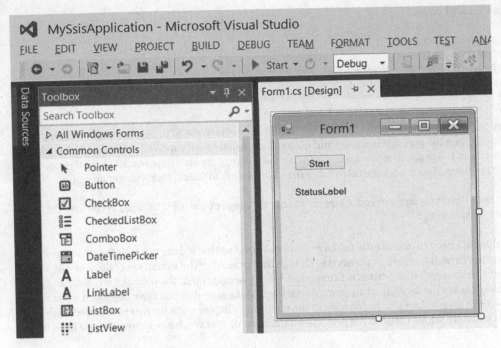

Figure 19-7. A simple form with just one button and a label

The Code

Double-click the Start button (btnStart) to create an onClick event handler. The code page opens and a new method is created, called btnStart_Click.

```
private void btnStart_Click(object sender, EventArgs e)
{
}
```

This is the VB.NET code:

```
Private Sub btnStart_Click(sender As Object, e As EventArgs) Handles _
                                                      btnStart.Click

End Sub
```

You will add the code to this method, but first you need to add some extra namespaces to shorten the code. For VB.NET projects, the imported namespace is a property of the project, but you can also add the imports code at the top of your code, like in a Script Task or a Script Component.

```
#region CustomNamespace
using System.Data.SqlClient;
using Microsoft.SqlServer.Management.IntegrationServices;
using System.Collections.ObjectModel;
#endregion
```

This is the VB.NET code:

```
#Region "CustomNamespace"
Imports System.Data.SqlClient
Imports Microsoft.SqlServer.Management.IntegrationServices
Imports System.Collections.ObjectModel
#End Region
```

Now back to the code for the button. This example first connects to the SQL Server instance where the catalog is located. Then the package is loaded and optional parameters are supplied. After that, the package is executed; but there is a problem if you want to wait for the package result. There is a 30-second timeout that cannot be changed. If your package takes more than 30 seconds to finish, then you get an error:

```
Timeout expired. The timeout period elapsed prior to completion of the operation or the
server is not responding.
```

To solve this, you need to execute the package asynchronized so that it does not wait for an answer. However, this is the default method, so no need to change the code. After the execution code, you can add a while loop that checks whether the status is Completed, which indicates that the package is finished.

In this code, you see the location of an example package. Make sure that you have deployed a test package to the SSISDB and changed the location in the code. You also see code for two parameters. Again, make sure that you have added those to the project and package, or that you have removed those lines from the code.

```
private void btnStart_Click(object sender, EventArgs e)
{
  // Connecting to the SQL Server instance where the catalog is located
  using (SqlConnection ssisConnection = new SqlConnection
       ("Data Source=.;Initial Catalog=master;Integrated Security=SSPI;"))
  {
    try
    {
      // SSIS server object with connection
      IntegrationServices ssisServer = new IntegrationServices(ssisConnection);

      // The reference to the package which you want to execute
      lblStatus.Text = "Loading package from catalog.";
      Form.ActiveForm.Refresh();
      PackageInfo ssisPackage = ssisServer.Catalogs["SSISDB"]
                                .Folders["Extending SSIS"]
                                .Projects["Chapter 19"]
                                .Packages["myPackage.dtsx"];

      // Setting parameters
      Collection<PackageInfo.ExecutionValueParameterSet> executionParameter =
                new Collection<PackageInfo.ExecutionValueParameterSet>();

      // Add execution parameter for an asynchronized (value=0, default)
      // or synchronized (value=1) execution. You could skip this code line.
      executionParameter.Add(new PackageInfo.ExecutionValueParameterSet
      {ObjectType = 50, ParameterName = "SYNCHRONIZED", ParameterValue = 0});
```

```csharp
// Add execution parameter (value) to override the default logging level
// (0=None, 1=Basic, 2=Performance, 3=Verbose)
executionParameter.Add(new PackageInfo.ExecutionValueParameterSet
{ObjectType = 50, ParameterName = "LOGGING_LEVEL", ParameterValue = 3});

// Add a project parameter (value) to fill a project parameter
executionParameter.Add(new PackageInfo.ExecutionValueParameterSet
{ObjectType = 20, ParameterName = "MyProjectParameter",
 ParameterValue = "some value"});

// Add a package parameter (value) to fill a package parameter
executionParameter.Add(new PackageInfo.ExecutionValueParameterSet
{ObjectType = 30, ParameterName = "MyPackageParameter",
 ParameterValue = "some value"});

// Execute package and return the ServerExecutionId
long executionIdentifier = ssisPackage.Execute(false,
                                        null,
                                        executionParameter);


// Get execution details with the ServerExecutionId from previous step
lblStatus.Text = "Executing package";
Form.ActiveForm.Refresh();
ExecutionOperation executionOperation = ssisServer.Catalogs["SSISDB"]
                            .Executions[executionIdentifier];


// Loop while the execution is not completed (timeout workaround)
while (!(executionOperation.Completed))
{
    // Refresh execution info
    executionOperation.Refresh();

    // Wait 5 seconds before refreshing
    // (you don't want to stress the server)
    System.Threading.Thread.Sleep(5000);
}
// Showing the ServerExecutionId
lblStatus.Text = "Execution " + executionOperation.Id.ToString() +
                 " finished: " + executionOperation.Status.ToString();

}
catch (Exception ex)
{
    // Log code for exceptions
    lblStatus.Text = "Error: " + ex.Message;
}
}
}
```

And this is the VB.NET code:

```vb
Private Sub btnStart_Click(sender As Object, e As EventArgs) _
                                    Handles btnStart.Click
  ' Connecting to the SQL Server instance where the catalog is located
  Using ssisConnection As New SqlConnection( _
          "Data Source=.;Initial Catalog=master;Integrated Security=SSPI;")
    Try
      ' SSIS server object with connection
      Dim ssisServer As New IntegrationServices(ssisConnection)

      ' The reference to the package which you want to execute
      lblStatus.Text = "Loading package from catalog."
      Form.ActiveForm.Refresh()
      Dim ssisPackage As PackageInfo = ssisServer.Catalogs("SSISDB") _
                                  .Folders("Extending SSIS") _
                                  .Projects("Chapter 19") _
                                  .Packages("myPackage.dtsx")

      ' Setting parameters
      Dim executionParameter As New Collection( _
                            Of PackageInfo.ExecutionValueParameterSet)()

      ' Add execution parameter for an asynchronized (value=0, default)
      ' or synchronized (value=1) execution. You could skip these code lines.
      executionParameter.Add(New PackageInfo.ExecutionValueParameterSet() _
      With { _
        .ObjectType = 50, _
        .ParameterName = "SYNCHRONIZED", _
        .ParameterValue = 0 _
      })

      ' Add execution parameter (value) to override the default logging level
      ' (0=None, 1=Basic, 2=Performance, 3=Verbose)
      executionParameter.Add(New PackageInfo.ExecutionValueParameterSet() _
      With { _
        .ObjectType = 50, _
        .ParameterName = "LOGGING_LEVEL", _
        .ParameterValue = 3 _
      })

      ' Add a project parameter (value) to fill a project parameter
      executionParameter.Add(New PackageInfo.ExecutionValueParameterSet() _
      With { _
        .ObjectType = 20, _
        .ParameterName = "MyProjectParameter", _
        .ParameterValue = "some value" _
      })

      ' Add a package parameter (value) to fill a package parameter
      executionParameter.Add(New PackageInfo.ExecutionValueParameterSet() _
```

```
    With { _
      .ObjectType = 30, _
      .ParameterName = "MyPackageParameter", _
      .ParameterValue = "some value" _
    })

    ' Execute package and return the ServerExecutionId
    Dim executionIdentifier As Long = ssisPackage.Execute(False, _
                                                Nothing, _
                                                executionParameter)

    ' Get execution details with the ServerExecutionId from the previous step
    lblStatus.Text = "Executing package"
    Form.ActiveForm.Refresh()
    Dim executionOperation As ExecutionOperation = ssisServer _
                                    .Catalogs("SSISDB") _
                                    .Executions(executionIdentifier)

    ' Loop while the execution is not completed
    While Not (executionOperation.Completed)
      ' Refresh execution info
      executionOperation.Refresh()

      ' Wait 5 seconds before refreshing
      ' (you don't want to stress the server)
      System.Threading.Thread.Sleep(5000)
    End While
    ' Showing the ServerExecutionId
    lblStatus.Text = "Execution " + executionOperation.Id.ToString() + _
                  " finished: " + executionOperation.Status.ToString()

  Catch ex As Exception
    ' Log code for exceptions
    lblStatus.Text = "Error: " + ex.Message
  End Try
End Using
End SubLogging
```

Showing the log is a little easier than in the previous example, but first you need to add a list box named lbLog to the form. It should look something like Figure 19-8.

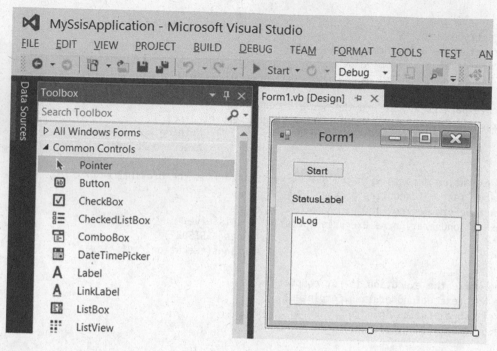

Figure 19-8. *The simple form extended with a list box for log messages*

To fill the list box, simply add the following loop, but make sure that the list box is cleared before doing it. You can add this code after showing the ServerExecutionId and the status.

```
// Clear listbox before adding log rows to it
lbLog.Items.Clear();

// Loop through the log and add the messages to the listbox
foreach (OperationMessage message in ssisServer.Catalogs["SSISDB"].
Executions[executionIdentifier].Messages)
{
    lbLog.Items.Add(message.MessageType.ToString() + ": " + message.Message);
}
```

And this is the VB.NET code:

```
' Clear listbox before adding log rows to it
lbLog.Items.Clear()

' Loop through the log and add the messages to the listbox
For Each message As OperationMessage In ssisServer.Catalogs("SSISDB") _
                                       .Executions(executionIdentifier) _
                                       .Messages
  lbLog.Items.Add(message.MessageType.ToString() + ": " + message.Message)
Next
```

The Results

Now run the application and click the Start button. Check the log in the list box (see Figure 19-9). You can compare it to the log in the catalog.

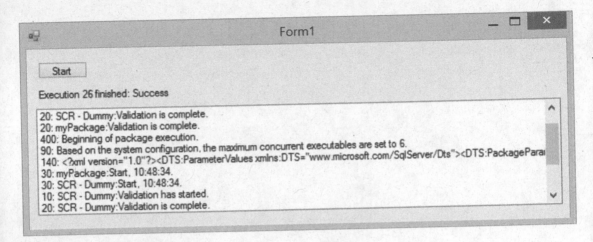

Figure 19-9. *The results*

Summary

In this chapter, you learned how to execute packages via a .NET application. You could create a web service that is used to execute packages remotely or you could create a Windows service that watches a certain folder and executes a package when a new file is dropped into that folder. The possibilities are endless.

Index

Get the eBook for only $5!

Why limit yourself?

Now you can take the weightless companion with you wherever you go and access your content on your PC, phone, tablet, or reader.

Since you've purchased this print book, we're happy to offer you the eBook in all 3 formats for just $5.

Convenient and fully searchable, the PDF version enables you to easily find and copy code—or perform examples by quickly toggling between instructions and applications. The MOBI format is ideal for your Kindle, while the ePUB can be utilized on a variety of mobile devices.

To learn more, go to www.apress.com/companion or contact support@apress.com.

Printed in the United States
By Bookmasters